CRYPTOCRACY
(*plural* cryptocracies)

n. A FORM OF GOVERNMENT
WHERE THE REAL LEADERS ARE
HIDDEN OR UNKNOWN.

CRYPTOCRACY™

WRITTEN BY

Van Jensen

ART BY

Pete Woods

LETTERING BY

Nate Piekos

OF BLAMBOT®

DARK HORSE BOOKS

PRESIDENT AND PUBLISHER Mike Richardson

EDITOR Spencer Cushing

ASSISTANT EDITOR Kevin Burkhalter

DESIGNER Anita Magaña

DIGITAL ART TECHNICIAN Melissa Martin

This volume collects the Dark Horse comic book series *Cryptocracy* #1–#6,
originally published June–November 2016.

Image Credit: NASA

Published by Dark Horse Books
A division of Dark Horse Comics, Inc.
10956 SE Main Street
Milwaukie, OR 97222

DarkHorse.com

International Licensing: 503-905-2377

To find a comics shop in your area,
call the Comic Shop Locater Service
toll-free at 1-888-266-4226.

First edition: March 2017
ISBN 978-1-50670-135-6

1 3 5 7 9 10 8 6 4 2
Printed in China

Names: Jensen, Van, author. | Woods, Pete, artist. | Piekos, Nate, letterer.
Title: Cryptocracy / script, Van Jensen ; art, Pete Woods ; lettering, Nate
   Piekos of Blambot ; cover art, Pete Woods.
Description: First edition. | Milwaukie, OR : Dark Horse Books, 2017. | "This
   volume collects the Dark Horse comic book series Cryptocracy #1-#6
   originally published June-November 2016"--Title page verso.
Identifiers: LCCN 2016044134 | ISBN 9781506701356 (paperback)
Subjects: LCSH: Comic books, strips, etc. | BISAC: COMICS & GRAPHIC NOVELS /
   Science Fiction.
Classification: LCC PN6728.C783 J46 2017 | DDC 741.5/973--dc23
LC record available at https://lccn.loc.gov/2016044134

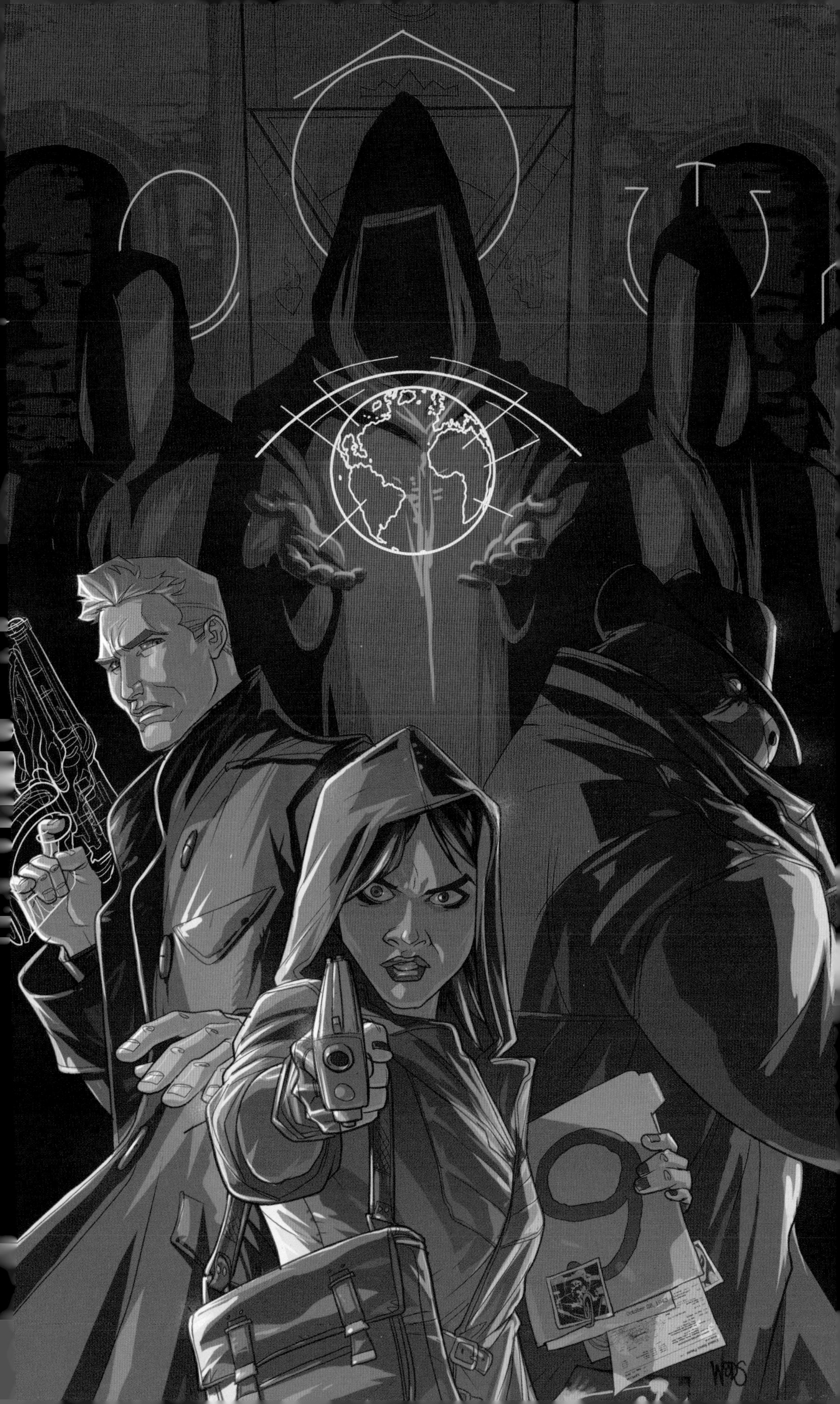

#1 THE ONION

NINE FAMILIES RULE THE WORLD. EACH ADHERES TO A STRICT ORGANIZATIONAL STRUCTURE.

009: ELDERS AND PRIESTS

The oldest Family members, with access to the most deeply hidden secrets.

008: SENIORS

Family members with leadership skills, tasked with the most difficult assignments.

007: FAMILY MEMBERS

Family members without leadership potential. Soldiers. Derogatorily called "cogs."

006: CHILDREN OF FAMILY MEMBERS

Taken to secret schools to be trained in the tasks of leadership.

005: CRYPTIDS

Creatures long thought extinct, most held in the Preserve.

004: ADVANCED AGENTS

Aware of the Families and active in high-level missions.

003: POLITICIANS AND BUSINESS LEADERS
Game pieces, but merely rooks and knights.

002: PAWNS

People used in Family tasks but oblivious of those whom they serve. Pawns of the lowest order.

001: MAJORITY OF HUMANS
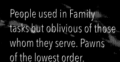
All 7.125 billion humans on Earth, the vast majority of whom know nothing of the Families' existence.

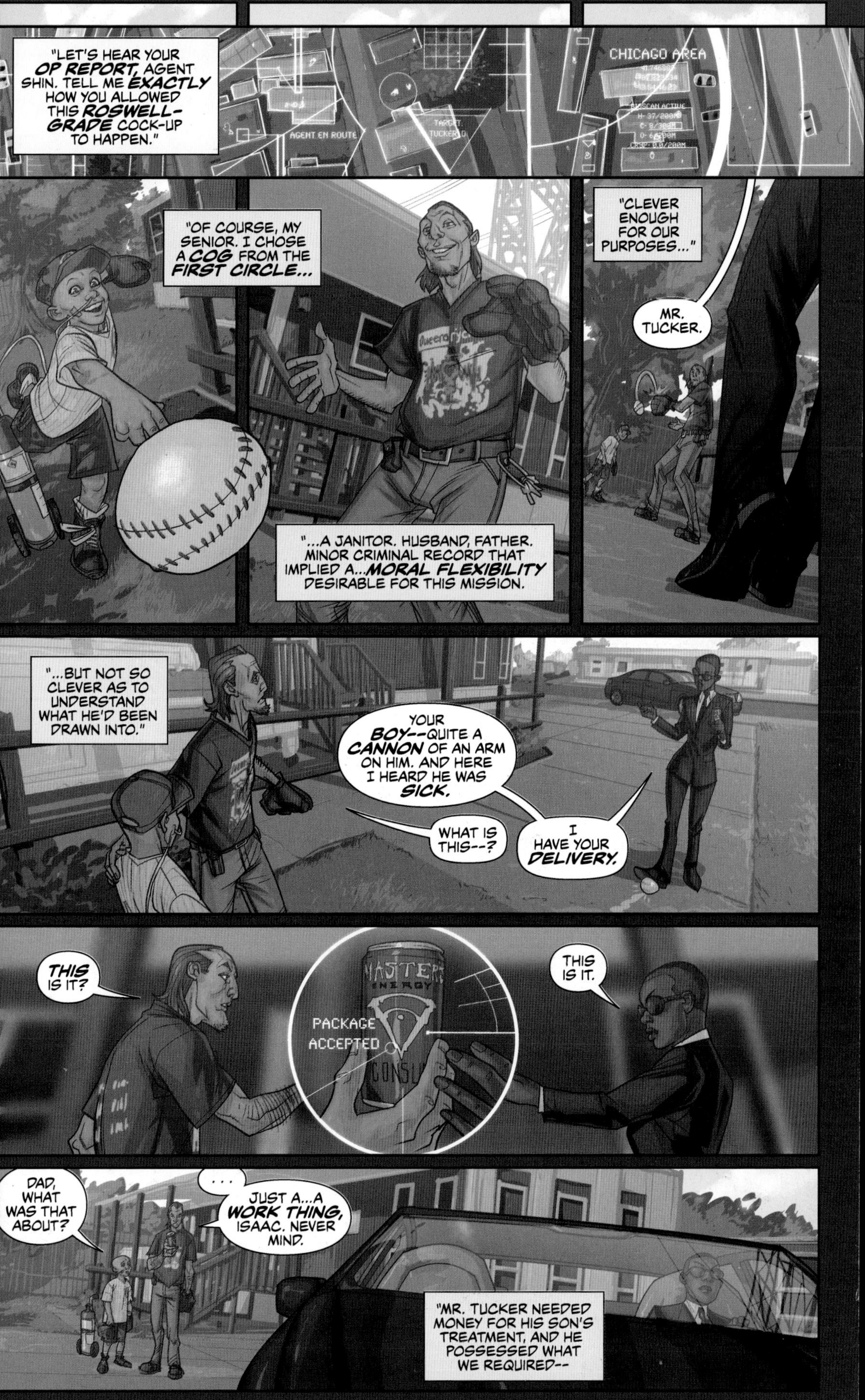
"LET'S HEAR YOUR OP REPORT, AGENT SHIN. TELL ME EXACTLY HOW YOU ALLOWED THIS ROSWELL-GRADE COCK-UP TO HAPPEN."
AGENT EN ROUTE
TARGET: TUCKER, D
CHICAGO AREA
BIOSCAN ACTIVE
"OF COURSE, MY SENIOR. I CHOSE A COG FROM THE FIRST CIRCLE...
"...A JANITOR. HUSBAND, FATHER. MINOR CRIMINAL RECORD THAT IMPLIED A...MORAL FLEXIBILITY DESIRABLE FOR THIS MISSION.
"CLEVER ENOUGH FOR OUR PURPOSES..."
MR. TUCKER.
"...BUT NOT SO CLEVER AS TO UNDERSTAND WHAT HE'D BEEN DRAWN INTO."
YOUR BOY--QUITE A CANNON OF AN ARM ON HIM. AND HERE I HEARD HE WAS SICK.
WHAT IS THIS--?
I HAVE YOUR DELIVERY.
THIS IS IT?
THIS IS IT.
MASTERS ENERGY
PACKAGE ACCEPTED
DAD, WHAT WAS THAT ABOUT?
. . .
JUST A...A WORK THING, ISAAC. NEVER MIND.
"MR. TUCKER NEEDED MONEY FOR HIS SON'S TREATMENT, AND HE POSSESSED WHAT WE REQUIRED--

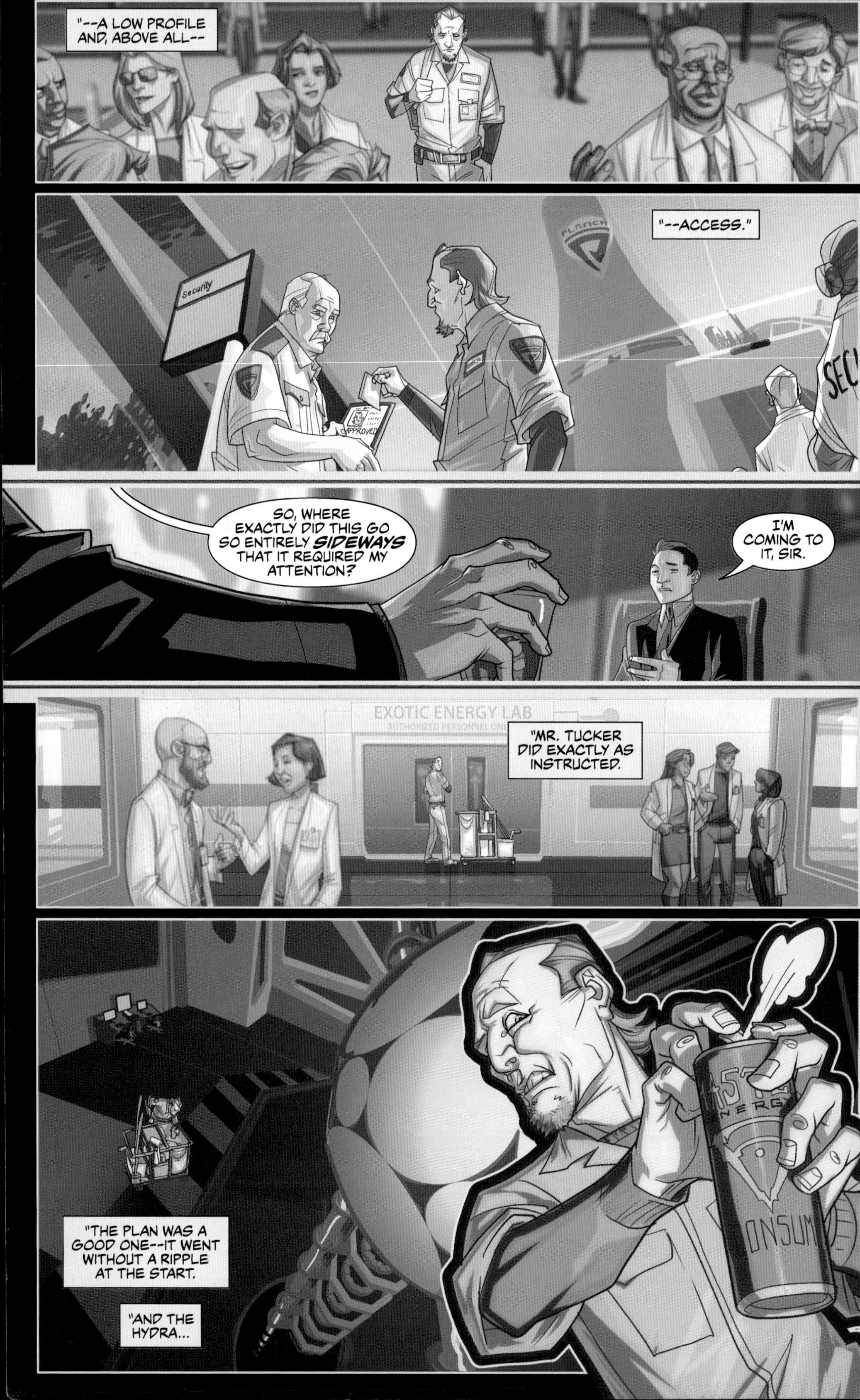
"--A LOW PROFILE AND, ABOVE ALL--
Security
APPROVED
"--ACCESS."
SO, WHERE EXACTLY DID THIS GO SO ENTIRELY SIDEWAYS THAT IT REQUIRED MY ATTENTION?
I'M COMING TO IT, SIR.
EXOTIC ENERGY LAB
"MR. TUCKER DID EXACTLY AS INSTRUCTED.
"THE PLAN WAS A GOOD ONE--IT WENT WITHOUT A RIPPLE AT THE START.
"AND THE HYDRA...

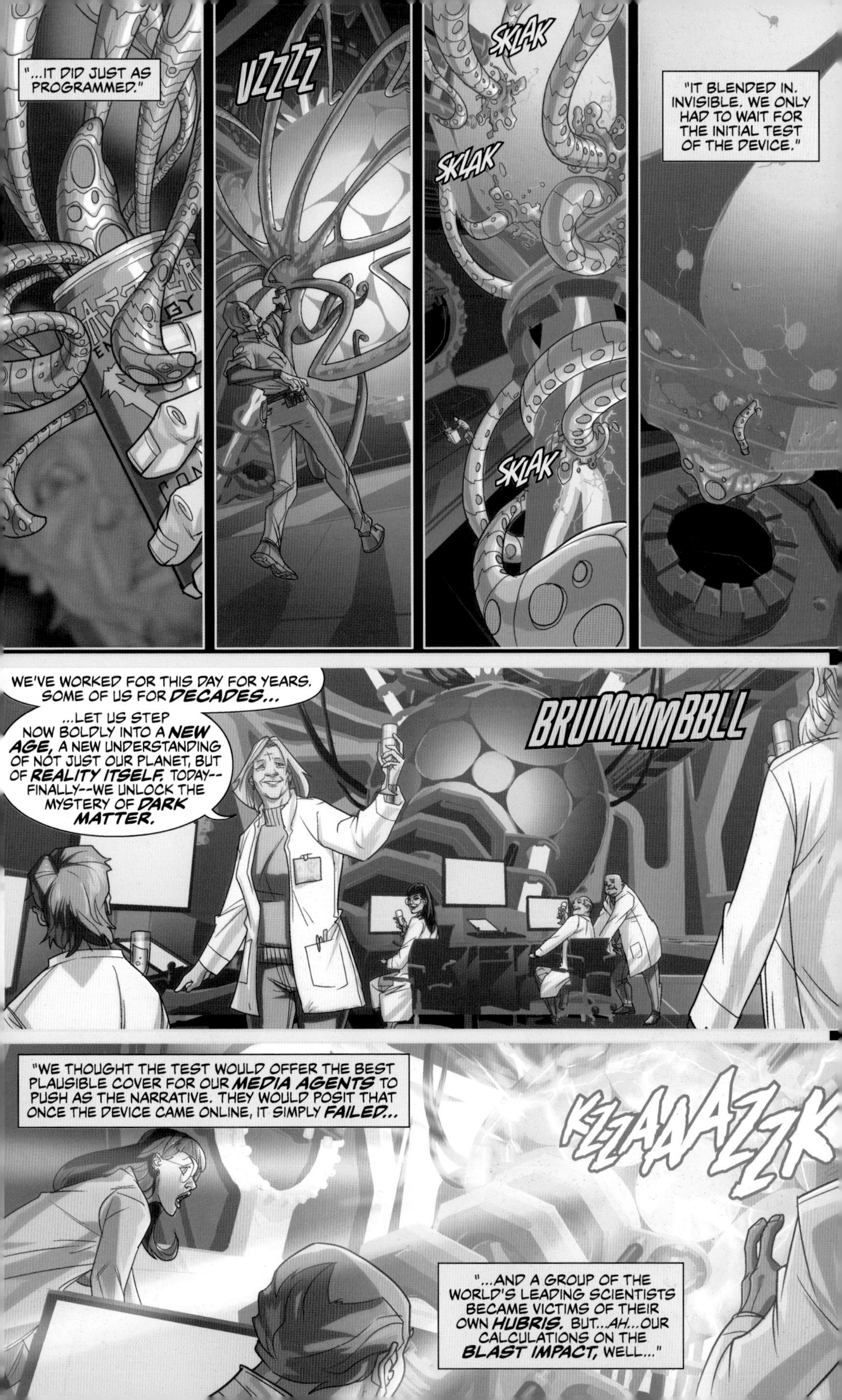
"...IT DID JUST AS PROGRAMMED."
VZZZZ
SKLAK
SKLAK
SKLAK
"IT BLENDED IN. INVISIBLE. WE ONLY HAD TO WAIT FOR THE INITIAL TEST OF THE DEVICE."
WE'VE WORKED FOR THIS DAY FOR YEARS. SOME OF US FOR DECADES...
...LET US STEP NOW BOLDLY INTO A NEW AGE, A NEW UNDERSTANDING OF NOT JUST OUR PLANET, BUT OF REALITY ITSELF. TODAY--FINALLY--WE UNLOCK THE MYSTERY OF DARK MATTER.
BRUMMMMBBLL
"WE THOUGHT THE TEST WOULD OFFER THE BEST PLAUSIBLE COVER FOR OUR MEDIA AGENTS TO PUSH AS THE NARRATIVE. THEY WOULD POSIT THAT ONCE THE DEVICE CAME ONLINE, IT SIMPLY FAILED...
KZZAAAZZK
"...AND A GROUP OF THE WORLD'S LEADING SCIENTISTS BECAME VICTIMS OF THEIR OWN HUBRIS. BUT...AH...OUR CALCULATIONS ON THE BLAST IMPACT, WELL..."

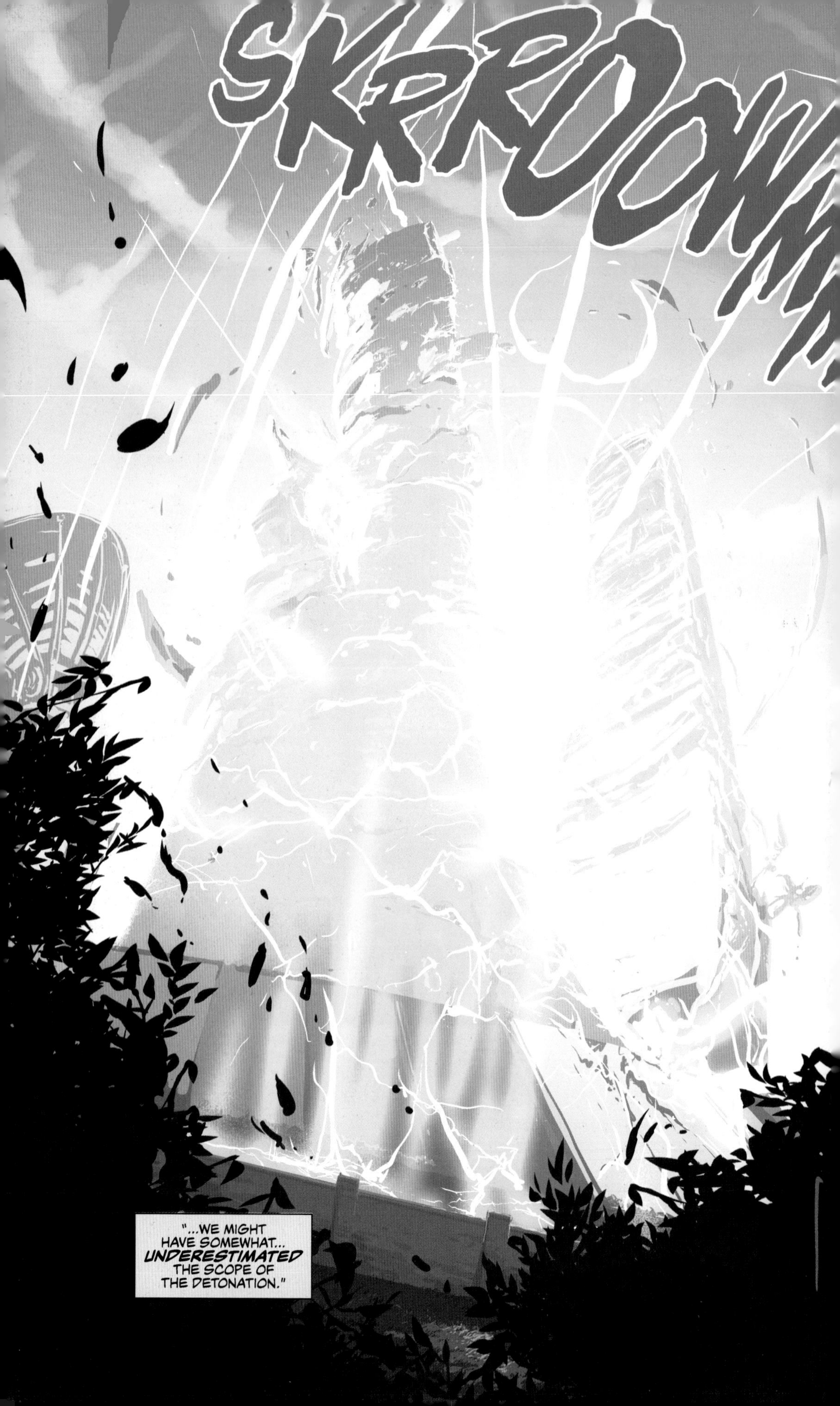
SKRROOOM
"...WE MIGHT HAVE SOMEWHAT... UNDERESTIMATED THE SCOPE OF THE DETONATION."

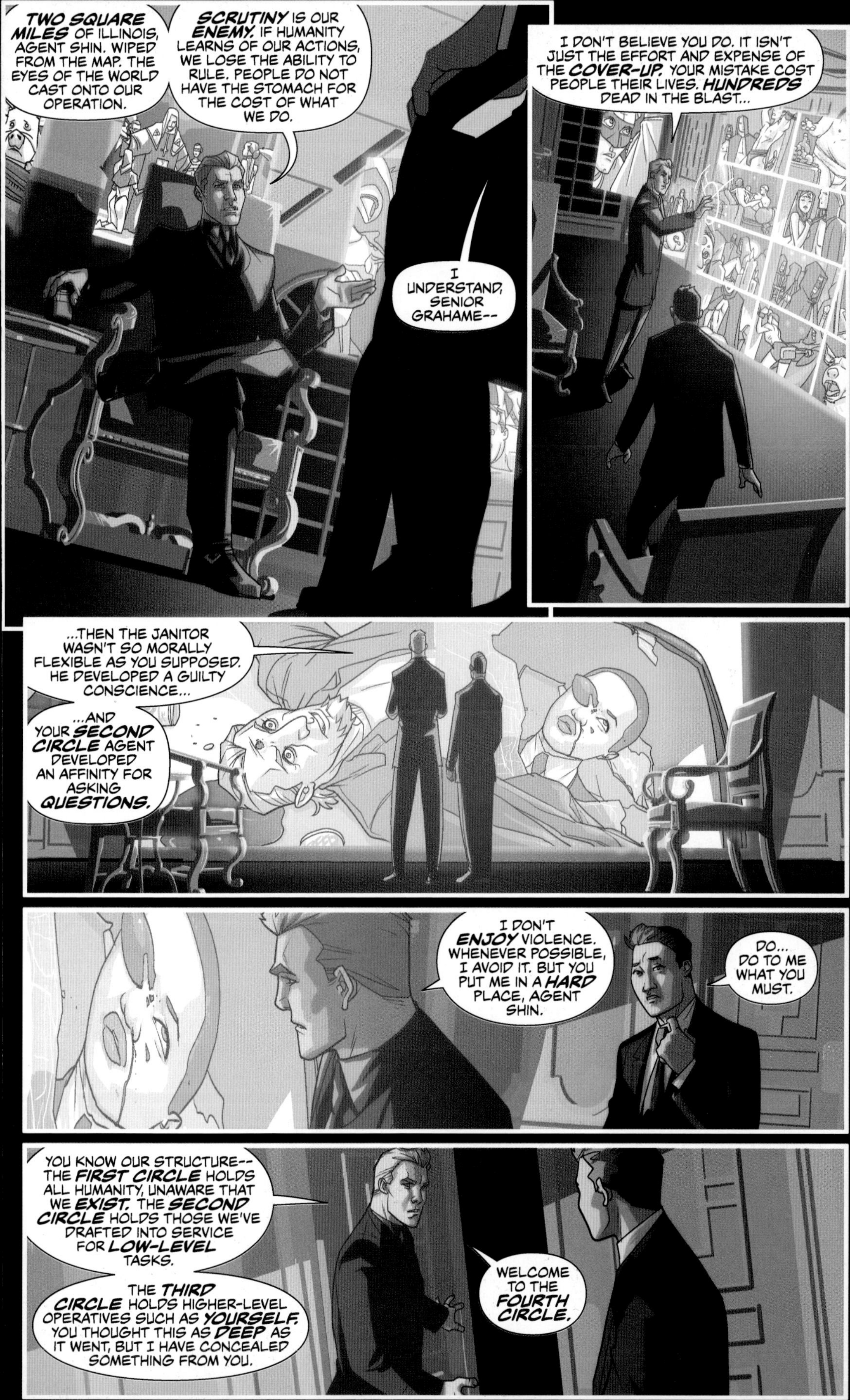

TWO SQUARE MILES OF ILLINOIS, AGENT SHIN. WIPED FROM THE MAP. THE EYES OF THE WORLD CAST ONTO OUR OPERATION.
SCRUTINY IS OUR ENEMY. IF HUMANITY LEARNS OF OUR ACTIONS, WE LOSE THE ABILITY TO RULE. PEOPLE DO NOT HAVE THE STOMACH FOR THE COST OF WHAT WE DO.
I UNDERSTAND, SENIOR GRAHAME--
I DON'T BELIEVE YOU DO. IT ISN'T JUST THE EFFORT AND EXPENSE OF THE COVER-UP. YOUR MISTAKE COST PEOPLE THEIR LIVES. HUNDREDS DEAD IN THE BLAST...
...THEN THE JANITOR WASN'T SO MORALLY FLEXIBLE AS YOU SUPPOSED. HE DEVELOPED A GUILTY CONSCIENCE...
...AND YOUR SECOND CIRCLE AGENT DEVELOPED AN AFFINITY FOR ASKING QUESTIONS.
I DON'T ENJOY VIOLENCE. WHENEVER POSSIBLE, I AVOID IT. BUT YOU PUT ME IN A HARD PLACE, AGENT SHIN.
DO... DO TO ME WHAT YOU MUST.
YOU KNOW OUR STRUCTURE-- THE FIRST CIRCLE HOLDS ALL HUMANITY, UNAWARE THAT WE EXIST. THE SECOND CIRCLE HOLDS THOSE WE'VE DRAFTED INTO SERVICE FOR LOW-LEVEL TASKS.
THE THIRD CIRCLE HOLDS HIGHER-LEVEL OPERATIVES SUCH AS YOURSELF. YOU THOUGHT THIS AS DEEP AS IT WENT, BUT I HAVE CONCEALED SOMETHING FROM YOU.
WELCOME TO THE FOURTH CIRCLE.

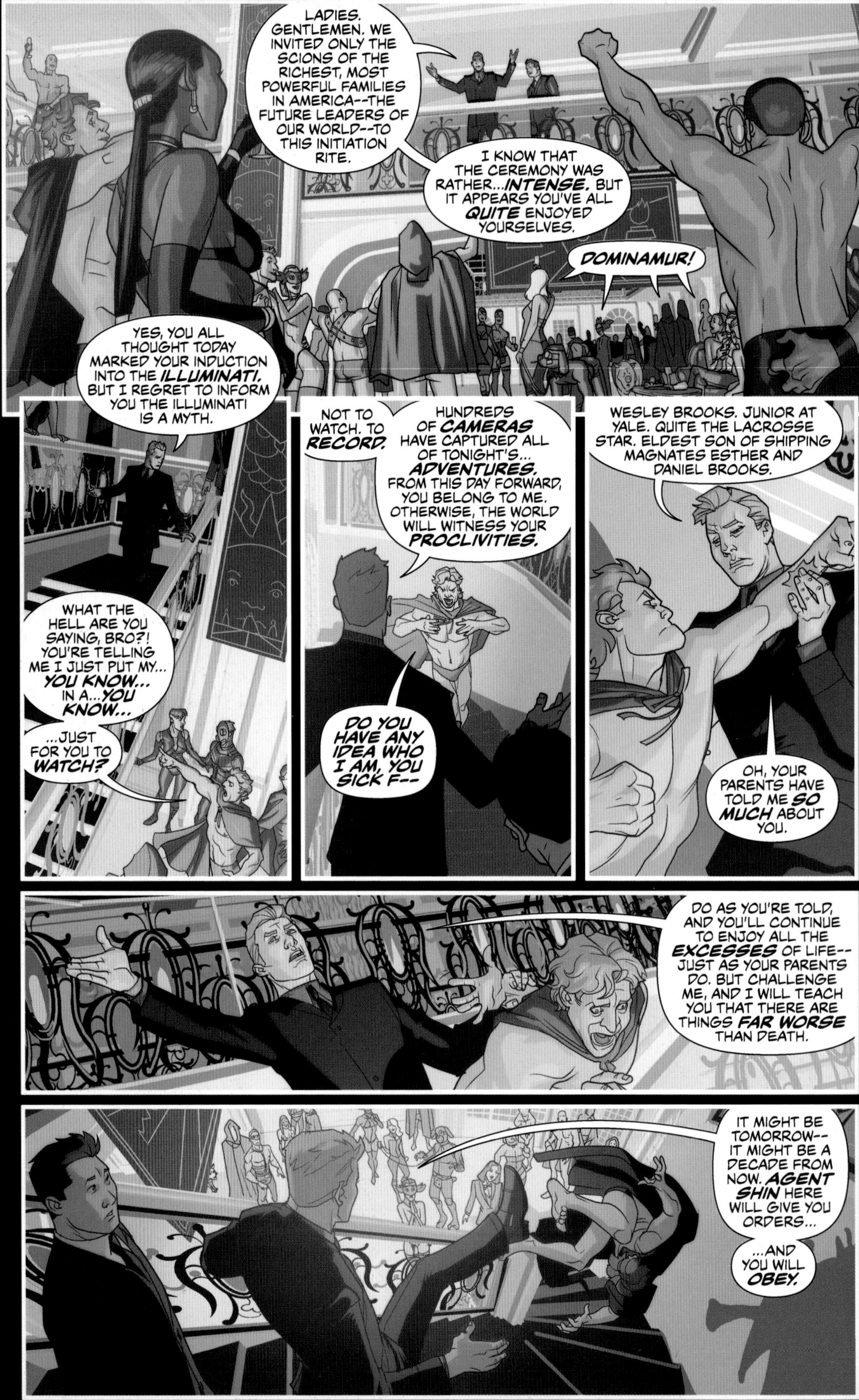
LADIES. GENTLEMEN. WE INVITED ONLY THE SCIONS OF THE RICHEST, MOST POWERFUL FAMILIES IN AMERICA--THE FUTURE LEADERS OF OUR WORLD--TO THIS INITIATION RITE.
I KNOW THAT THE CEREMONY WAS RATHER...INTENSE. BUT IT APPEARS YOU'VE ALL QUITE ENJOYED YOURSELVES.
DOMINAMUR!
YES, YOU ALL THOUGHT TODAY MARKED YOUR INDUCTION INTO THE ILLUMINATI. BUT I REGRET TO INFORM YOU THE ILLUMINATI IS A MYTH.
WHAT THE HELL ARE YOU SAYING, BRO?! YOU'RE TELLING ME I JUST PUT MY... YOU KNOW... IN A...YOU KNOW...
...JUST FOR YOU TO WATCH?
NOT TO WATCH. TO RECORD.
HUNDREDS OF CAMERAS HAVE CAPTURED ALL OF TONIGHT'S... ADVENTURES. FROM THIS DAY FORWARD, YOU BELONG TO ME. OTHERWISE, THE WORLD WILL WITNESS YOUR PROCLIVITIES.
DO YOU HAVE ANY IDEA WHO I AM, YOU SICK F--
WESLEY BROOKS. JUNIOR AT YALE. QUITE THE LACROSSE STAR. ELDEST SON OF SHIPPING MAGNATES ESTHER AND DANIEL BROOKS.
OH, YOUR PARENTS HAVE TOLD ME SO MUCH ABOUT YOU.
DO AS YOU'RE TOLD, AND YOU'LL CONTINUE TO ENJOY ALL THE EXCESSES OF LIFE--JUST AS YOUR PARENTS DO. BUT CHALLENGE ME, AND I WILL TEACH YOU THAT THERE ARE THINGS FAR WORSE THAN DEATH.
IT MIGHT BE TOMORROW--IT MIGHT BE A DECADE FROM NOW. AGENT SHIN HERE WILL GIVE YOU ORDERS...
...AND YOU WILL OBEY.

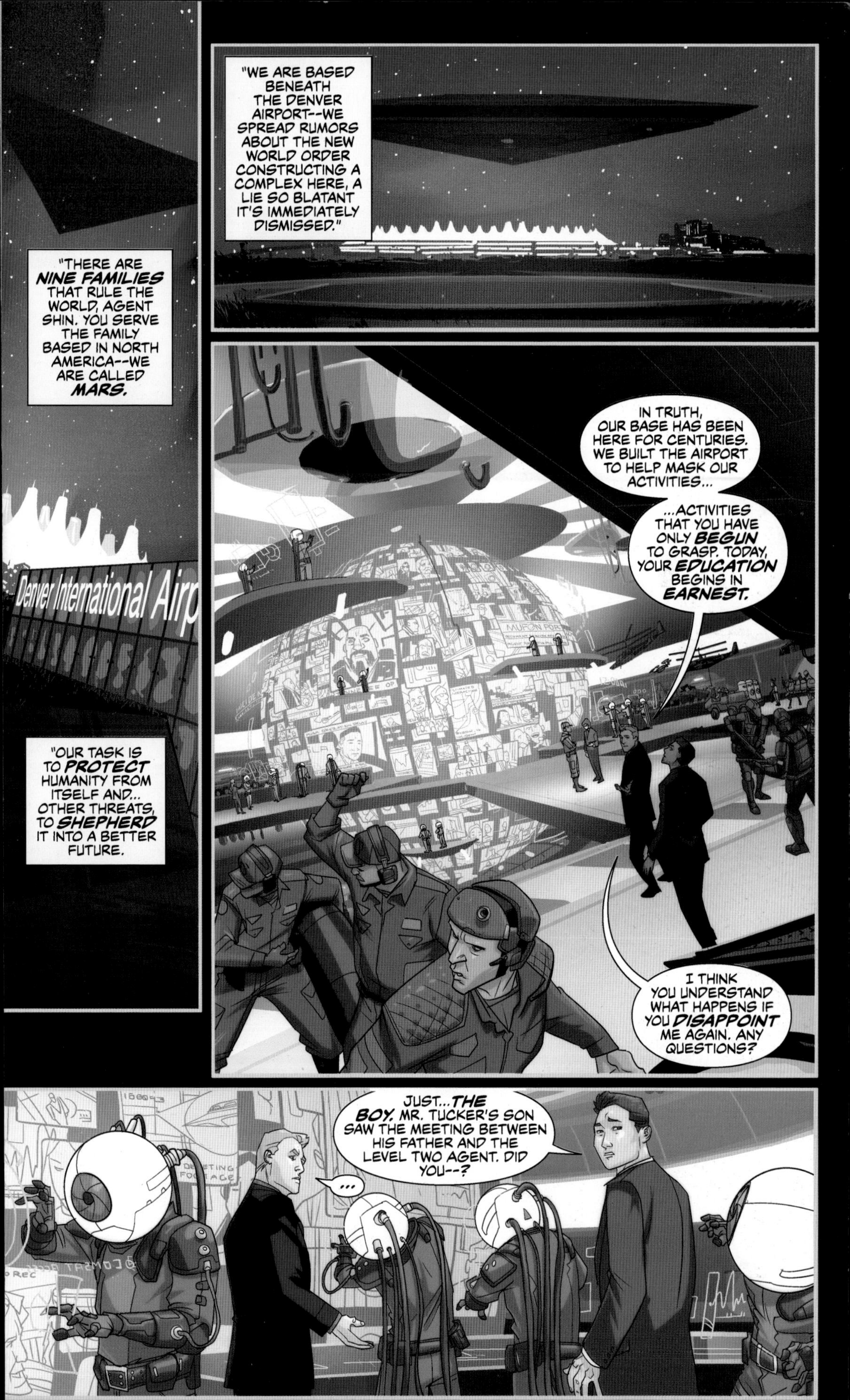
"THERE ARE NINE FAMILIES THAT RULE THE WORLD, AGENT SHIN. YOU SERVE THE FAMILY BASED IN NORTH AMERICA--WE ARE CALLED MARS.
"WE ARE BASED BENEATH THE DENVER AIRPORT--WE SPREAD RUMORS ABOUT THE NEW WORLD ORDER CONSTRUCTING A COMPLEX HERE, A LIE SO BLATANT IT'S IMMEDIATELY DISMISSED."
Denver International Airp
"OUR TASK IS TO PROTECT HUMANITY FROM ITSELF AND... OTHER THREATS, TO SHEPHERD IT INTO A BETTER FUTURE.
IN TRUTH, OUR BASE HAS BEEN HERE FOR CENTURIES. WE BUILT THE AIRPORT TO HELP MASK OUR ACTIVITIES...
...ACTIVITIES THAT YOU HAVE ONLY BEGUN TO GRASP. TODAY, YOUR EDUCATION BEGINS IN EARNEST.
I THINK YOU UNDERSTAND WHAT HAPPENS IF YOU DISAPPOINT ME AGAIN. ANY QUESTIONS?
JUST...THE BOY. MR. TUCKER'S SON SAW THE MEETING BETWEEN HIS FATHER AND THE LEVEL TWO AGENT. DID YOU--?
...

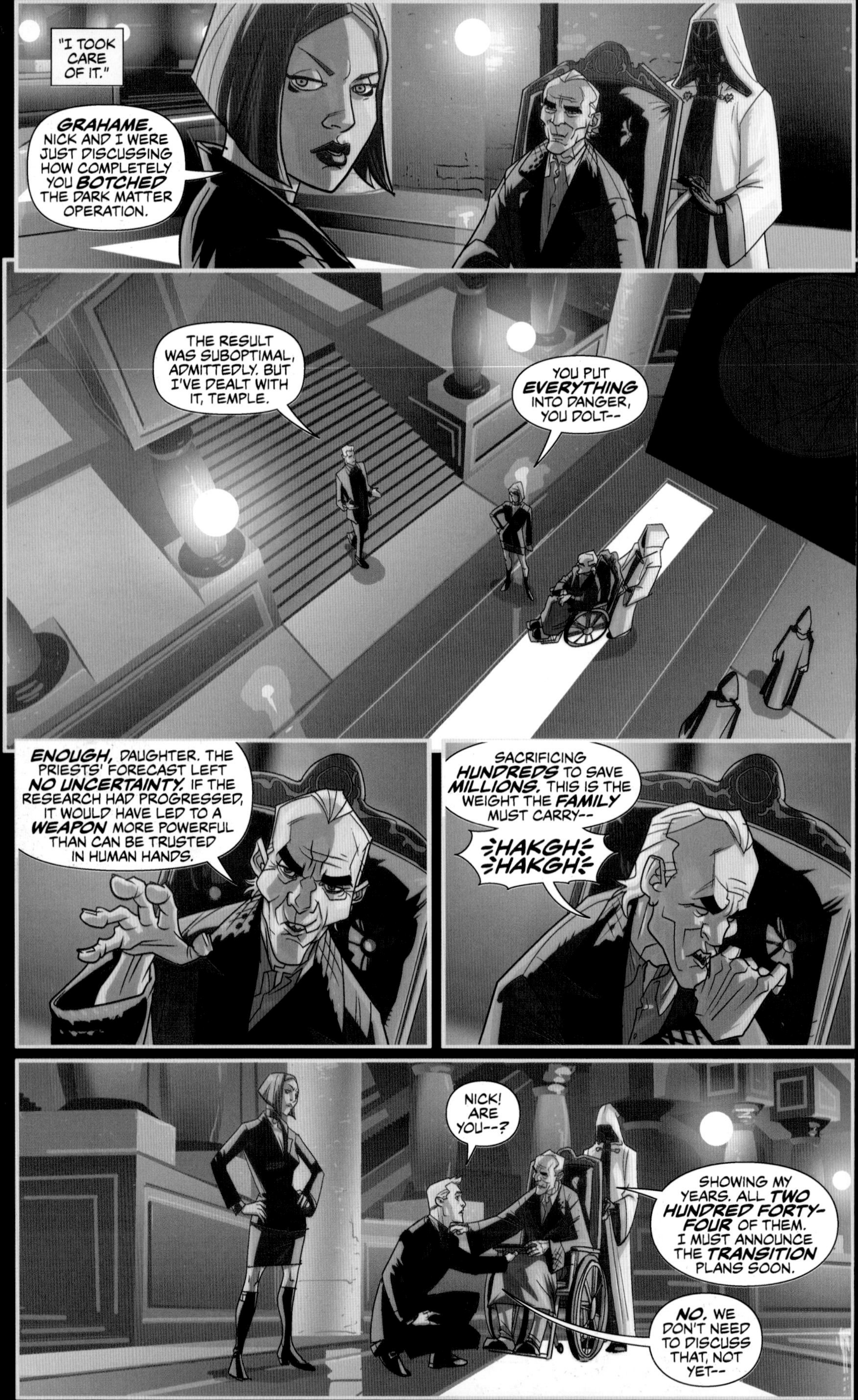
"I TOOK CARE OF IT."
GRAHAME. NICK AND I WERE JUST DISCUSSING HOW COMPLETELY YOU BOTCHED THE DARK MATTER OPERATION.
THE RESULT WAS SUBOPTIMAL, ADMITTEDLY. BUT I'VE DEALT WITH IT, TEMPLE.
YOU PUT EVERYTHING INTO DANGER, YOU DOLT--
ENOUGH, DAUGHTER. THE PRIESTS' FORECAST LEFT NO UNCERTAINTY. IF THE RESEARCH HAD PROGRESSED, IT WOULD HAVE LED TO A WEAPON MORE POWERFUL THAN CAN BE TRUSTED IN HUMAN HANDS.
SACRIFICING HUNDREDS TO SAVE MILLIONS. THIS IS THE WEIGHT THE FAMILY MUST CARRY--
HAKGH HAKGH
NICK! ARE YOU--?
SHOWING MY YEARS. ALL TWO HUNDRED FORTY-FOUR OF THEM. I MUST ANNOUNCE THE TRANSITION PLANS SOON.
NO. WE DON'T NEED TO DISCUSS THAT, NOT YET--

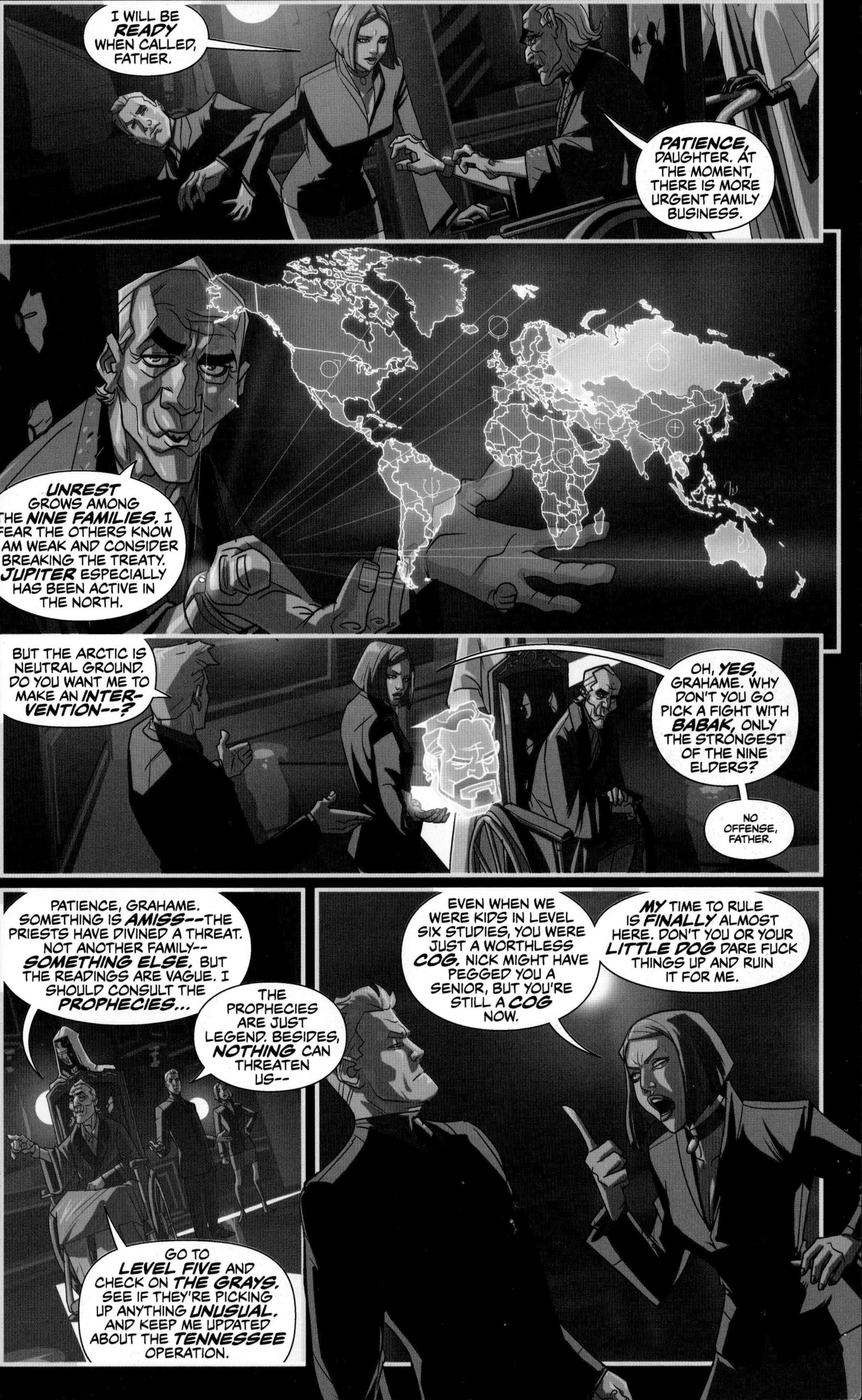
I WILL BE READY WHEN CALLED, FATHER.
PATIENCE, DAUGHTER. AT THE MOMENT, THERE IS MORE URGENT FAMILY BUSINESS.
UNREST GROWS AMONG THE NINE FAMILIES. I FEAR THE OTHERS KNOW I AM WEAK AND CONSIDER BREAKING THE TREATY. JUPITER ESPECIALLY HAS BEEN ACTIVE IN THE NORTH.
BUT THE ARCTIC IS NEUTRAL GROUND. DO YOU WANT ME TO MAKE AN INTER-VENTION--?
OH, YES, GRAHAME. WHY DON'T YOU GO PICK A FIGHT WITH BABAK, ONLY THE STRONGEST OF THE NINE ELDERS?
NO OFFENSE, FATHER.
PATIENCE, GRAHAME. SOMETHING IS AMISS--THE PRIESTS HAVE DIVINED A THREAT. NOT ANOTHER FAMILY-- SOMETHING ELSE. BUT THE READINGS ARE VAGUE. I SHOULD CONSULT THE PROPHECIES...
THE PROPHECIES ARE JUST LEGEND. BESIDES, NOTHING CAN THREATEN US--
GO TO LEVEL FIVE AND CHECK ON THE GRAYS. SEE IF THEY'RE PICKING UP ANYTHING UNUSUAL. AND KEEP ME UPDATED ABOUT THE TENNESSEE OPERATION.
EVEN WHEN WE WERE KIDS IN LEVEL SIX STUDIES, YOU WERE JUST A WORTHLESS COG. NICK MIGHT HAVE PEGGED YOU A SENIOR, BUT YOU'RE STILL A COG NOW.
MY TIME TO RULE IS FINALLY ALMOST HERE. DON'T YOU OR YOUR LITTLE DOG DARE FUCK THINGS UP AND RUIN IT FOR ME.

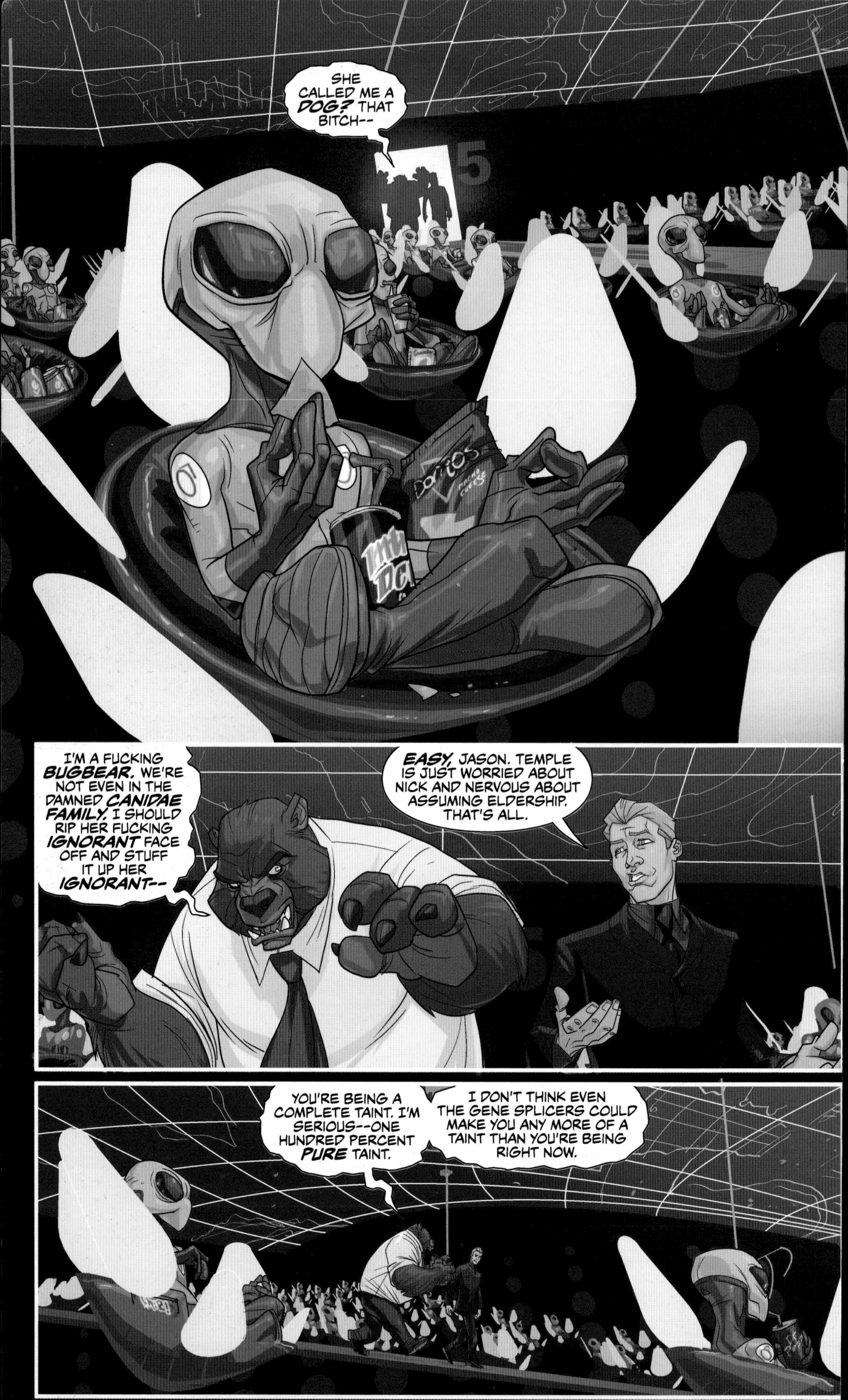
SHE CALLED ME A DOG? THAT BITCH--
I'M A FUCKING BUGBEAR. WE'RE NOT EVEN IN THE DAMNED CANIDAE FAMILY. I SHOULD RIP HER FUCKING IGNORANT FACE OFF AND STUFF IT UP HER IGNORANT--
EASY, JASON. TEMPLE IS JUST WORRIED ABOUT NICK AND NERVOUS ABOUT ASSUMING ELDERSHIP. THAT'S ALL.
YOU'RE BEING A COMPLETE TAINT. I'M SERIOUS--ONE HUNDRED PERCENT PURE TAINT.
I DON'T THINK EVEN THE GENE SPLICERS COULD MAKE YOU ANY MORE OF A TAINT THAN YOU'RE BEING RIGHT NOW.

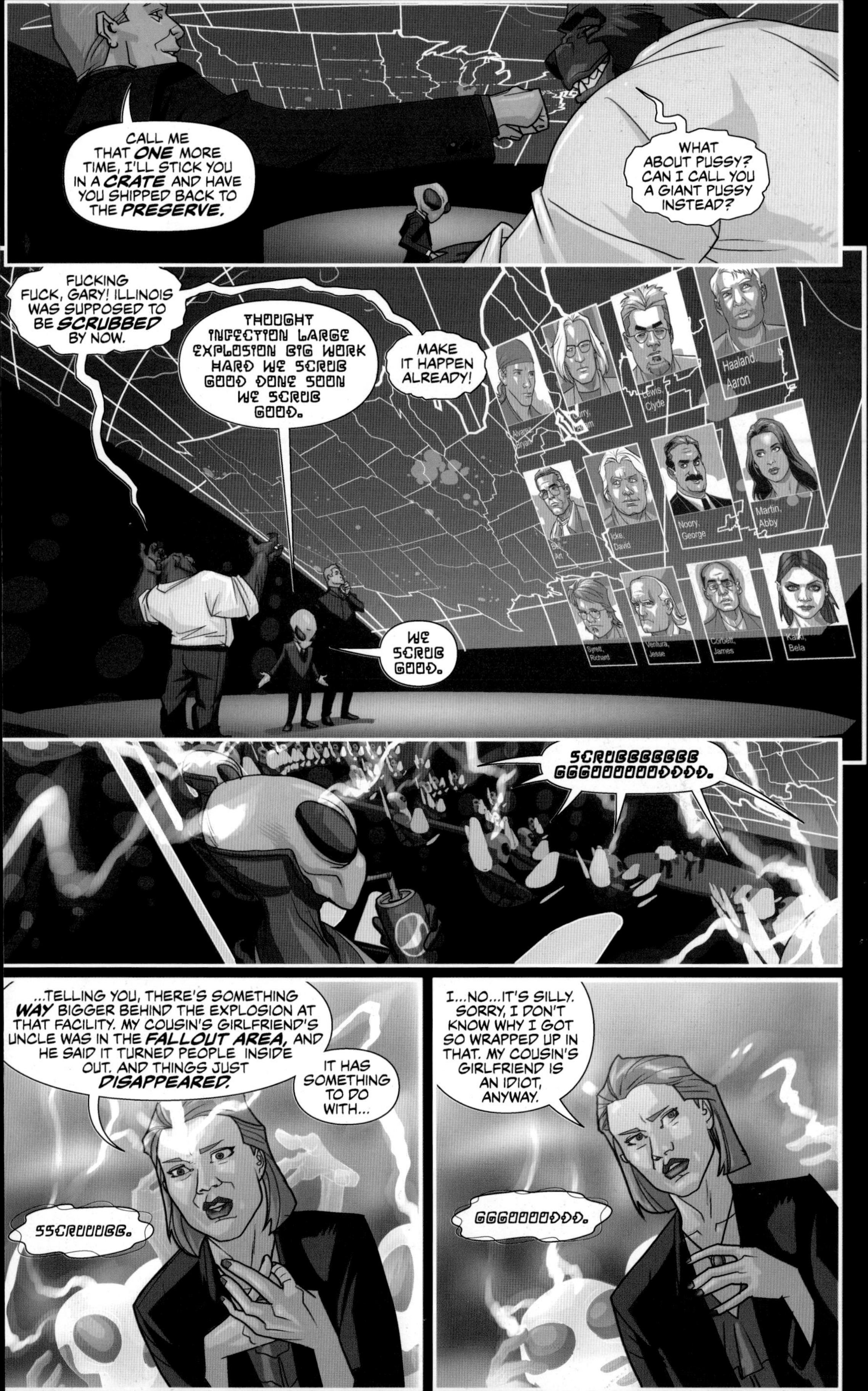
CALL ME THAT ONE MORE TIME, I'LL STICK YOU IN A CRATE AND HAVE YOU SHIPPED BACK TO THE PRESERVE.
WHAT ABOUT PUSSY? CAN I CALL YOU A GIANT PUSSY INSTEAD?
FUCKING FUCK, GARY! ILLINOIS WAS SUPPOSED TO BE SCRUBBED BY NOW.
THOUGHT INFECTION LARGE EXPLOSION BIG WORK HARD WE SCRUB GOOD DONE SOON WE SCRUB GOOD.
MAKE IT HAPPEN ALREADY!
Lewis, Clyde
Haaland, Aaron
Icke, David
Noory, George
Martin, Abby
Syrett, Richard
Ventura, Jesse
Corbett, James
WE SCRUB GOOD.
SCRUBBBBBBB GGGUUUUUUDDDD.
...TELLING YOU, THERE'S SOMETHING WAY BIGGER BEHIND THE EXPLOSION AT THAT FACILITY. MY COUSIN'S GIRLFRIEND'S UNCLE WAS IN THE FALLOUT AREA, AND HE SAID IT TURNED PEOPLE INSIDE OUT. AND THINGS JUST DISAPPEARED.
IT HAS SOMETHING TO DO WITH...
SSCRUUUBB.
I...NO...IT'S SILLY. SORRY, I DON'T KNOW WHY I GOT SO WRAPPED UP IN THAT. MY COUSIN'S GIRLFRIEND IS AN IDIOT, ANYWAY.
GGGUUUUDDD.

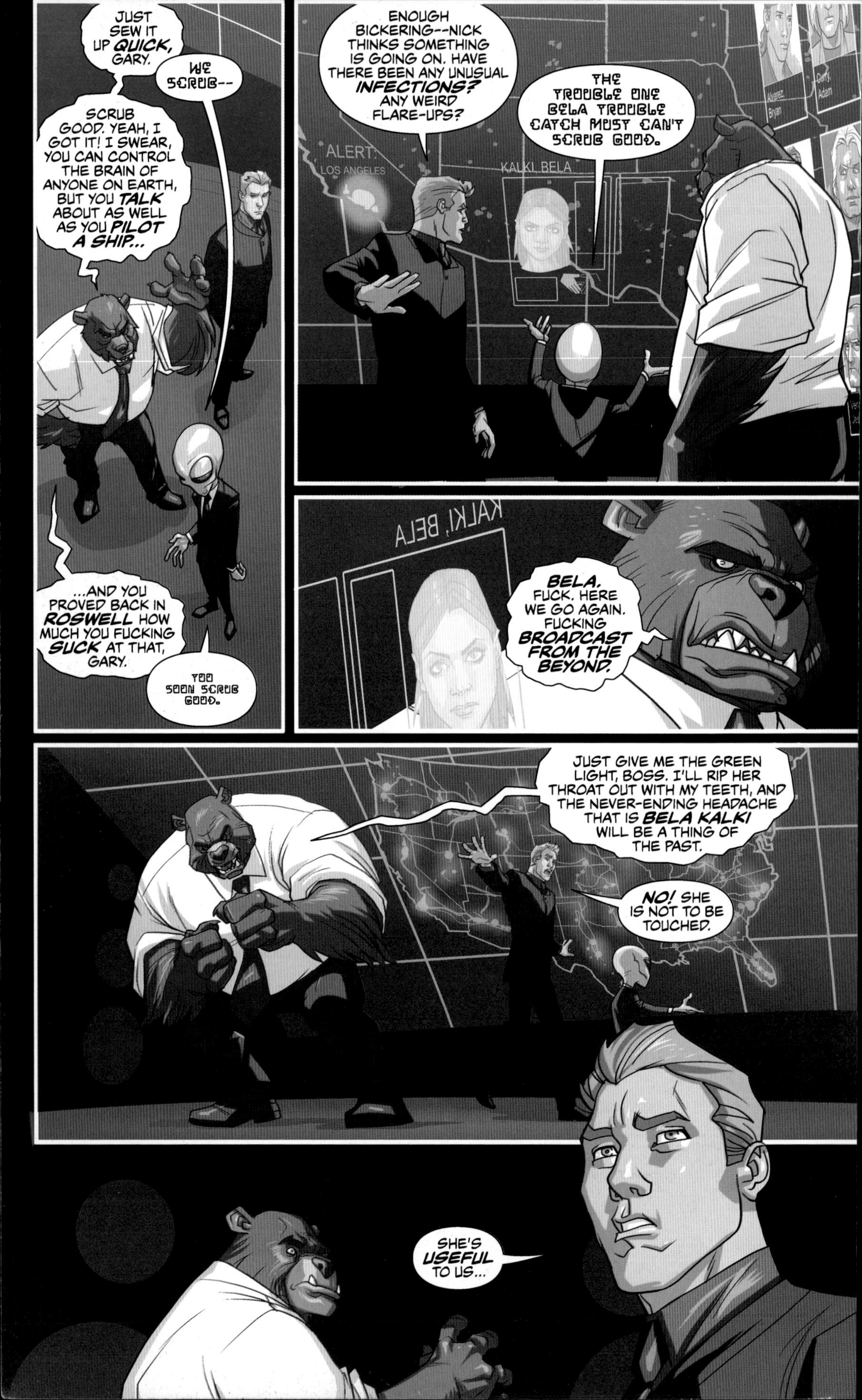
JUST SEW IT UP QUICK, GARY.
WE SCRUB--
SCRUB GOOD. YEAH, I GOT IT! I SWEAR, YOU CAN CONTROL THE BRAIN OF ANYONE ON EARTH, BUT YOU TALK ABOUT AS WELL AS YOU PILOT A SHIP...
...AND YOU PROVED BACK IN ROSWELL HOW MUCH YOU FUCKING SUCK AT THAT, GARY.
TOO SOON SCRUB GOOD.
ENOUGH BICKERING--NICK THINKS SOMETHING IS GOING ON. HAVE THERE BEEN ANY UNUSUAL INFECTIONS? ANY WEIRD FLARE-UPS?
ALERT:
LOS ANGELES
KALKI, BELA
Alvarez, Bryan
Curry, Adam
THE TROUBLE ONE BELA TROUBLE CATCH MUST CAN'T SCRUB GOOD.
BELA. FUCK. HERE WE GO AGAIN. FUCKING BROADCAST FROM THE BEYOND.
JUST GIVE ME THE GREEN LIGHT, BOSS. I'LL RIP HER THROAT OUT WITH MY TEETH, AND THE NEVER-ENDING HEADACHE THAT IS BELA KALKI WILL BE A THING OF THE PAST.
NO! SHE IS NOT TO BE TOUCHED.
SHE'S USEFUL TO US...

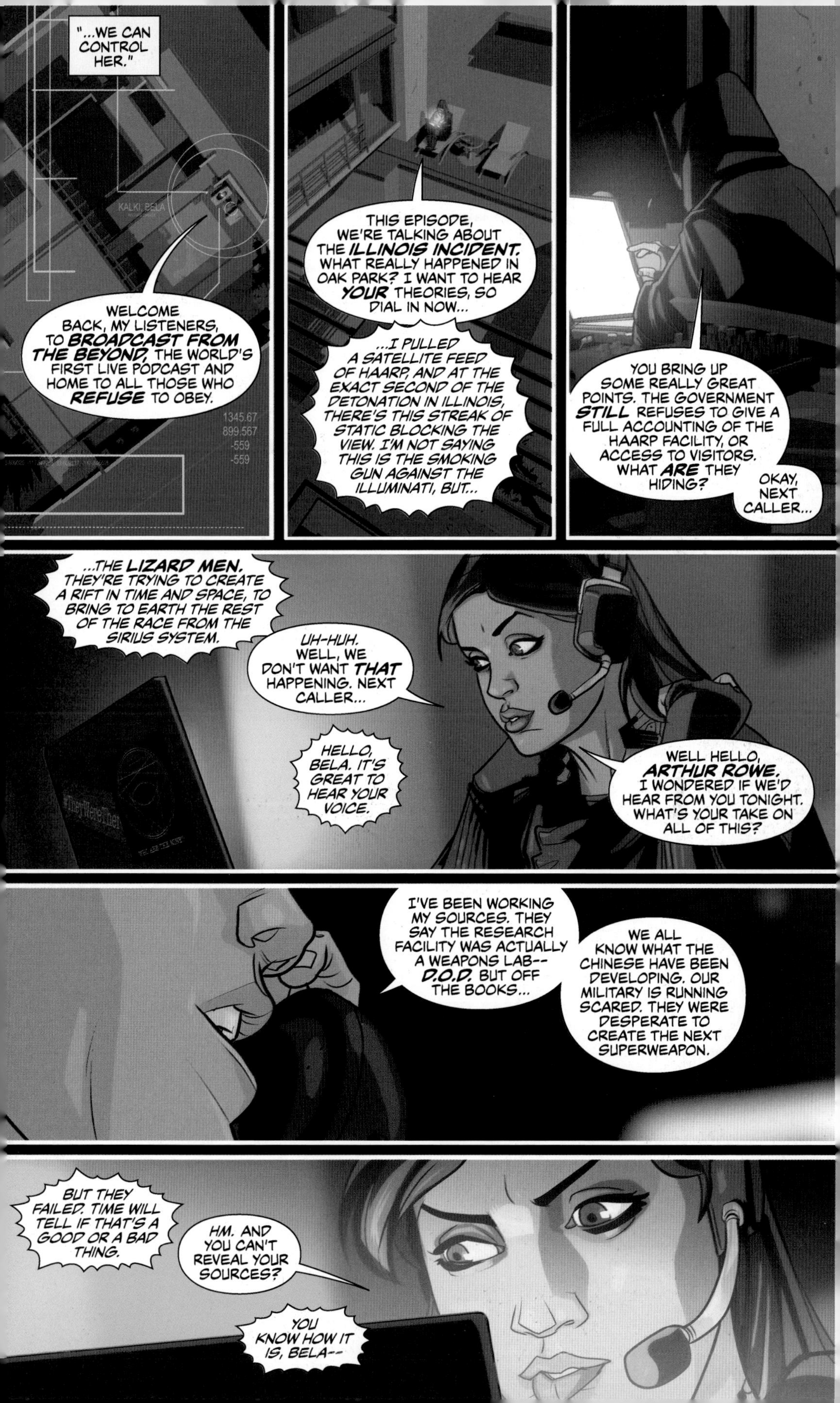

"...WE CAN CONTROL HER."
KALKI, BELA
WELCOME BACK, MY LISTENERS, TO BROADCAST FROM THE BEYOND, THE WORLD'S FIRST LIVE PODCAST AND HOME TO ALL THOSE WHO REFUSE TO OBEY.
1345.67
899.567
-559
-559
THIS EPISODE, WE'RE TALKING ABOUT THE ILLINOIS INCIDENT. WHAT REALLY HAPPENED IN OAK PARK? I WANT TO HEAR YOUR THEORIES, SO DIAL IN NOW...
...I PULLED A SATELLITE FEED OF HAARP, AND AT THE EXACT SECOND OF THE DETONATION IN ILLINOIS, THERE'S THIS STREAK OF STATIC BLOCKING THE VIEW. I'M NOT SAYING THIS IS THE SMOKING GUN AGAINST THE ILLUMINATI, BUT...
YOU BRING UP SOME REALLY GREAT POINTS. THE GOVERNMENT STILL REFUSES TO GIVE A FULL ACCOUNTING OF THE HAARP FACILITY, OR ACCESS TO VISITORS. WHAT ARE THEY HIDING?
OKAY, NEXT CALLER...
...THE LIZARD MEN. THEY'RE TRYING TO CREATE A RIFT IN TIME AND SPACE, TO BRING TO EARTH THE REST OF THE RACE FROM THE SIRIUS SYSTEM.
UH-HUH. WELL, WE DON'T WANT THAT HAPPENING. NEXT CALLER...
HELLO, BELA. IT'S GREAT TO HEAR YOUR VOICE.
WELL HELLO, ARTHUR ROWE. I WONDERED IF WE'D HEAR FROM YOU TONIGHT. WHAT'S YOUR TAKE ON ALL OF THIS?
I'VE BEEN WORKING MY SOURCES. THEY SAY THE RESEARCH FACILITY WAS ACTUALLY A WEAPONS LAB-- D.O.D. BUT OFF THE BOOKS...
WE ALL KNOW WHAT THE CHINESE HAVE BEEN DEVELOPING. OUR MILITARY IS RUNNING SCARED. THEY WERE DESPERATE TO CREATE THE NEXT SUPERWEAPON.
BUT THEY FAILED. TIME WILL TELL IF THAT'S A GOOD OR A BAD THING.
HM. AND YOU CAN'T REVEAL YOUR SOURCES?
YOU KNOW HOW IT IS, BELA--

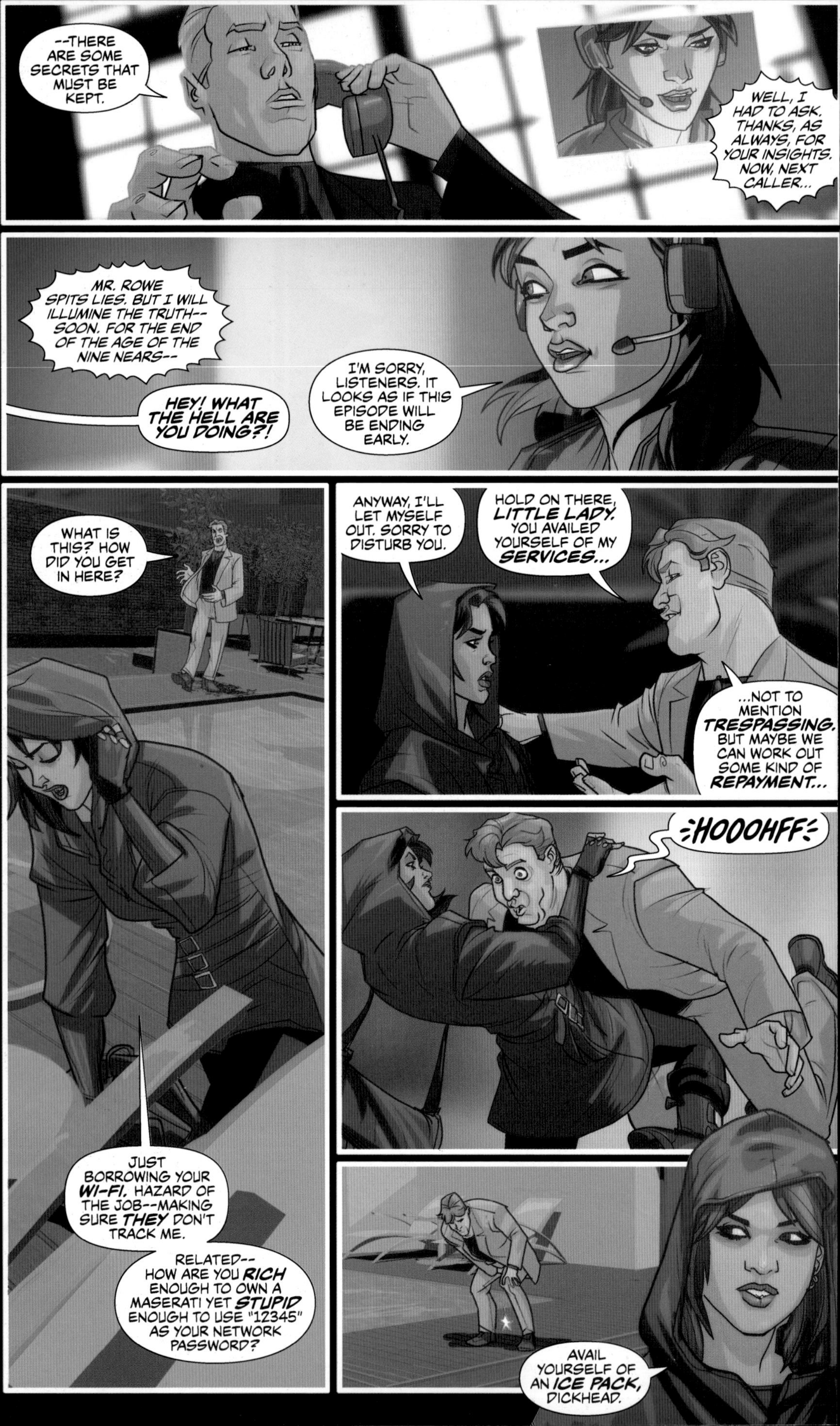
--THERE ARE SOME SECRETS THAT MUST BE KEPT.
WELL, I HAD TO ASK. THANKS, AS ALWAYS, FOR YOUR INSIGHTS. NOW, NEXT CALLER...
MR. ROWE SPITS LIES. BUT I WILL ILLUMINE THE TRUTH--SOON. FOR THE END OF THE AGE OF THE NINE NEARS--
HEY! WHAT THE HELL ARE YOU DOING?!
I'M SORRY, LISTENERS. IT LOOKS AS IF THIS EPISODE WILL BE ENDING EARLY.
WHAT IS THIS? HOW DID YOU GET IN HERE?
JUST BORROWING YOUR WI-FI. HAZARD OF THE JOB--MAKING SURE THEY DON'T TRACK ME.
RELATED--HOW ARE YOU RICH ENOUGH TO OWN A MASERATI YET STUPID ENOUGH TO USE "12345" AS YOUR NETWORK PASSWORD?
ANYWAY, I'LL LET MYSELF OUT. SORRY TO DISTURB YOU.
HOLD ON THERE, LITTLE LADY. YOU AVAILED YOURSELF OF MY SERVICES...
...NOT TO MENTION TRESPASSING. BUT MAYBE WE CAN WORK OUT SOME KIND OF REPAYMENT...
HOOOHFF
AVAIL YOURSELF OF AN ICE PACK, DICKHEAD.

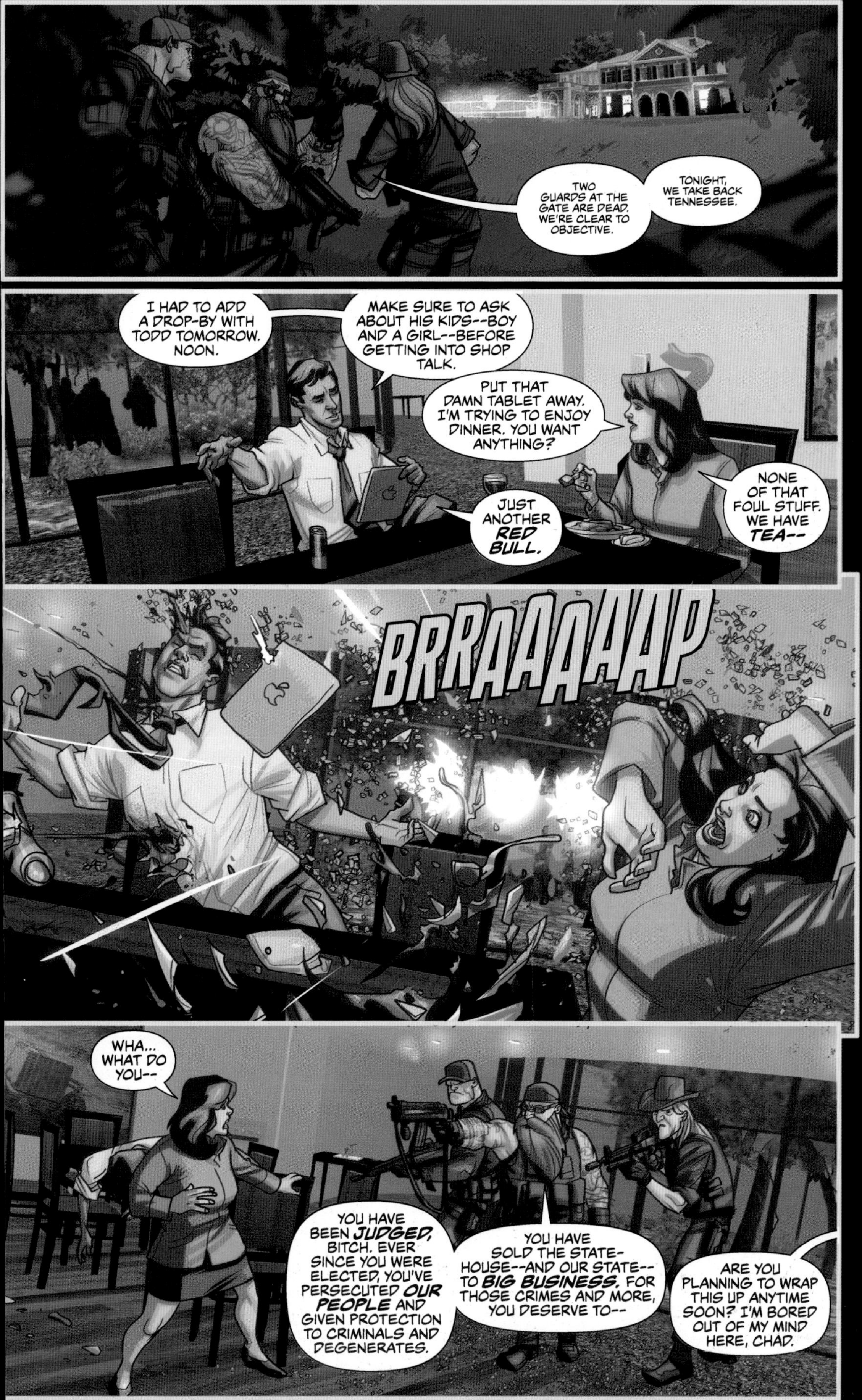
TWO GUARDS AT THE GATE ARE DEAD. WE'RE CLEAR TO OBJECTIVE.
TONIGHT, WE TAKE BACK TENNESSEE.
I HAD TO ADD A DROP-BY WITH TODD TOMORROW. NOON.
MAKE SURE TO ASK ABOUT HIS KIDS--BOY AND A GIRL--BEFORE GETTING INTO SHOP TALK.
PUT THAT DAMN TABLET AWAY. I'M TRYING TO ENJOY DINNER. YOU WANT ANYTHING?
JUST ANOTHER RED BULL.
NONE OF THAT FOUL STUFF. WE HAVE TEA--
BRRAAAAAAP
WHA... WHAT DO YOU--
YOU HAVE BEEN JUDGED, BITCH. EVER SINCE YOU WERE ELECTED, YOU'VE PERSECUTED OUR PEOPLE AND GIVEN PROTECTION TO CRIMINALS AND DEGENERATES.
YOU HAVE SOLD THE STATE-HOUSE--AND OUR STATE--TO BIG BUSINESS. FOR THOSE CRIMES AND MORE, YOU DESERVE TO--
ARE YOU PLANNING TO WRAP THIS UP ANYTIME SOON? I'M BORED OUT OF MY MIND HERE, CHAD.

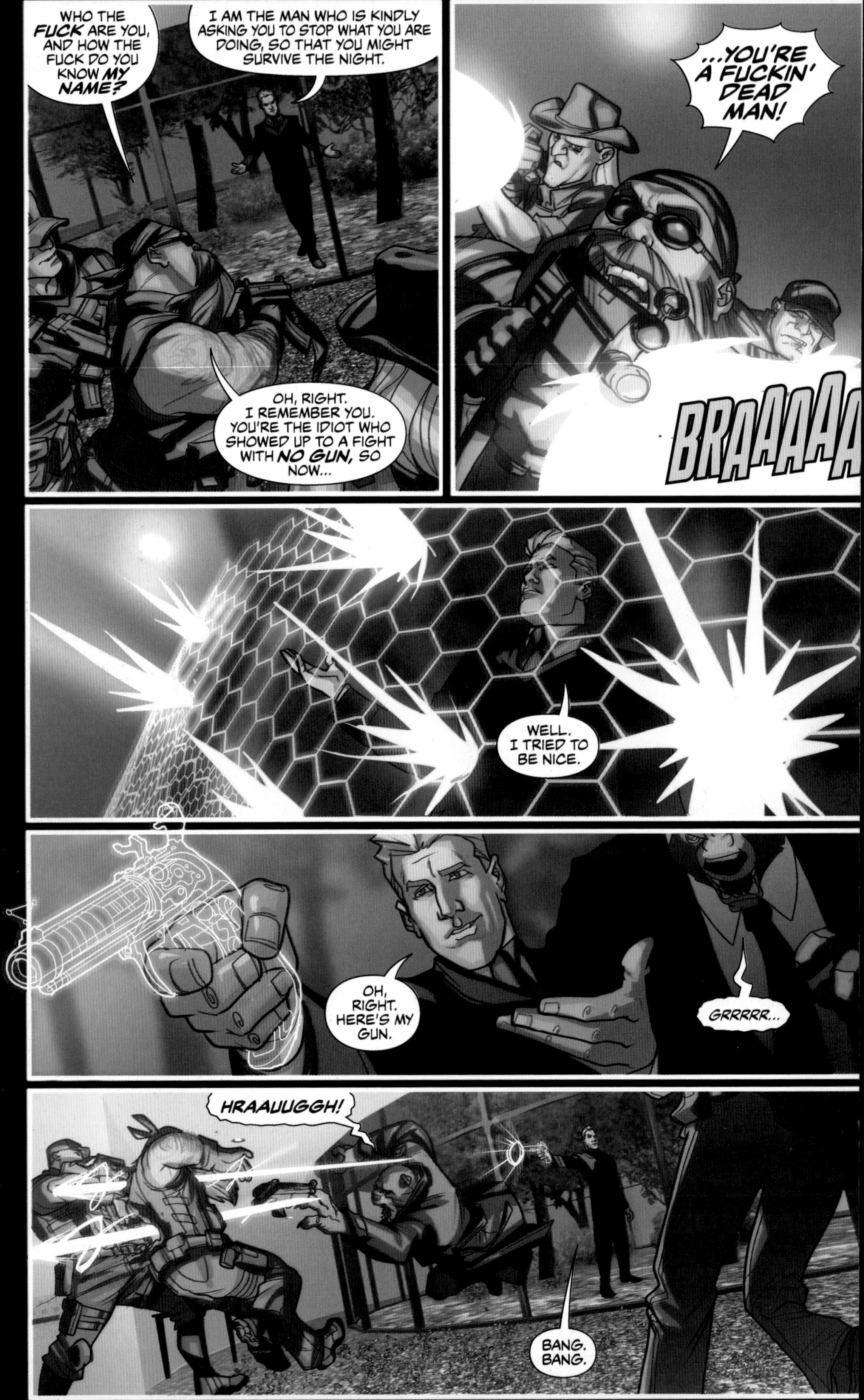
WHO THE FUCK ARE YOU, AND HOW THE FUCK DO YOU KNOW MY NAME?
I AM THE MAN WHO IS KINDLY ASKING YOU TO STOP WHAT YOU ARE DOING, SO THAT YOU MIGHT SURVIVE THE NIGHT.
OH, RIGHT. I REMEMBER YOU. YOU'RE THE IDIOT WHO SHOWED UP TO A FIGHT WITH NO GUN, SO NOW...
...YOU'RE A FUCKIN' DEAD MAN!
BRAAAAAA
WELL. I TRIED TO BE NICE.
OH, RIGHT. HERE'S MY GUN.
GRRRRR...
HRAAUUGGH!
BANG. BANG.

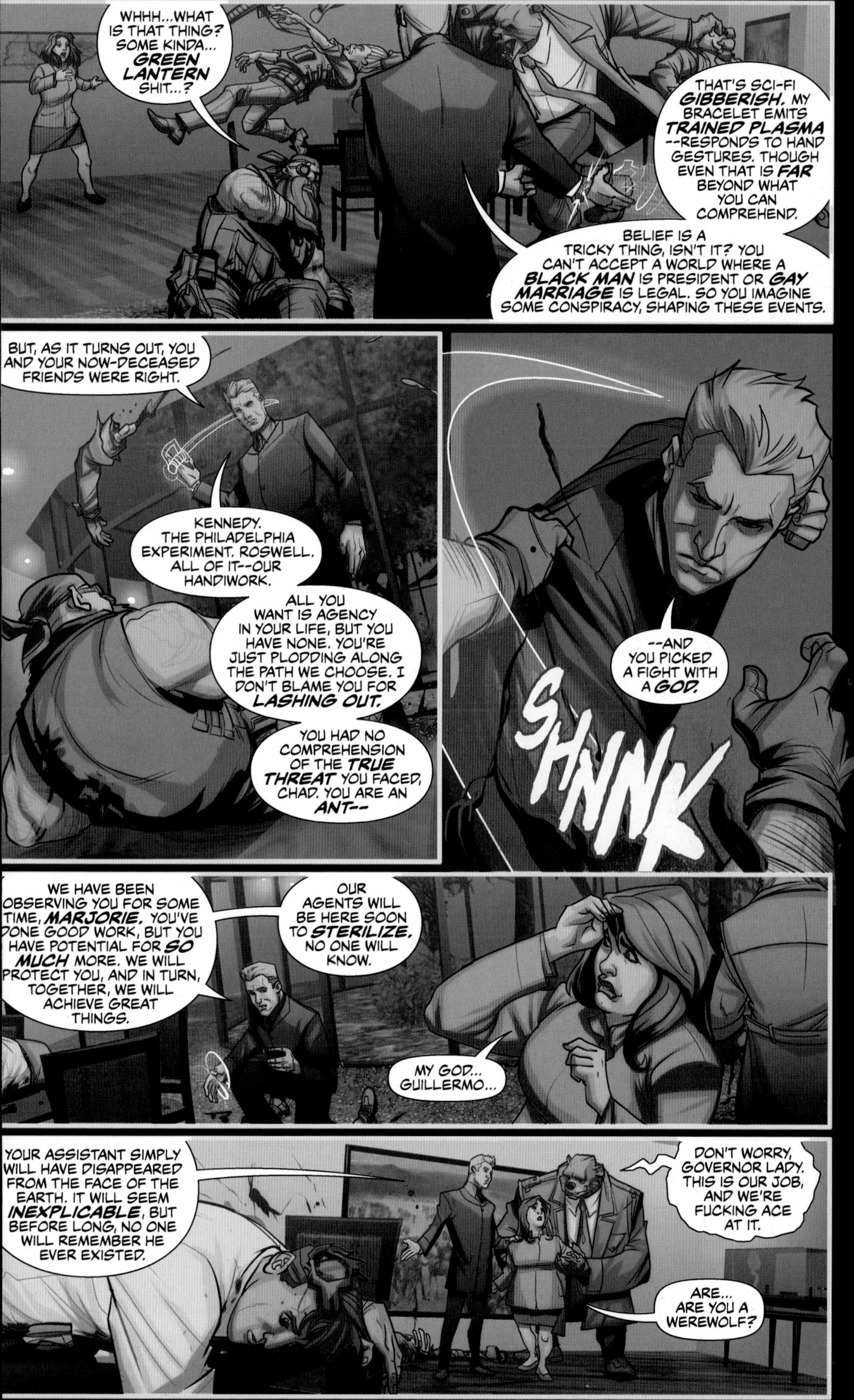
WHHH...WHAT IS THAT THING? SOME KINDA... GREEN LANTERN SHIT...?
THAT'S SCI-FI GIBBERISH. MY BRACELET EMITS TRAINED PLASMA --RESPONDS TO HAND GESTURES. THOUGH EVEN THAT IS FAR BEYOND WHAT YOU CAN COMPREHEND.
BELIEF IS A TRICKY THING, ISN'T IT? YOU CAN'T ACCEPT A WORLD WHERE A BLACK MAN IS PRESIDENT OR GAY MARRIAGE IS LEGAL. SO YOU IMAGINE SOME CONSPIRACY, SHAPING THESE EVENTS.
BUT, AS IT TURNS OUT, YOU AND YOUR NOW-DECEASED FRIENDS WERE RIGHT.
KENNEDY. THE PHILADELPHIA EXPERIMENT. ROSWELL. ALL OF IT--OUR HANDIWORK.
ALL YOU WANT IS AGENCY IN YOUR LIFE, BUT YOU HAVE NONE. YOU'RE JUST PLODDING ALONG THE PATH WE CHOOSE. I DON'T BLAME YOU FOR LASHING OUT.
YOU HAD NO COMPREHENSION OF THE TRUE THREAT YOU FACED, CHAD. YOU ARE AN ANT--
--AND YOU PICKED A FIGHT WITH A GOD.
SHNNK
WE HAVE BEEN OBSERVING YOU FOR SOME TIME, MARJORIE. YOU'VE DONE GOOD WORK, BUT YOU HAVE POTENTIAL FOR SO MUCH MORE. WE WILL PROTECT YOU, AND IN TURN, TOGETHER, WE WILL ACHIEVE GREAT THINGS.
OUR AGENTS WILL BE HERE SOON TO STERILIZE. NO ONE WILL KNOW.
MY GOD... GUILLERMO...
YOUR ASSISTANT SIMPLY WILL HAVE DISAPPEARED FROM THE FACE OF THE EARTH. IT WILL SEEM INEXPLICABLE, BUT BEFORE LONG, NO ONE WILL REMEMBER HE EVER EXISTED.
DON'T WORRY, GOVERNOR LADY. THIS IS OUR JOB, AND WE'RE FUCKING ACE AT IT.
ARE... ARE YOU A WEREWOLF?

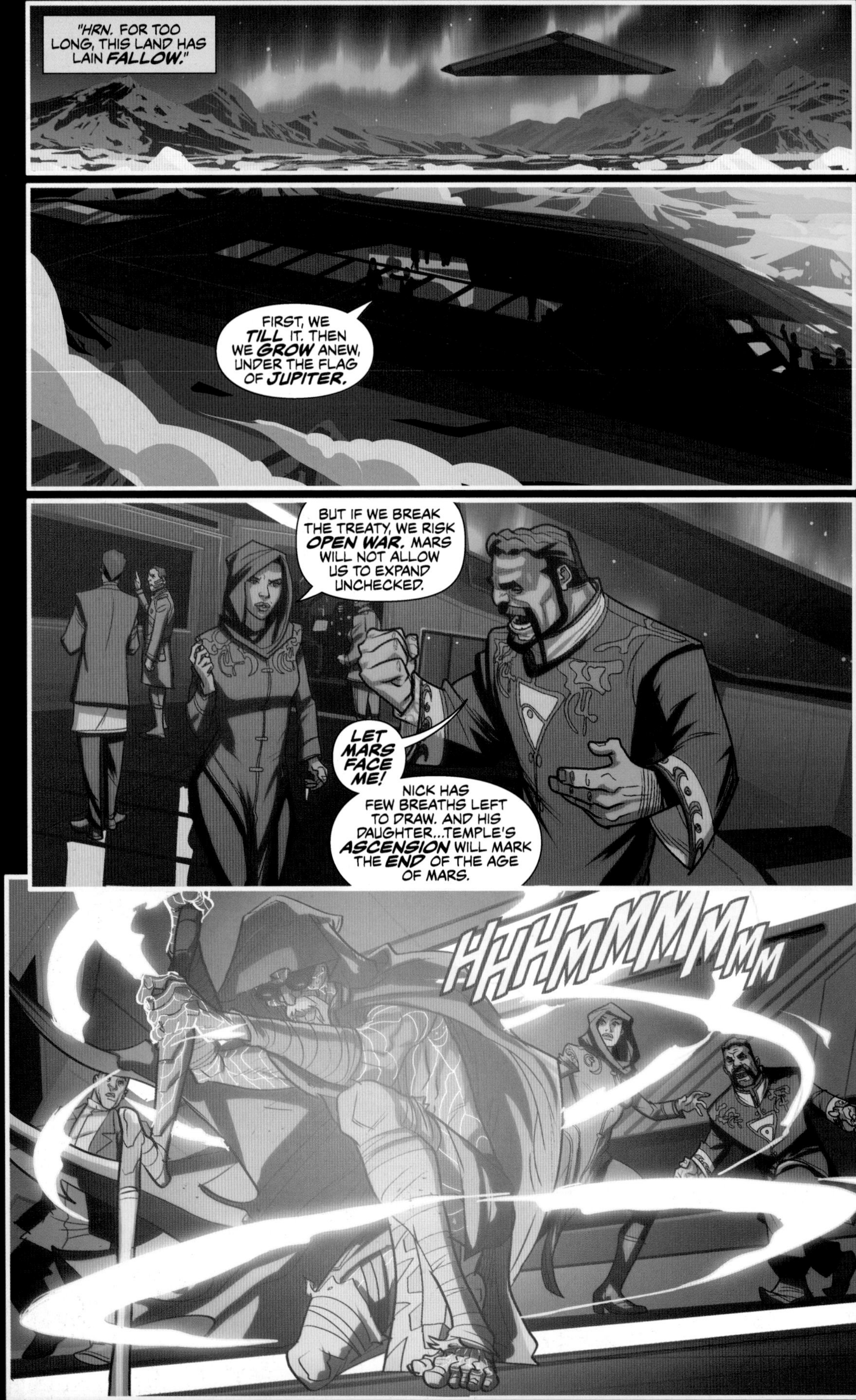
"HRN. FOR TOO LONG, THIS LAND HAS LAIN FALLOW."
FIRST, WE TILL IT. THEN WE GROW ANEW, UNDER THE FLAG OF JUPITER.
BUT IF WE BREAK THE TREATY, WE RISK OPEN WAR. MARS WILL NOT ALLOW US TO EXPAND UNCHECKED.
LET MARS FACE ME!
NICK HAS FEW BREATHS LEFT TO DRAW. AND HIS DAUGHTER...TEMPLE'S ASCENSION WILL MARK THE END OF THE AGE OF MARS.
HHHMMMMMMM

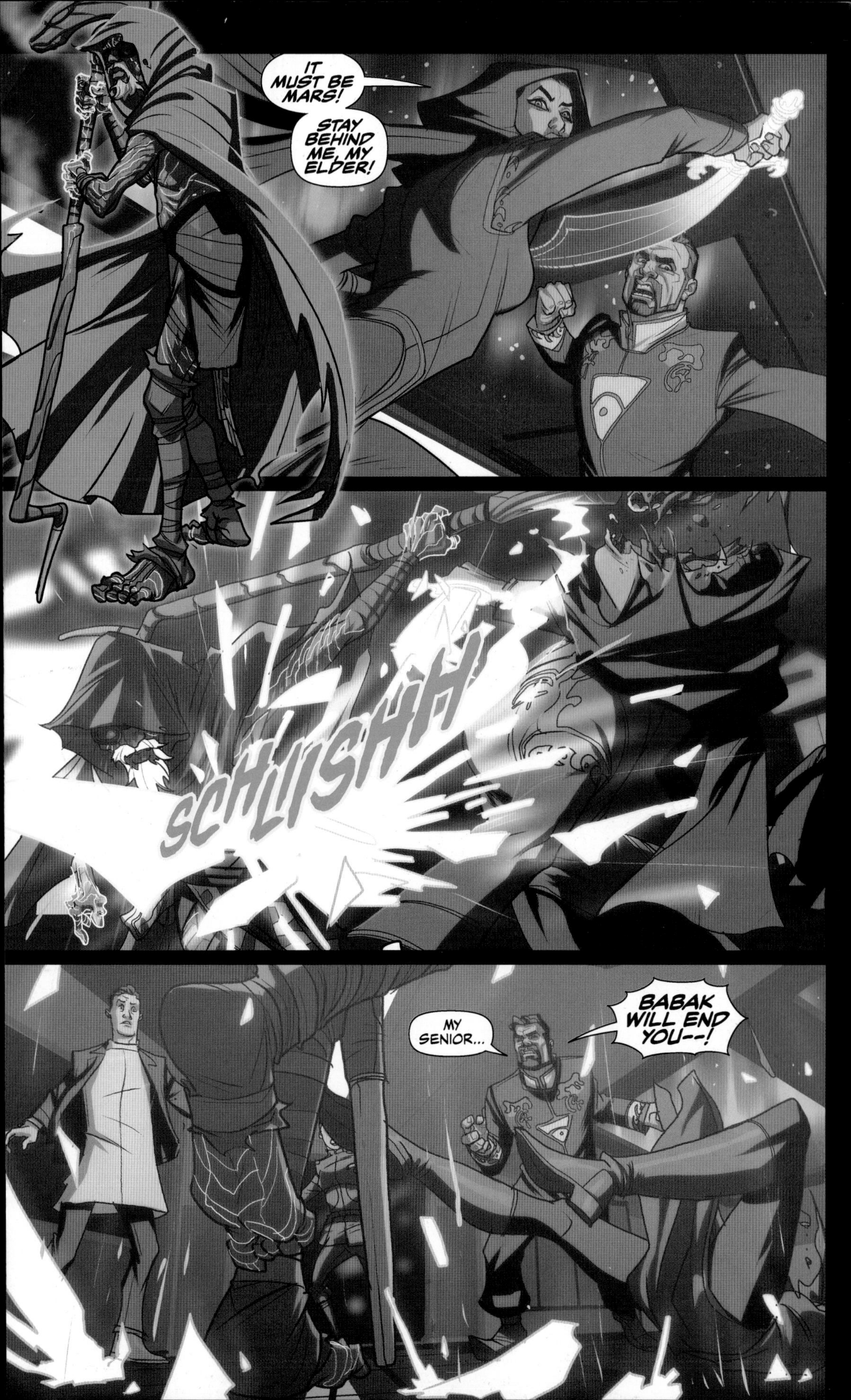
IT MUST BE MARS!
STAY BEHIND ME, MY ELDER!
SCHLISHH
MY SENIOR...
BABAK WILL END YOU--!

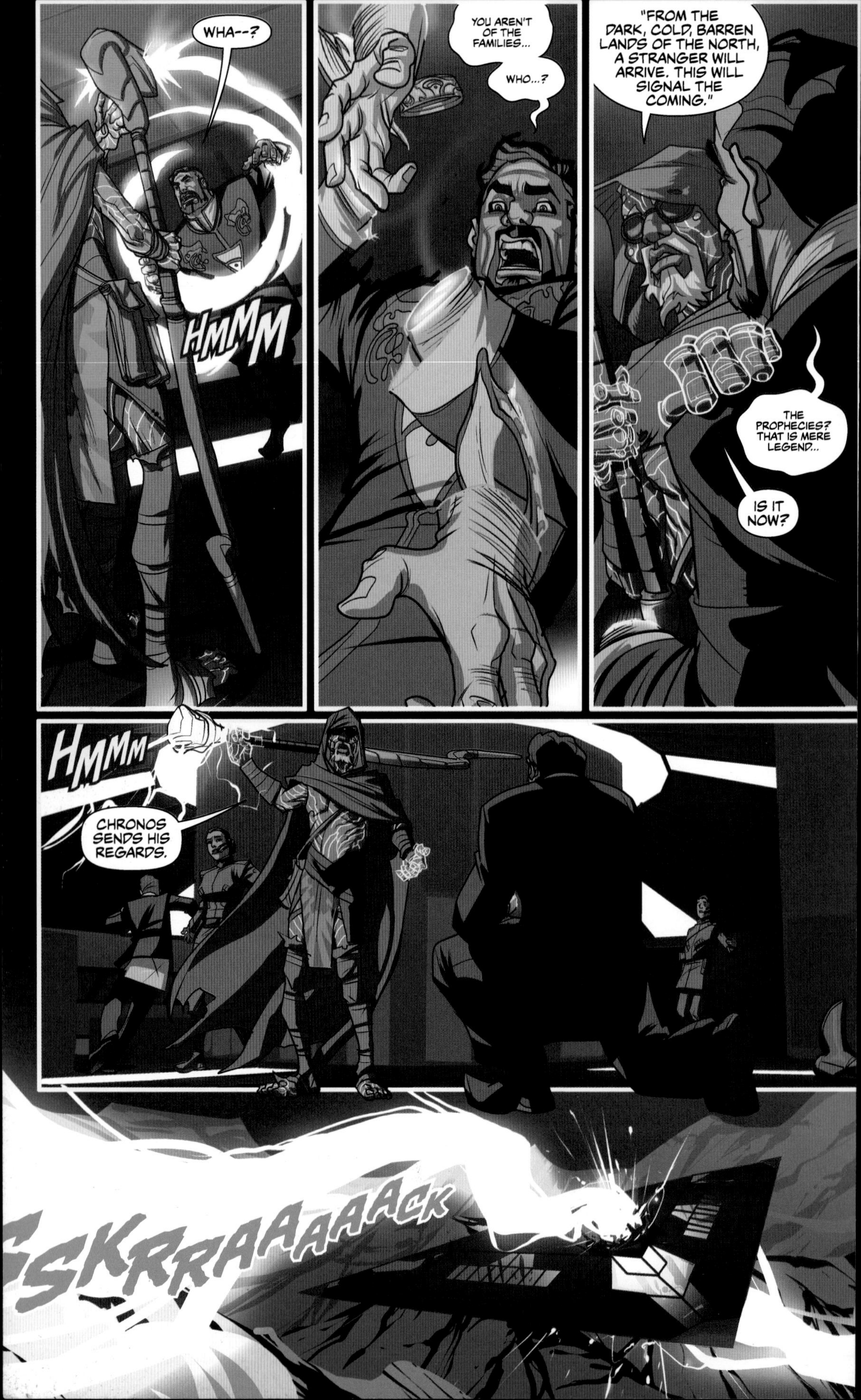
WHA--?
HMMM
YOU AREN'T OF THE FAMILIES...
WHO...?
"FROM THE DARK, COLD, BARREN LANDS OF THE NORTH, A STRANGER WILL ARRIVE. THIS WILL SIGNAL THE COMING."
THE PROPHECIES? THAT IS MERE LEGEND...
IS IT NOW?
HMMM
CHRONOS SENDS HIS REGARDS.
SKRRAAAAAACK

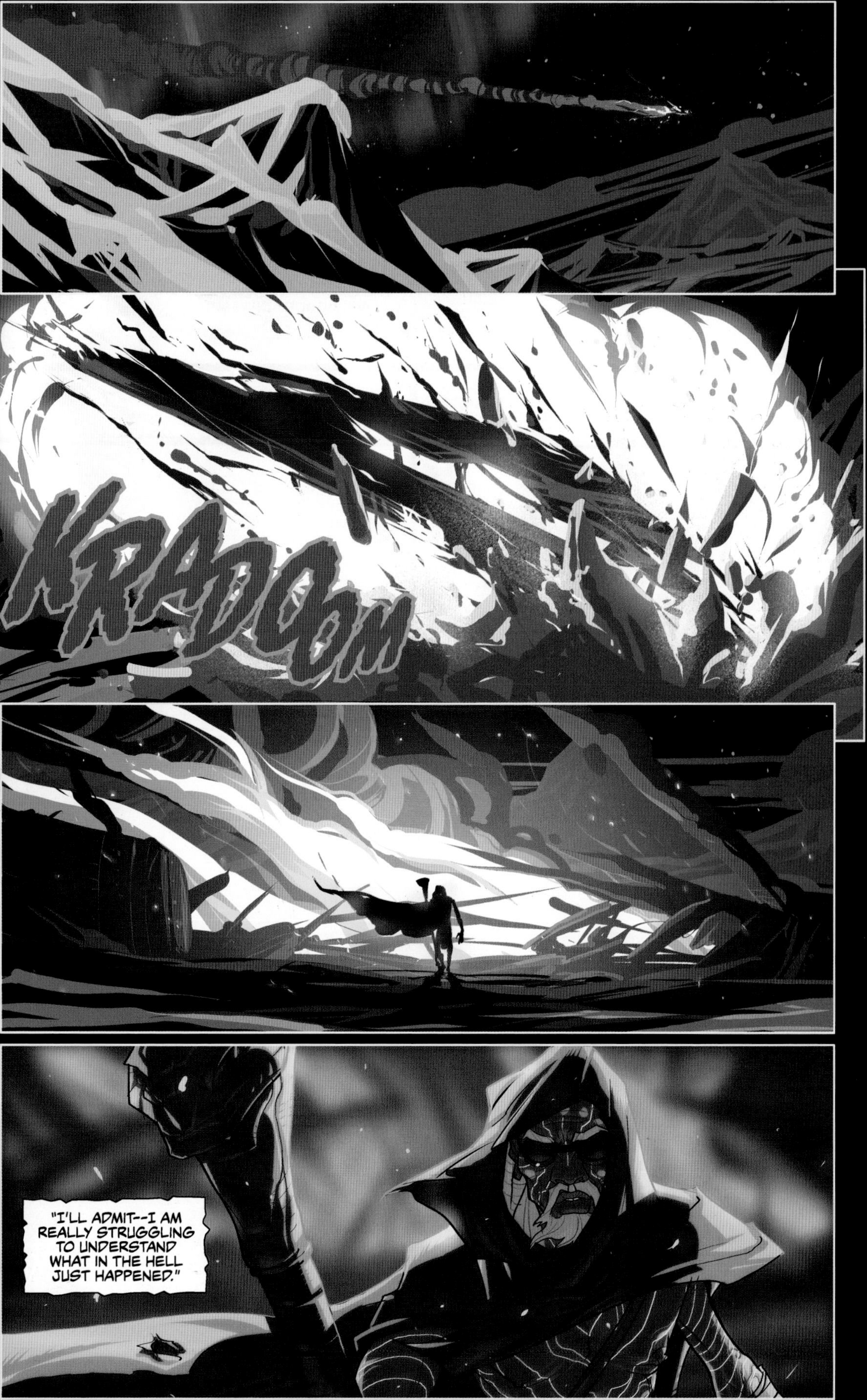
KRADOOM
"I'LL ADMIT--I AM REALLY STRUGGLING TO UNDERSTAND WHAT IN THE HELL JUST HAPPENED."

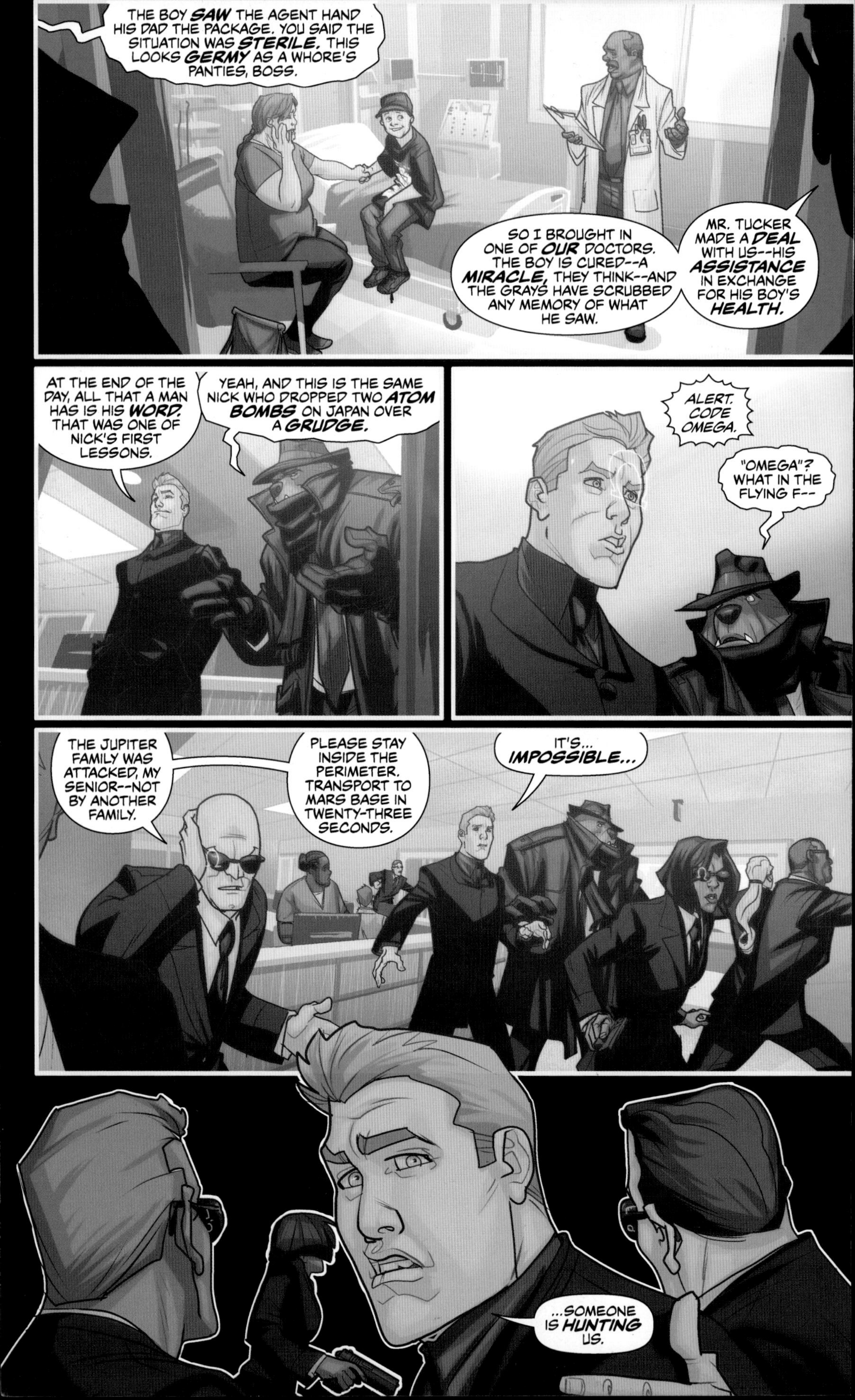
THE BOY SAW THE AGENT HAND HIS DAD THE PACKAGE. YOU SAID THE SITUATION WAS STERILE. THIS LOOKS GERMY AS A WHORE'S PANTIES, BOSS.
SO I BROUGHT IN ONE OF OUR DOCTORS. THE BOY IS CURED--A MIRACLE, THEY THINK--AND THE GRAYS HAVE SCRUBBED ANY MEMORY OF WHAT HE SAW.
MR. TUCKER MADE A DEAL WITH US--HIS ASSISTANCE IN EXCHANGE FOR HIS BOY'S HEALTH.
AT THE END OF THE DAY, ALL THAT A MAN HAS IS HIS WORD. THAT WAS ONE OF NICK'S FIRST LESSONS.
YEAH, AND THIS IS THE SAME NICK WHO DROPPED TWO ATOM BOMBS ON JAPAN OVER A GRUDGE.
ALERT. CODE OMEGA.
"OMEGA"? WHAT IN THE FLYING F--
THE JUPITER FAMILY WAS ATTACKED, MY SENIOR--NOT BY ANOTHER FAMILY.
PLEASE STAY INSIDE THE PERIMETER. TRANSPORT TO MARS BASE IN TWENTY-THREE SECONDS.
IT'S... IMPOSSIBLE...
...SOMEONE IS HUNTING US.

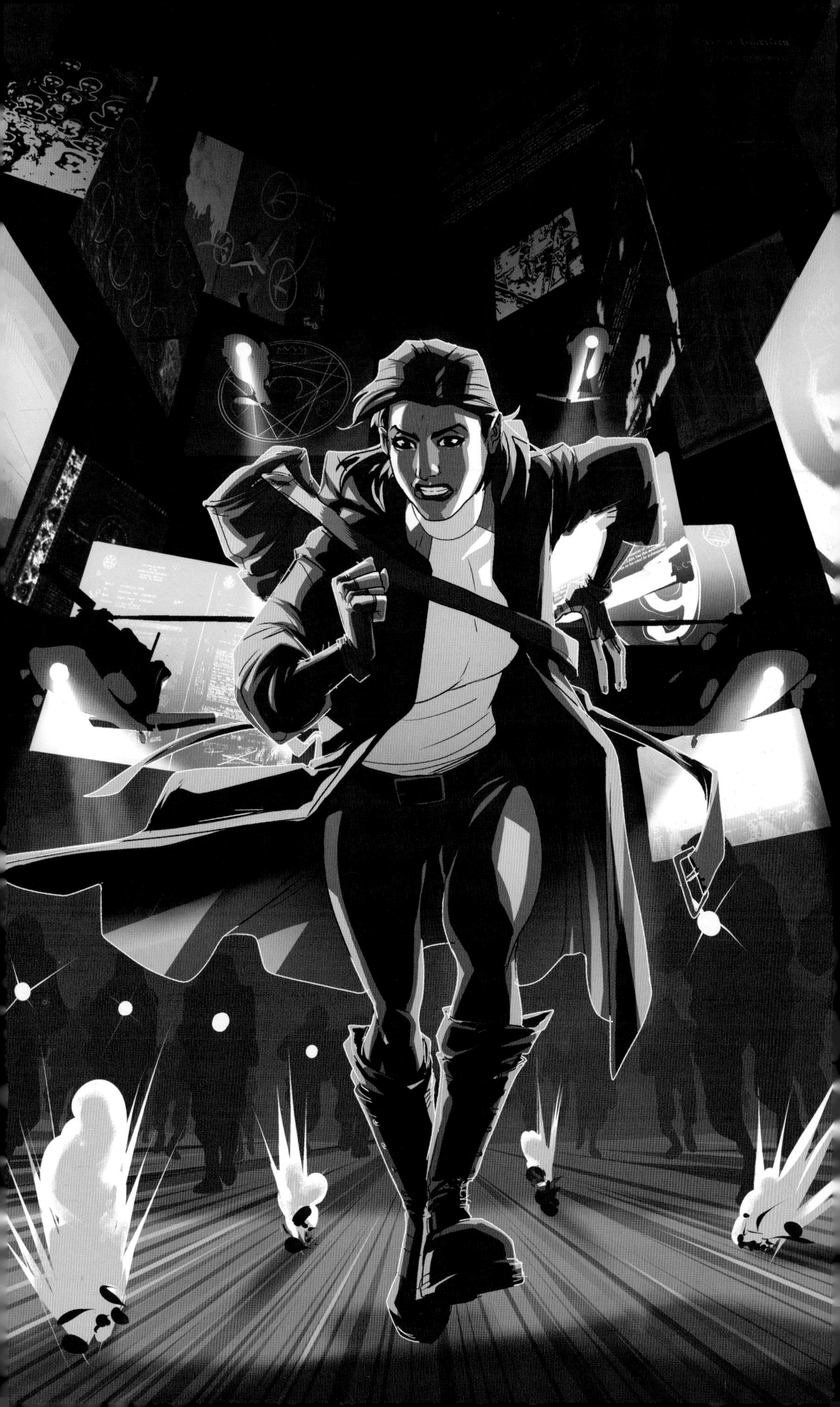

#2 FEINT

NINE FAMILIES RULE THE WORLD. ONE ELDER LEADS EACH FAMILY IN OVERSEEING ITS TERRITORY.

JUPITER

The Fifth Family. Ruled by Babak. At least up until he was killed by the mysterious figure known as "Hum."

URANUS

The Seventh Family. Ruled by Galina. A harsh, ruthless Family, determined to use its resources against the others.

MERCURY

The First Family. Ruled by Mum, one of the oldest Elders. Once the most powerful Family, though now overshadowed.

GAIA

The Third Family. Ruled by Sajjan, an old rival of Nick's. Gaia is home to the Preserve, ancient home of the cryptid races.

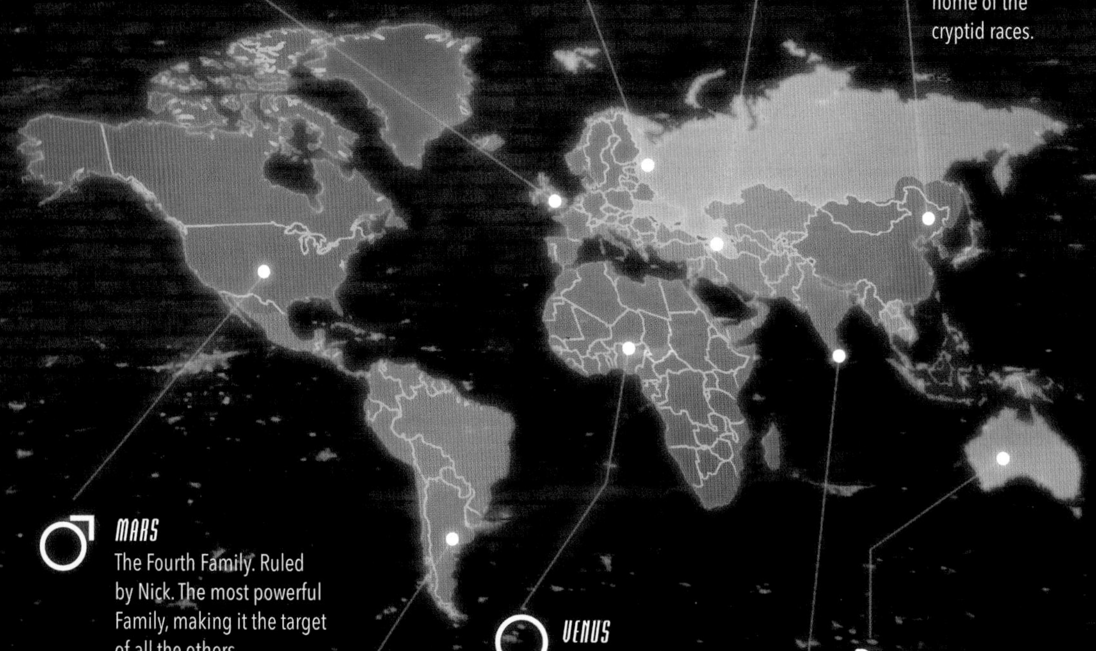

MARS

The Fourth Family. Ruled by Nick. The most powerful Family, making it the target of all the others.

VENUS

The Second Family. Ruled by Achebe, a young Elder eager to expand her Family's operation.

PLUTO

The Ninth Family. Ruled by Diggory. A laughingstock among the others. Pluto has always been the least of the Families.

NEPTUNE

The Eighth Family. Ruled by Tecocol. A once-great Family that has become all but irrelevant in the shadow of Mars.

SATURN

The Sixth Family. Ruled by Dilipa. The most peaceful of the Families.

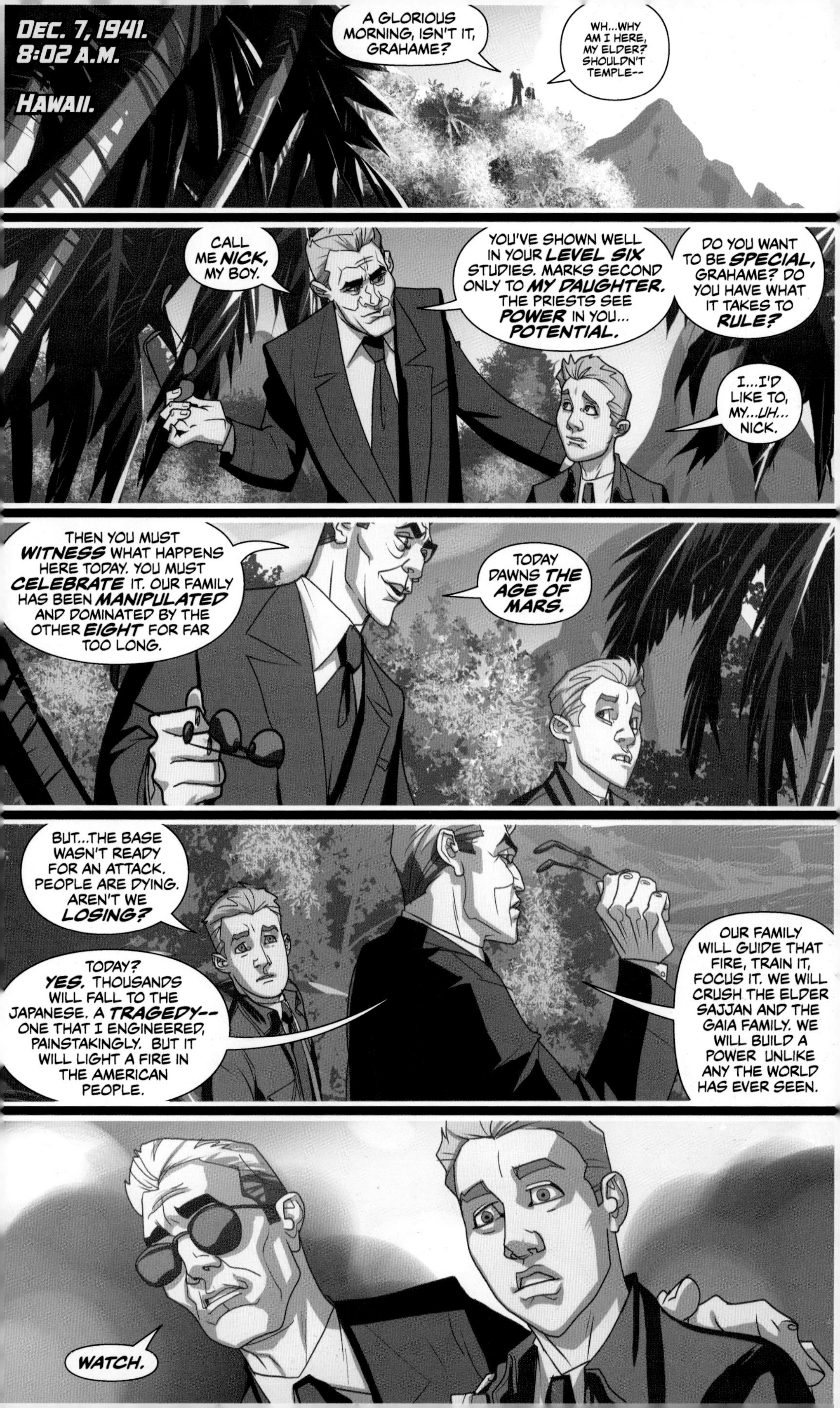
DEC. 7, 1941.
8:02 A.M.
HAWAII.
A GLORIOUS MORNING, ISN'T IT, GRAHAME?
WH...WHY AM I HERE, MY ELDER? SHOULDN'T TEMPLE--
CALL ME NICK, MY BOY.
YOU'VE SHOWN WELL IN YOUR LEVEL SIX STUDIES. MARKS SECOND ONLY TO MY DAUGHTER. THE PRIESTS SEE POWER IN YOU... POTENTIAL.
DO YOU WANT TO BE SPECIAL, GRAHAME? DO YOU HAVE WHAT IT TAKES TO RULE?
I...I'D LIKE TO, MY...UH... NICK.
THEN YOU MUST WITNESS WHAT HAPPENS HERE TODAY. YOU MUST CELEBRATE IT. OUR FAMILY HAS BEEN MANIPULATED AND DOMINATED BY THE OTHER EIGHT FOR FAR TOO LONG.
TODAY DAWNS THE AGE OF MARS.
BUT...THE BASE WASN'T READY FOR AN ATTACK. PEOPLE ARE DYING. AREN'T WE LOSING?
TODAY? YES. THOUSANDS WILL FALL TO THE JAPANESE. A TRAGEDY-- ONE THAT I ENGINEERED, PAINSTAKINGLY. BUT IT WILL LIGHT A FIRE IN THE AMERICAN PEOPLE.
OUR FAMILY WILL GUIDE THAT FIRE, TRAIN IT, FOCUS IT. WE WILL CRUSH THE ELDER SAJJAN AND THE GAIA FAMILY. WE WILL BUILD A POWER UNLIKE ANY THE WORLD HAS EVER SEEN.
WATCH.

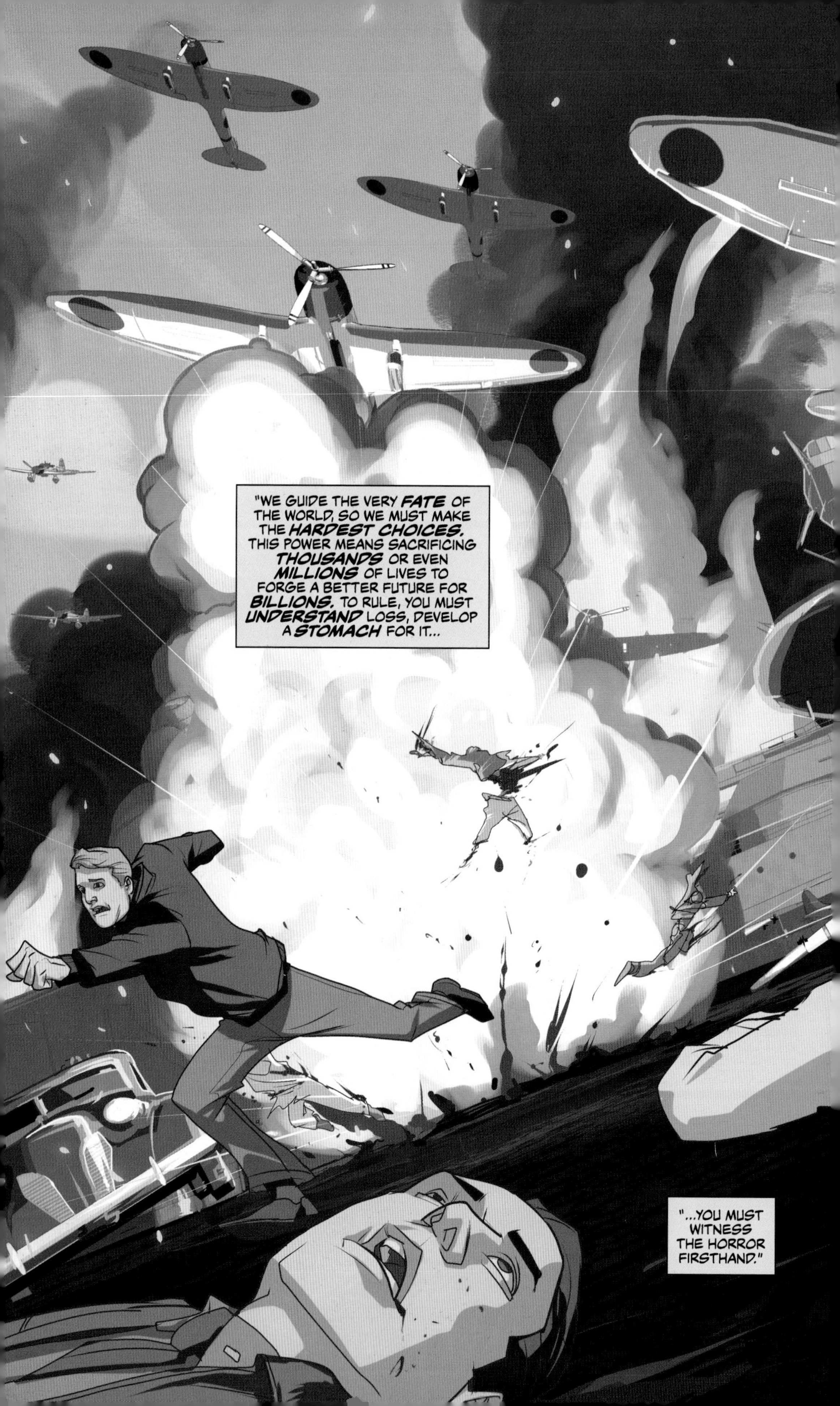
"WE GUIDE THE VERY FATE OF THE WORLD, SO WE MUST MAKE THE HARDEST CHOICES. THIS POWER MEANS SACRIFICING THOUSANDS OR EVEN MILLIONS OF LIVES TO FORGE A BETTER FUTURE FOR BILLIONS. TO RULE, YOU MUST UNDERSTAND LOSS, DEVELOP A STOMACH FOR IT...
"...YOU MUST WITNESS THE HORROR FIRSTHAND."

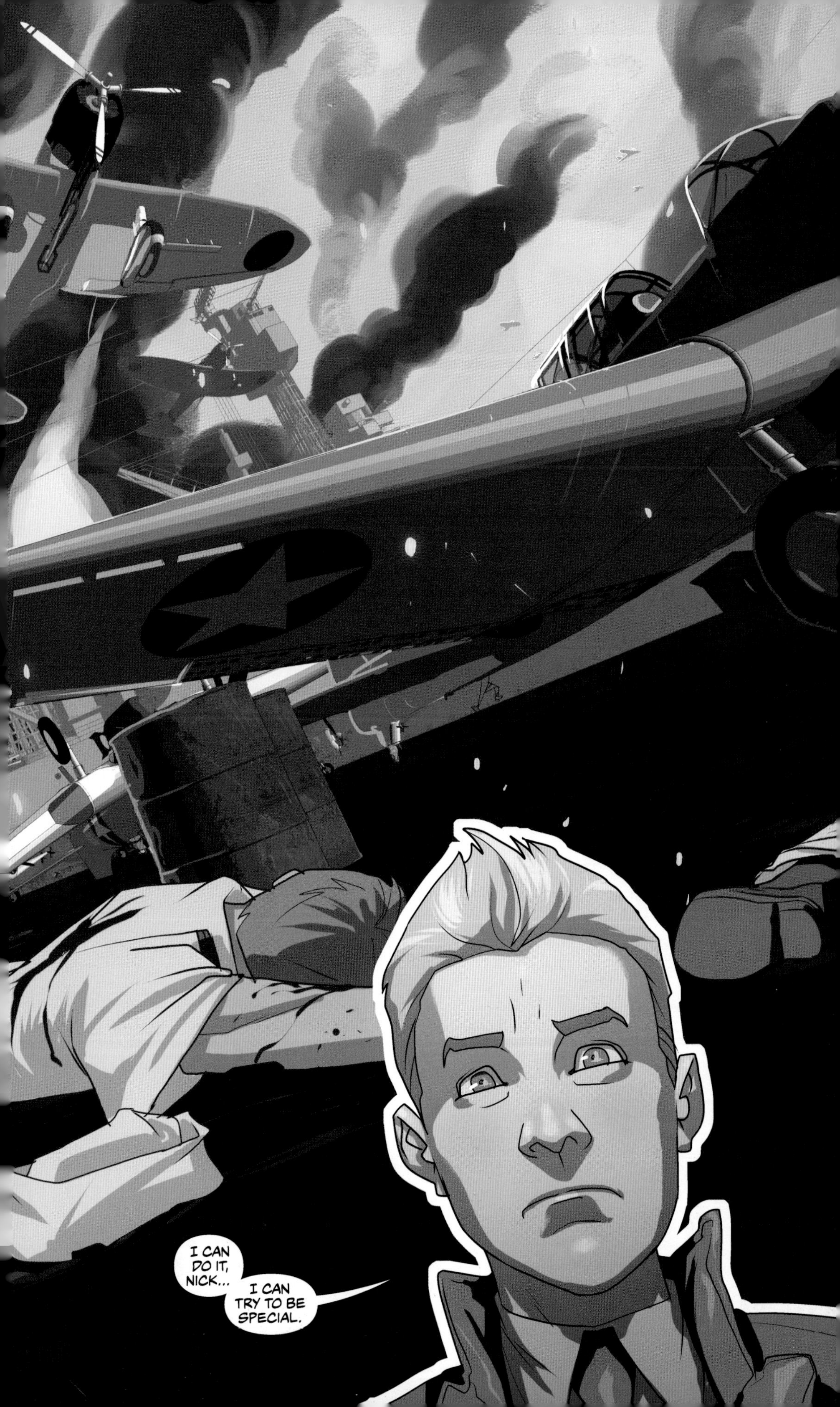

I CAN DO IT, NICK...
I CAN TRY TO BE SPECIAL.

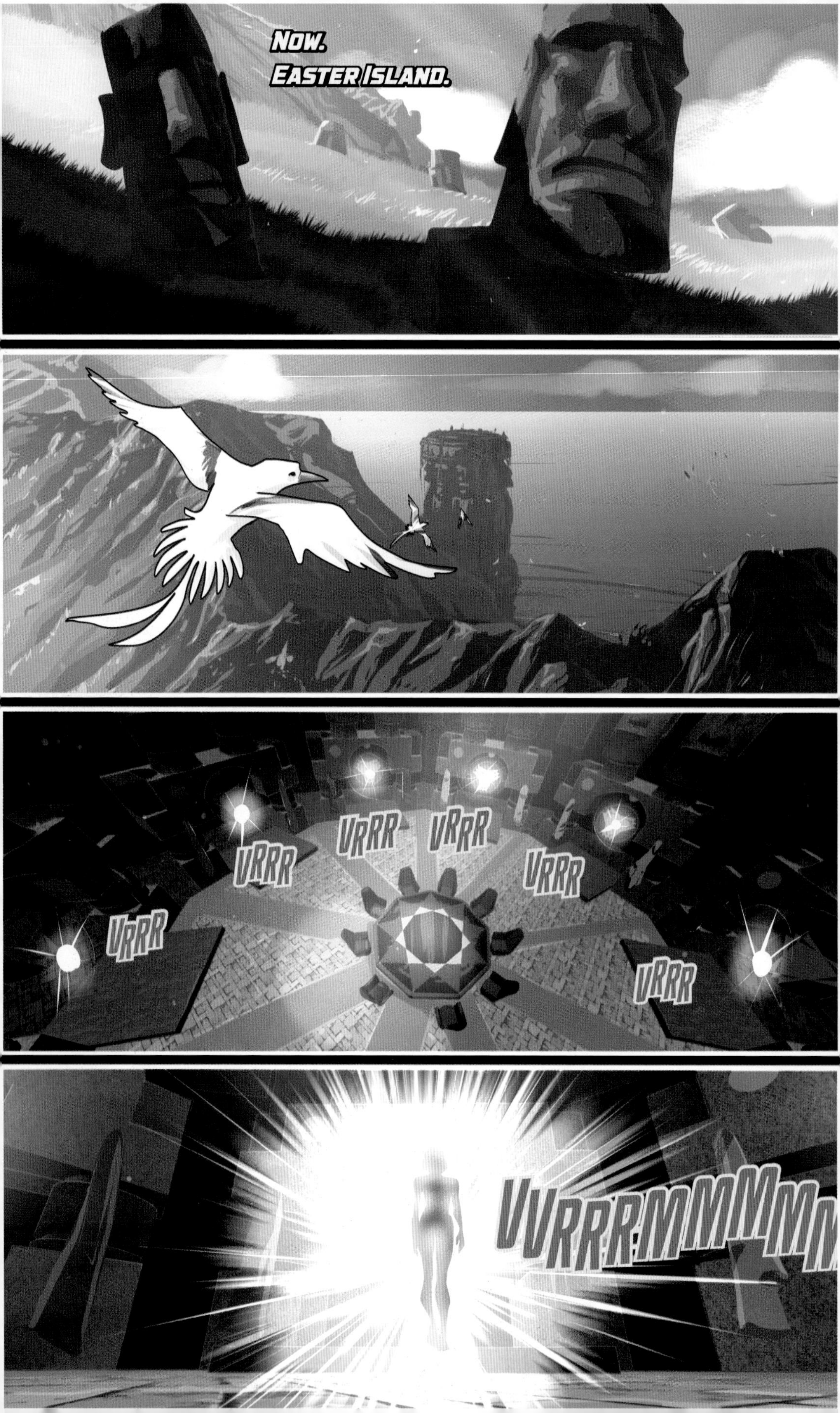

NOW.
EASTER ISLAND.
VRRR
VRRR
VRRR
VRRR
VRRR
VRRR
VVRRRMMMMMM

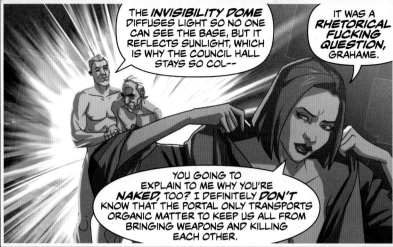

BRR.

WE CONTROL THE **WHOLE FUCKING WORLD**, AND WE CAN'T AFFORD SOME HEATERS FOR THIS **SHITHOLE**?

THE **INVISIBILITY DOME** DIFFUSES LIGHT SO NO ONE CAN SEE THE BASE, BUT IT REFLECTS SUNLIGHT, WHICH IS WHY THE COUNCIL HALL STAYS SO COL--

IT WAS A **RHETORICAL FUCKING QUESTION**, GRAHAME.

YOU GOING TO EXPLAIN TO ME WHY YOU'RE **NAKED**, TOO? I DEFINITELY **DON'T** KNOW THAT THE PORTAL ONLY TRANSPORTS ORGANIC MATTER TO KEEP US ALL FROM BRINGING WEAPONS AND KILLING EACH OTHER.

DAUGHTER, **BEHAVE**--

--THE **NINE** ARE GATHERED.

I AM ZAREH. I...I HAVE BEEN APPOINTED JUPITER'S NEW ELDER, SINCE BABAK WAS... **MURDERED**...

WELCOME. ALL IN THE SATURN FAMILY MOURNED HIM.

OF COURSE... THANK YOU FOR--

NOW **COVER** YOURSELF AND TAKE YOUR PLACE AT THE TABLE. YOU NEED TO **ACCOUNT FOR** YOUR FAMILY'S FAILURE.

Y...YES.

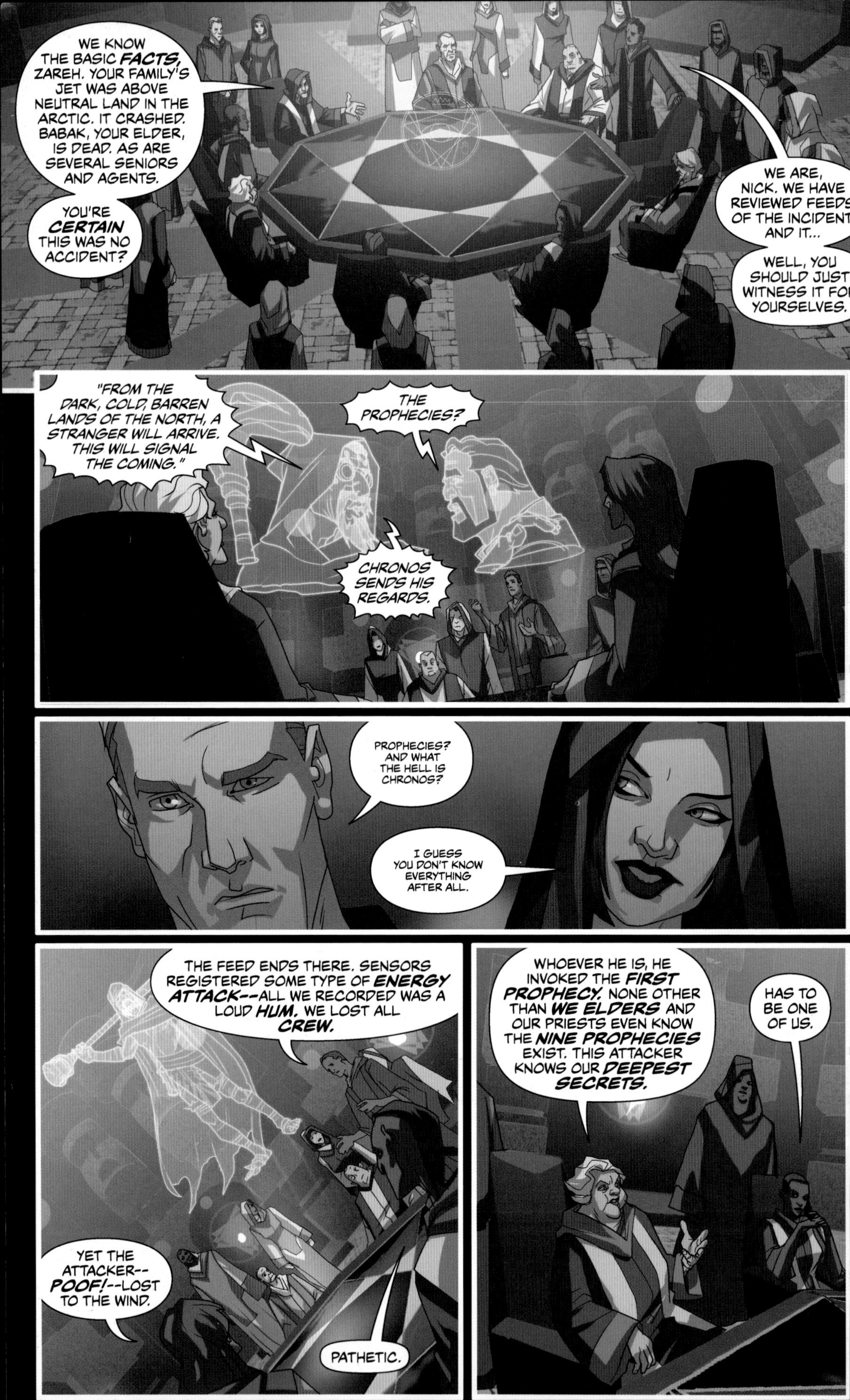

WE KNOW THE BASIC FACTS, ZAREH. YOUR FAMILY'S JET WAS ABOVE NEUTRAL LAND IN THE ARCTIC. IT CRASHED. BABAK, YOUR ELDER, IS DEAD. AS ARE SEVERAL SENIORS AND AGENTS.
YOU'RE CERTAIN THIS WAS NO ACCIDENT?
WE ARE, NICK. WE HAVE REVIEWED FEEDS OF THE INCIDENT AND IT...
WELL, YOU SHOULD JUST WITNESS IT FOR YOURSELVES.
"FROM THE DARK, COLD, BARREN LANDS OF THE NORTH, A STRANGER WILL ARRIVE. THIS WILL SIGNAL THE COMING."
THE PROPHECIES?
CHRONOS SENDS HIS REGARDS.
PROPHECIES? AND WHAT THE HELL IS CHRONOS?
I GUESS YOU DON'T KNOW EVERYTHING AFTER ALL.
THE FEED ENDS THERE. SENSORS REGISTERED SOME TYPE OF ENERGY ATTACK--ALL WE RECORDED WAS A LOUD HUM. WE LOST ALL CREW.
YET THE ATTACKER--POOF!--LOST TO THE WIND.
PATHETIC.
WHOEVER HE IS, HE INVOKED THE FIRST PROPHECY. NONE OTHER THAN WE ELDERS AND OUR PRIESTS EVEN KNOW THE NINE PROPHECIES EXIST. THIS ATTACKER KNOWS OUR DEEPEST SECRETS.
HAS TO BE ONE OF US.

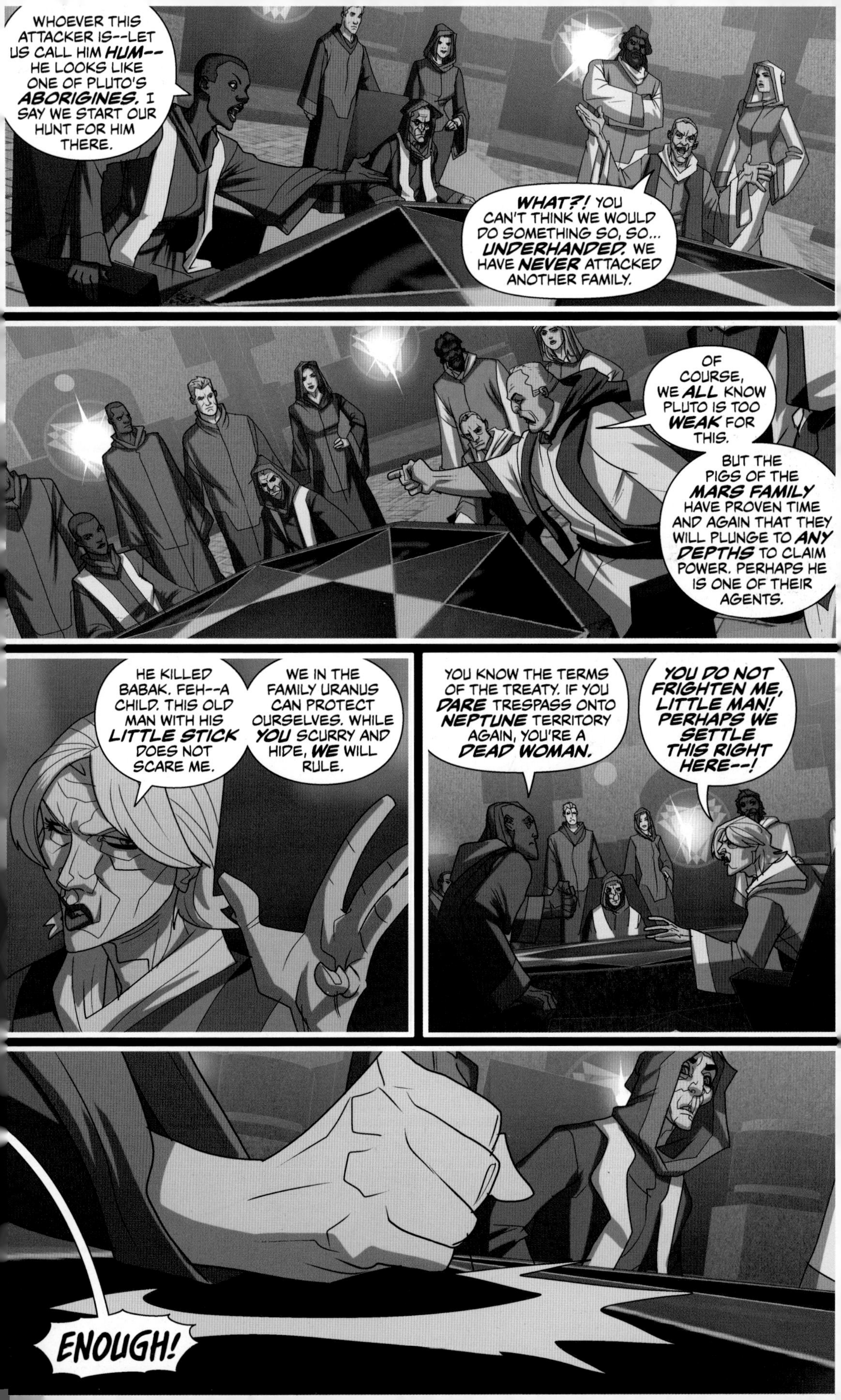
WHOEVER THIS ATTACKER IS--LET US CALL HIM HUM--HE LOOKS LIKE ONE OF PLUTO'S ABORIGINES. I SAY WE START OUR HUNT FOR HIM THERE.
WHAT?! YOU CAN'T THINK WE WOULD DO SOMETHING SO, SO... UNDERHANDED. WE HAVE NEVER ATTACKED ANOTHER FAMILY.
OF COURSE, WE ALL KNOW PLUTO IS TOO WEAK FOR THIS.
BUT THE PIGS OF THE MARS FAMILY HAVE PROVEN TIME AND AGAIN THAT THEY WILL PLUNGE TO ANY DEPTHS TO CLAIM POWER. PERHAPS HE IS ONE OF THEIR AGENTS.
HE KILLED BABAK. FEH--A CHILD. THIS OLD MAN WITH HIS LITTLE STICK DOES NOT SCARE ME.
WE IN THE FAMILY URANUS CAN PROTECT OURSELVES. WHILE YOU SCURRY AND HIDE, WE WILL RULE.
YOU KNOW THE TERMS OF THE TREATY. IF YOU DARE TRESPASS ONTO NEPTUNE TERRITORY AGAIN, YOU'RE A DEAD WOMAN.
YOU DO NOT FRIGHTEN ME, LITTLE MAN! PERHAPS WE SETTLE THIS RIGHT HERE--!
ENOUGH!

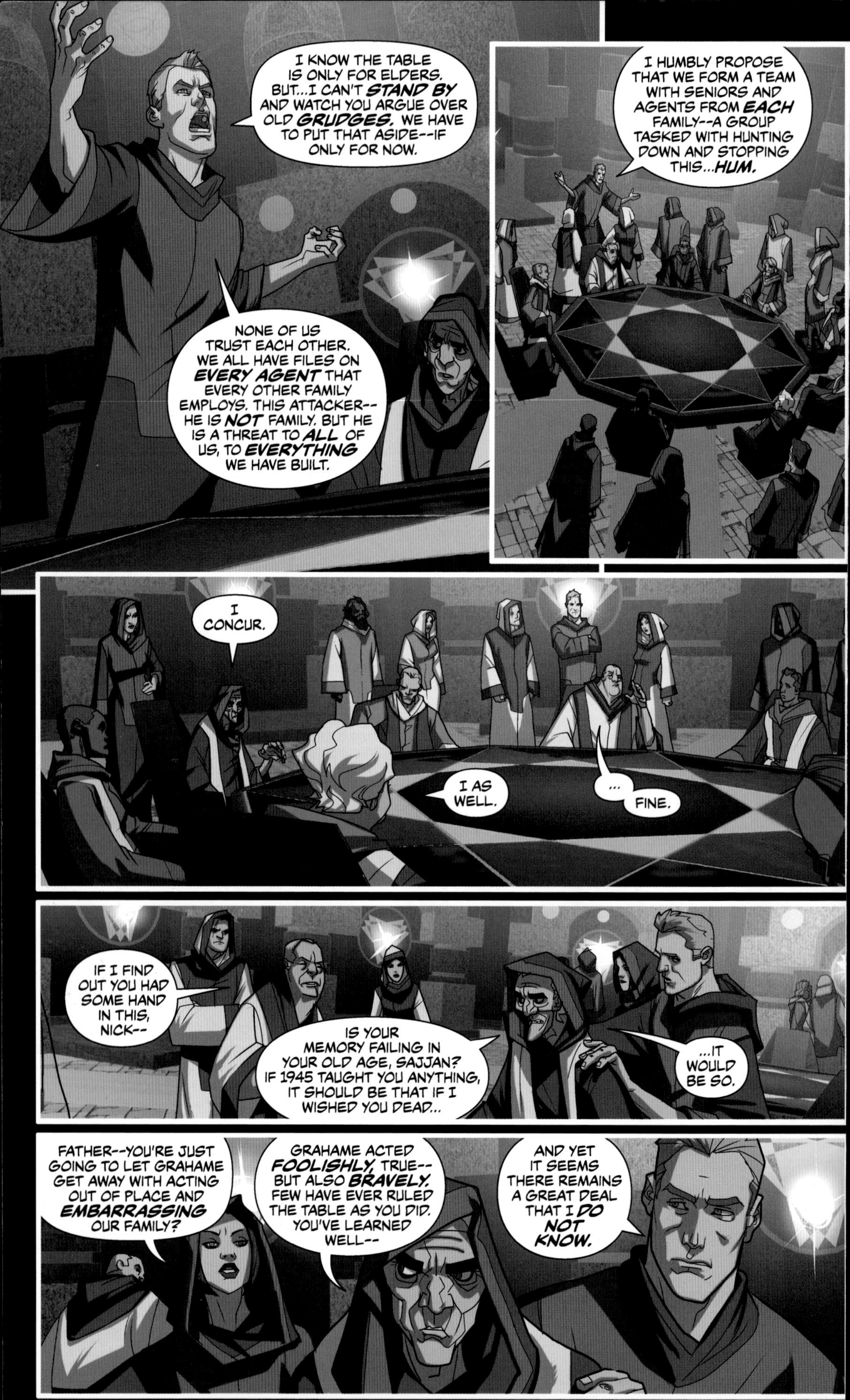
I KNOW THE TABLE IS ONLY FOR ELDERS. BUT...I CAN'T STAND BY AND WATCH YOU ARGUE OVER OLD GRUDGES. WE HAVE TO PUT THAT ASIDE--IF ONLY FOR NOW.
NONE OF US TRUST EACH OTHER. WE ALL HAVE FILES ON EVERY AGENT THAT EVERY OTHER FAMILY EMPLOYS. THIS ATTACKER--HE IS NOT FAMILY. BUT HE IS A THREAT TO ALL OF US, TO EVERYTHING WE HAVE BUILT.
I HUMBLY PROPOSE THAT WE FORM A TEAM WITH SENIORS AND AGENTS FROM EACH FAMILY--A GROUP TASKED WITH HUNTING DOWN AND STOPPING THIS...HUM.
I CONCUR.
I AS WELL.
...
FINE.
IF I FIND OUT YOU HAD SOME HAND IN THIS, NICK--
IS YOUR MEMORY FAILING IN YOUR OLD AGE, SAJJAN? IF 1945 TAUGHT YOU ANYTHING, IT SHOULD BE THAT IF I WISHED YOU DEAD...
...IT WOULD BE SO.
FATHER--YOU'RE JUST GOING TO LET GRAHAME GET AWAY WITH ACTING OUT OF PLACE AND EMBARRASSING OUR FAMILY?
GRAHAME ACTED FOOLISHLY, TRUE--BUT ALSO BRAVELY. FEW HAVE EVER RULED THE TABLE AS YOU DID. YOU'VE LEARNED WELL--
AND YET IT SEEMS THERE REMAINS A GREAT DEAL THAT I DO NOT KNOW.

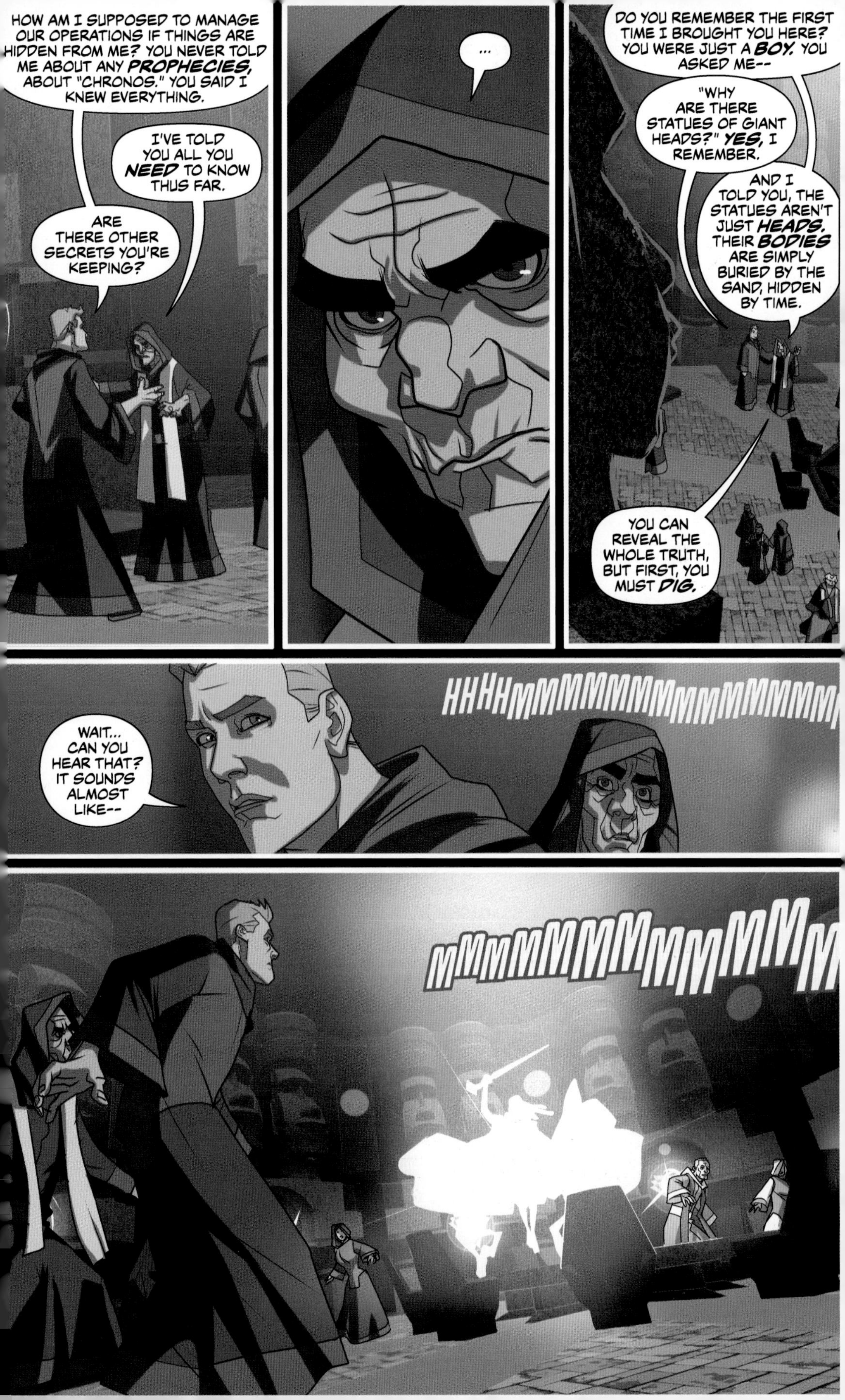
HOW AM I SUPPOSED TO MANAGE OUR OPERATIONS IF THINGS ARE HIDDEN FROM ME? YOU NEVER TOLD ME ABOUT ANY PROPHECIES, ABOUT "CHRONOS." YOU SAID I KNEW EVERYTHING.
I'VE TOLD YOU ALL YOU NEED TO KNOW THUS FAR.
ARE THERE OTHER SECRETS YOU'RE KEEPING?
...
DO YOU REMEMBER THE FIRST TIME I BROUGHT YOU HERE? YOU WERE JUST A BOY. YOU ASKED ME--
"WHY ARE THERE STATUES OF GIANT HEADS?" YES, I REMEMBER.
AND I TOLD YOU, THE STATUES AREN'T JUST HEADS. THEIR BODIES ARE SIMPLY BURIED BY THE SAND, HIDDEN BY TIME.
YOU CAN REVEAL THE WHOLE TRUTH, BUT FIRST, YOU MUST DIG.
HHHHMMMMMMMMMMMMMMMMM
WAIT... CAN YOU HEAR THAT? IT SOUNDS ALMOST LIKE--
MMMMMMMMMMMMMMMMMM

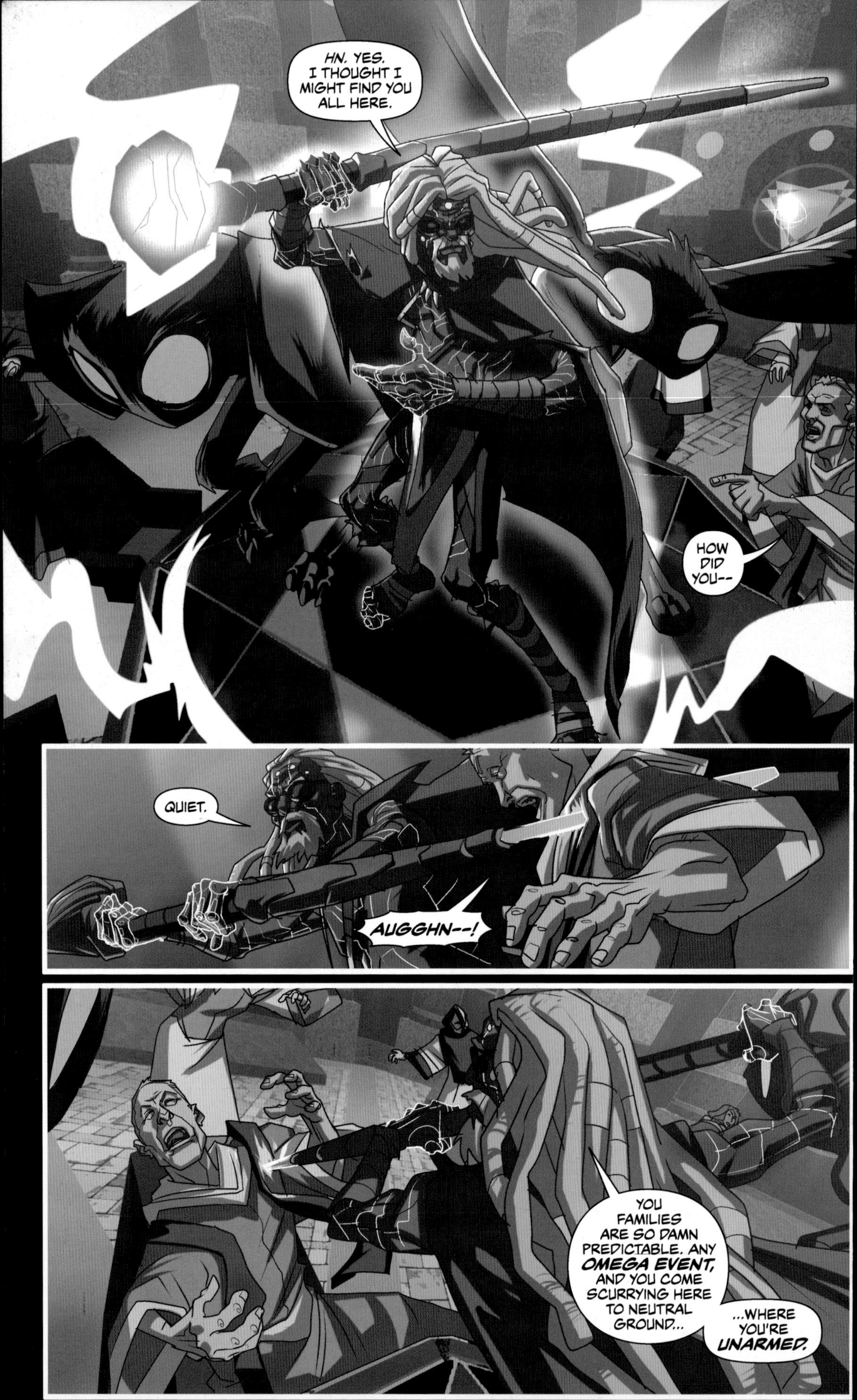
HN. YES. I THOUGHT I MIGHT FIND YOU ALL HERE.
HOW DID YOU--
QUIET.
AUGGHN--!
YOU FAMILIES ARE SO DAMN PREDICTABLE. ANY OMEGA EVENT, AND YOU COME SCURRYING HERE TO NEUTRAL GROUND...
...WHERE YOU'RE UNARMED.

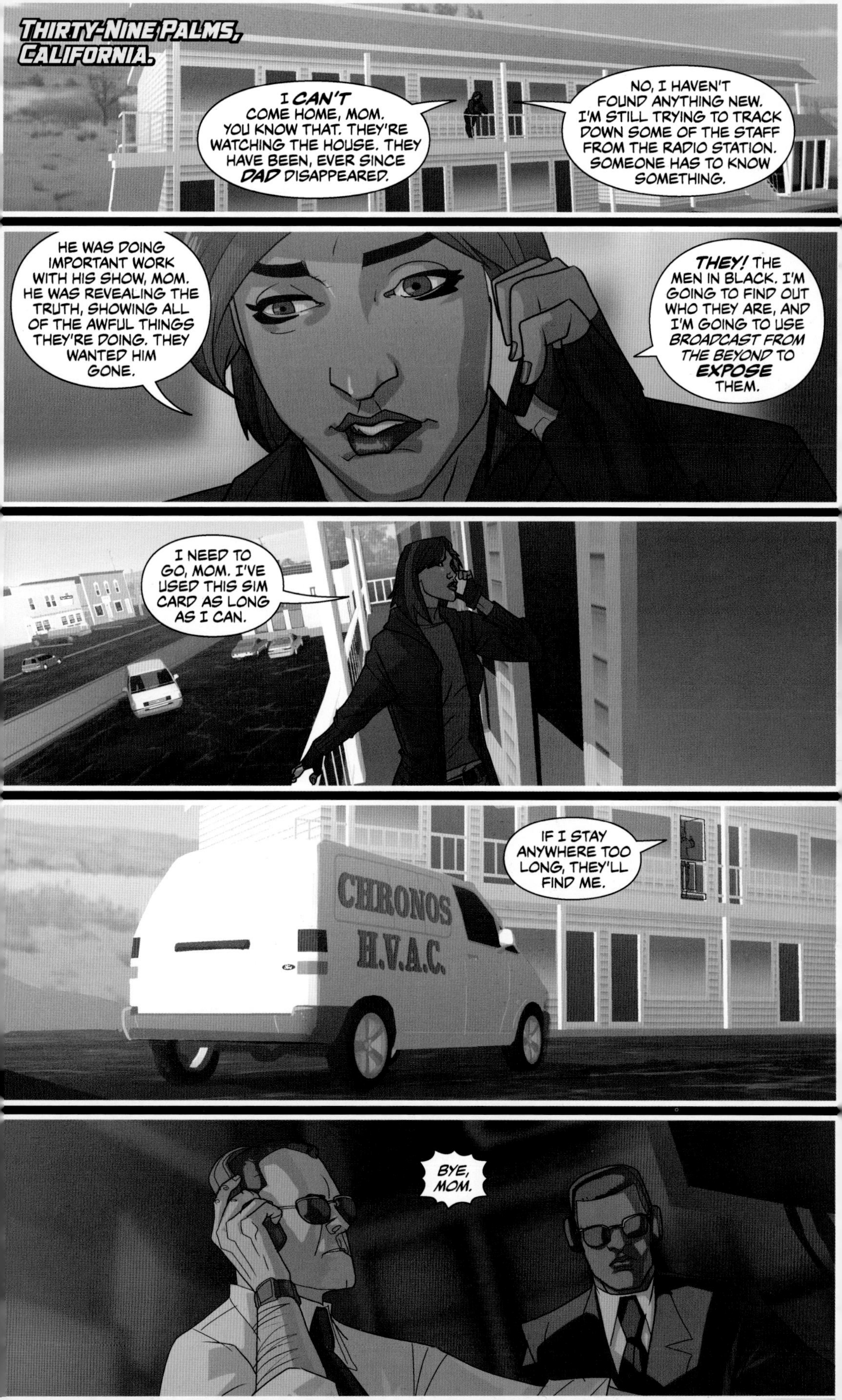
THIRTY-NINE PALMS, CALIFORNIA.
I CAN'T COME HOME, MOM. YOU KNOW THAT. THEY'RE WATCHING THE HOUSE. THEY HAVE BEEN, EVER SINCE DAD DISAPPEARED.
NO, I HAVEN'T FOUND ANYTHING NEW. I'M STILL TRYING TO TRACK DOWN SOME OF THE STAFF FROM THE RADIO STATION. SOMEONE HAS TO KNOW SOMETHING.
HE WAS DOING IMPORTANT WORK WITH HIS SHOW, MOM. HE WAS REVEALING THE TRUTH, SHOWING ALL OF THE AWFUL THINGS THEY'RE DOING. THEY WANTED HIM GONE.
THEY! THE MEN IN BLACK. I'M GOING TO FIND OUT WHO THEY ARE, AND I'M GOING TO USE BROADCAST FROM THE BEYOND TO EXPOSE THEM.
I NEED TO GO, MOM. I'VE USED THIS SIM CARD AS LONG AS I CAN.
CHRONOS H.V.A.C.
IF I STAY ANYWHERE TOO LONG, THEY'LL FIND ME.
BYE, MOM.

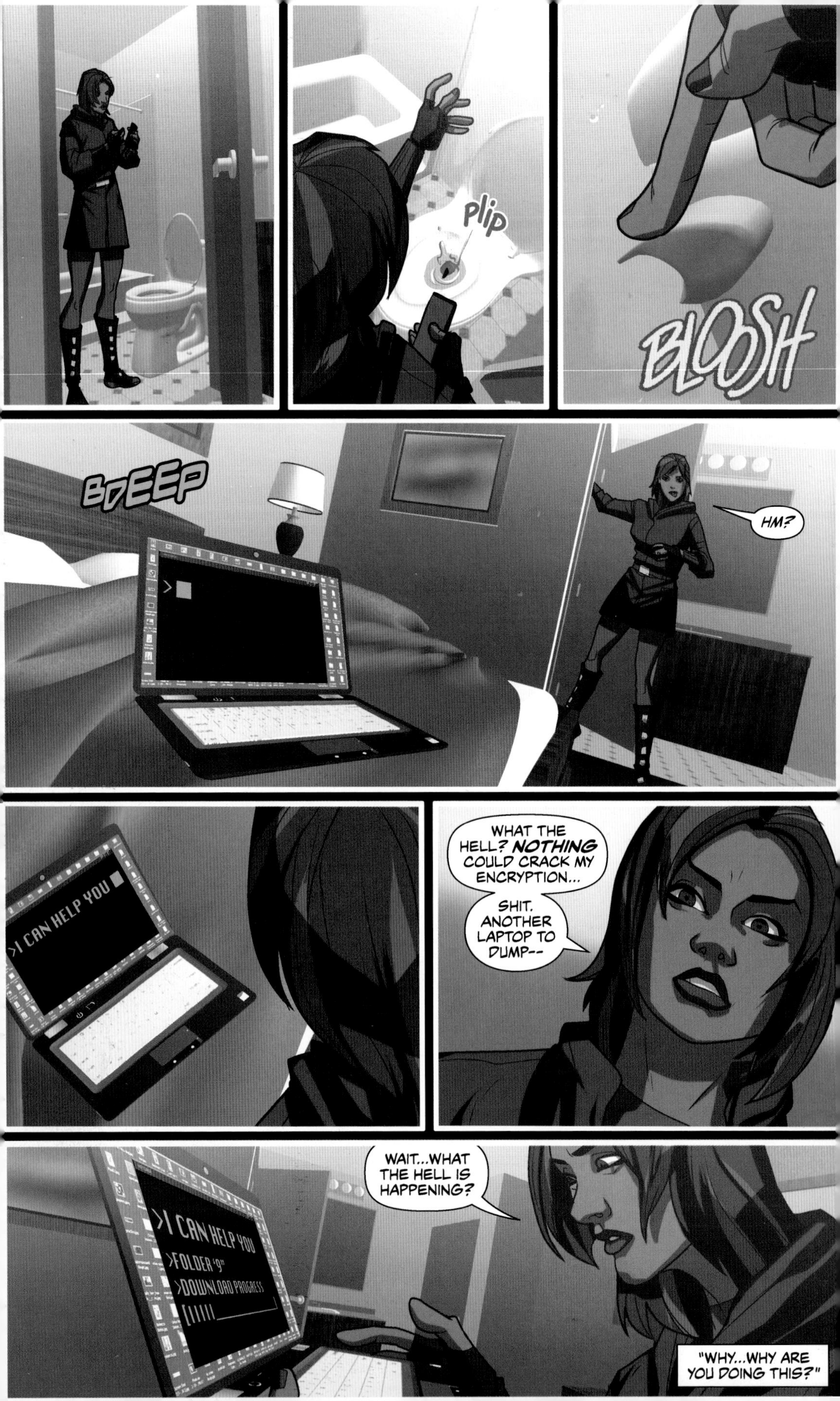

PLIP
BLOOSH
BDEEP
>
HM?
>I CAN HELP YOU
WHAT THE HELL? NOTHING COULD CRACK MY ENCRYPTION...
SHIT. ANOTHER LAPTOP TO DUMP--
>I CAN HELP YOU
>FOLDER "9"
>DOWNLOAD PROGRESS
[IIIII______]
WAIT...WHAT THE HELL IS HAPPENING?
"WHY...WHY ARE YOU DOING THIS?"

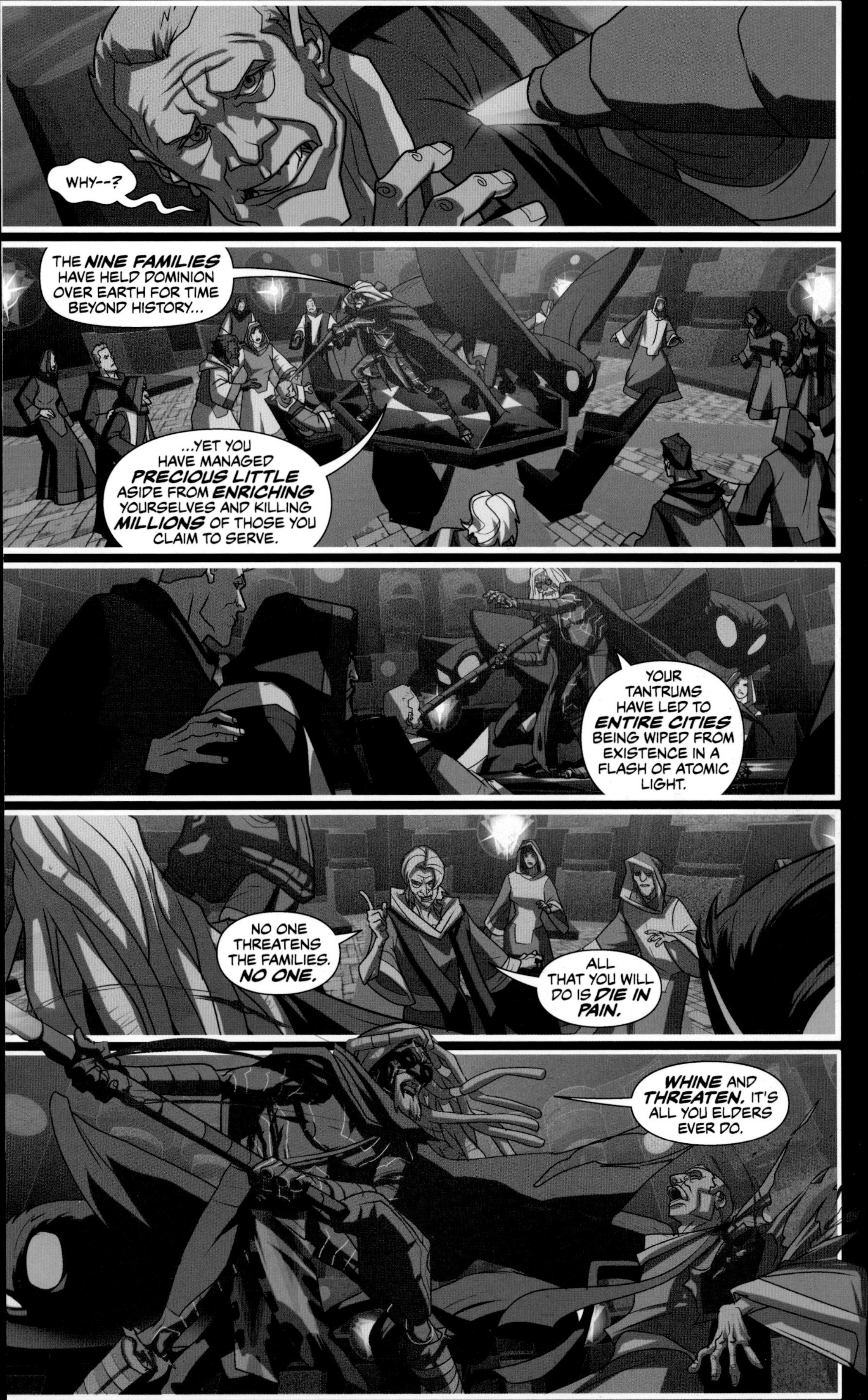
WHY--?
THE NINE FAMILIES HAVE HELD DOMINION OVER EARTH FOR TIME BEYOND HISTORY...
...YET YOU HAVE MANAGED PRECIOUS LITTLE ASIDE FROM ENRICHING YOURSELVES AND KILLING MILLIONS OF THOSE YOU CLAIM TO SERVE.
YOUR TANTRUMS HAVE LED TO ENTIRE CITIES BEING WIPED FROM EXISTENCE IN A FLASH OF ATOMIC LIGHT.
NO ONE THREATENS THE FAMILIES. NO ONE.
ALL THAT YOU WILL DO IS DIE IN PAIN.
WHINE AND THREATEN. IT'S ALL YOU ELDERS EVER DO.

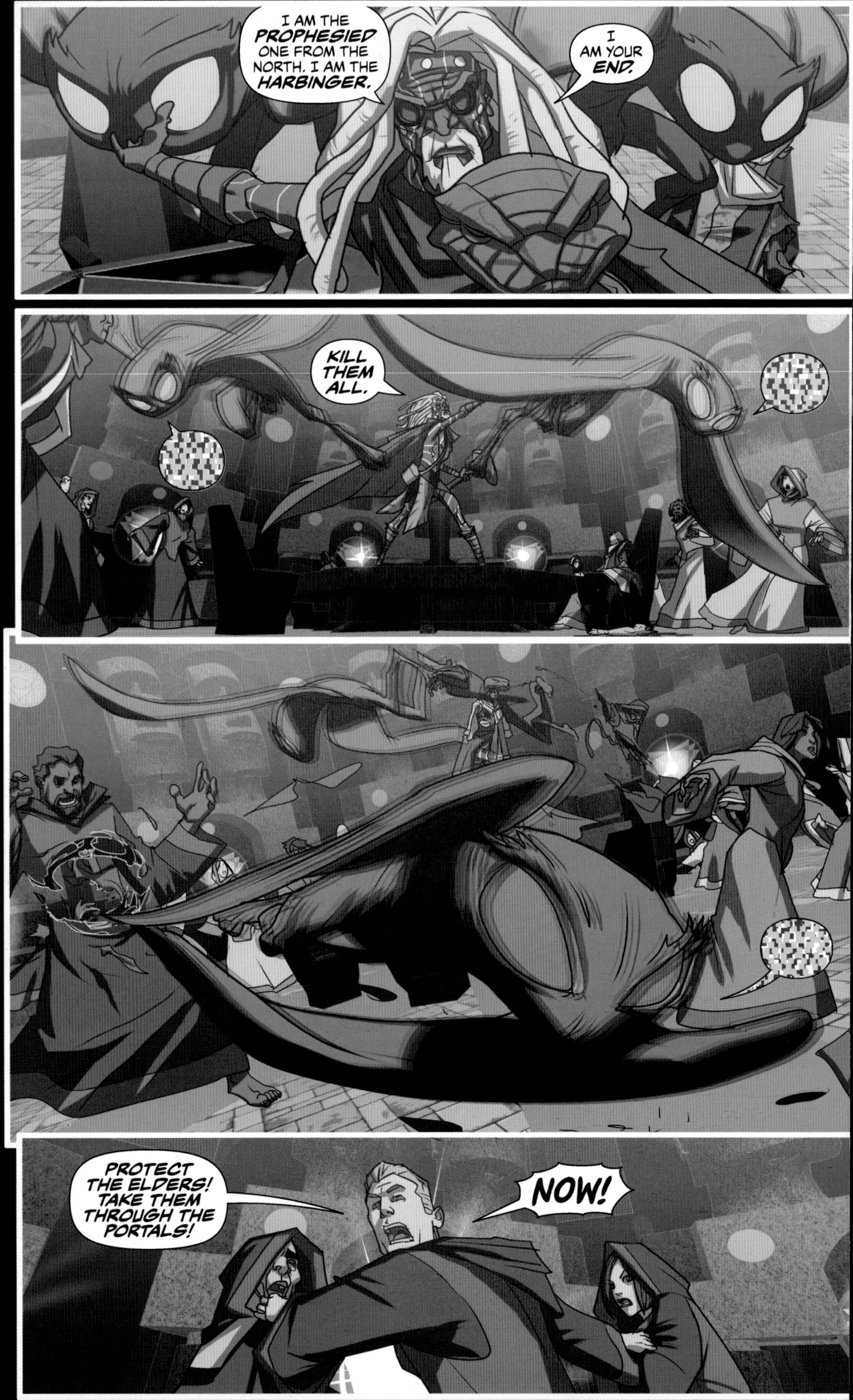
I AM THE PROPHESIED ONE FROM THE NORTH. I AM THE HARBINGER.
I AM YOUR END.
KILL THEM ALL.
PROTECT THE ELDERS! TAKE THEM THROUGH THE PORTALS!
NOW!

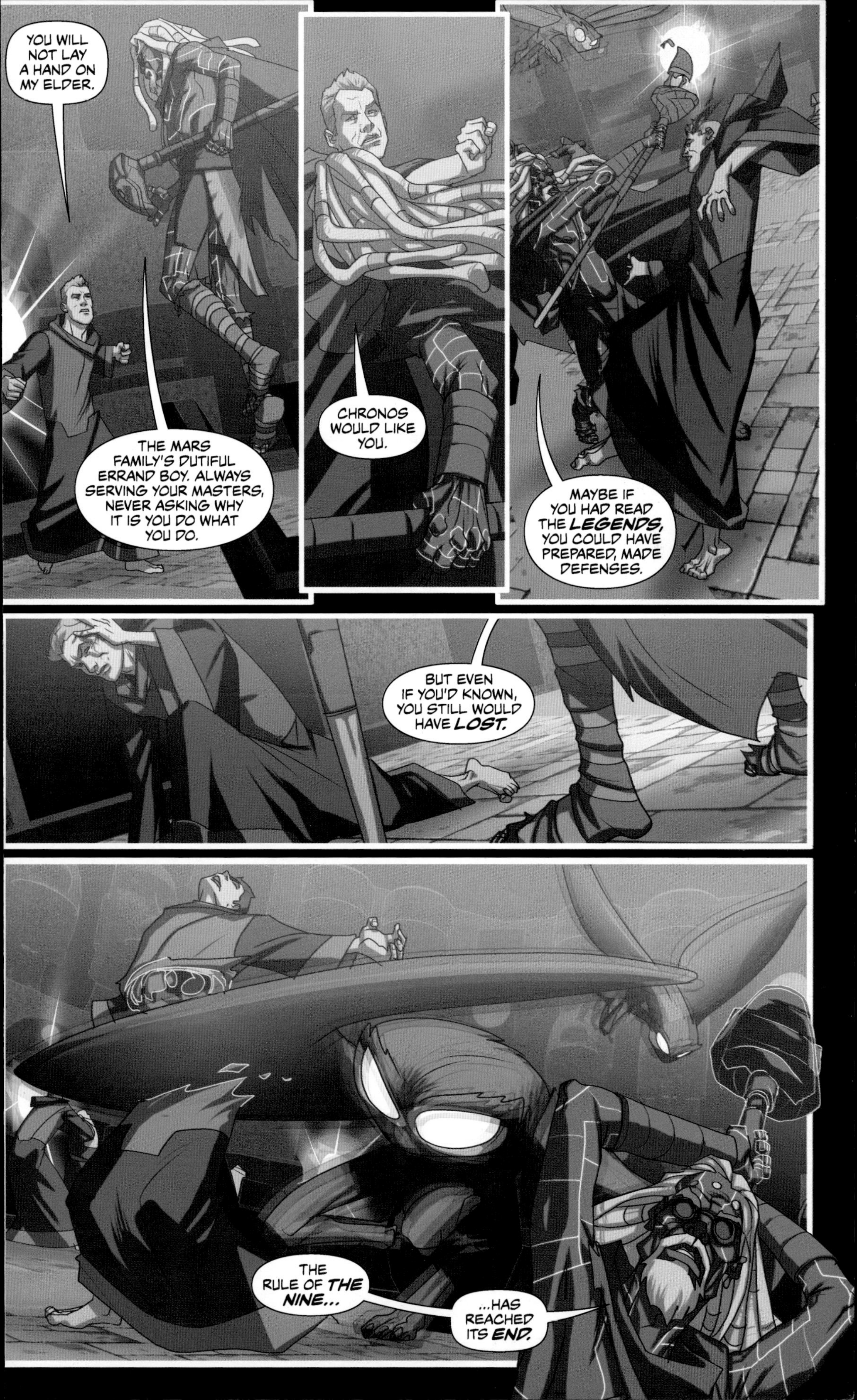
YOU WILL NOT LAY A HAND ON MY ELDER.
THE MARS FAMILY'S DUTIFUL ERRAND BOY. ALWAYS SERVING YOUR MASTERS, NEVER ASKING WHY IT IS YOU DO WHAT YOU DO.
CHRONOS WOULD LIKE YOU.
MAYBE IF YOU HAD READ THE LEGENDS, YOU COULD HAVE PREPARED, MADE DEFENSES.
BUT EVEN IF YOU'D KNOWN, YOU STILL WOULD HAVE LOST.
THE RULE OF THE NINE...
...HAS REACHED ITS END.

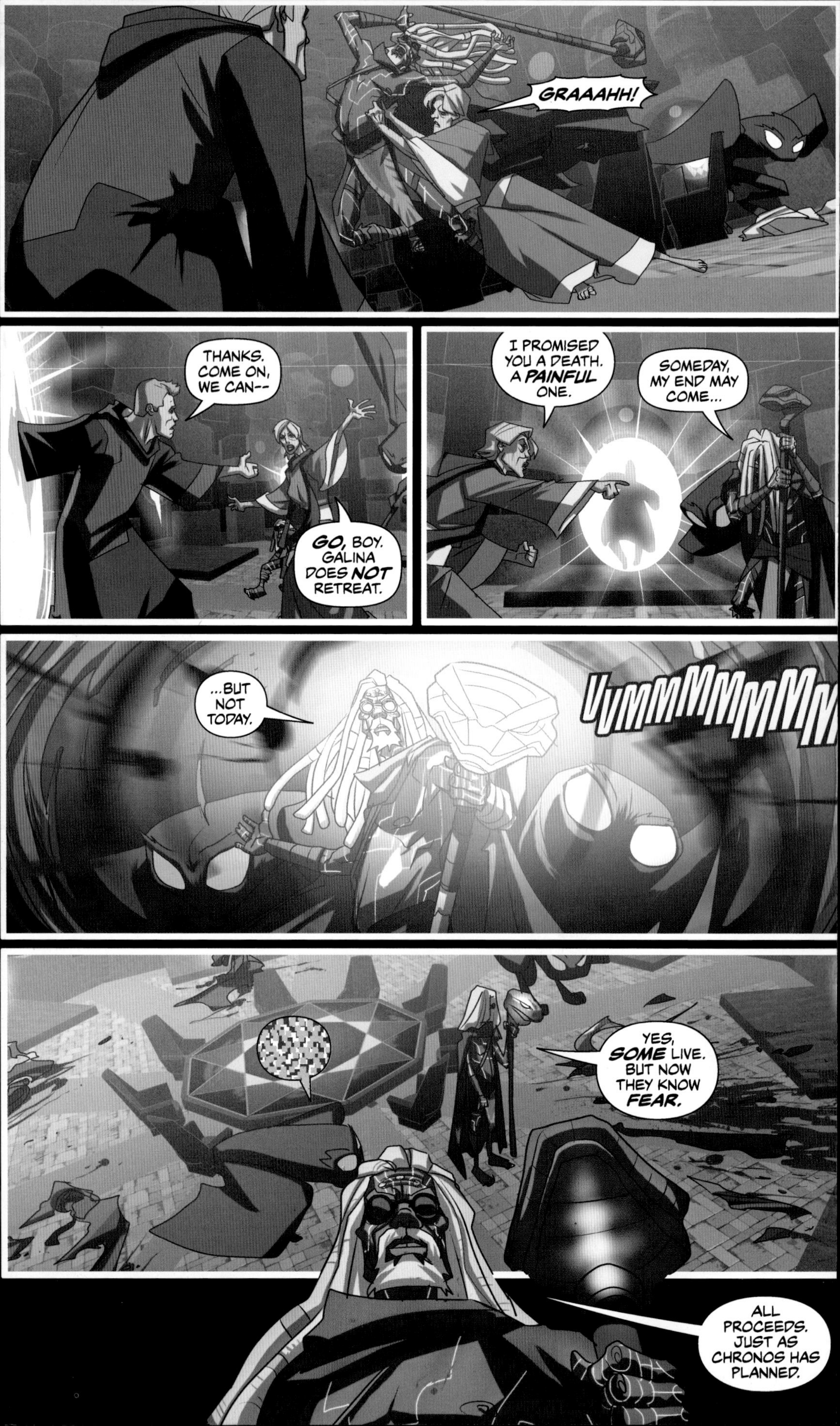
GRAAAHH!
THANKS. COME ON, WE CAN--
GO, BOY. GALINA DOES NOT RETREAT.
I PROMISED YOU A DEATH. A PAINFUL ONE.
SOMEDAY, MY END MAY COME...
...BUT NOT TODAY.
VVMMMMMMMMN
YES, SOME LIVE. BUT NOW THEY KNOW FEAR.
ALL PROCEEDS. JUST AS CHRONOS HAS PLANNED.

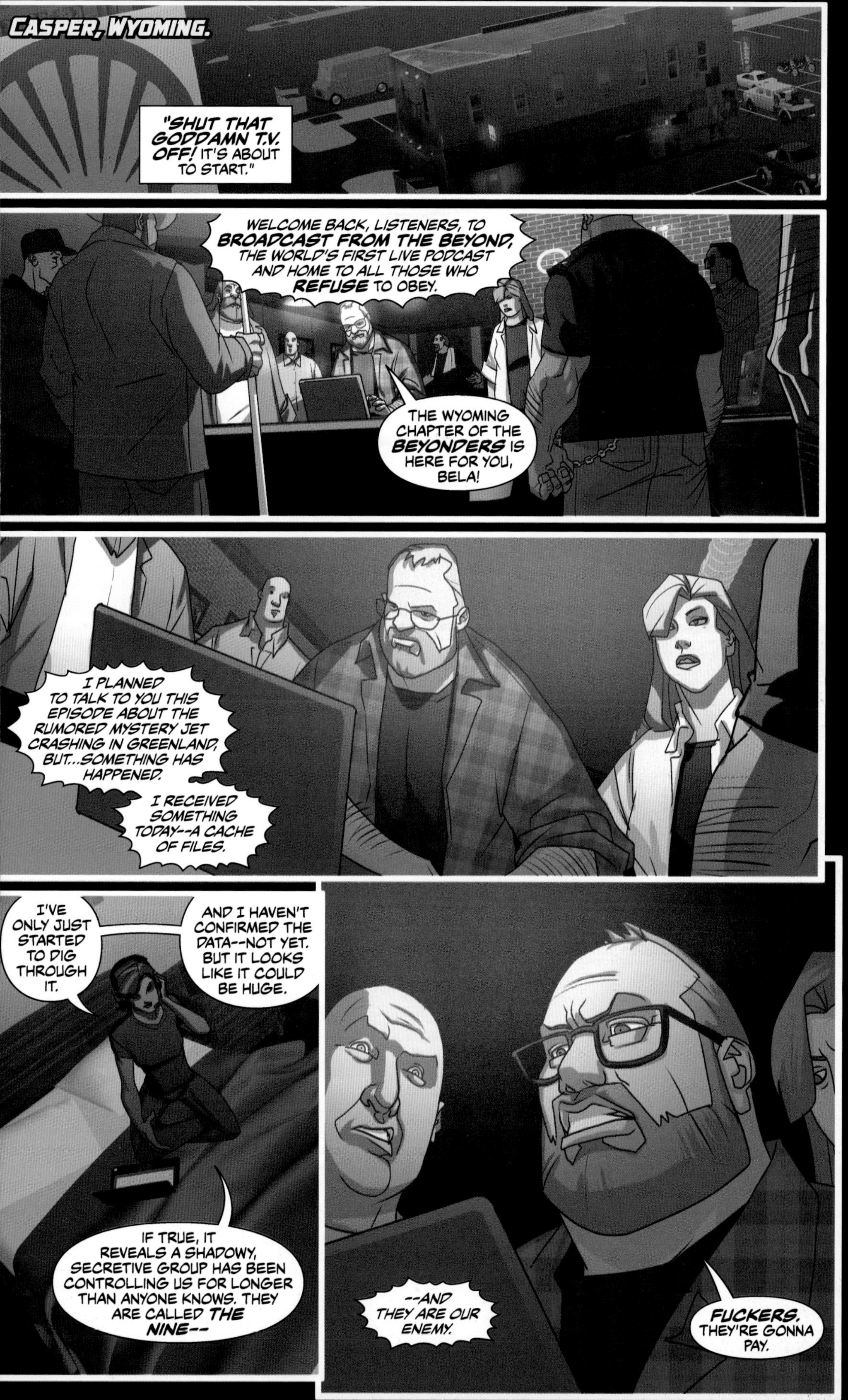
CASPER, WYOMING.
"SHUT THAT GODDAMN T.V. OFF! IT'S ABOUT TO START."
WELCOME BACK, LISTENERS, TO BROADCAST FROM THE BEYOND, THE WORLD'S FIRST LIVE PODCAST AND HOME TO ALL THOSE WHO REFUSE TO OBEY.
THE WYOMING CHAPTER OF THE BEYONDERS IS HERE FOR YOU, BELA!
I PLANNED TO TALK TO YOU THIS EPISODE ABOUT THE RUMORED MYSTERY JET CRASHING IN GREENLAND, BUT...SOMETHING HAS HAPPENED.
I RECEIVED SOMETHING TODAY--A CACHE OF FILES.
I'VE ONLY JUST STARTED TO DIG THROUGH IT.
AND I HAVEN'T CONFIRMED THE DATA--NOT YET. BUT IT LOOKS LIKE IT COULD BE HUGE.
IF TRUE, IT REVEALS A SHADOWY, SECRETIVE GROUP HAS BEEN CONTROLLING US FOR LONGER THAN ANYONE KNOWS. THEY ARE CALLED THE NINE--
--AND THEY ARE OUR ENEMY.
FUCKERS. THEY'RE GONNA PAY.

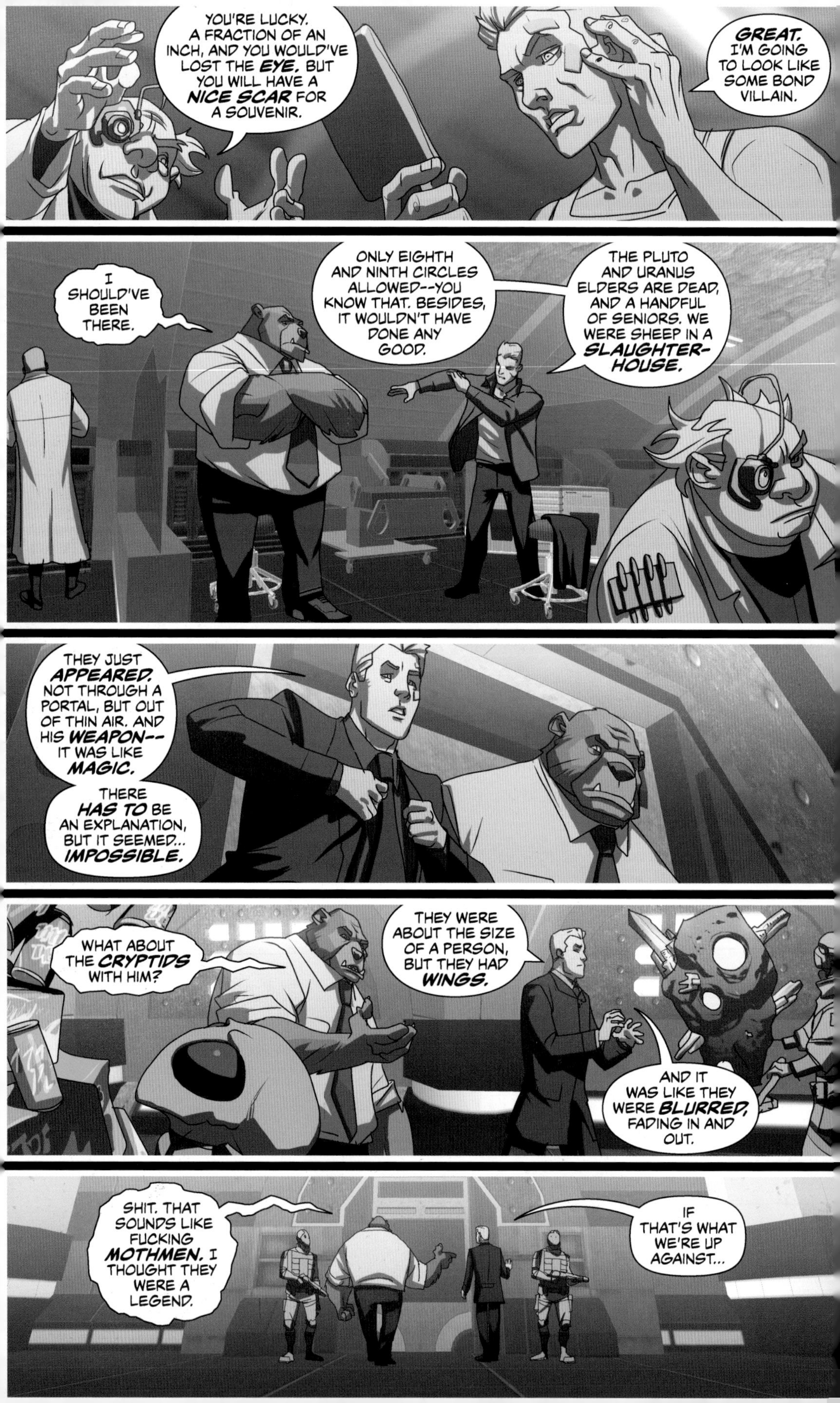
YOU'RE LUCKY. A FRACTION OF AN INCH, AND YOU WOULD'VE LOST THE EYE. BUT YOU WILL HAVE A NICE SCAR FOR A SOUVENIR.
GREAT. I'M GOING TO LOOK LIKE SOME BOND VILLAIN.
I SHOULD'VE BEEN THERE.
ONLY EIGHTH AND NINTH CIRCLES ALLOWED--YOU KNOW THAT. BESIDES, IT WOULDN'T HAVE DONE ANY GOOD.
THE PLUTO AND URANUS ELDERS ARE DEAD, AND A HANDFUL OF SENIORS. WE WERE SHEEP IN A SLAUGHTER-HOUSE.
THEY JUST APPEARED. NOT THROUGH A PORTAL, BUT OUT OF THIN AIR. AND HIS WEAPON-- IT WAS LIKE MAGIC.
THERE HAS TO BE AN EXPLANATION, BUT IT SEEMED... IMPOSSIBLE.
WHAT ABOUT THE CRYPTIDS WITH HIM?
THEY WERE ABOUT THE SIZE OF A PERSON, BUT THEY HAD WINGS.
AND IT WAS LIKE THEY WERE BLURRED, FADING IN AND OUT.
SHIT. THAT SOUNDS LIKE FUCKING MOTHMEN. I THOUGHT THEY WERE A LEGEND.
IF THAT'S WHAT WE'RE UP AGAINST...

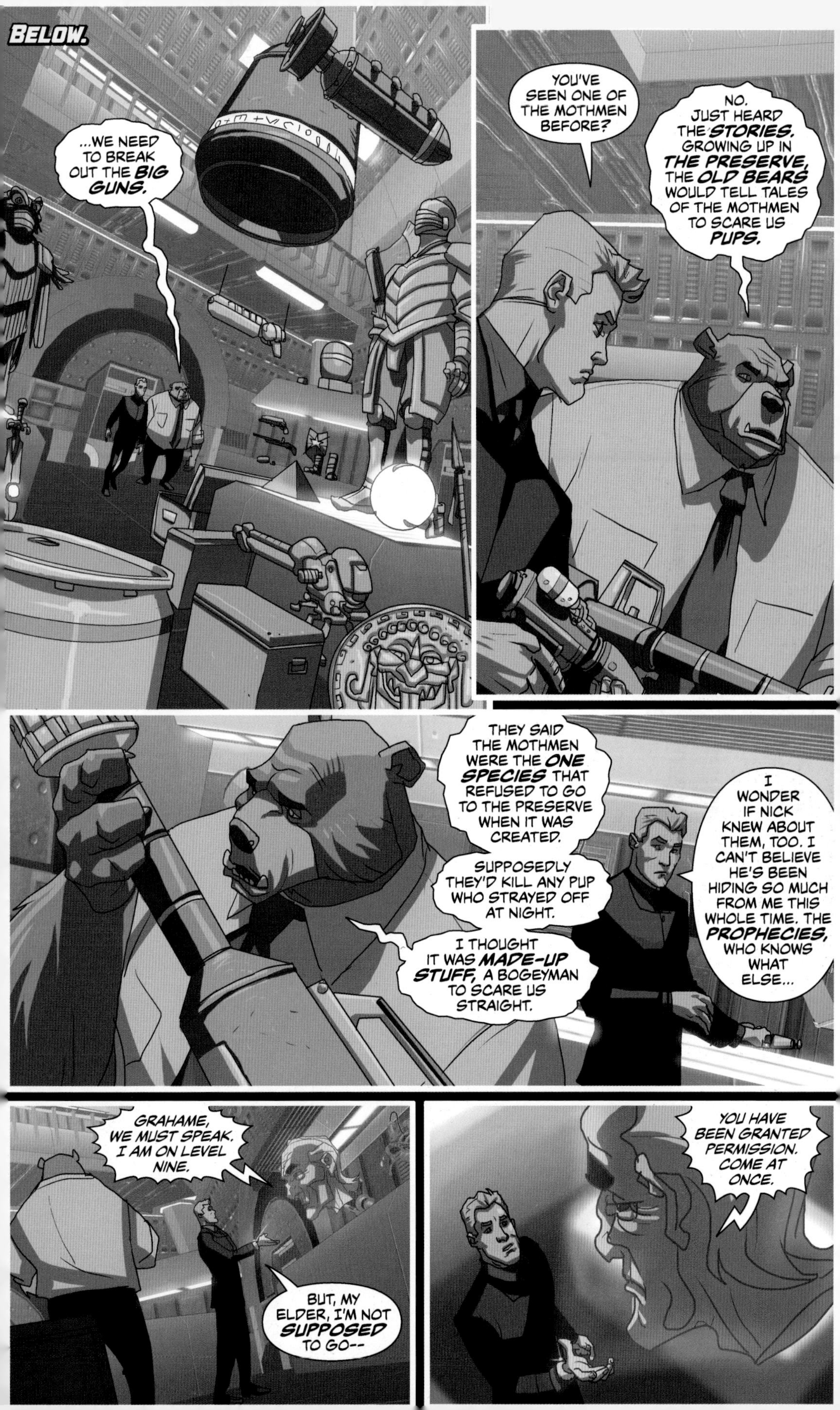
BELOW.
...WE NEED TO BREAK OUT THE BIG GUNS.
YOU'VE SEEN ONE OF THE MOTHMEN BEFORE?
NO. JUST HEARD THE STORIES. GROWING UP IN THE PRESERVE, THE OLD BEARS WOULD TELL TALES OF THE MOTHMEN TO SCARE US PUPS.
THEY SAID THE MOTHMEN WERE THE ONE SPECIES THAT REFUSED TO GO TO THE PRESERVE WHEN IT WAS CREATED.
SUPPOSEDLY THEY'D KILL ANY PUP WHO STRAYED OFF AT NIGHT.
I THOUGHT IT WAS MADE-UP STUFF, A BOGEYMAN TO SCARE US STRAIGHT.
I WONDER IF NICK KNEW ABOUT THEM, TOO. I CAN'T BELIEVE HE'S BEEN HIDING SO MUCH FROM ME THIS WHOLE TIME. THE PROPHECIES, WHO KNOWS WHAT ELSE...
GRAHAME, WE MUST SPEAK. I AM ON LEVEL NINE.
BUT, MY ELDER, I'M NOT SUPPOSED TO GO--
YOU HAVE BEEN GRANTED PERMISSION. COME AT ONCE.

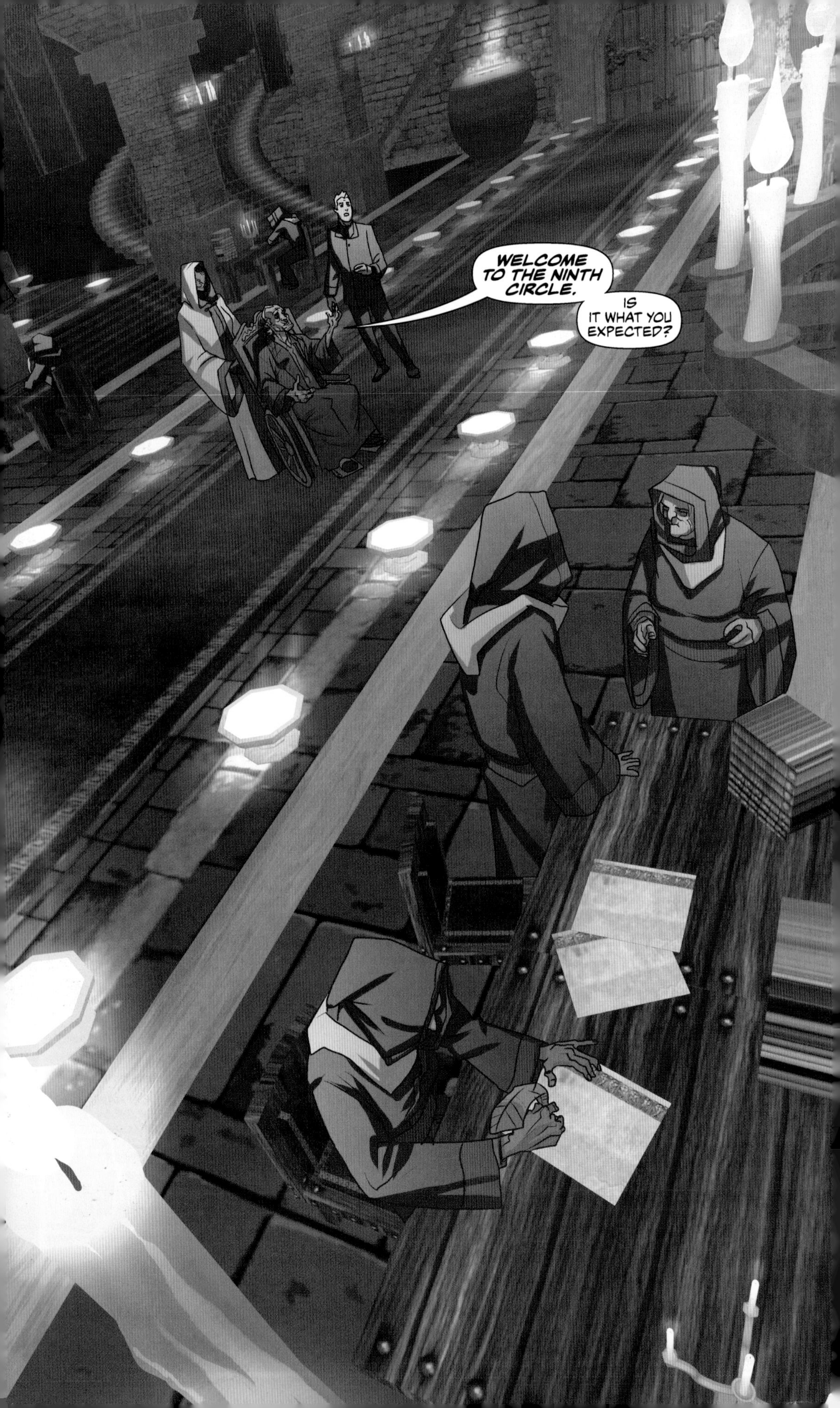
WELCOME TO THE NINTH CIRCLE.
IS IT WHAT YOU EXPECTED?

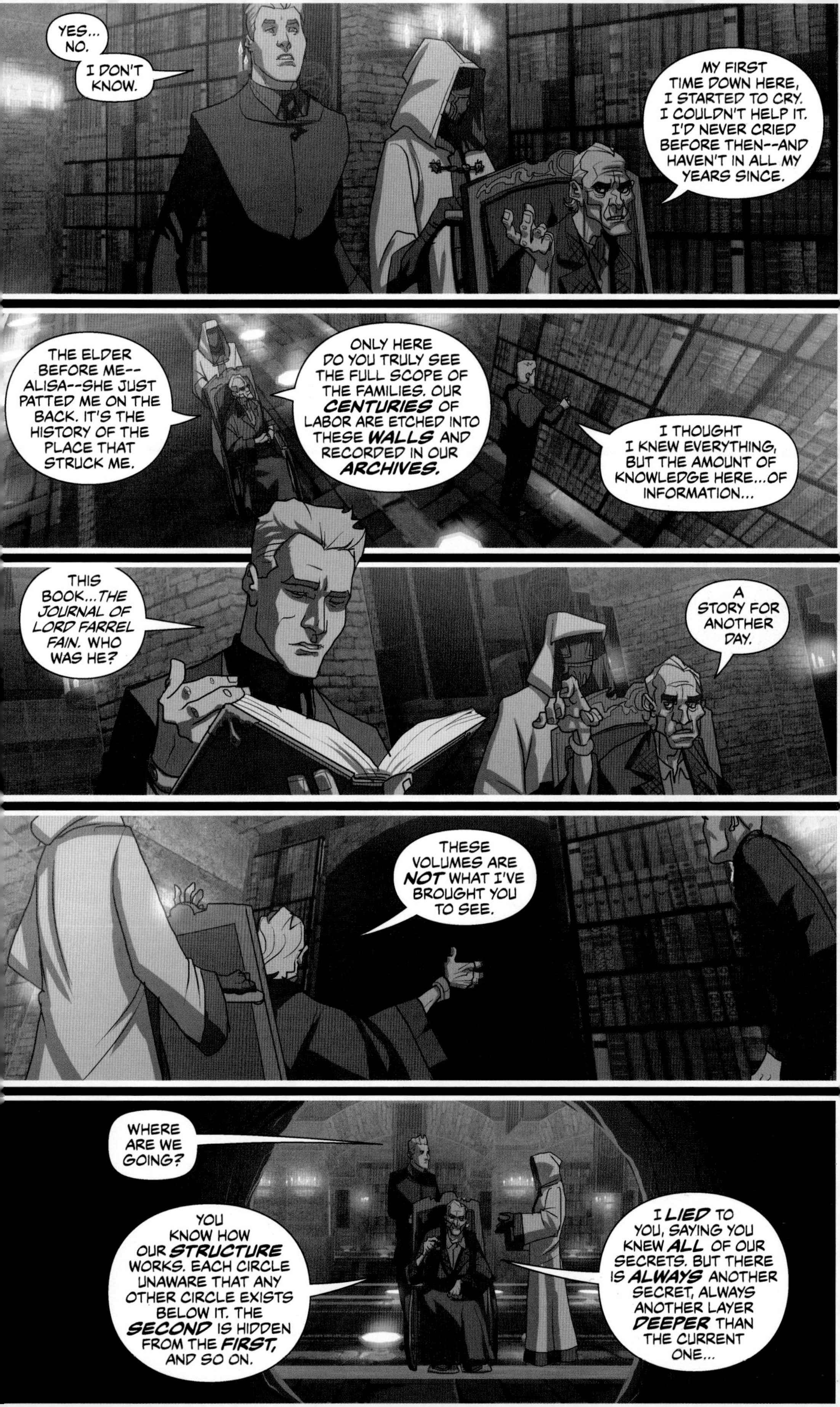
YES... NO.
I DON'T KNOW.
MY FIRST TIME DOWN HERE, I STARTED TO CRY. I COULDN'T HELP IT. I'D NEVER CRIED BEFORE THEN--AND HAVEN'T IN ALL MY YEARS SINCE.
THE ELDER BEFORE ME--ALISA--SHE JUST PATTED ME ON THE BACK. IT'S THE HISTORY OF THE PLACE THAT STRUCK ME.
ONLY HERE DO YOU TRULY SEE THE FULL SCOPE OF THE FAMILIES. OUR CENTURIES OF LABOR ARE ETCHED INTO THESE WALLS AND RECORDED IN OUR ARCHIVES.
I THOUGHT I KNEW EVERYTHING, BUT THE AMOUNT OF KNOWLEDGE HERE...OF INFORMATION...
THIS BOOK...THE JOURNAL OF LORD FARREL FAIN. WHO WAS HE?
A STORY FOR ANOTHER DAY.
THESE VOLUMES ARE NOT WHAT I'VE BROUGHT YOU TO SEE.
WHERE ARE WE GOING?
YOU KNOW HOW OUR STRUCTURE WORKS. EACH CIRCLE UNAWARE THAT ANY OTHER CIRCLE EXISTS BELOW IT. THE SECOND IS HIDDEN FROM THE FIRST, AND SO ON.
I LIED TO YOU, SAYING YOU KNEW ALL OF OUR SECRETS. BUT THERE IS ALWAYS ANOTHER SECRET, ALWAYS ANOTHER LAYER DEEPER THAN THE CURRENT ONE...

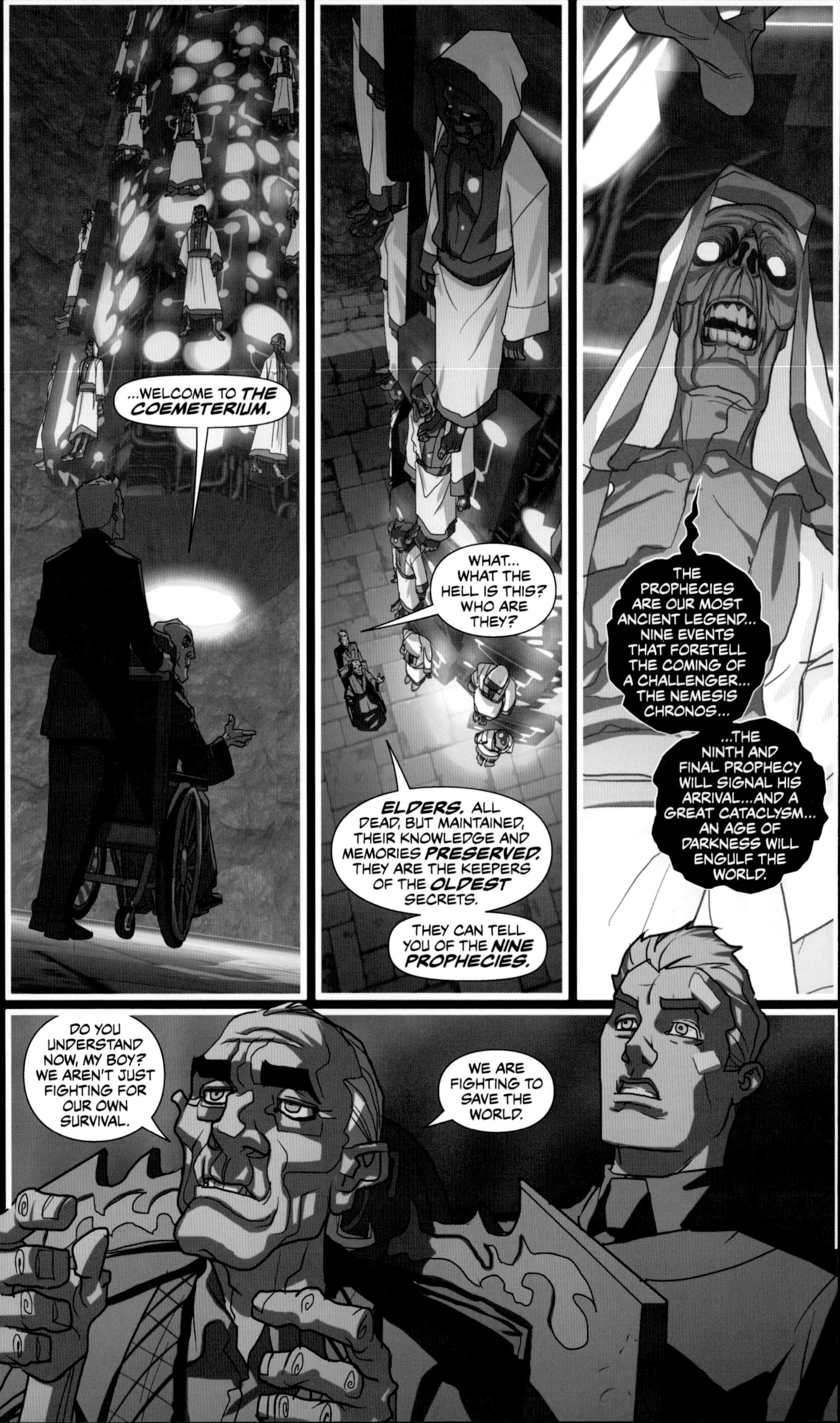
...WELCOME TO THE COEMETERIUM.
WHAT... WHAT THE HELL IS THIS? WHO ARE THEY?
ELDERS. ALL DEAD, BUT MAINTAINED, THEIR KNOWLEDGE AND MEMORIES PRESERVED. THEY ARE THE KEEPERS OF THE OLDEST SECRETS.
THEY CAN TELL YOU OF THE NINE PROPHECIES.
THE PROPHECIES ARE OUR MOST ANCIENT LEGEND... NINE EVENTS THAT FORETELL THE COMING OF A CHALLENGER... THE NEMESIS CHRONOS...
...THE NINTH AND FINAL PROPHECY WILL SIGNAL HIS ARRIVAL...AND A GREAT CATACLYSM... AN AGE OF DARKNESS WILL ENGULF THE WORLD.
DO YOU UNDERSTAND NOW, MY BOY? WE AREN'T JUST FIGHTING FOR OUR OWN SURVIVAL.
WE ARE FIGHTING TO SAVE THE WORLD.

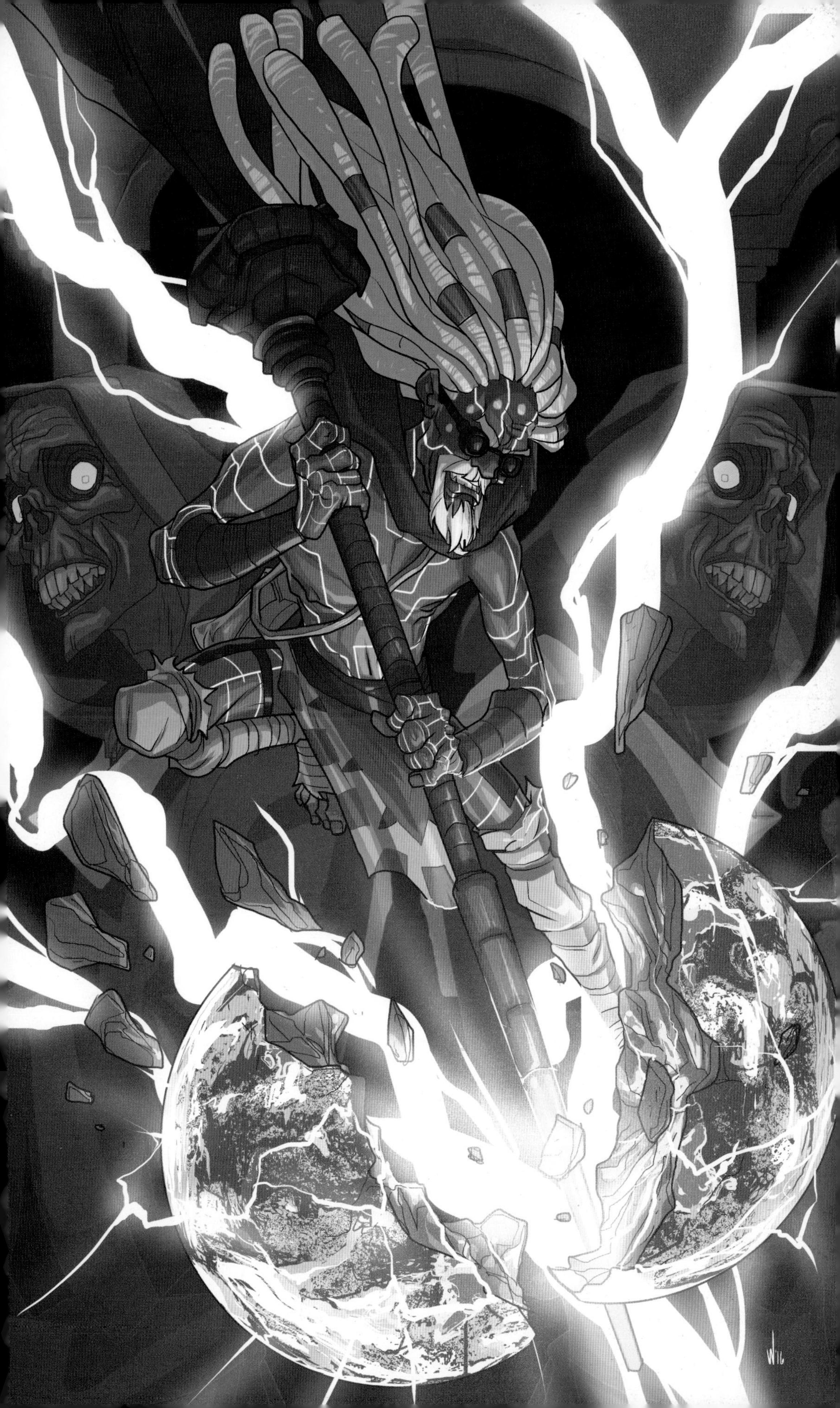

#3 HISTORY

NINE FAMILIES RULE THE WORLD. ONE ELDER LEADS EACH IN OVERSEEING THE FAMILY'S TERRITORY.

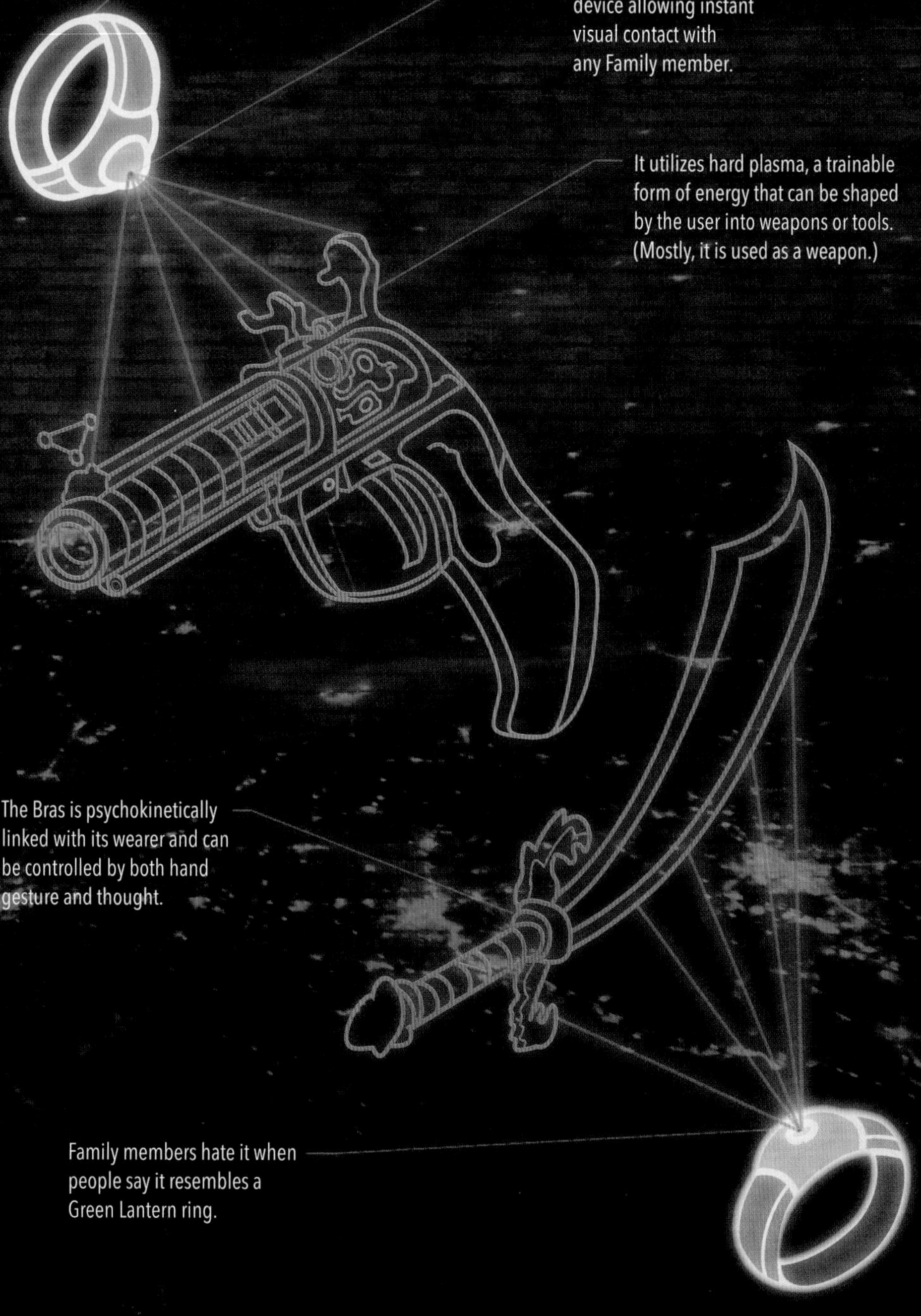

Each Elder and Senior is trained in the use of a Bras (also called a bracelet), to be worn on the right wrist.
The Bras is primarily a communication device allowing instant visual contact with any Family member.
It utilizes hard plasma, a trainable form of energy that can be shaped by the user into weapons or tools. (Mostly, it is used as a weapon.)
The Bras is psychokinetically linked with its wearer and can be controlled by both hand gesture and thought.
Family members hate it when people say it resembles a Green Lantern ring.

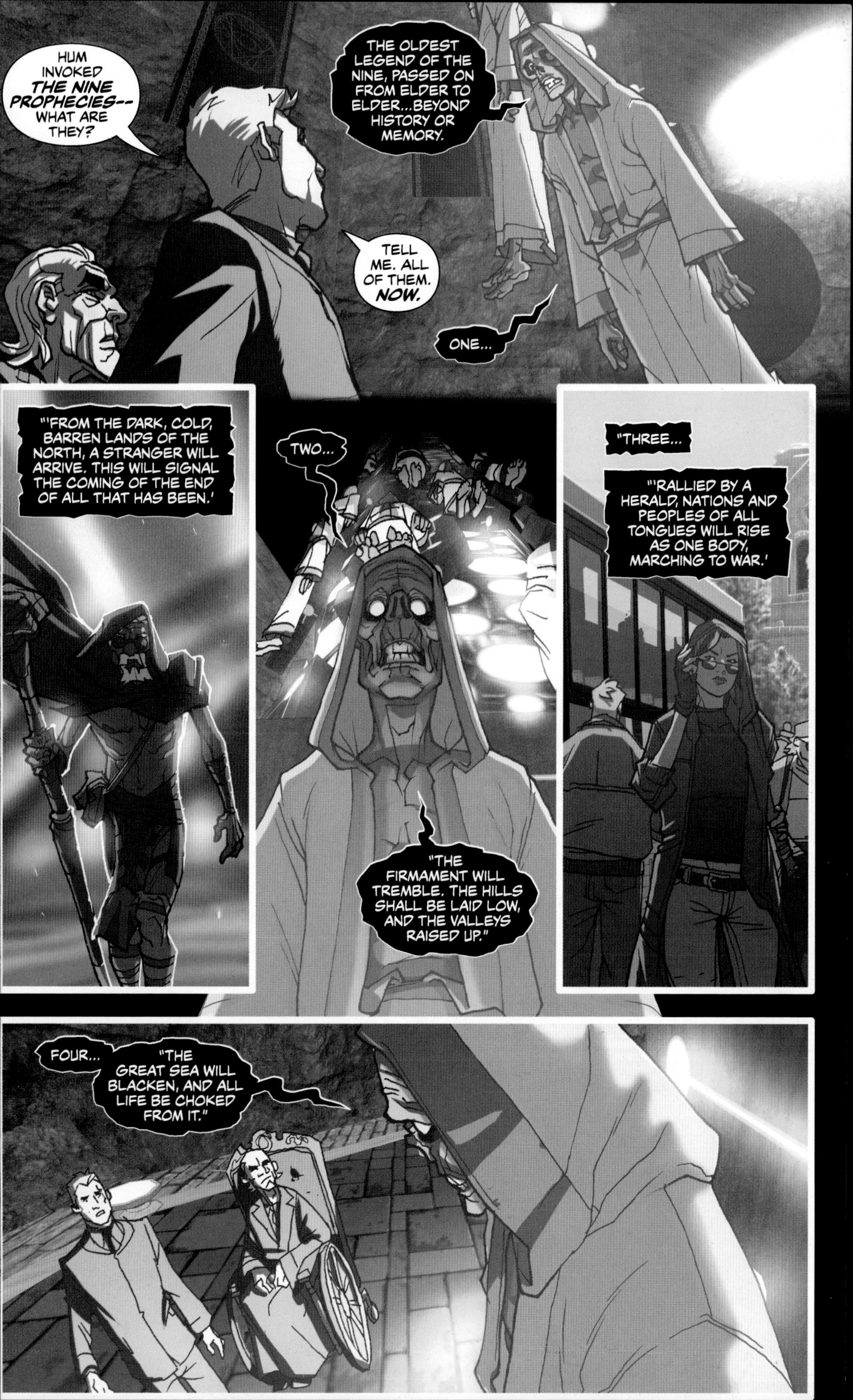
HUM INVOKED THE NINE PROPHECIES-- WHAT ARE THEY?
THE OLDEST LEGEND OF THE NINE, PASSED ON FROM ELDER TO ELDER...BEYOND HISTORY OR MEMORY.
TELL ME. ALL OF THEM. NOW.
ONE...
"'FROM THE DARK, COLD, BARREN LANDS OF THE NORTH, A STRANGER WILL ARRIVE. THIS WILL SIGNAL THE COMING OF THE END OF ALL THAT HAS BEEN.'
TWO...
"THE FIRMAMENT WILL TREMBLE. THE HILLS SHALL BE LAID LOW, AND THE VALLEYS RAISED UP."
"THREE...
"'RALLIED BY A HERALD, NATIONS AND PEOPLES OF ALL TONGUES WILL RISE AS ONE BODY, MARCHING TO WAR.'
FOUR...
"THE GREAT SEA WILL BLACKEN, AND ALL LIFE BE CHOKED FROM IT."

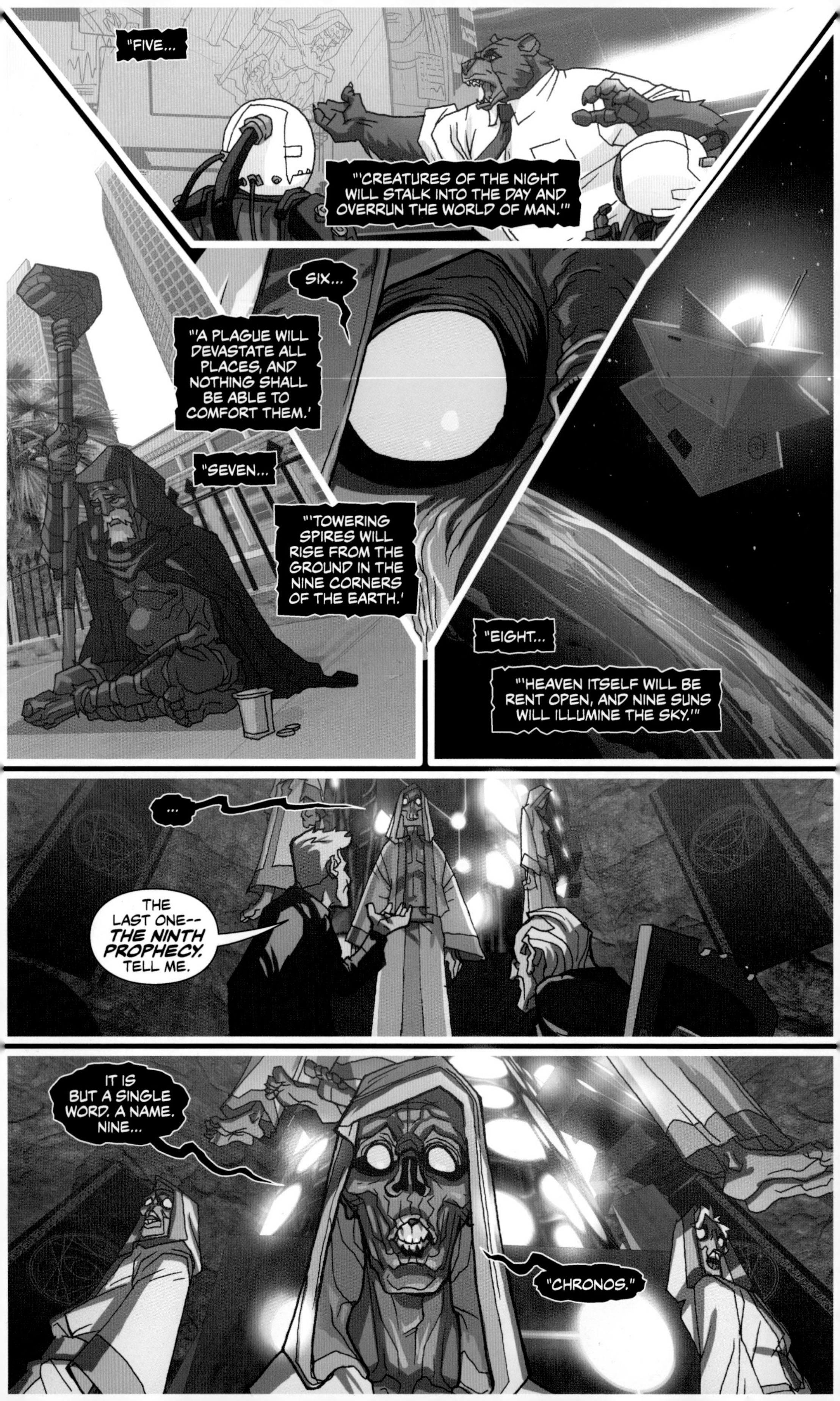
"FIVE...
"'CREATURES OF THE NIGHT WILL STALK INTO THE DAY AND OVERRUN THE WORLD OF MAN.'"
SIX...
"'A PLAGUE WILL DEVASTATE ALL PLACES, AND NOTHING SHALL BE ABLE TO COMFORT THEM.'
"SEVEN...
"'TOWERING SPIRES WILL RISE FROM THE GROUND IN THE NINE CORNERS OF THE EARTH.'
"EIGHT...
"'HEAVEN ITSELF WILL BE RENT OPEN, AND NINE SUNS WILL ILLUMINE THE SKY.'"
...
THE LAST ONE-- *THE NINTH PROPHECY.* TELL ME.
IT IS BUT A SINGLE WORD. A NAME. NINE...
"CHRONOS."

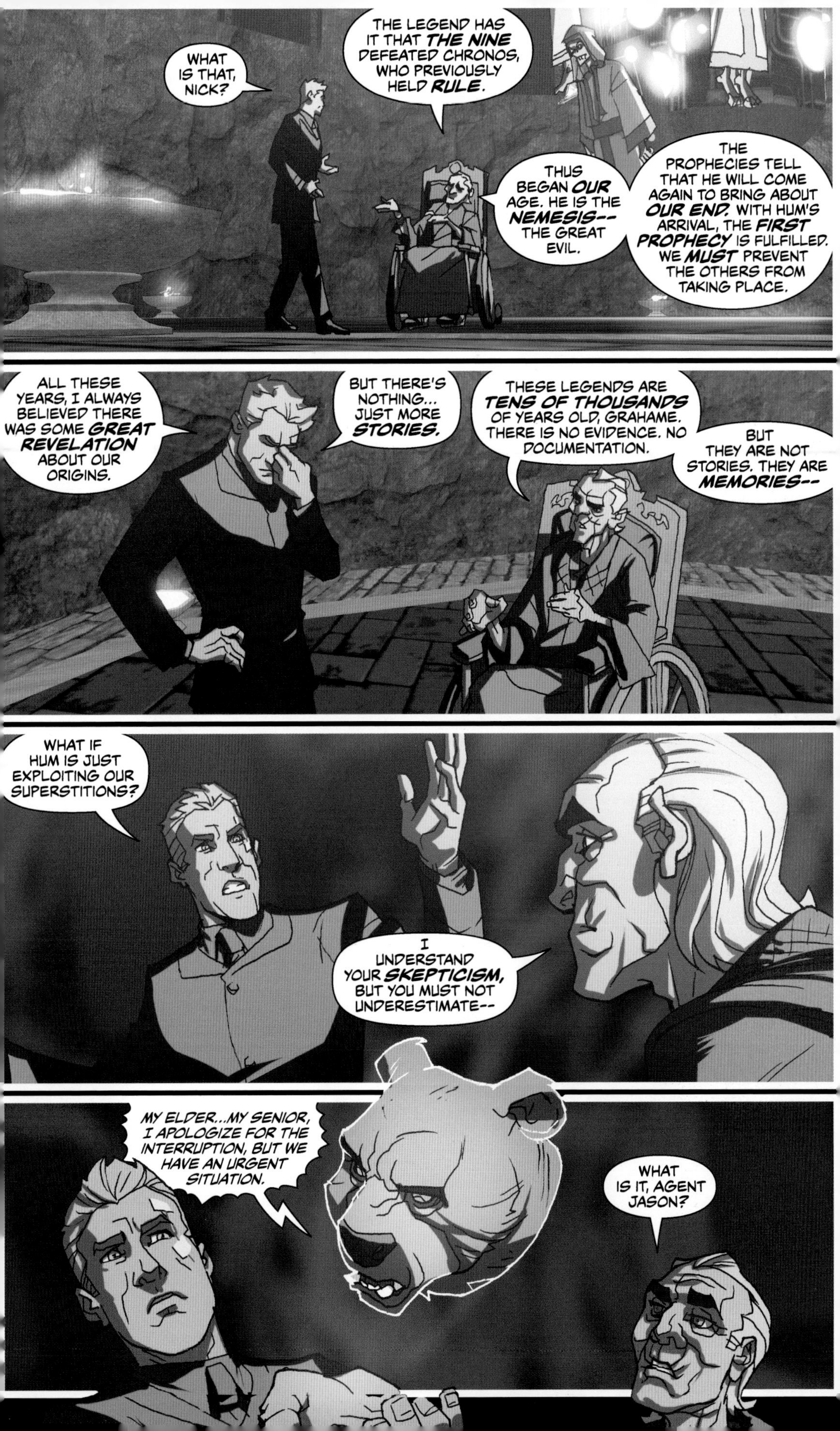

WHAT IS THAT, NICK?
THE LEGEND HAS IT THAT THE NINE DEFEATED CHRONOS, WHO PREVIOUSLY HELD RULE.
THUS BEGAN OUR AGE. HE IS THE NEMESIS-- THE GREAT EVIL.
THE PROPHECIES TELL THAT HE WILL COME AGAIN TO BRING ABOUT OUR END. WITH HUM'S ARRIVAL, THE FIRST PROPHECY IS FULFILLED. WE MUST PREVENT THE OTHERS FROM TAKING PLACE.
ALL THESE YEARS, I ALWAYS BELIEVED THERE WAS SOME GREAT REVELATION ABOUT OUR ORIGINS.
BUT THERE'S NOTHING... JUST MORE STORIES.
THESE LEGENDS ARE TENS OF THOUSANDS OF YEARS OLD, GRAHAME. THERE IS NO EVIDENCE. NO DOCUMENTATION.
BUT THEY ARE NOT STORIES. THEY ARE MEMORIES--
WHAT IF HUM IS JUST EXPLOITING OUR SUPERSTITIONS?
I UNDERSTAND YOUR SKEPTICISM, BUT YOU MUST NOT UNDERESTIMATE--
MY ELDER...MY SENIOR, I APOLOGIZE FOR THE INTERRUPTION, BUT WE HAVE AN URGENT SITUATION.
WHAT IS IT, AGENT JASON?

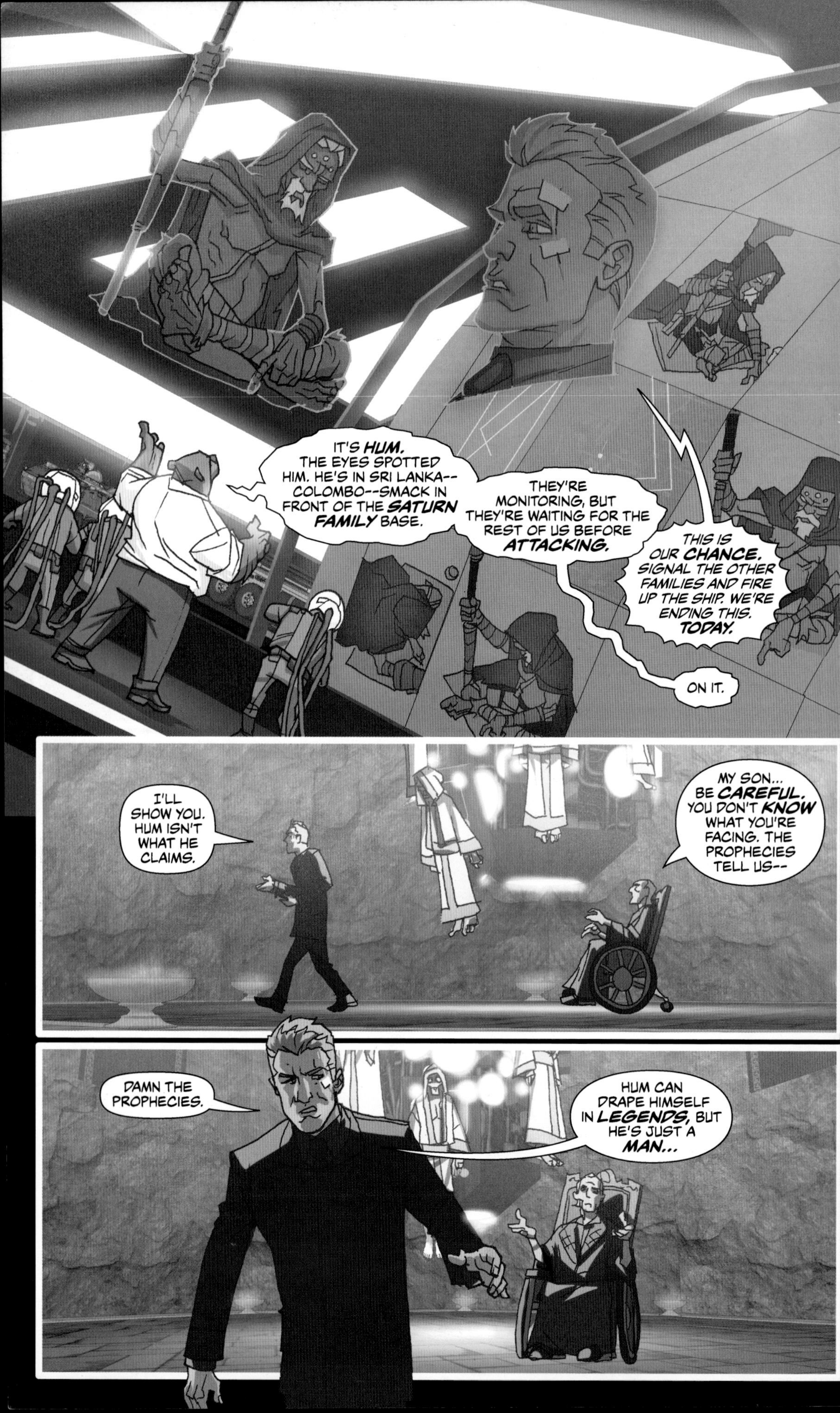
IT'S HUM. THE EYES SPOTTED HIM. HE'S IN SRI LANKA-- COLOMBO--SMACK IN FRONT OF THE SATURN FAMILY BASE.
THEY'RE MONITORING, BUT THEY'RE WAITING FOR THE REST OF US BEFORE ATTACKING.
THIS IS OUR CHANCE. SIGNAL THE OTHER FAMILIES AND FIRE UP THE SHIP. WE'RE ENDING THIS. TODAY.
ON IT.
I'LL SHOW YOU. HUM ISN'T WHAT HE CLAIMS.
MY SON... BE CAREFUL. YOU DON'T KNOW WHAT YOU'RE FACING. THE PROPHECIES TELL US--
DAMN THE PROPHECIES.
HUM CAN DRAPE HIMSELF IN LEGENDS, BUT HE'S JUST A MAN...

"...AND MEN CAN BE KILLED."

I'M IN POSITION AT THE LIBRARY. ONE CASUALTY--A LIBRARIAN WHO ASKED TOO MANY QUESTIONS. **OPERATION CENSOR** IS A GO. GIVE ME TWO MINUTES...

"...AND THAT BITCH IS DEAD."

WHO ARE YOU?

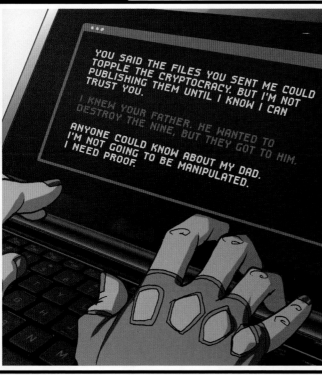

YOU SAID THE FILES YOU SENT ME COULD TOPPLE THE CRYPTOCRACY. BUT I'M NOT PUBLISHING THEM UNTIL I KNOW I CAN TRUST YOU.

I KNEW YOUR FATHER. HE WANTED TO DESTROY THE NINE, BUT THEY GOT TO HIM.

ANYONE COULD KNOW ABOUT MY DAD. I'M NOT GOING TO BE MANIPULATED. I NEED PROOF.

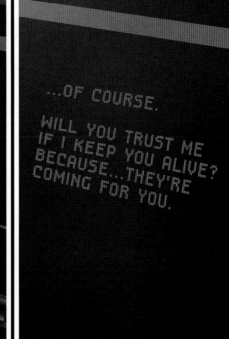

...OF COURSE.

WILL YOU TRUST ME IF I KEEP YOU ALIVE? BECAUSE...THEY'RE COMING FOR YOU.

NO...

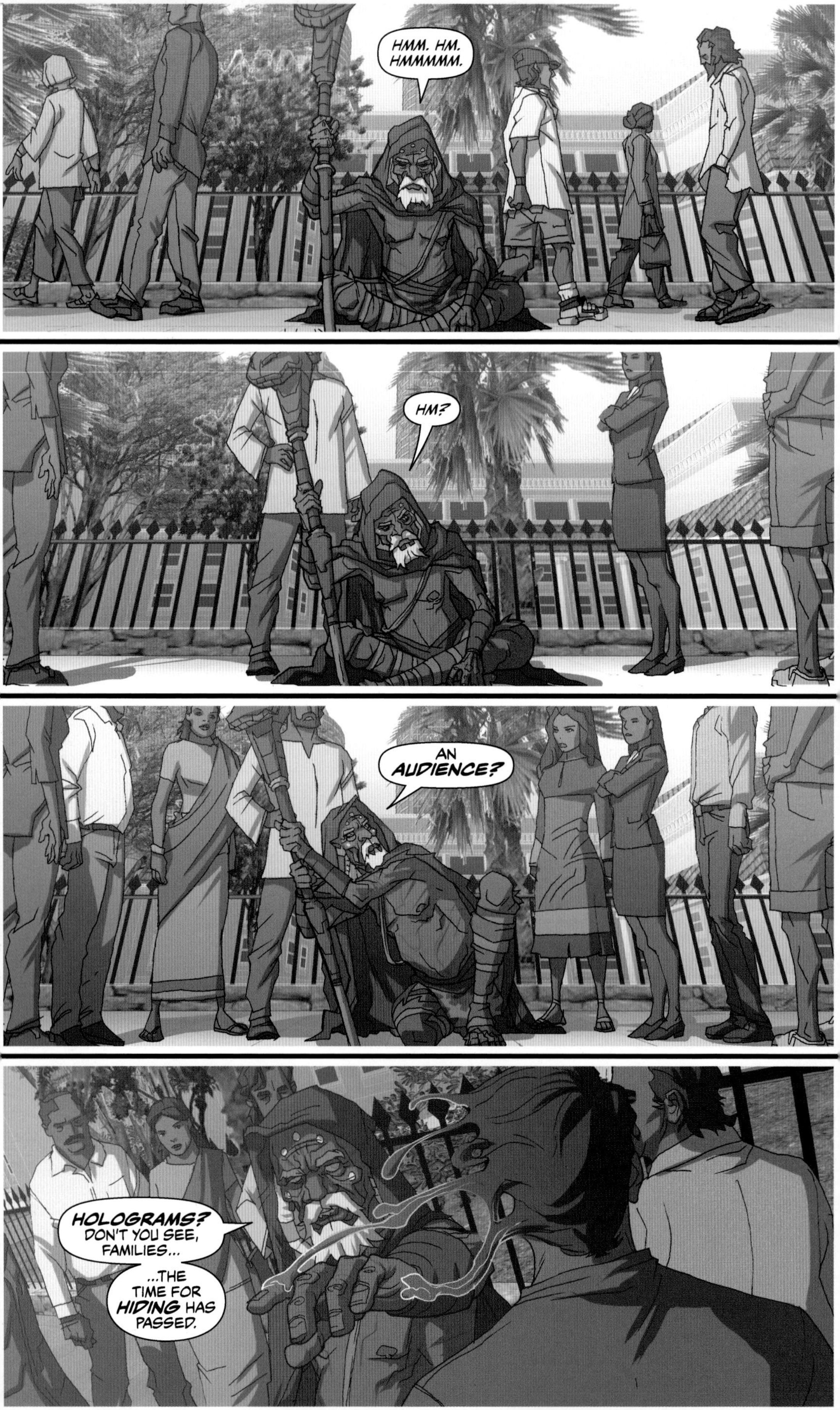

HMM. HM. HMMMMM.
HM?
AN AUDIENCE?
HOLOGRAMS? DON'T YOU SEE, FAMILIES...
...THE TIME FOR HIDING HAS PASSED.

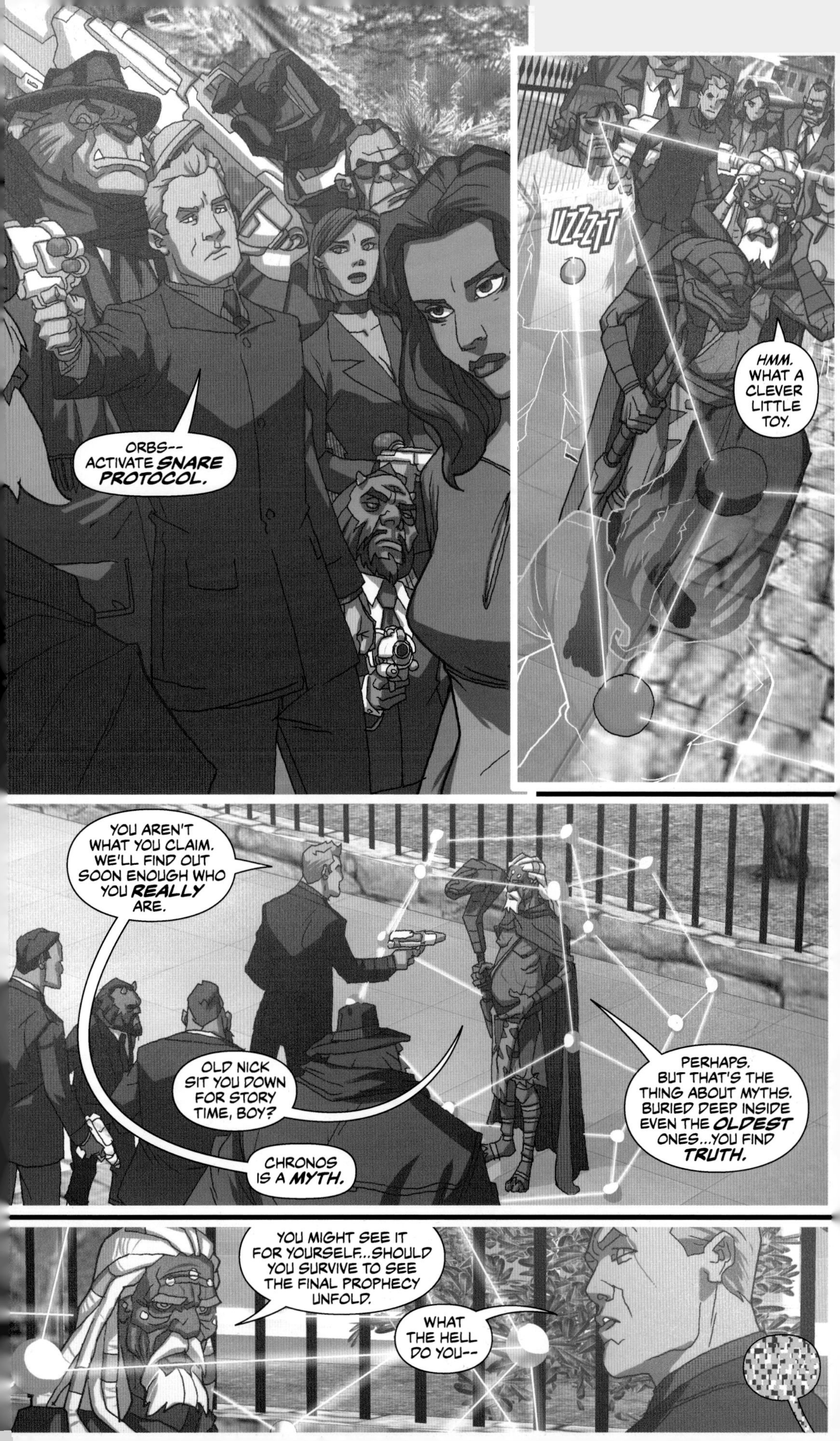
ORBS-- ACTIVATE SNARE PROTOCOL.
VZZZT
HMM. WHAT A CLEVER LITTLE TOY.
YOU AREN'T WHAT YOU CLAIM. WE'LL FIND OUT SOON ENOUGH WHO YOU REALLY ARE.
OLD NICK SIT YOU DOWN FOR STORY TIME, BOY?
CHRONOS IS A MYTH.
PERHAPS. BUT THAT'S THE THING ABOUT MYTHS. BURIED DEEP INSIDE EVEN THE OLDEST ONES...YOU FIND TRUTH.
YOU MIGHT SEE IT FOR YOURSELF...SHOULD YOU SURVIVE TO SEE THE FINAL PROPHECY UNFOLD.
WHAT THE HELL DO YOU--

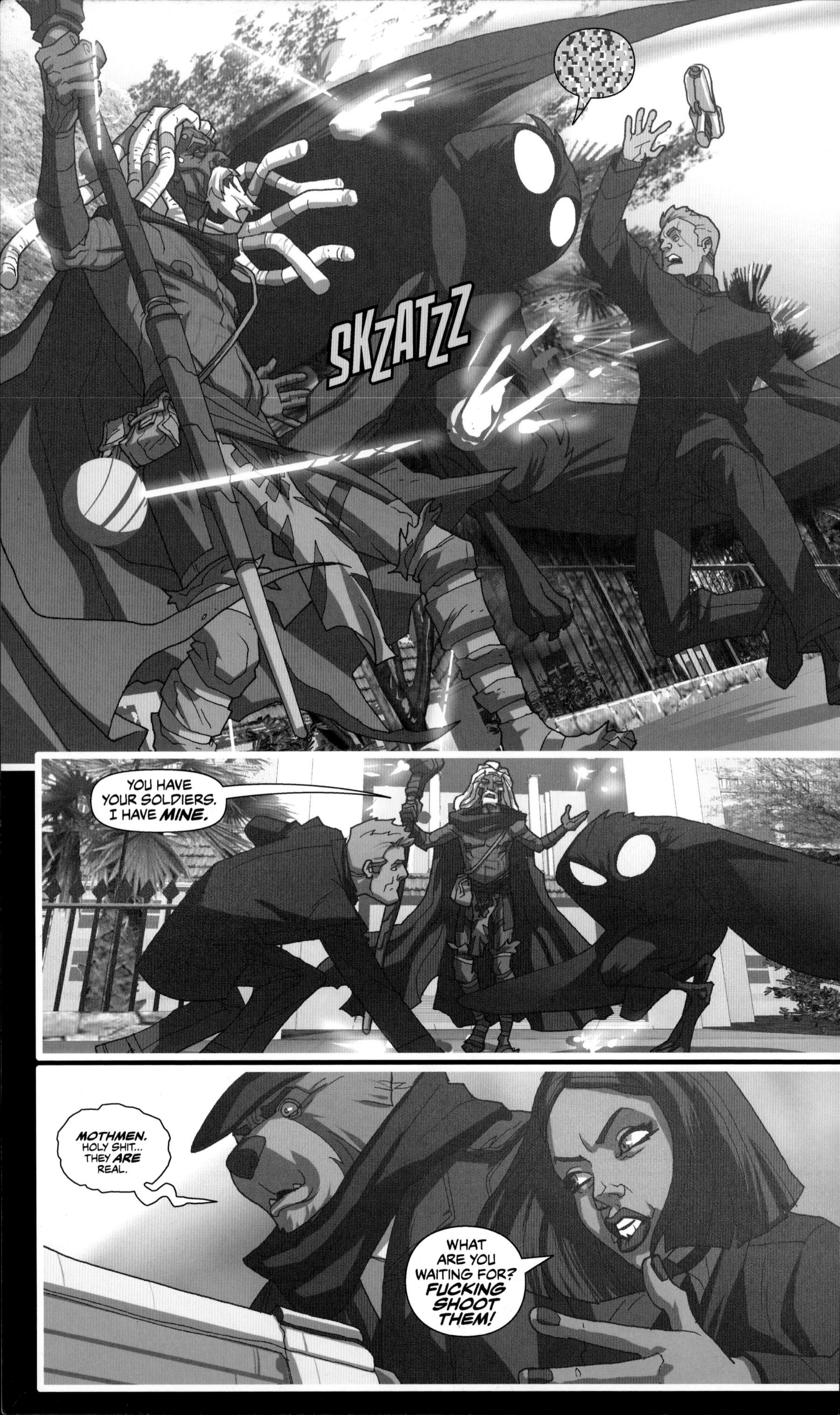
SKZATZZ
YOU HAVE YOUR SOLDIERS. I HAVE MINE.
MOTHMEN. HOLY SHIT... THEY ARE REAL.
WHAT ARE YOU WAITING FOR? FUCKING SHOOT THEM!

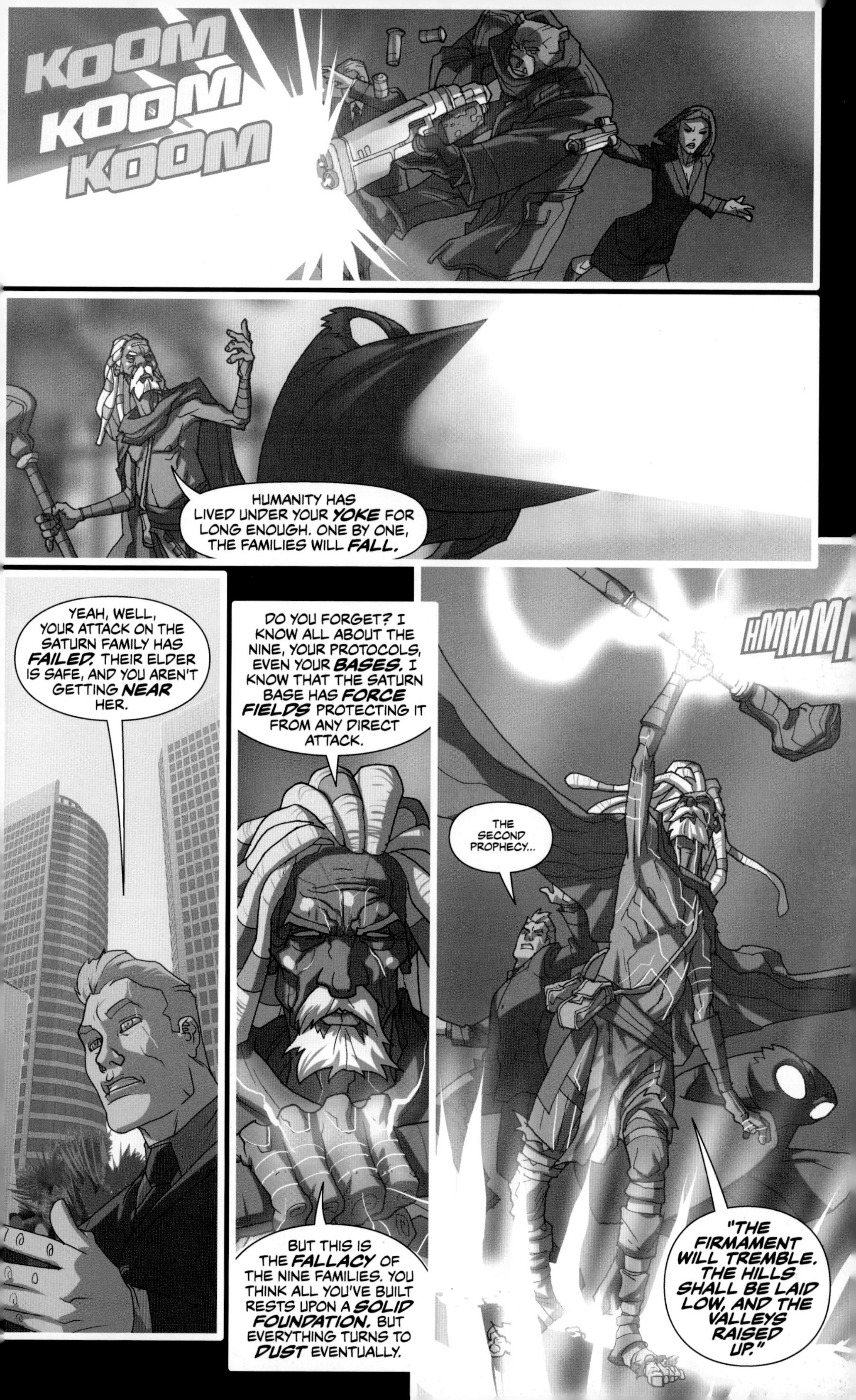
KOOM KOOM KOOM
HUMANITY HAS LIVED UNDER YOUR YOKE FOR LONG ENOUGH. ONE BY ONE, THE FAMILIES WILL FALL.
YEAH, WELL, YOUR ATTACK ON THE SATURN FAMILY HAS FAILED. THEIR ELDER IS SAFE, AND YOU AREN'T GETTING NEAR HER.
DO YOU FORGET? I KNOW ALL ABOUT THE NINE, YOUR PROTOCOLS, EVEN YOUR BASES. I KNOW THAT THE SATURN BASE HAS FORCE FIELDS PROTECTING IT FROM ANY DIRECT ATTACK.
BUT THIS IS THE FALLACY OF THE NINE FAMILIES. YOU THINK ALL YOU'VE BUILT RESTS UPON A SOLID FOUNDATION. BUT EVERYTHING TURNS TO DUST EVENTUALLY.
HMMMM
THE SECOND PROPHECY...
"THE FIRMAMENT WILL TREMBLE. THE HILLS SHALL BE LAID LOW, AND THE VALLEYS RAISED UP."

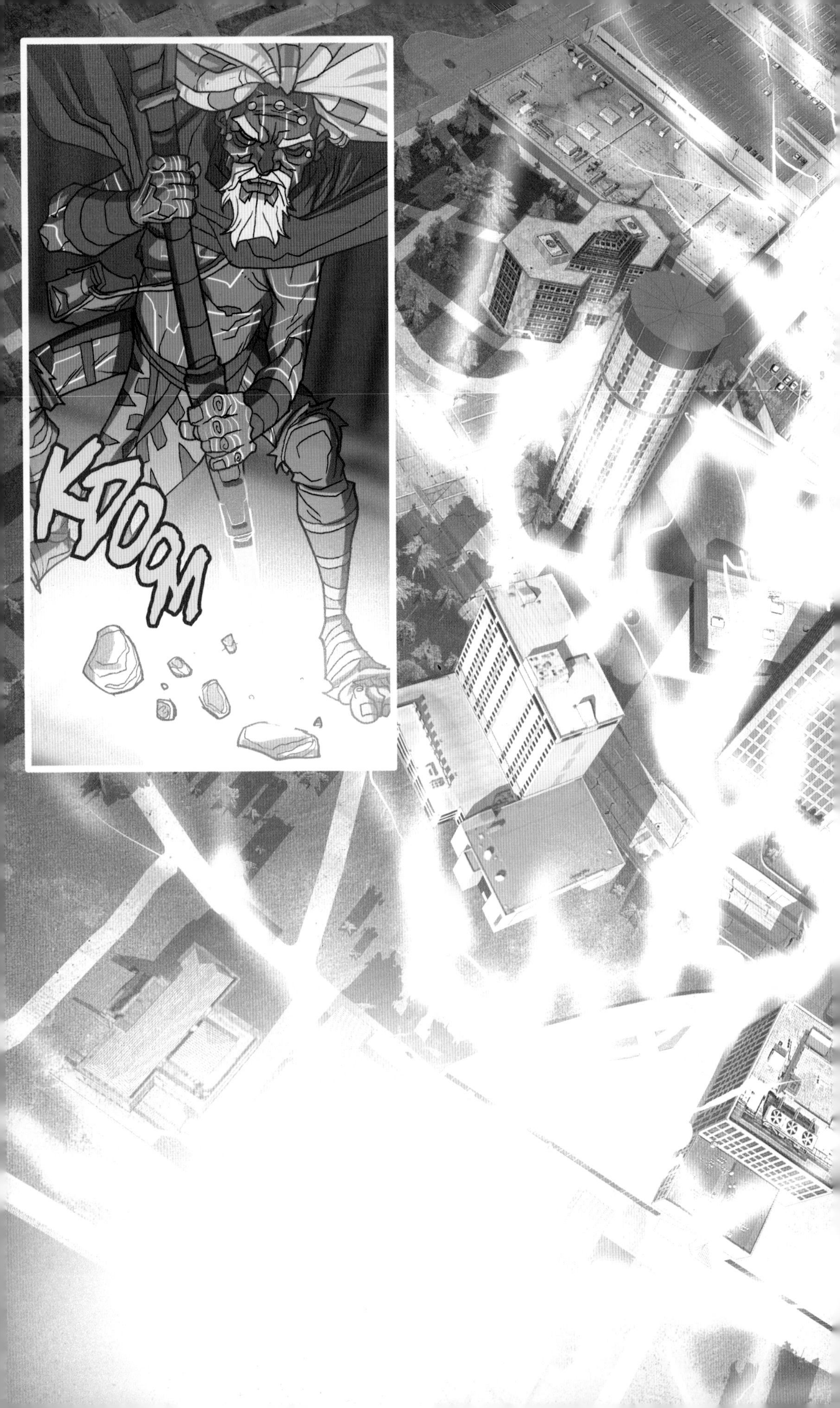
KDOOM

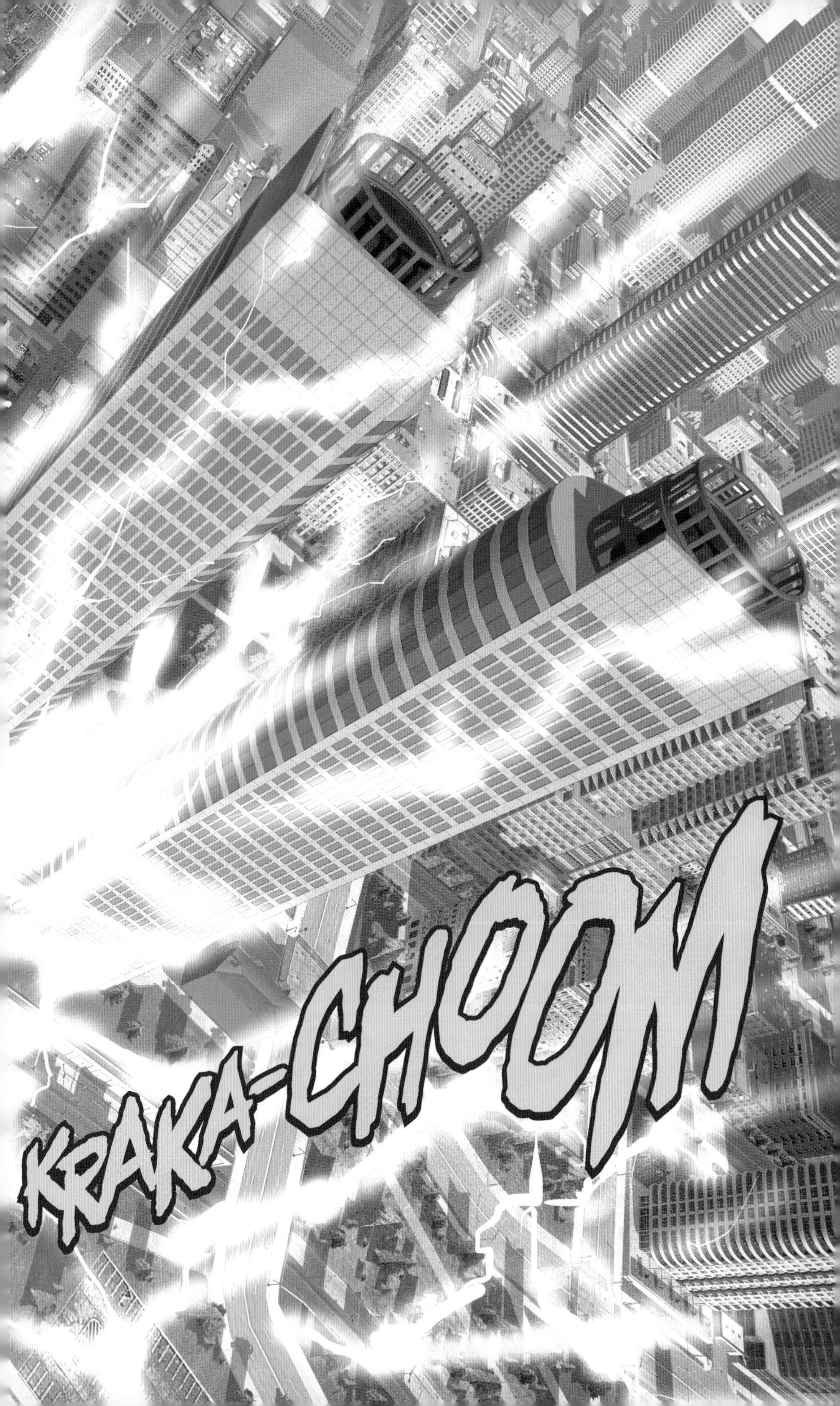
KRAKA-CHOOM

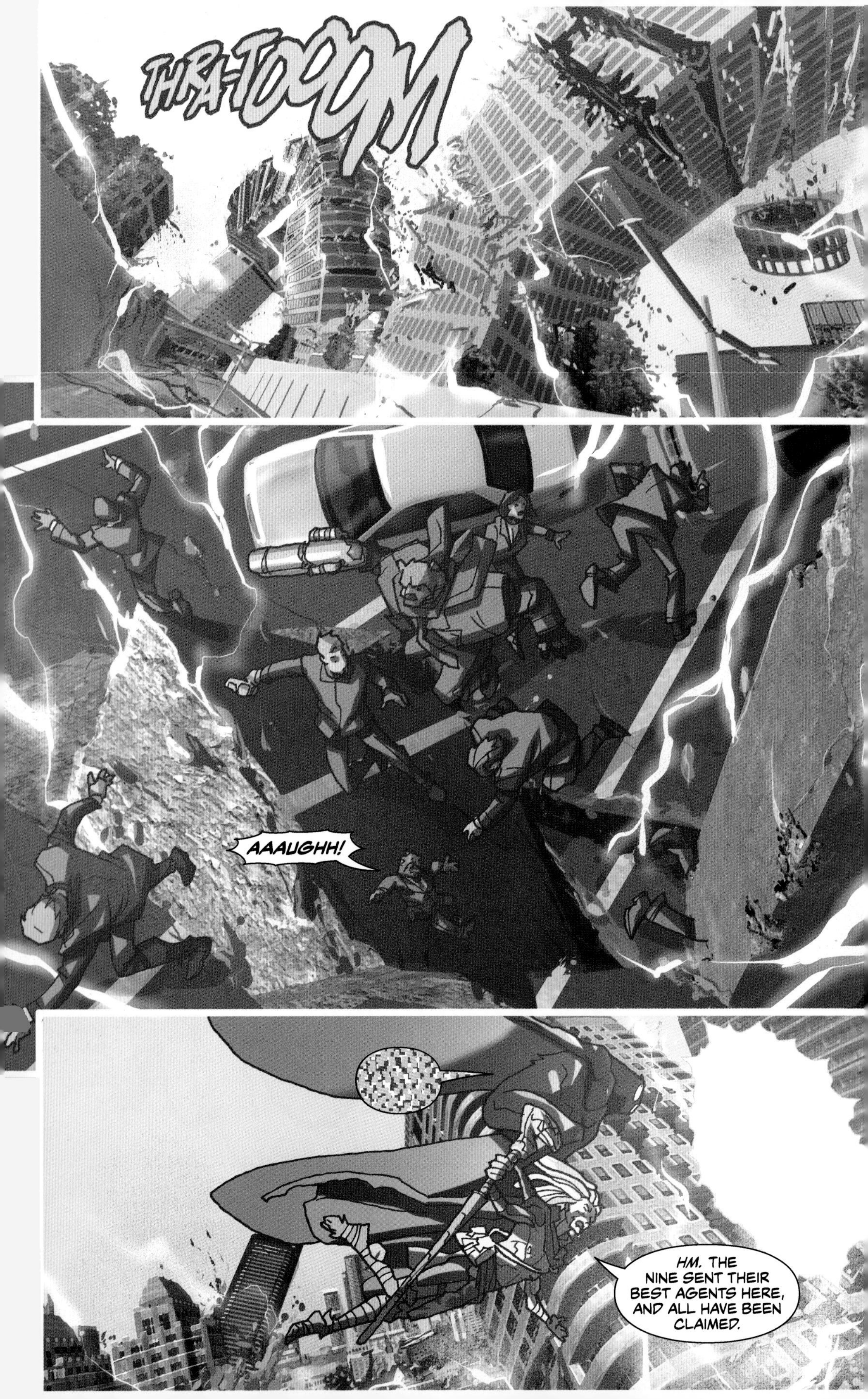
THRA-TOOOM
AAAUGHH!
HM. THE NINE SENT THEIR BEST AGENTS HERE, AND ALL HAVE BEEN CLAIMED.

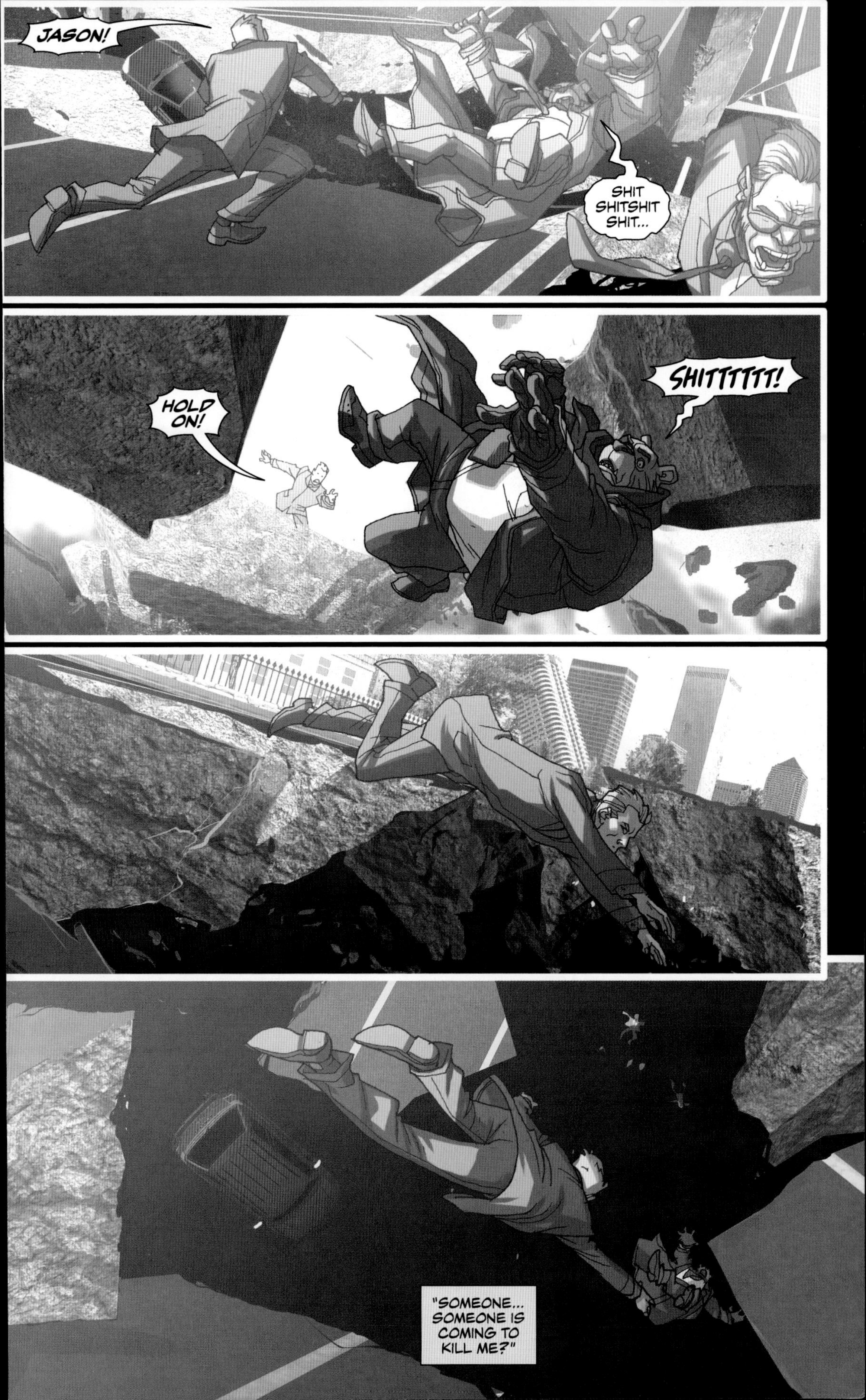
JASON!
SHIT SHITSHIT SHIT...
HOLD ON!
SHITTTTTT!
"SOMEONE... SOMEONE IS COMING TO KILL ME?"

SHIT SHIT SHIT SHIT DOUBLE SHIT

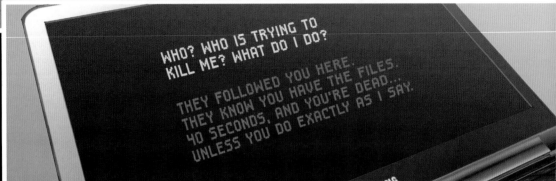

WHO? WHO IS TRYING TO KILL ME? WHAT DO I DO?

THEY FOLLOWED YOU HERE. THEY KNOW YOU HAVE THE FILES. 40 SECONDS, AND YOU'RE DEAD... UNLESS YOU DO EXACTLY AS I SAY.

THERE.

PHUT PHUT

TARGET ON THE RUN, BUT I HAVE HER PINNED DOWN.

NOTHING MAJOR. SOME LOOSE ENDS TIDIED UP.

PHUT PHUT

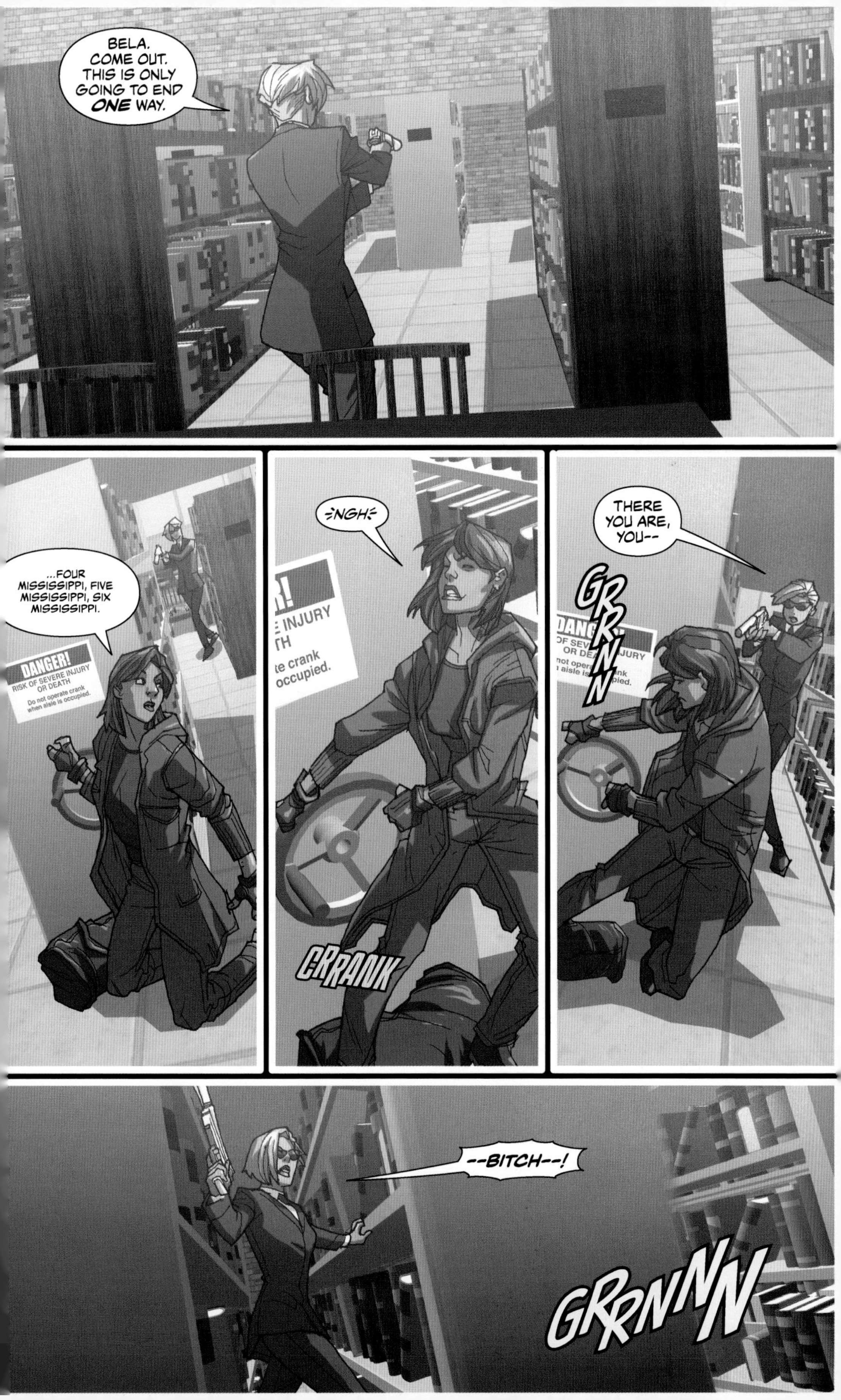

BELA. COME OUT. THIS IS ONLY GOING TO END ONE WAY.
...FOUR MISSISSIPPI, FIVE MISSISSIPPI, SIX MISSISSIPPI.
DANGER!
RISK OF SEVERE INJURY OR DEATH
Do not operate crank when aisle is occupied.
NGH
CRRANK
THERE YOU ARE, YOU--
GRRNNN
--BITCH--!
GRRNNNN

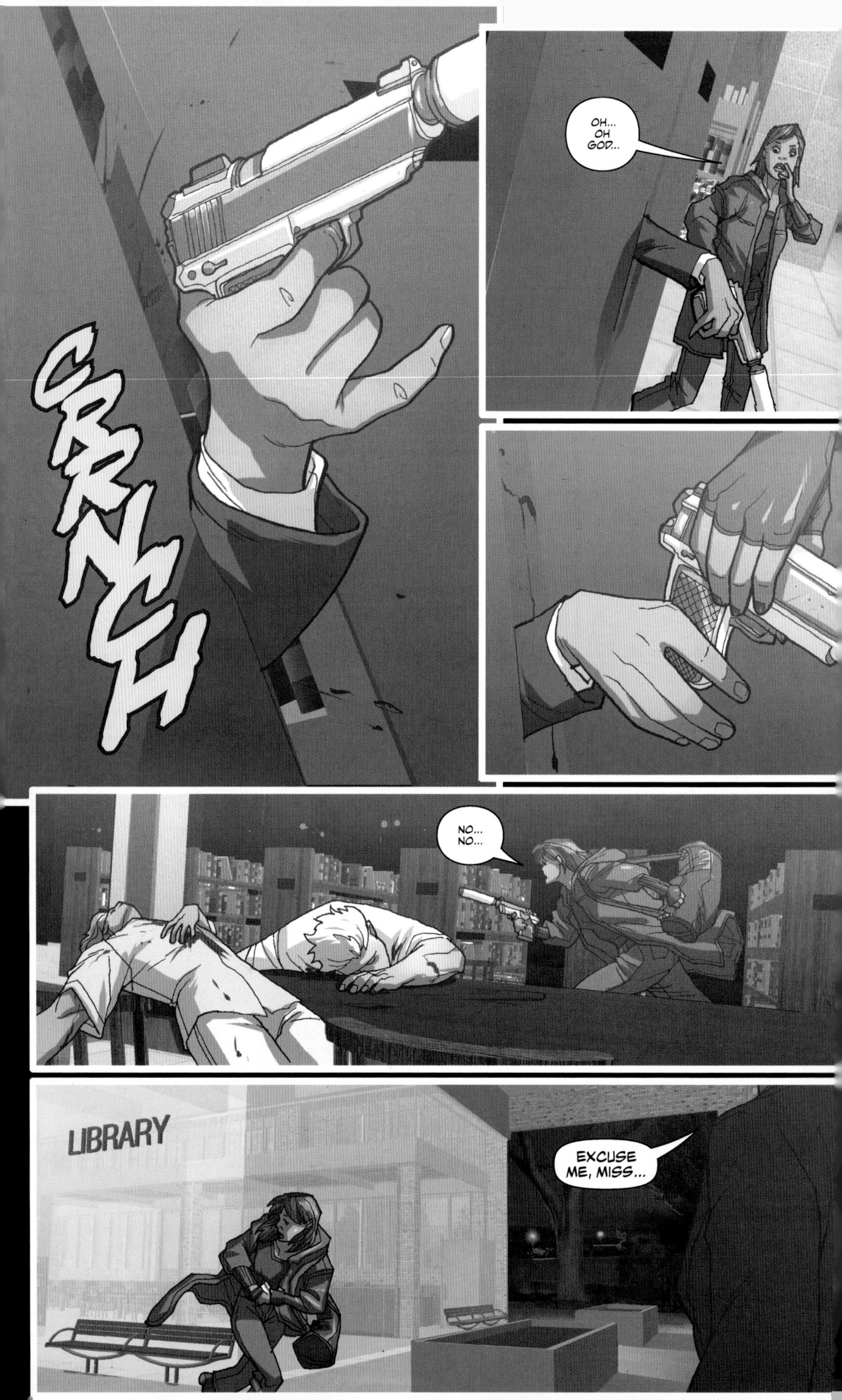
CRRNCH
OH... OH GOD...
NO... NO...
LIBRARY
EXCUSE ME, MISS...

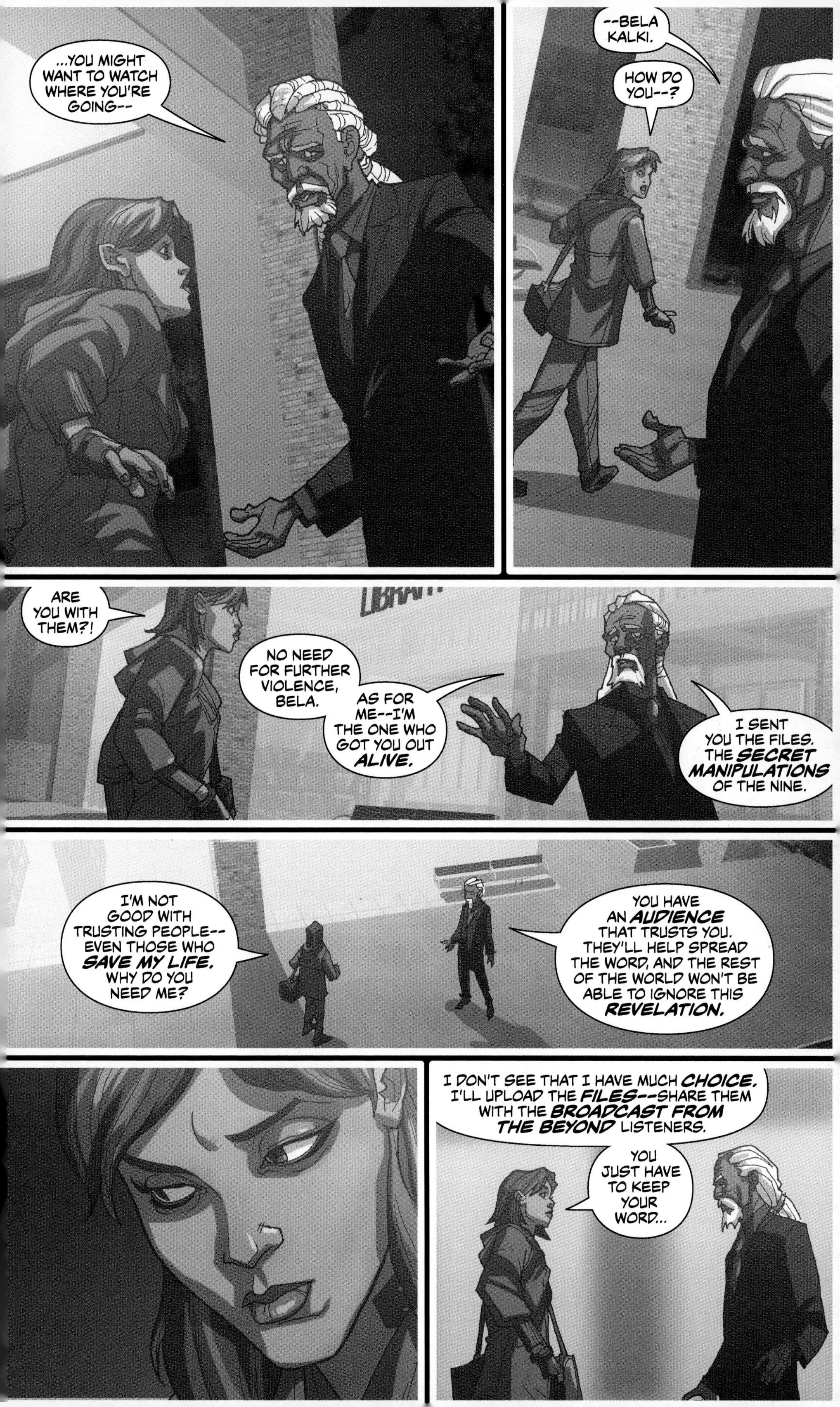
...YOU MIGHT WANT TO WATCH WHERE YOU'RE GOING--
--BELA KALKI.
HOW DO YOU--?
ARE YOU WITH THEM?!
NO NEED FOR FURTHER VIOLENCE, BELA.
AS FOR ME--I'M THE ONE WHO GOT YOU OUT ALIVE.
I SENT YOU THE FILES. THE SECRET MANIPULATIONS OF THE NINE.
I'M NOT GOOD WITH TRUSTING PEOPLE--EVEN THOSE WHO SAVE MY LIFE. WHY DO YOU NEED ME?
YOU HAVE AN AUDIENCE THAT TRUSTS YOU. THEY'LL HELP SPREAD THE WORD, AND THE REST OF THE WORLD WON'T BE ABLE TO IGNORE THIS REVELATION.
I DON'T SEE THAT I HAVE MUCH CHOICE. I'LL UPLOAD THE FILES--SHARE THEM WITH THE BROADCAST FROM THE BEYOND LISTENERS.
YOU JUST HAVE TO KEEP YOUR WORD...

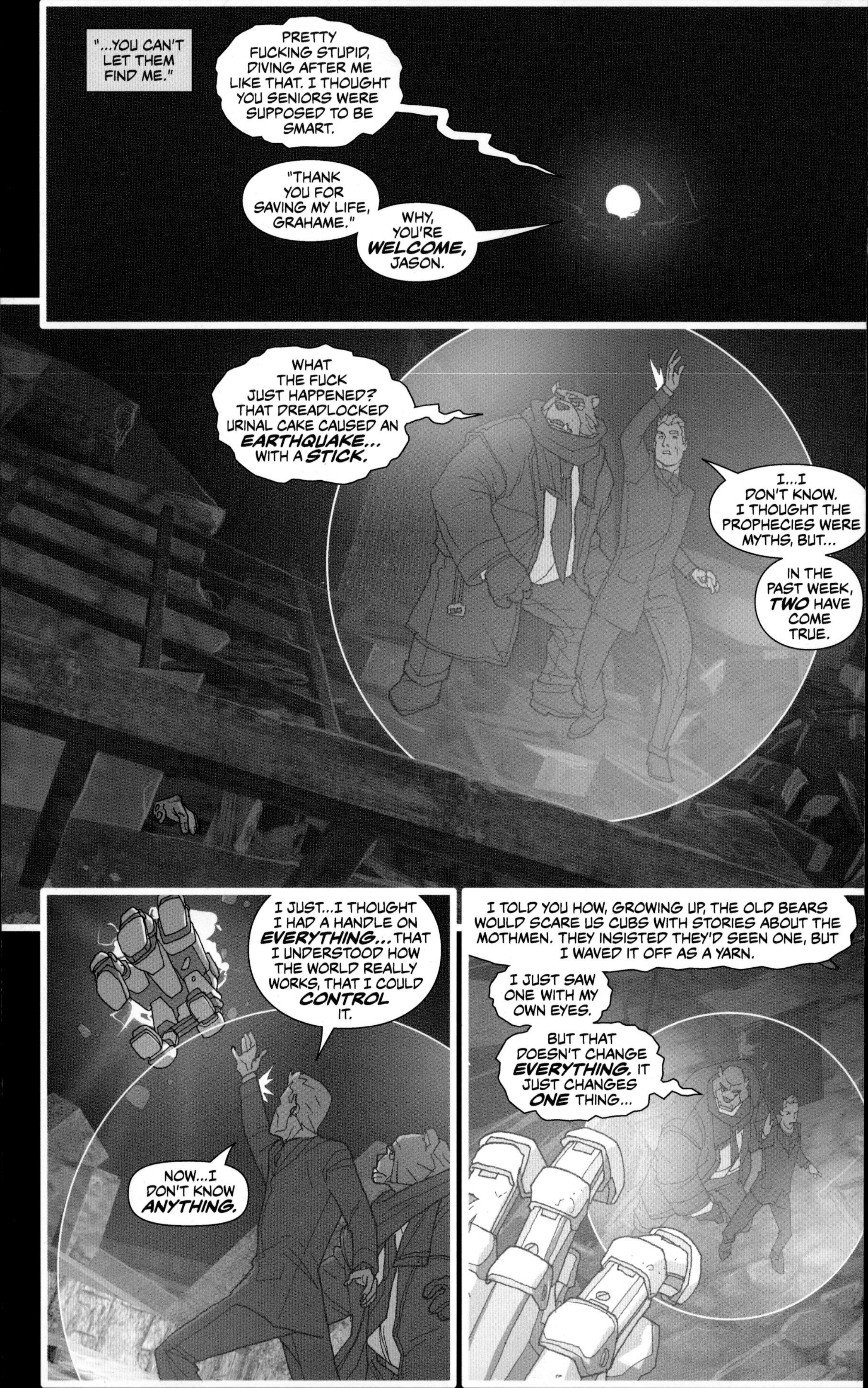
"...YOU CAN'T LET THEM FIND ME."
PRETTY FUCKING STUPID, DIVING AFTER ME LIKE THAT. I THOUGHT YOU SENIORS WERE SUPPOSED TO BE SMART.
"THANK YOU FOR SAVING MY LIFE, GRAHAME."
WHY, YOU'RE WELCOME, JASON.
WHAT THE FUCK JUST HAPPENED? THAT DREADLOCKED URINAL CAKE CAUSED AN EARTHQUAKE... WITH A STICK.
I...I DON'T KNOW. I THOUGHT THE PROPHECIES WERE MYTHS, BUT...
IN THE PAST WEEK, TWO HAVE COME TRUE.
I JUST...I THOUGHT I HAD A HANDLE ON EVERYTHING...THAT I UNDERSTOOD HOW THE WORLD REALLY WORKS, THAT I COULD CONTROL IT.
NOW...I DON'T KNOW ANYTHING.
I TOLD YOU HOW, GROWING UP, THE OLD BEARS WOULD SCARE US CUBS WITH STORIES ABOUT THE MOTHMEN. THEY INSISTED THEY'D SEEN ONE, BUT I WAVED IT OFF AS A YARN.
I JUST SAW ONE WITH MY OWN EYES.
BUT THAT DOESN'T CHANGE EVERYTHING. IT JUST CHANGES ONE THING...

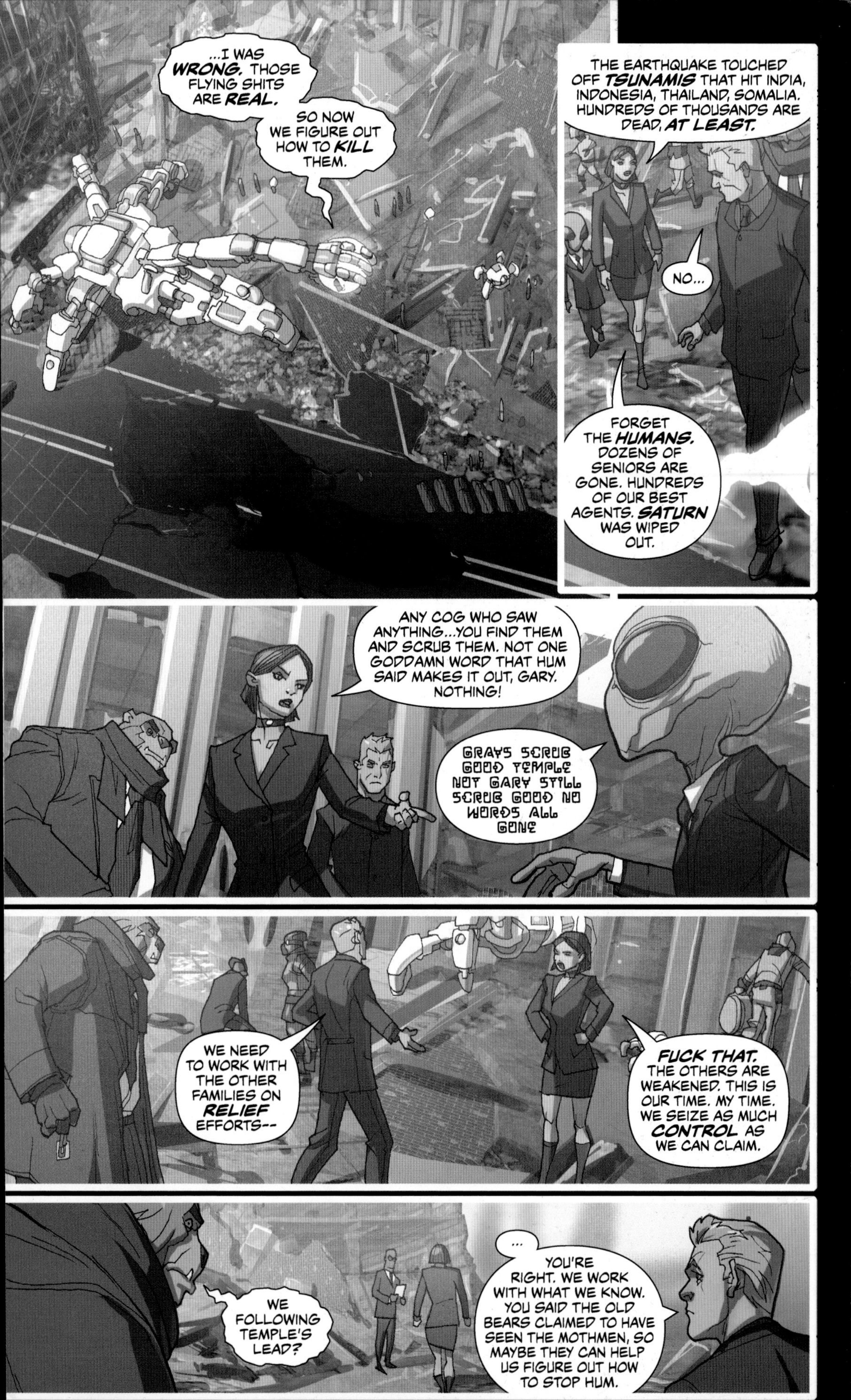
...I WAS WRONG. THOSE FLYING SHITS ARE REAL.
SO NOW WE FIGURE OUT HOW TO KILL THEM.
THE EARTHQUAKE TOUCHED OFF TSUNAMIS THAT HIT INDIA, INDONESIA, THAILAND, SOMALIA. HUNDREDS OF THOUSANDS ARE DEAD, AT LEAST.
NO...
FORGET THE HUMANS. DOZENS OF SENIORS ARE GONE. HUNDREDS OF OUR BEST AGENTS. SATURN WAS WIPED OUT.
ANY COG WHO SAW ANYTHING...YOU FIND THEM AND SCRUB THEM. NOT ONE GODDAMN WORD THAT HUM SAID MAKES IT OUT, GARY. NOTHING!
GRAYS SCRUB GOOD TEMPLE NOT GARY STILL SCRUB GOOD NO WORDS ALL GONE
WE NEED TO WORK WITH THE OTHER FAMILIES ON RELIEF EFFORTS--
FUCK THAT. THE OTHERS ARE WEAKENED. THIS IS OUR TIME. MY TIME. WE SEIZE AS MUCH CONTROL AS WE CAN CLAIM.
WE FOLLOWING TEMPLE'S LEAD?
...
YOU'RE RIGHT. WE WORK WITH WHAT WE KNOW. YOU SAID THE OLD BEARS CLAIMED TO HAVE SEEN THE MOTHMEN, SO MAYBE THEY CAN HELP US FIGURE OUT HOW TO STOP HUM.

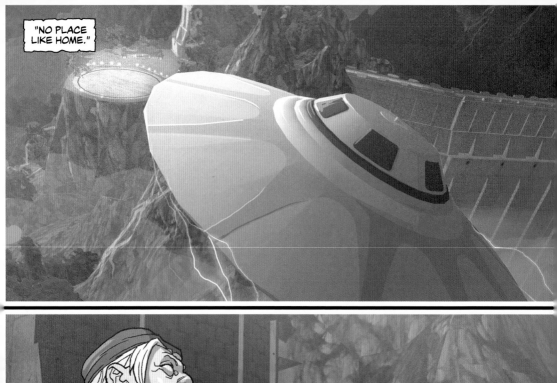

"NO PLACE LIKE HOME."

I SHOULD HAVE SHOT YOU MARS BASTARDS OUT OF THE SKY. AFTER WHAT NICK DID TO HIROSHIMA... NAGASAKI...

IT WAS *SEVENTY* YEARS AGO, OKAY?! WE'RE AT *WAR,* VINH. HOWEVER MUCH WE HATE EACH OTHER, WE *HAVE TO* SET THAT ASIDE.

BESIDES, THE PRESERVE IS NEUTRAL GROUND.

WE'VE HEARD OF SATURN'S FALL. THIS IS WHAT COMES OF MARS'S DOMINANCE, OF NICK'S RULE.

RUIN, ALL IN RUIN.

IT ISN'T FINISHED YET.

NO. YOU ARE HERE, WHAT--CHASING *GHOSTS?*

JUST OPEN THE DOORS, WILL YA?

WATCH YOUR STEP, GRAHAME. THE *RESIDENTS* AREN'T ALL AS WELL BEHAVED AS YOUR *PET.*

GRRRRRR

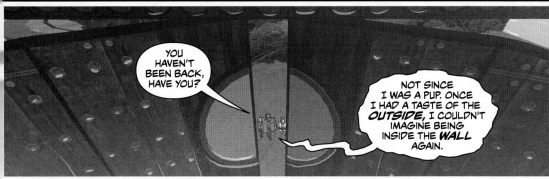

YOU HAVEN'T BEEN BACK, HAVE YOU?

NOT SINCE I WAS A PUP. ONCE I HAD A TASTE OF THE *OUTSIDE*, I COULDN'T IMAGINE BEING INSIDE THE *WALL* AGAIN.

BACK THEN, EVERYTHING SEEMED SO HUGE. COMING BACK...

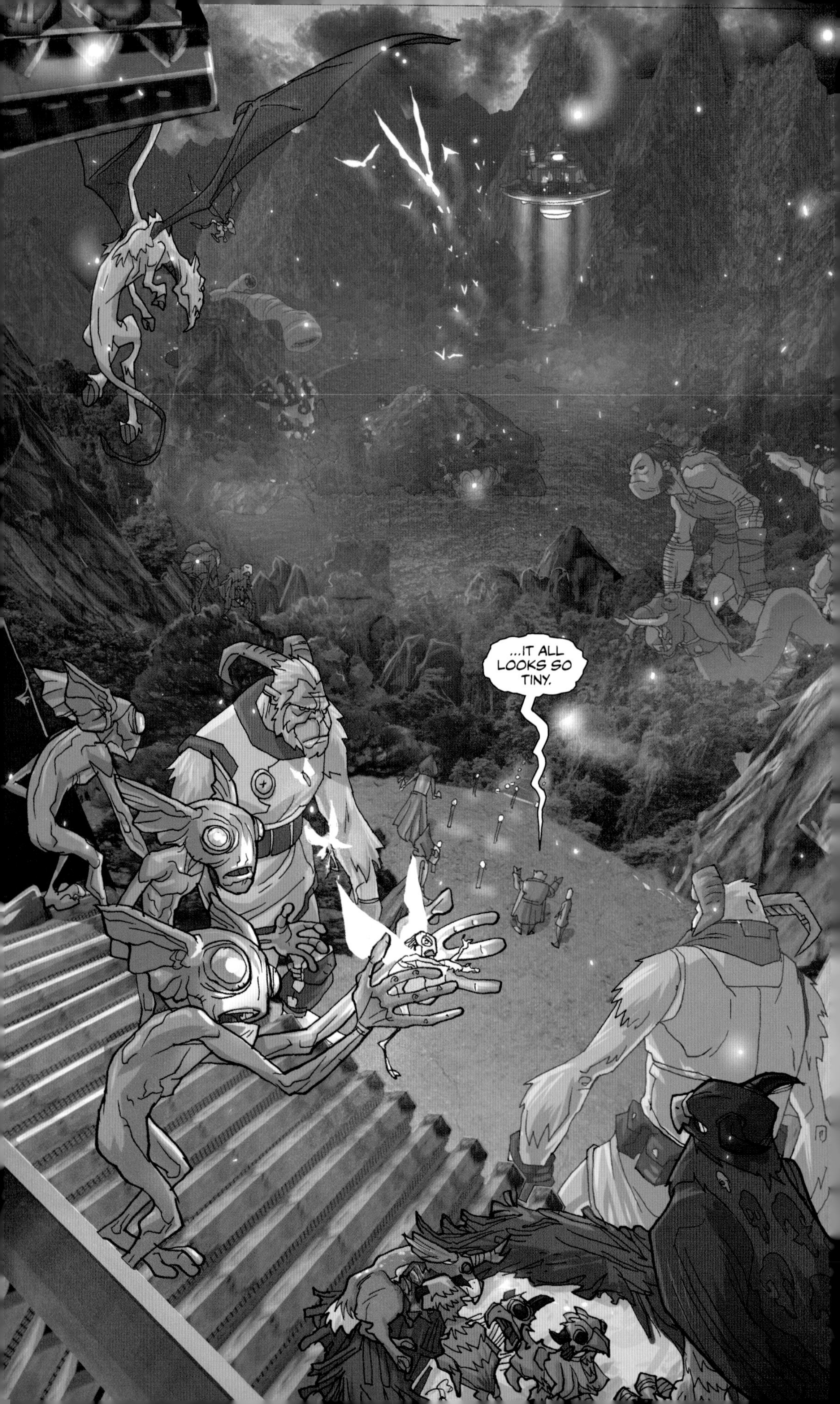
...IT ALL LOOKS SO TINY.

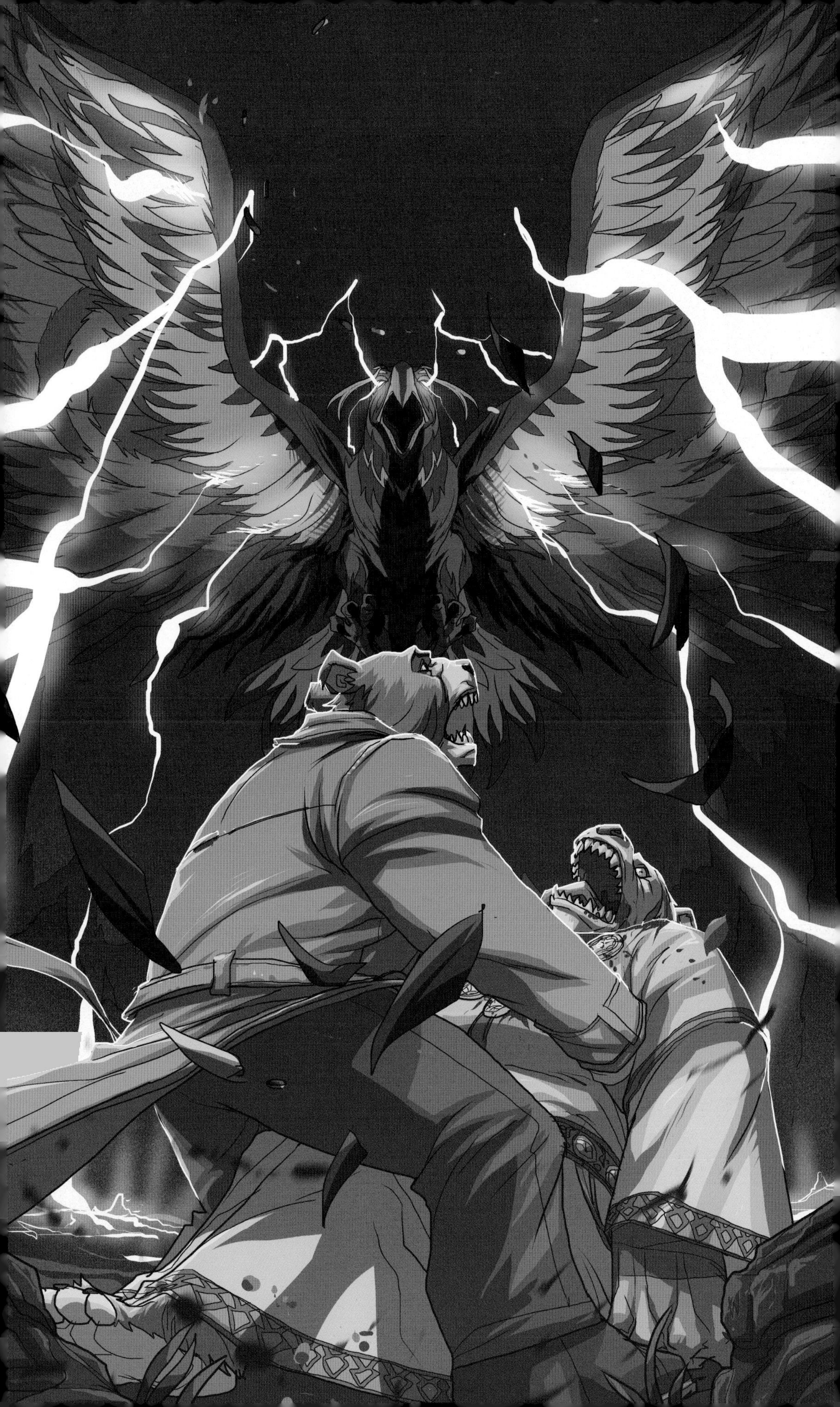

#4 PROGENY

NINE FAMILIES RULE THE WORLD. EACH OPERATES OUT OF A SECRET BASE IN THEIR TERRITORY.

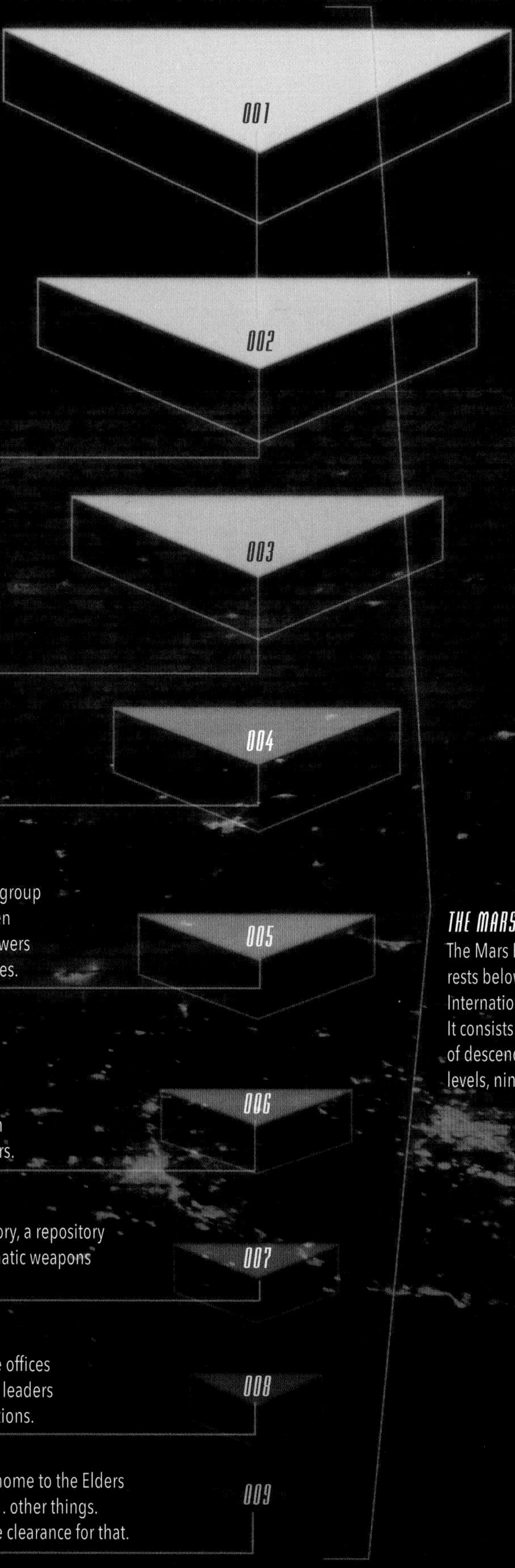

001
002
003
004
005
006
007
008
009

The first and second levels house basic Family operations, mostly staffed by non-Family members and nonleadership Family members, known as "Cogs."

The third level is home to "the Eyes," technicians who spend every hour of every day scouring endless streams of video surveillance collected around the world, looking for threats.

The fourth level is a barracks for Family operatives.

The fifth level holds "the Grays," a group of cryptids, often called "little green men," who use their telepathic powers to hide the existence of the Families.

The sixth level is home to classrooms for Family children as they train to become Seniors.

The seventh level holds the armory, a repository of the deadliest and most enigmatic weapons the world has ever seen.

The eighth level holds the offices of the Seniors, the Family leaders who plan all major operations.

The ninth level is home to the Elders and Priests. And . . . other things. But you don't have clearance for that.

THE MARS FAMILY BASE

The Mars Family base rests below Denver International Airport. It consists of a series of descending levels, nine in total.

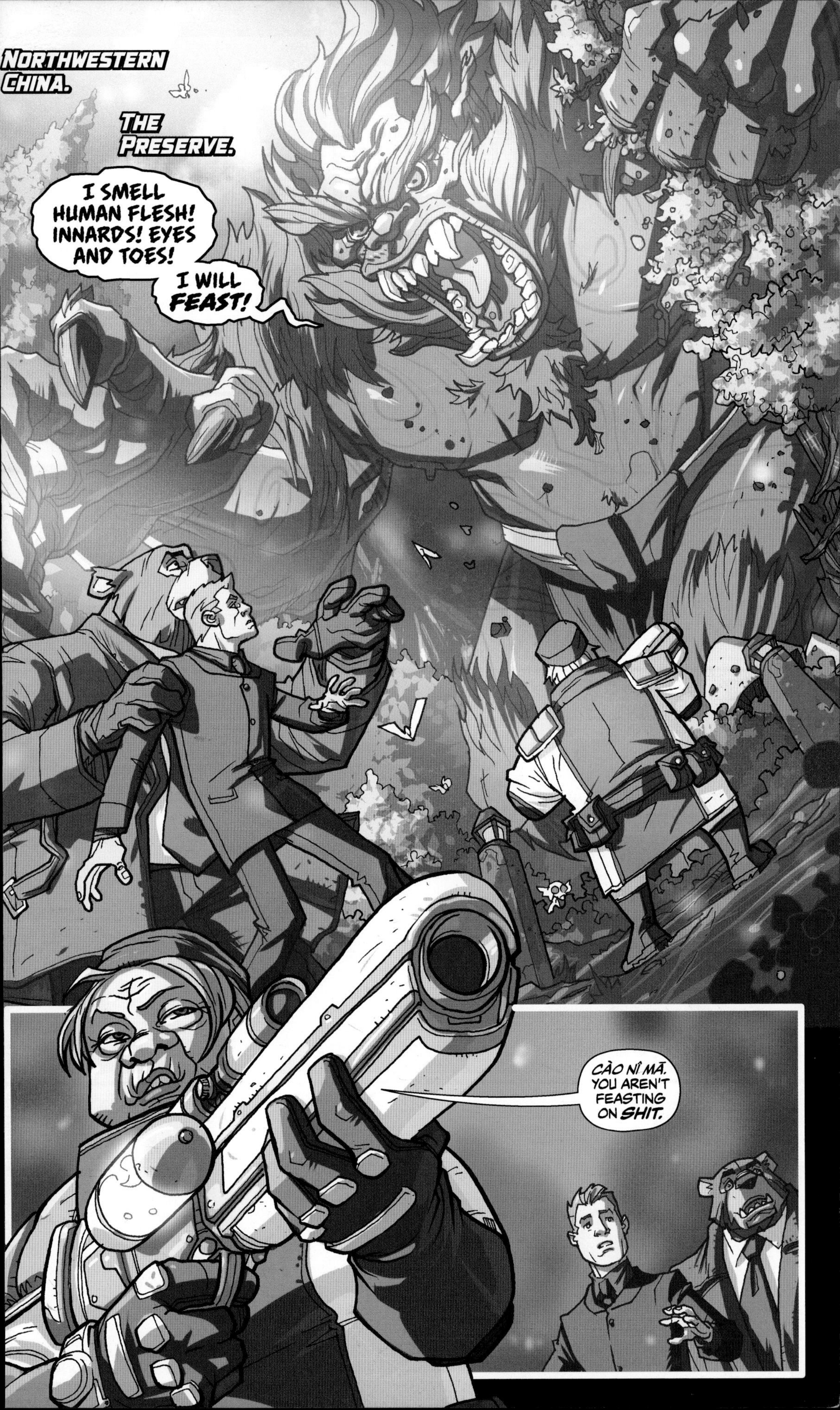

NORTHWESTERN CHINA.
THE PRESERVE.
I SMELL HUMAN FLESH! INNARDS! EYES AND TOES!
I WILL FEAST!
CÀO NÍ MĀ. YOU AREN'T FEASTING ON SHIT.

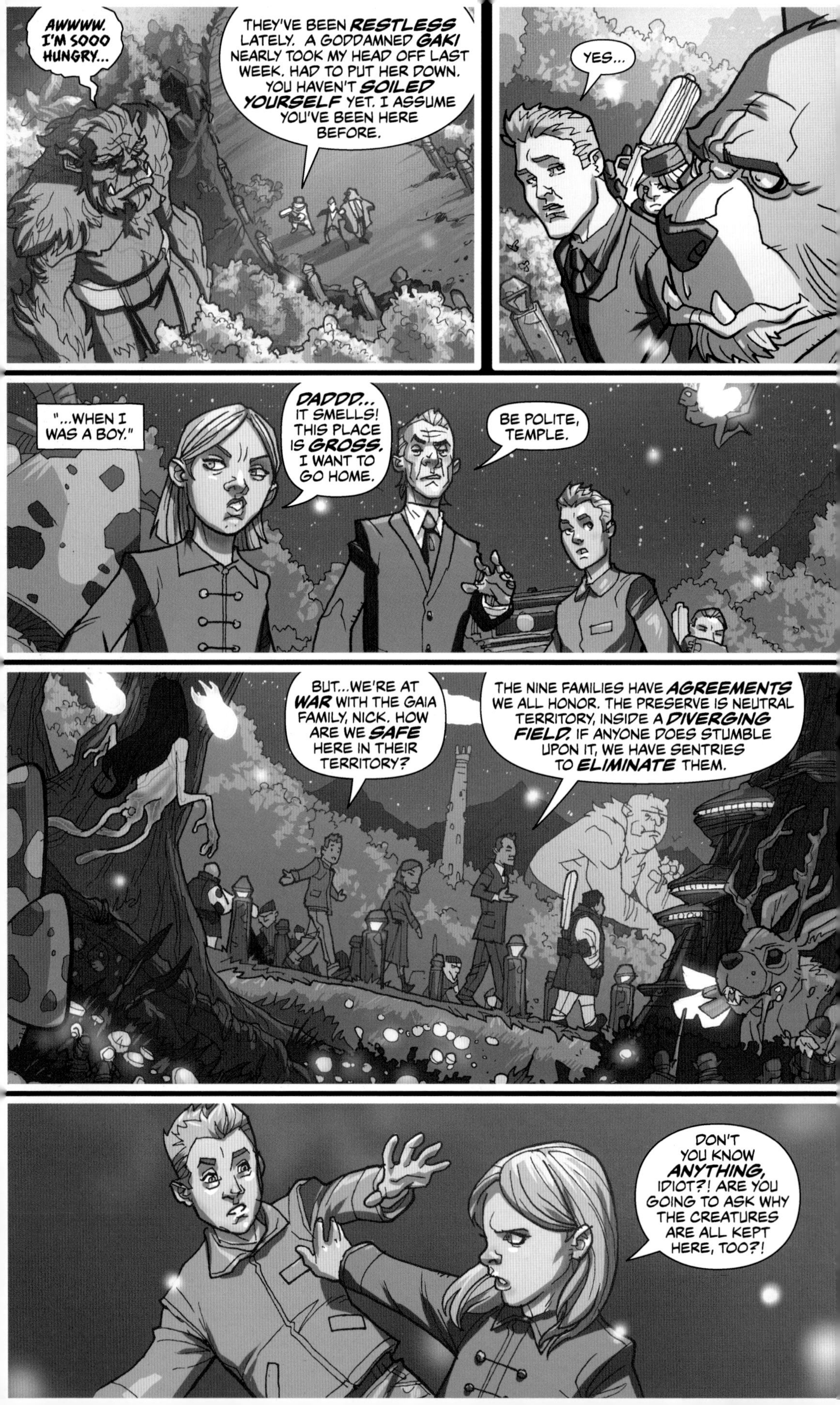
AWWWW. I'M SOOO HUNGRY...
THEY'VE BEEN RESTLESS LATELY. A GODDAMNED GAKI NEARLY TOOK MY HEAD OFF LAST WEEK. HAD TO PUT HER DOWN. YOU HAVEN'T SOILED YOURSELF YET. I ASSUME YOU'VE BEEN HERE BEFORE.
YES...
"...WHEN I WAS A BOY."
DADDD... IT SMELLS! THIS PLACE IS GROSS. I WANT TO GO HOME.
BE POLITE, TEMPLE.
BUT...WE'RE AT WAR WITH THE GAIA FAMILY, NICK. HOW ARE WE SAFE HERE IN THEIR TERRITORY?
THE NINE FAMILIES HAVE AGREEMENTS WE ALL HONOR. THE PRESERVE IS NEUTRAL TERRITORY, INSIDE A DIVERGING FIELD. IF ANYONE DOES STUMBLE UPON IT, WE HAVE SENTRIES TO ELIMINATE THEM.
DON'T YOU KNOW ANYTHING, IDIOT?! ARE YOU GOING TO ASK WHY THE CREATURES ARE ALL KEPT HERE, TOO?!

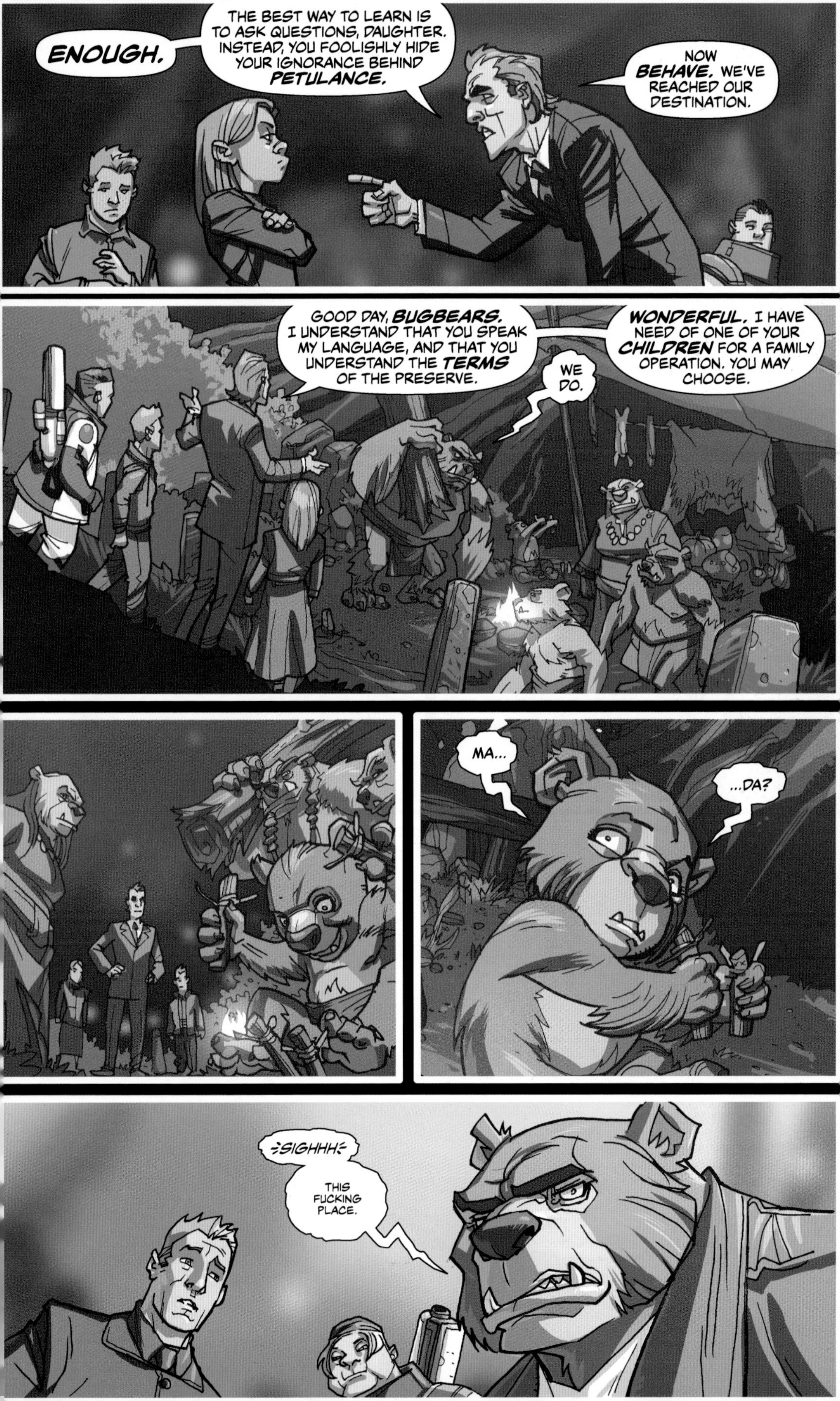
ENOUGH.
THE BEST WAY TO LEARN IS TO ASK QUESTIONS, DAUGHTER. INSTEAD, YOU FOOLISHLY HIDE YOUR IGNORANCE BEHIND PETULANCE.
NOW BEHAVE. WE'VE REACHED OUR DESTINATION.
GOOD DAY, BUGBEARS. I UNDERSTAND THAT YOU SPEAK MY LANGUAGE, AND THAT YOU UNDERSTAND THE TERMS OF THE PRESERVE.
WE DO.
WONDERFUL. I HAVE NEED OF ONE OF YOUR CHILDREN FOR A FAMILY OPERATION. YOU MAY CHOOSE.
MA...
...DA?
SIGHHH
THIS FUCKING PLACE.

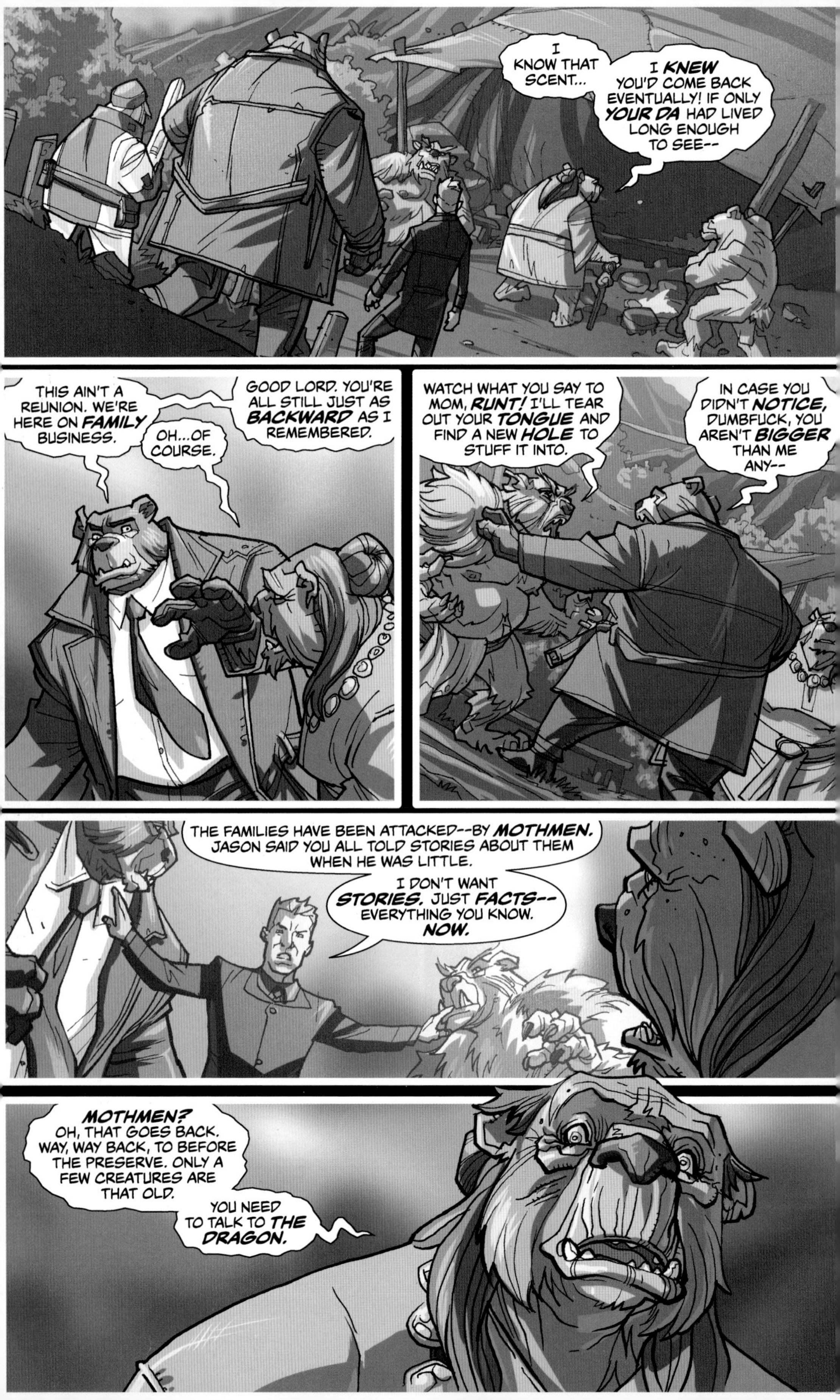
I KNOW THAT SCENT...
I KNEW YOU'D COME BACK EVENTUALLY! IF ONLY YOUR DA HAD LIVED LONG ENOUGH TO SEE--
THIS AIN'T A REUNION. WE'RE HERE ON FAMILY BUSINESS.
OH...OF COURSE.
GOOD LORD. YOU'RE ALL STILL JUST AS BACKWARD AS I REMEMBERED.
WATCH WHAT YOU SAY TO MOM, RUNT! I'LL TEAR OUT YOUR TONGUE AND FIND A NEW HOLE TO STUFF IT INTO.
IN CASE YOU DIDN'T NOTICE, DUMBFUCK, YOU AREN'T BIGGER THAN ME ANY--
THE FAMILIES HAVE BEEN ATTACKED--BY MOTHMEN. JASON SAID YOU ALL TOLD STORIES ABOUT THEM WHEN HE WAS LITTLE.
I DON'T WANT STORIES. JUST FACTS-- EVERYTHING YOU KNOW. NOW.
MOTHMEN? OH, THAT GOES BACK. WAY, WAY BACK, TO BEFORE THE PRESERVE. ONLY A FEW CREATURES ARE THAT OLD.
YOU NEED TO TALK TO THE DRAGON.

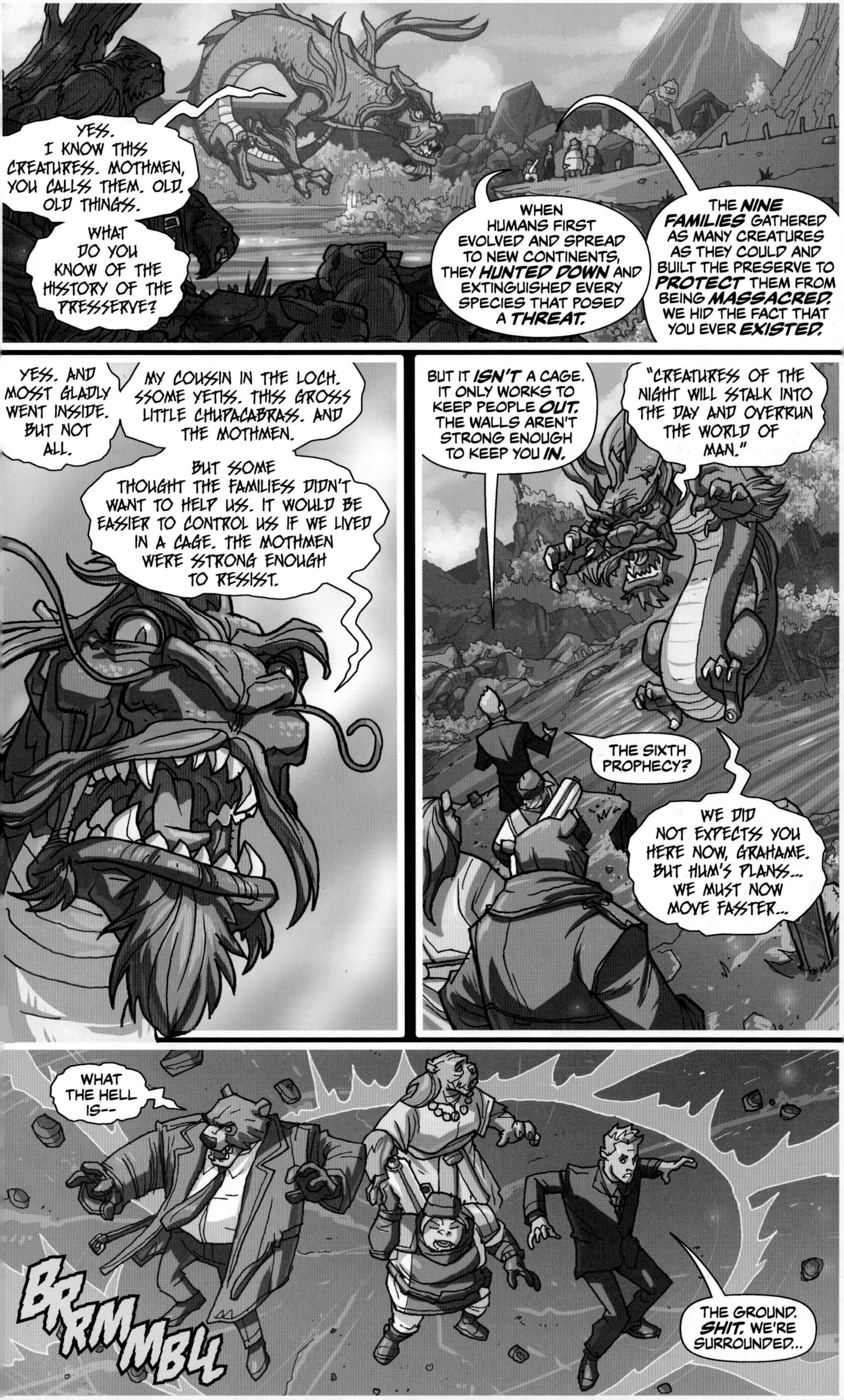

YESS. I KNOW THISS CREATURESS. MOTHMEN, YOU CALLSS THEM. OLD. OLD THINGSS.
WHAT DO YOU KNOW OF THE HISSTORY OF THE PRESSSERVE?
WHEN HUMANS FIRST EVOLVED AND SPREAD TO NEW CONTINENTS, THEY HUNTED DOWN AND EXTINGUISHED EVERY SPECIES THAT POSED A THREAT.
THE NINE FAMILIES GATHERED AS MANY CREATURES AS THEY COULD AND BUILT THE PRESERVE TO PROTECT THEM FROM BEING MASSACRED. WE HID THE FACT THAT YOU EVER EXISTED.
YESS. AND MOSST GLADLY WENT INSSIDE. BUT NOT ALL.
MY COUSSIN IN THE LOCH. SSOME YETISS. THISS GROSSS LITTLE CHUPACABRASS. AND THE MOTHMEN.
BUT SSOME THOUGHT THE FAMILIESS DIDN'T WANT TO HELP USS. IT WOULD BE EASSIER TO CONTROL USS IF WE LIVED IN A CAGE. THE MOTHMEN WERE SSTRONG ENOUGH TO RESSISST.
BUT IT ISN'T A CAGE. IT ONLY WORKS TO KEEP PEOPLE OUT. THE WALLS AREN'T STRONG ENOUGH TO KEEP YOU IN.
"CREATURESS OF THE NIGHT WILL SSTALK INTO THE DAY AND OVERRUN THE WORLD OF MAN."
THE SIXTH PROPHECY?
WE DID NOT EXPECTSS YOU HERE NOW, GRAHAME. BUT HUM'S PLANSS... WE MUST NOW MOVE FASSTER...
WHAT THE HELL IS--
BRRMMBLL
THE GROUND. SHIT, WE'RE SURROUNDED...

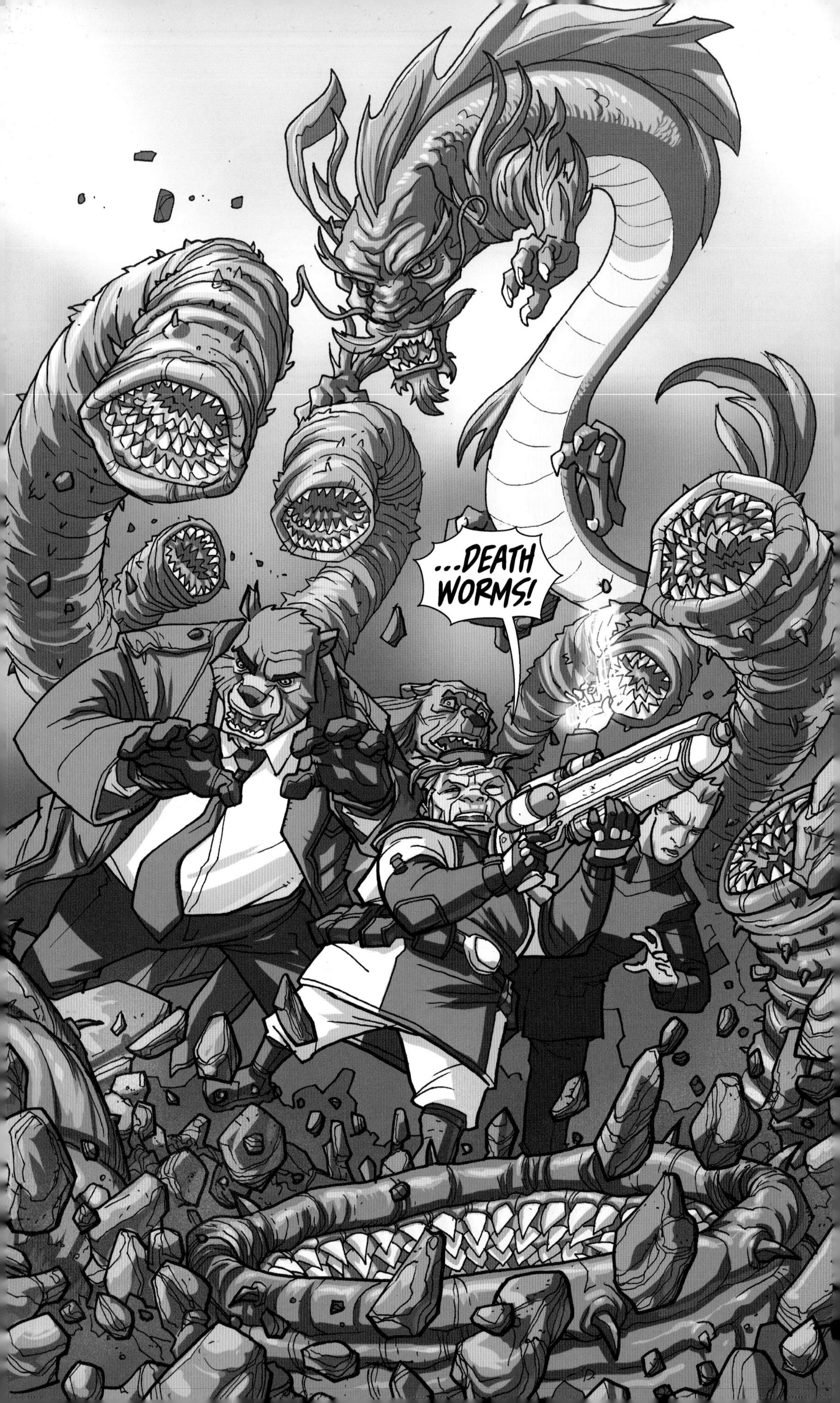
...DEATH WORMS!

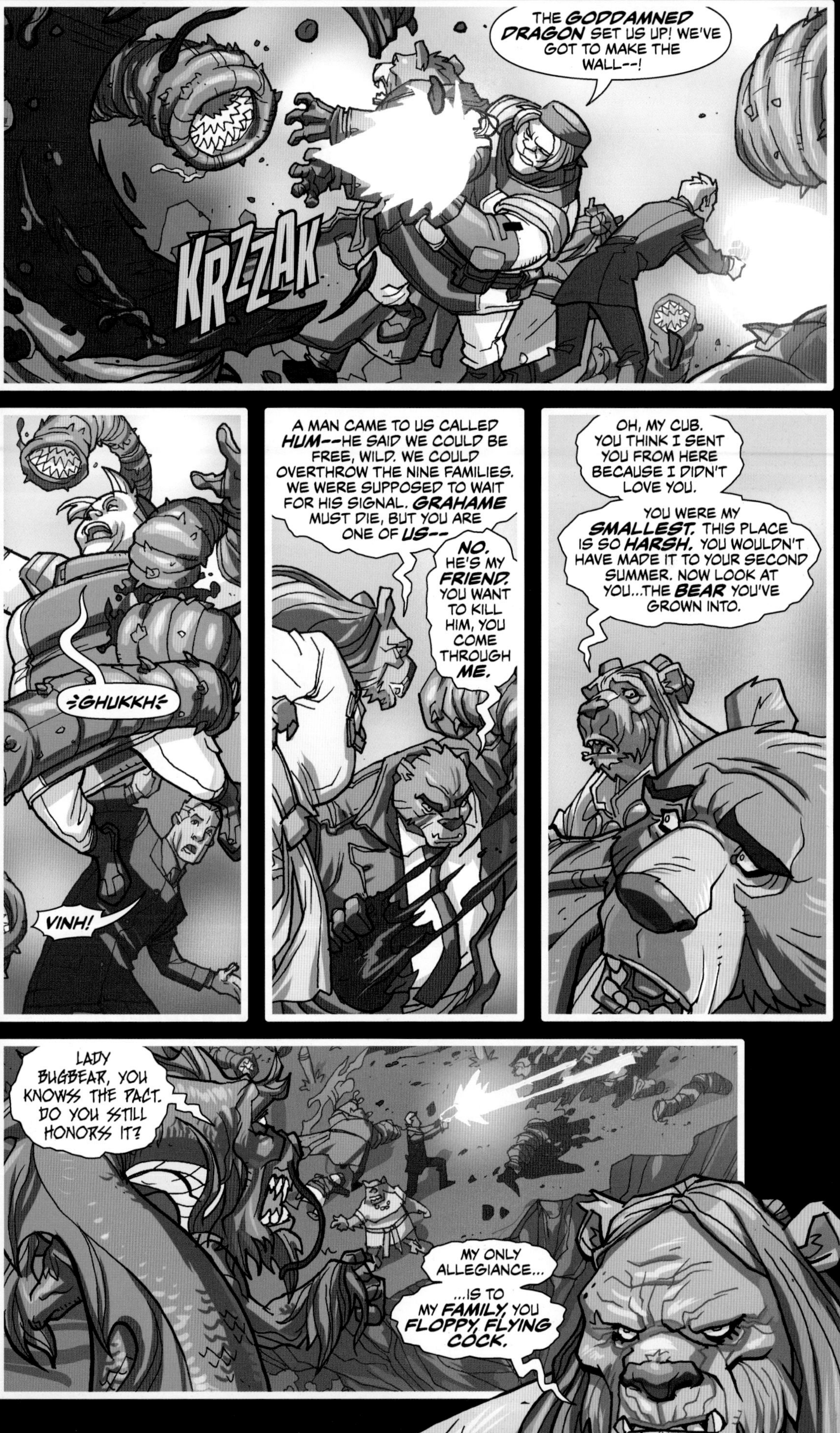
THE GODDAMNED DRAGON SET US UP! WE'VE GOT TO MAKE THE WALL--!
KRZZAK
:GHUKKH:
VINH!
A MAN CAME TO US CALLED HUM--HE SAID WE COULD BE FREE, WILD. WE COULD OVERTHROW THE NINE FAMILIES. WE WERE SUPPOSED TO WAIT FOR HIS SIGNAL. GRAHAME MUST DIE, BUT YOU ARE ONE OF US--
NO. HE'S MY FRIEND. YOU WANT TO KILL HIM, YOU COME THROUGH ME.
OH, MY CUB. YOU THINK I SENT YOU FROM HERE BECAUSE I DIDN'T LOVE YOU.
YOU WERE MY SMALLEST. THIS PLACE IS SO HARSH. YOU WOULDN'T HAVE MADE IT TO YOUR SECOND SUMMER. NOW LOOK AT YOU...THE BEAR YOU'VE GROWN INTO.
LADY BUGBEAR, YOU KNOWSS THE PACT. DO YOU SSTILL HONORSS IT?
MY ONLY ALLEGIANCE...
...IS TO MY FAMILY, YOU FLOPPY, FLYING COCK.

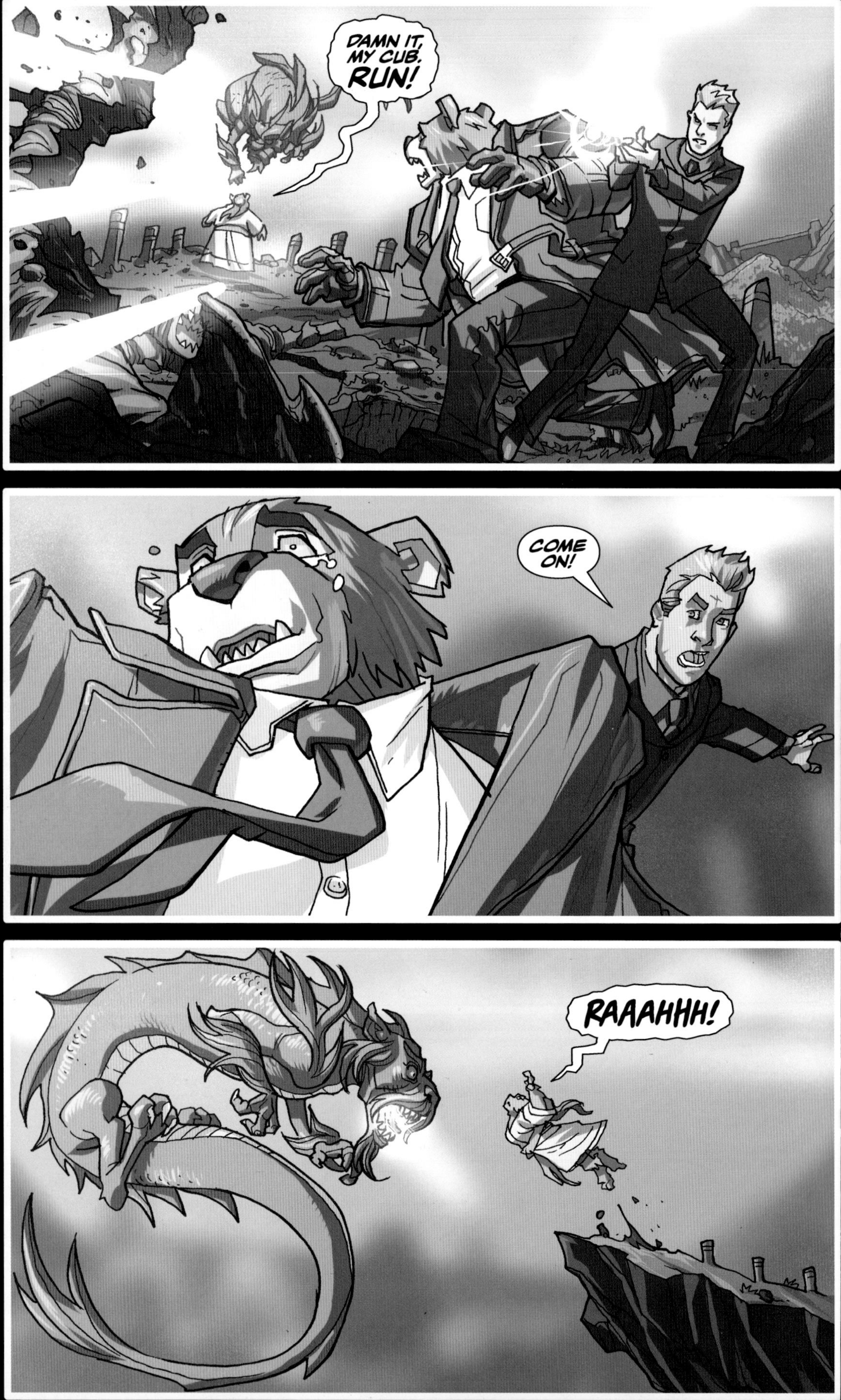
DAMN IT, MY CUB. RUN!
COME ON!
RAAAHHH!

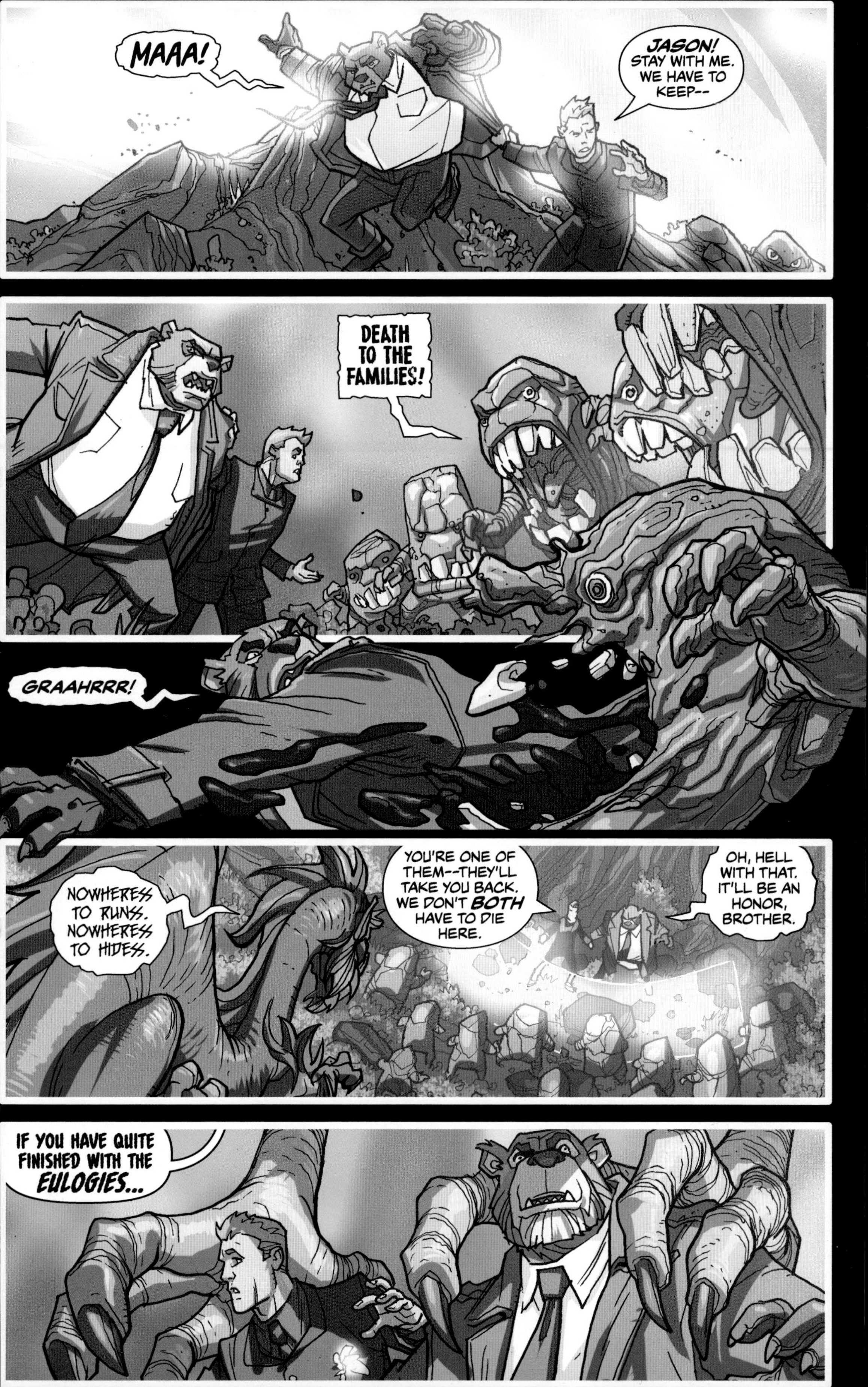
MAAA!
JASON! STAY WITH ME. WE HAVE TO KEEP--
DEATH TO THE FAMILIES!
GRAAHRRR!
NOWHERESS TO RUNSS. NOWHERESS TO HIDESS.
YOU'RE ONE OF THEM--THEY'LL TAKE YOU BACK. WE DON'T BOTH HAVE TO DIE HERE.
OH, HELL WITH THAT. IT'LL BE AN HONOR, BROTHER.
IF YOU HAVE QUITE FINISHED WITH THE EULOGIES...

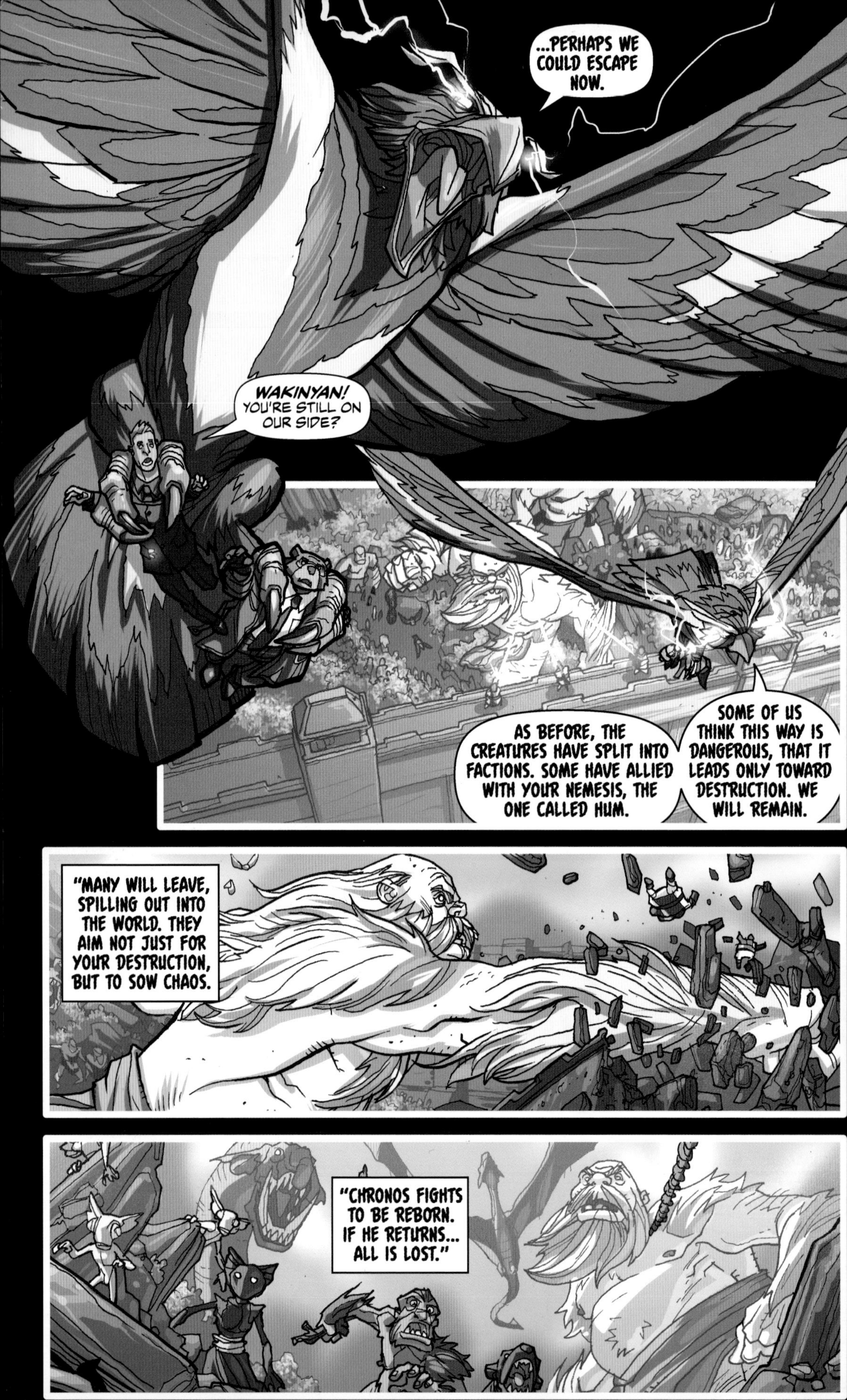
...PERHAPS WE COULD ESCAPE NOW.
WAKINYAN! YOU'RE STILL ON OUR SIDE?
AS BEFORE, THE CREATURES HAVE SPLIT INTO FACTIONS. SOME HAVE ALLIED WITH YOUR NEMESIS, THE ONE CALLED HUM.
SOME OF US THINK THIS WAY IS DANGEROUS, THAT IT LEADS ONLY TOWARD DESTRUCTION. WE WILL REMAIN.
"MANY WILL LEAVE, SPILLING OUT INTO THE WORLD. THEY AIM NOT JUST FOR YOUR DESTRUCTION, BUT TO SOW CHAOS.
"CHRONOS FIGHTS TO BE REBORN. IF HE RETURNS... ALL IS LOST."

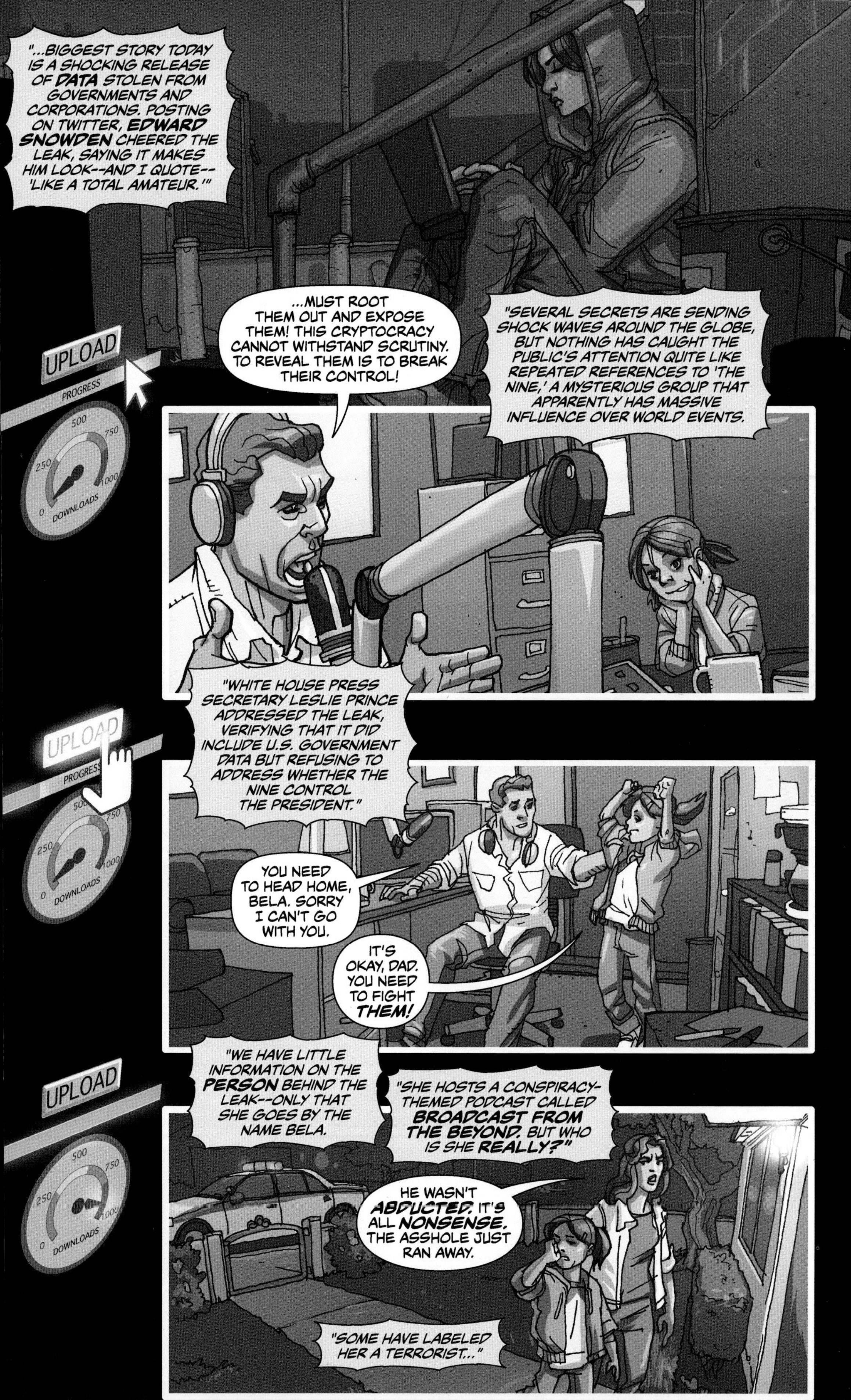
"...BIGGEST STORY TODAY IS A SHOCKING RELEASE OF DATA STOLEN FROM GOVERNMENTS AND CORPORATIONS. POSTING ON TWITTER, EDWARD SNOWDEN CHEERED THE LEAK, SAYING IT MAKES HIM LOOK--AND I QUOTE--'LIKE A TOTAL AMATEUR.'"
UPLOAD
PROGRESS
0
250
500
750
1000
DOWNLOADS
...MUST ROOT THEM OUT AND EXPOSE THEM! THIS CRYPTOCRACY CANNOT WITHSTAND SCRUTINY. TO REVEAL THEM IS TO BREAK THEIR CONTROL!
"SEVERAL SECRETS ARE SENDING SHOCK WAVES AROUND THE GLOBE, BUT NOTHING HAS CAUGHT THE PUBLIC'S ATTENTION QUITE LIKE REPEATED REFERENCES TO 'THE NINE,' A MYSTERIOUS GROUP THAT APPARENTLY HAS MASSIVE INFLUENCE OVER WORLD EVENTS.
"WHITE HOUSE PRESS SECRETARY LESLIE PRINCE ADDRESSED THE LEAK, VERIFYING THAT IT DID INCLUDE U.S. GOVERNMENT DATA BUT REFUSING TO ADDRESS WHETHER THE NINE CONTROL THE PRESIDENT."
YOU NEED TO HEAD HOME, BELA. SORRY I CAN'T GO WITH YOU.
IT'S OKAY, DAD. YOU NEED TO FIGHT THEM!
"WE HAVE LITTLE INFORMATION ON THE PERSON BEHIND THE LEAK--ONLY THAT SHE GOES BY THE NAME BELA.
"SHE HOSTS A CONSPIRACY-THEMED PODCAST CALLED BROADCAST FROM THE BEYOND. BUT WHO IS SHE REALLY?"
HE WASN'T ABDUCTED. IT'S ALL NONSENSE. THE ASSHOLE JUST RAN AWAY.
"SOME HAVE LABELED HER A TERRORIST..."

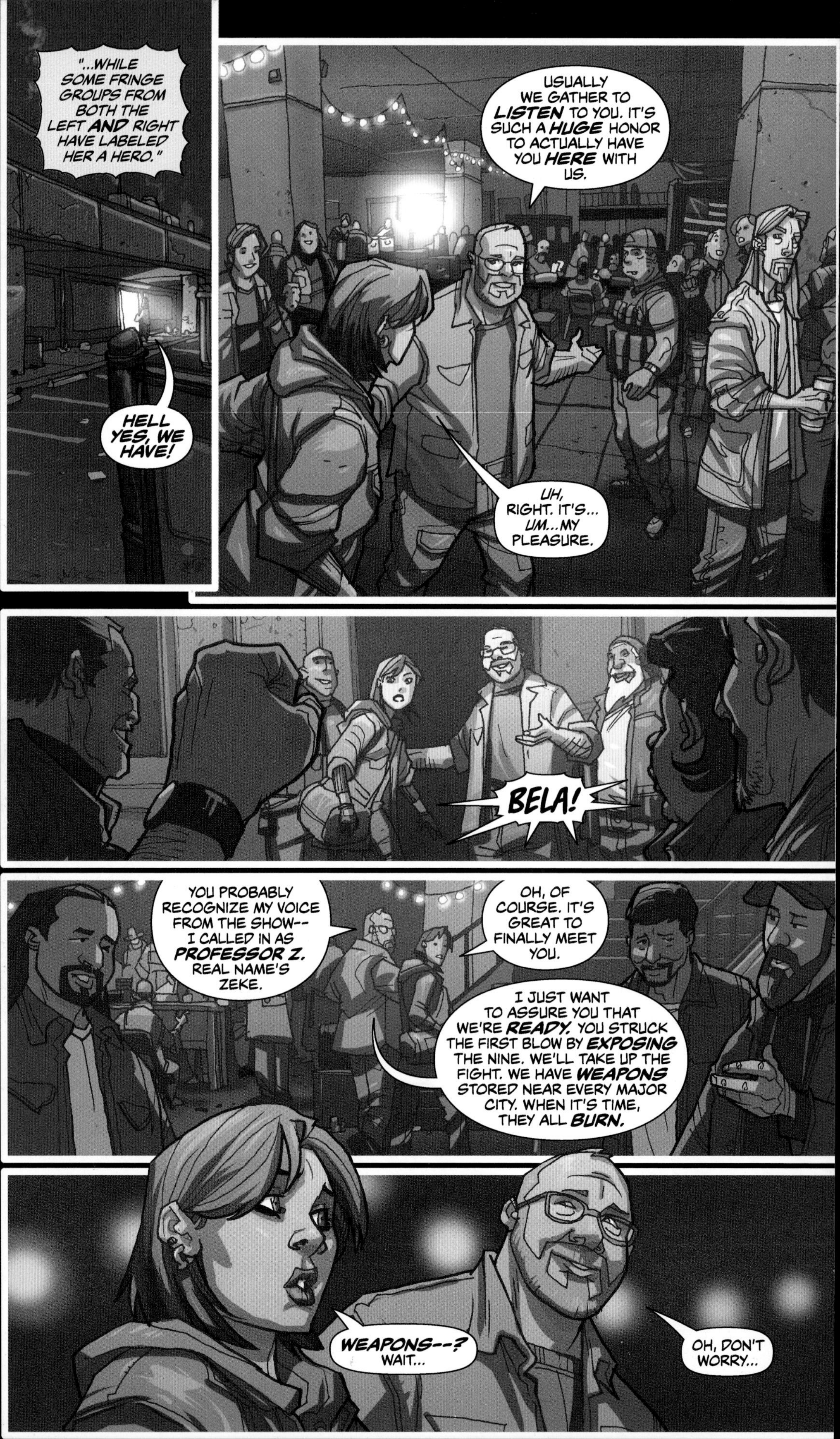

"...WHILE SOME FRINGE GROUPS FROM BOTH THE LEFT AND RIGHT HAVE LABELED HER A HERO."
HELL YES, WE HAVE!
USUALLY WE GATHER TO LISTEN TO YOU. IT'S SUCH A HUGE HONOR TO ACTUALLY HAVE YOU HERE WITH US.
UH, RIGHT. IT'S... UM...MY PLEASURE.
BELA!
YOU PROBABLY RECOGNIZE MY VOICE FROM THE SHOW-- I CALLED IN AS PROFESSOR Z. REAL NAME'S ZEKE.
OH, OF COURSE. IT'S GREAT TO FINALLY MEET YOU.
I JUST WANT TO ASSURE YOU THAT WE'RE READY. YOU STRUCK THE FIRST BLOW BY EXPOSING THE NINE. WE'LL TAKE UP THE FIGHT. WE HAVE WEAPONS STORED NEAR EVERY MAJOR CITY. WHEN IT'S TIME, THEY ALL BURN.
WEAPONS--? WAIT...
OH, DON'T WORRY...

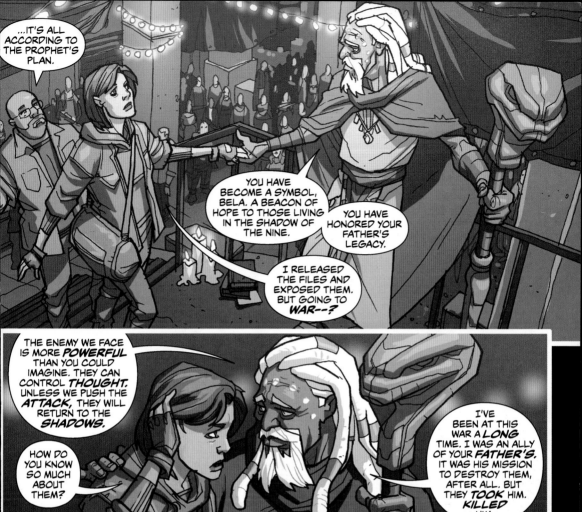

...IT'S ALL ACCORDING TO THE PROPHET'S PLAN.

YOU HAVE BECOME A SYMBOL, BELA. A BEACON OF HOPE TO THOSE LIVING IN THE SHADOW OF THE NINE.

YOU HAVE HONORED YOUR FATHER'S LEGACY.

I RELEASED THE FILES AND EXPOSED THEM. BUT GOING TO WAR--?

THE ENEMY WE FACE IS MORE POWERFUL THAN YOU COULD IMAGINE. THEY CAN CONTROL THOUGHT. UNLESS WE PUSH THE ATTACK, THEY WILL RETURN TO THE SHADOWS.

HOW DO YOU KNOW SO MUCH ABOUT THEM?

I'VE BEEN AT THIS WAR A LONG TIME. I WAS AN ALLY OF YOUR FATHER'S. IT WAS HIS MISSION TO DESTROY THEM, AFTER ALL. BUT THEY TOOK HIM. KILLED HIM.

...NOW WE CLAIM REVENGE.

DOWN WITH THE NINE!

DOWN WITH THE NINE!

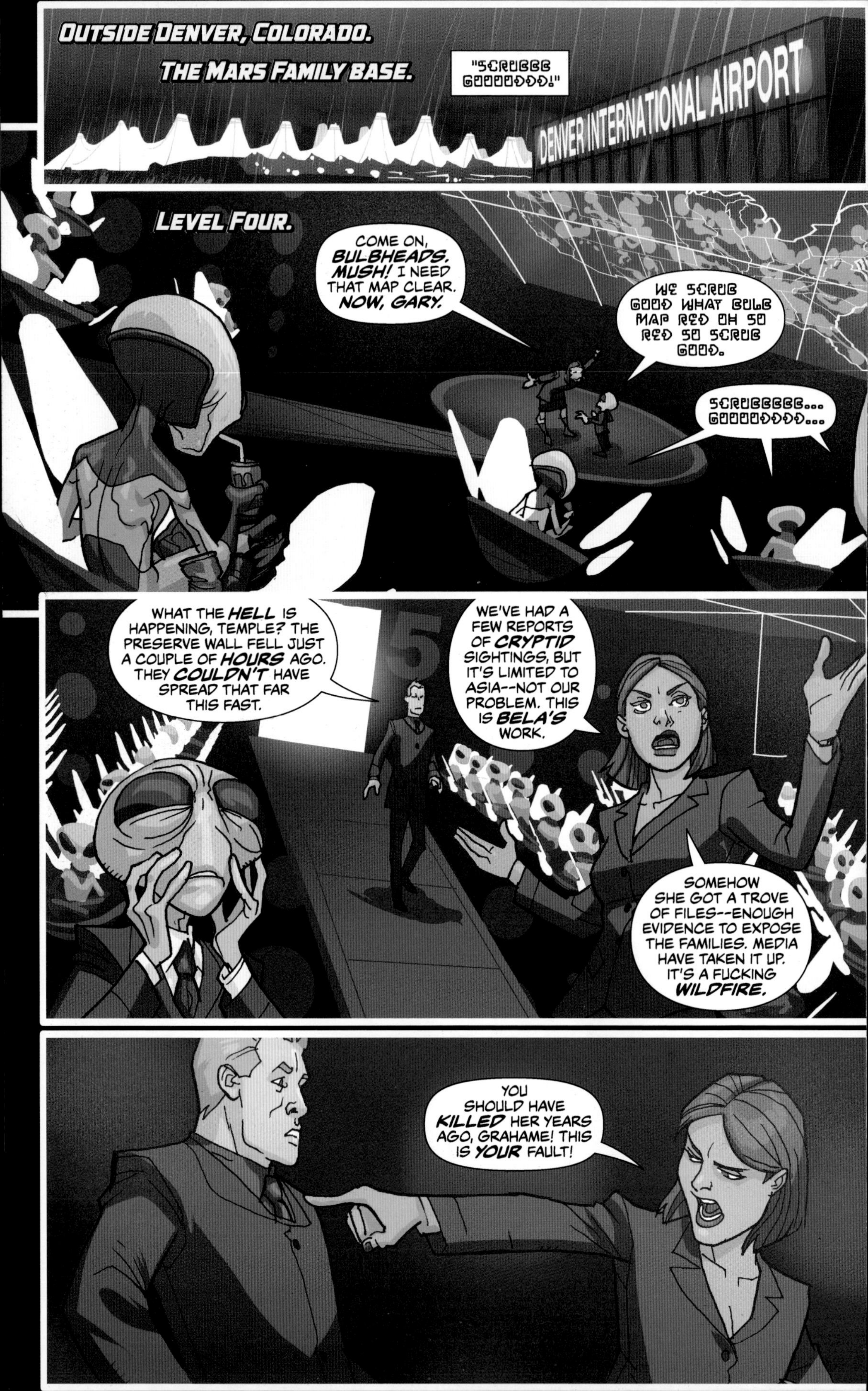

OUTSIDE DENVER, COLORADO.
THE MARS FAMILY BASE.
"SCRUBBB GUUUUDDD!"
DENVER INTERNATIONAL AIRPORT
LEVEL FOUR.
COME ON, BULBHEADS. MUSH! I NEED THAT MAP CLEAR. NOW, GARY.
WE SCRUB GOOD WHAT BULB MAP RED OH SO RED SO SCRUB GOOD.
SCRUBBBBB... GUUUUDDD...
WHAT THE HELL IS HAPPENING, TEMPLE? THE PRESERVE WALL FELL JUST A COUPLE OF HOURS AGO. THEY COULDN'T HAVE SPREAD THAT FAR THIS FAST.
WE'VE HAD A FEW REPORTS OF CRYPTID SIGHTINGS, BUT IT'S LIMITED TO ASIA--NOT OUR PROBLEM. THIS IS BELA'S WORK.
SOMEHOW SHE GOT A TROVE OF FILES--ENOUGH EVIDENCE TO EXPOSE THE FAMILIES. MEDIA HAVE TAKEN IT UP. IT'S A FUCKING WILDFIRE.
YOU SHOULD HAVE KILLED HER YEARS AGO, GRAHAME! THIS IS YOUR FAULT!

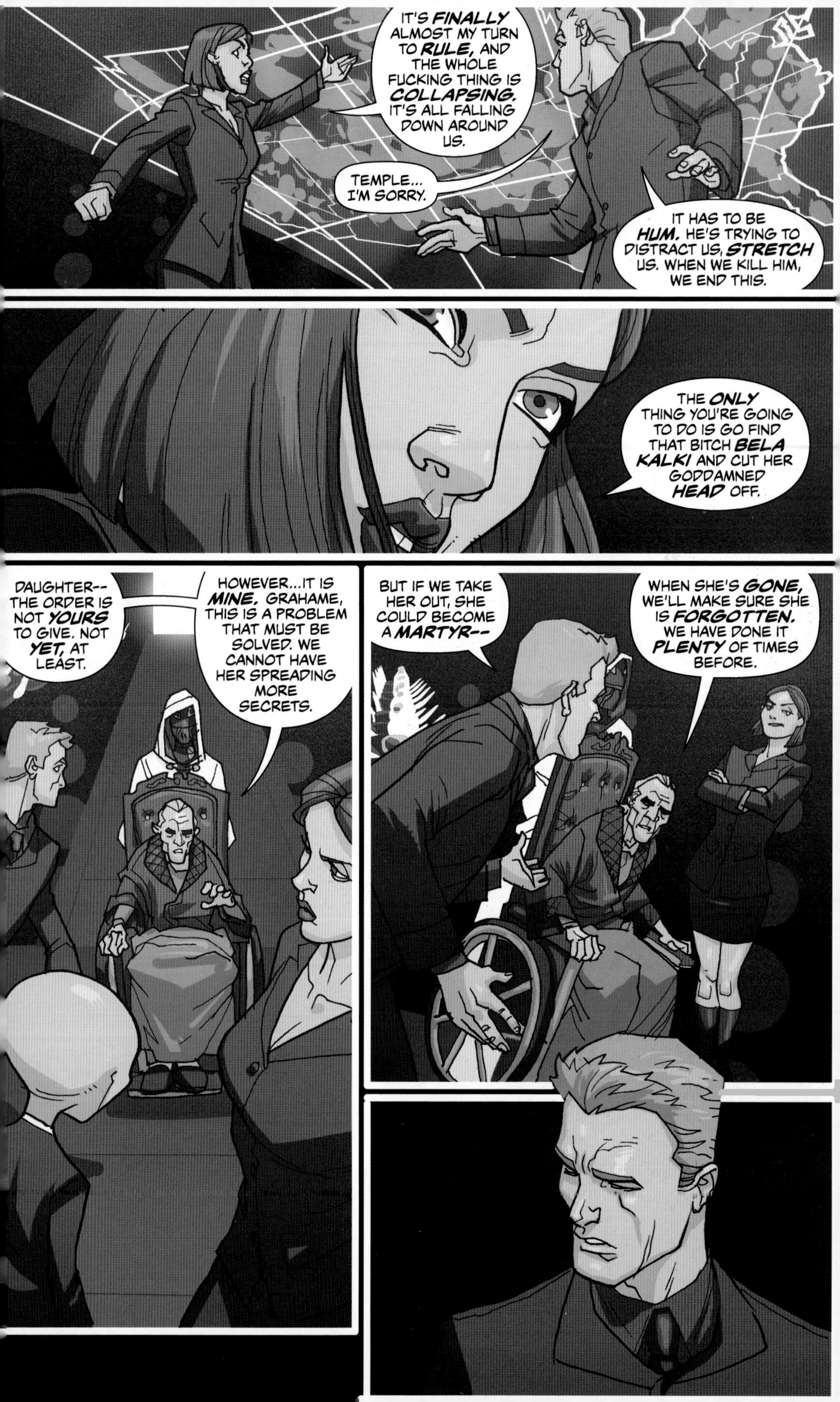
IT'S FINALLY ALMOST MY TURN TO RULE, AND THE WHOLE FUCKING THING IS COLLAPSING. IT'S ALL FALLING DOWN AROUND US.
TEMPLE... I'M SORRY.
IT HAS TO BE HUM. HE'S TRYING TO DISTRACT US, STRETCH US. WHEN WE KILL HIM, WE END THIS.
THE ONLY THING YOU'RE GOING TO DO IS GO FIND THAT BITCH BELA KALKI AND CUT HER GODDAMNED HEAD OFF.
DAUGHTER-- THE ORDER IS NOT YOURS TO GIVE. NOT YET, AT LEAST.
HOWEVER...IT IS MINE. GRAHAME, THIS IS A PROBLEM THAT MUST BE SOLVED. WE CANNOT HAVE HER SPREADING MORE SECRETS.
BUT IF WE TAKE HER OUT, SHE COULD BECOME A MARTYR--
WHEN SHE'S GONE, WE'LL MAKE SURE SHE IS FORGOTTEN. WE HAVE DONE IT PLENTY OF TIMES BEFORE.

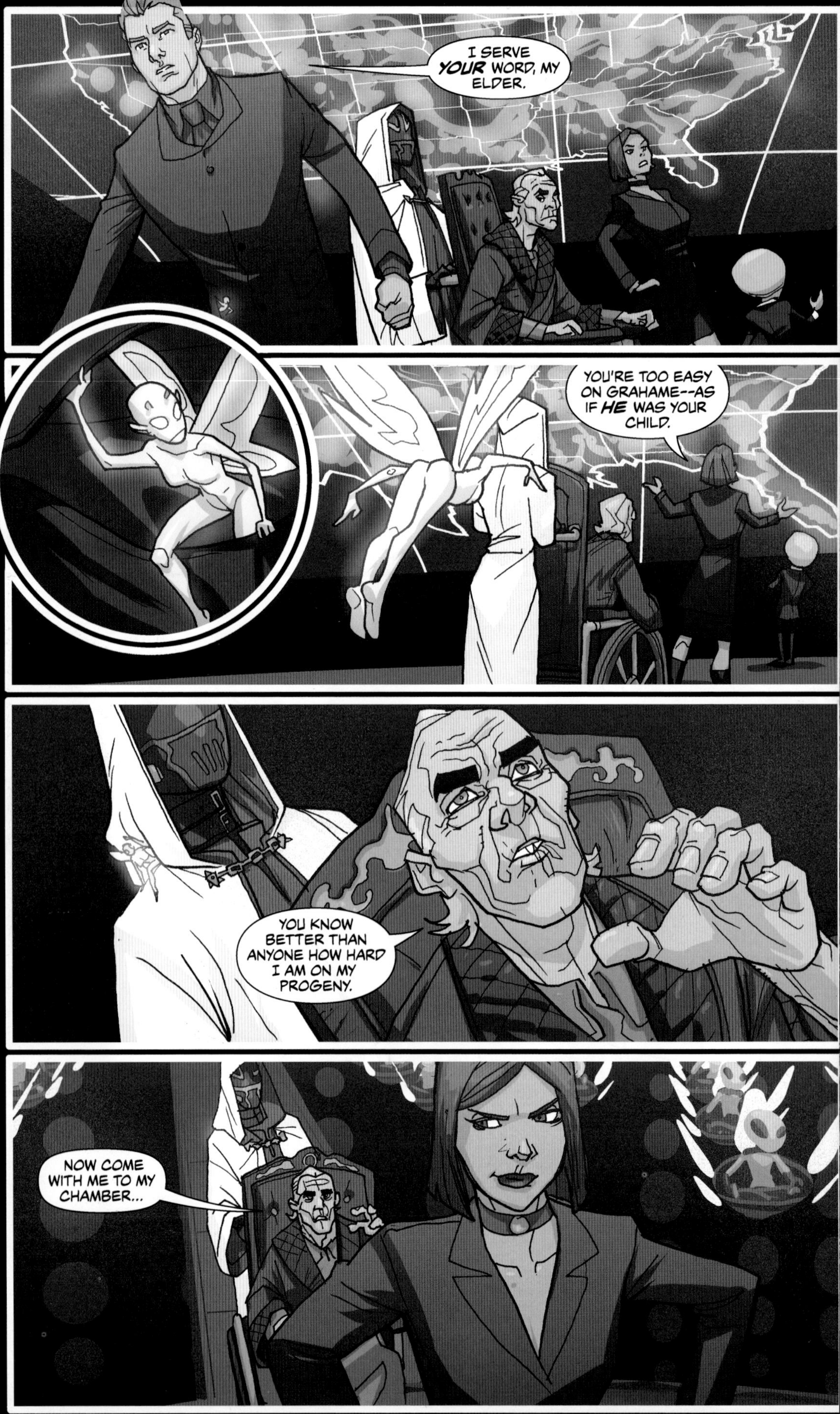
I SERVE YOUR WORD, MY ELDER.
YOU'RE TOO EASY ON GRAHAME--AS IF HE WAS YOUR CHILD.
YOU KNOW BETTER THAN ANYONE HOW HARD I AM ON MY PROGENY.
NOW COME WITH ME TO MY CHAMBER...

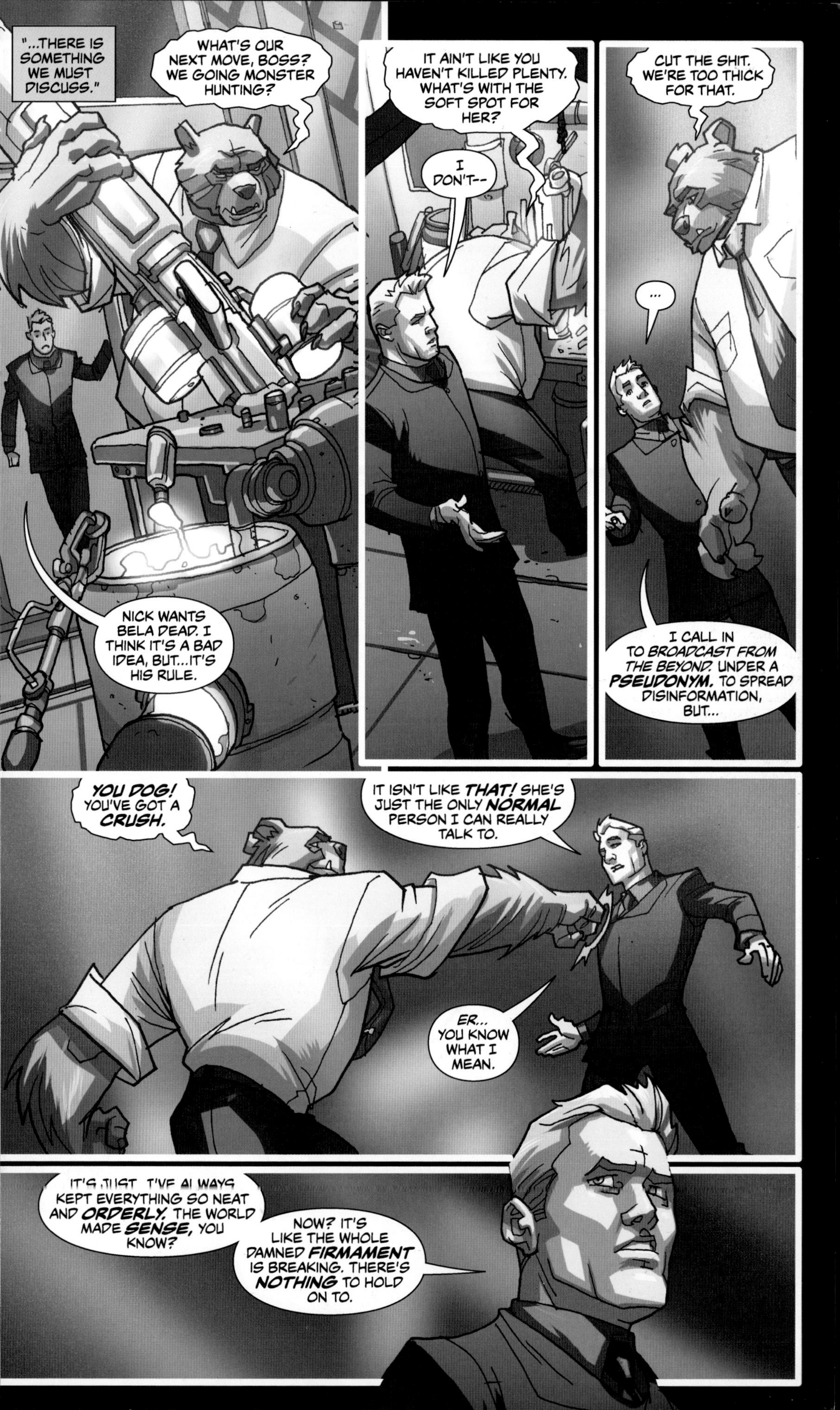
"...THERE IS SOMETHING WE MUST DISCUSS."
WHAT'S OUR NEXT MOVE, BOSS? WE GOING MONSTER HUNTING?
NICK WANTS BELA DEAD. I THINK IT'S A BAD IDEA, BUT...IT'S HIS RULE.
IT AIN'T LIKE YOU HAVEN'T KILLED PLENTY. WHAT'S WITH THE SOFT SPOT FOR HER?
I DON'T--
CUT THE SHIT. WE'RE TOO THICK FOR THAT.
...
I CALL IN TO BROADCAST FROM THE BEYOND UNDER A PSEUDONYM, TO SPREAD DISINFORMATION, BUT...
YOU DOG! YOU'VE GOT A CRUSH.
IT ISN'T LIKE THAT! SHE'S JUST THE ONLY NORMAL PERSON I CAN REALLY TALK TO.
ER... YOU KNOW WHAT I MEAN.
IT'S JUST, I'VE ALWAYS KEPT EVERYTHING SO NEAT AND ORDERLY. THE WORLD MADE SENSE, YOU KNOW?
NOW? IT'S LIKE THE WHOLE DAMNED FIRMAMENT IS BREAKING. THERE'S NOTHING TO HOLD ON TO.

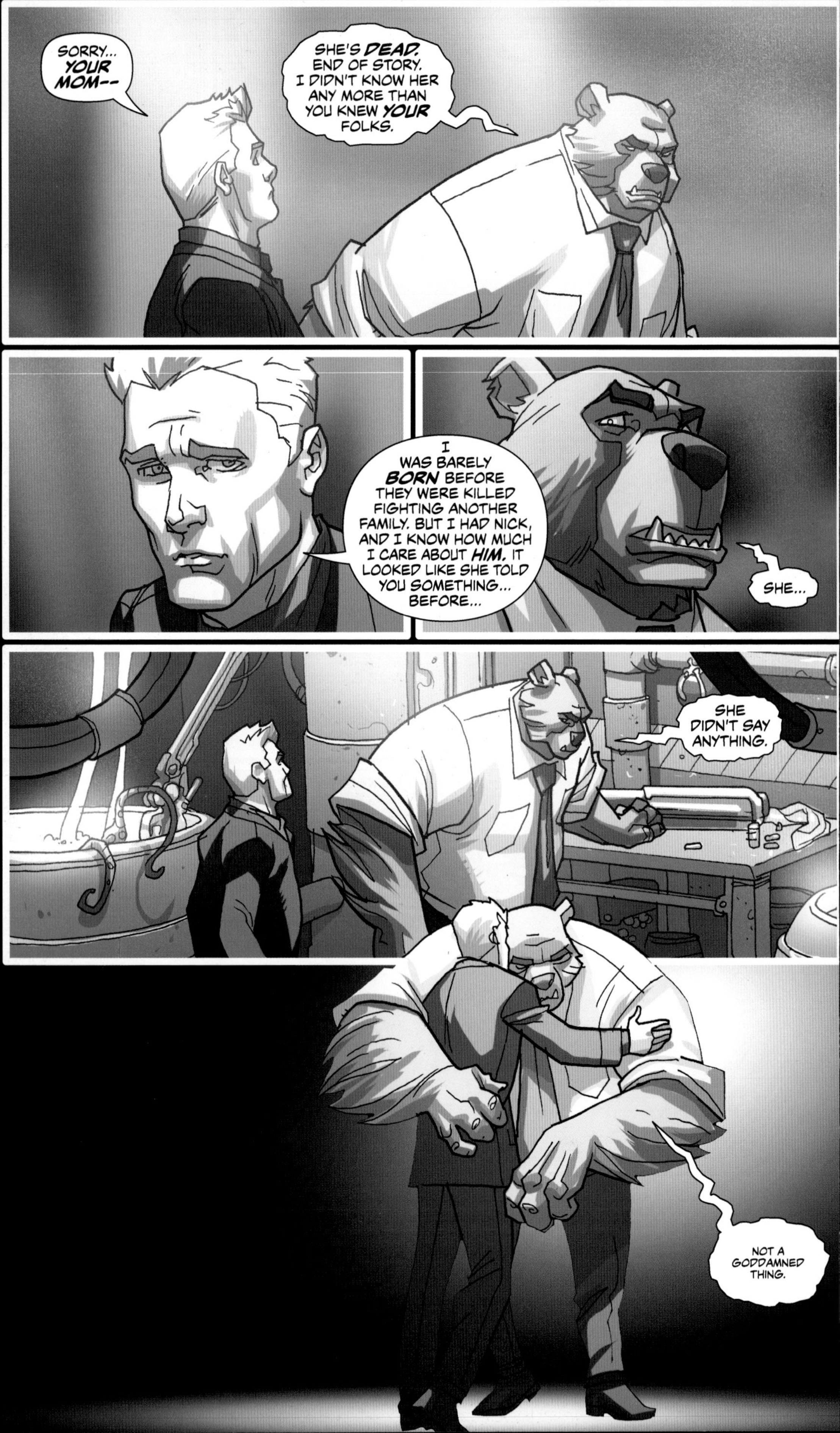
SORRY... YOUR MOM--
SHE'S DEAD. END OF STORY. I DIDN'T KNOW HER ANY MORE THAN YOU KNEW YOUR FOLKS.
I WAS BARELY BORN BEFORE THEY WERE KILLED FIGHTING ANOTHER FAMILY. BUT I HAD NICK, AND I KNOW HOW MUCH I CARE ABOUT HIM. IT LOOKED LIKE SHE TOLD YOU SOMETHING... BEFORE...
SHE...
SHE DIDN'T SAY ANYTHING.
NOT A GODDAMNED THING.

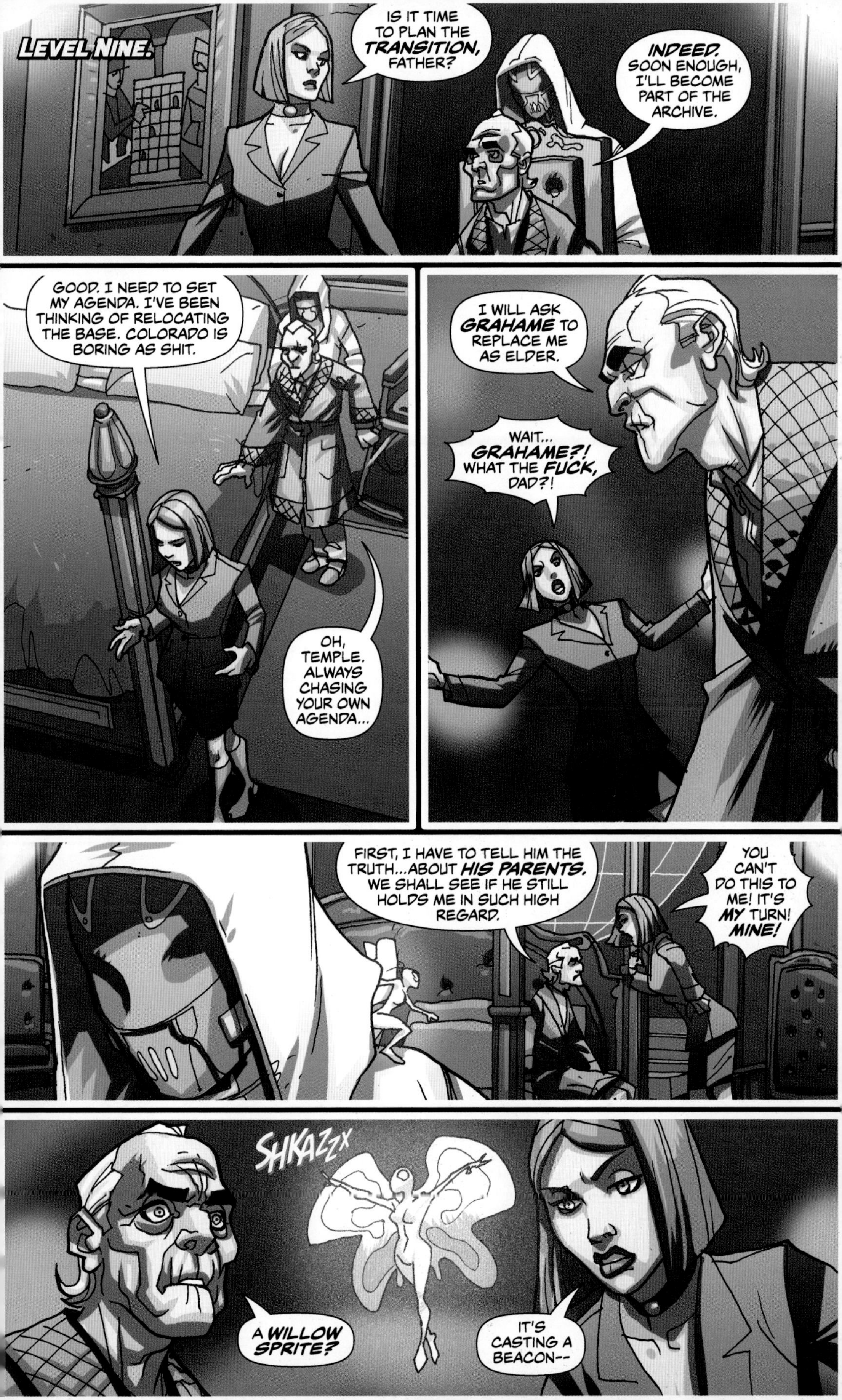

LEVEL NINE.
IS IT TIME TO PLAN THE TRANSITION, FATHER?
INDEED. SOON ENOUGH, I'LL BECOME PART OF THE ARCHIVE.
GOOD. I NEED TO SET MY AGENDA. I'VE BEEN THINKING OF RELOCATING THE BASE. COLORADO IS BORING AS SHIT.
OH, TEMPLE. ALWAYS CHASING YOUR OWN AGENDA...
I WILL ASK GRAHAME TO REPLACE ME AS ELDER.
WAIT... GRAHAME?! WHAT THE FUCK, DAD?!
FIRST, I HAVE TO TELL HIM THE TRUTH...ABOUT HIS PARENTS. WE SHALL SEE IF HE STILL HOLDS ME IN SUCH HIGH REGARD.
YOU CAN'T DO THIS TO ME! IT'S MY TURN! MINE!
SHKAZZX
A WILLOW SPRITE?
IT'S CASTING A BEACON--

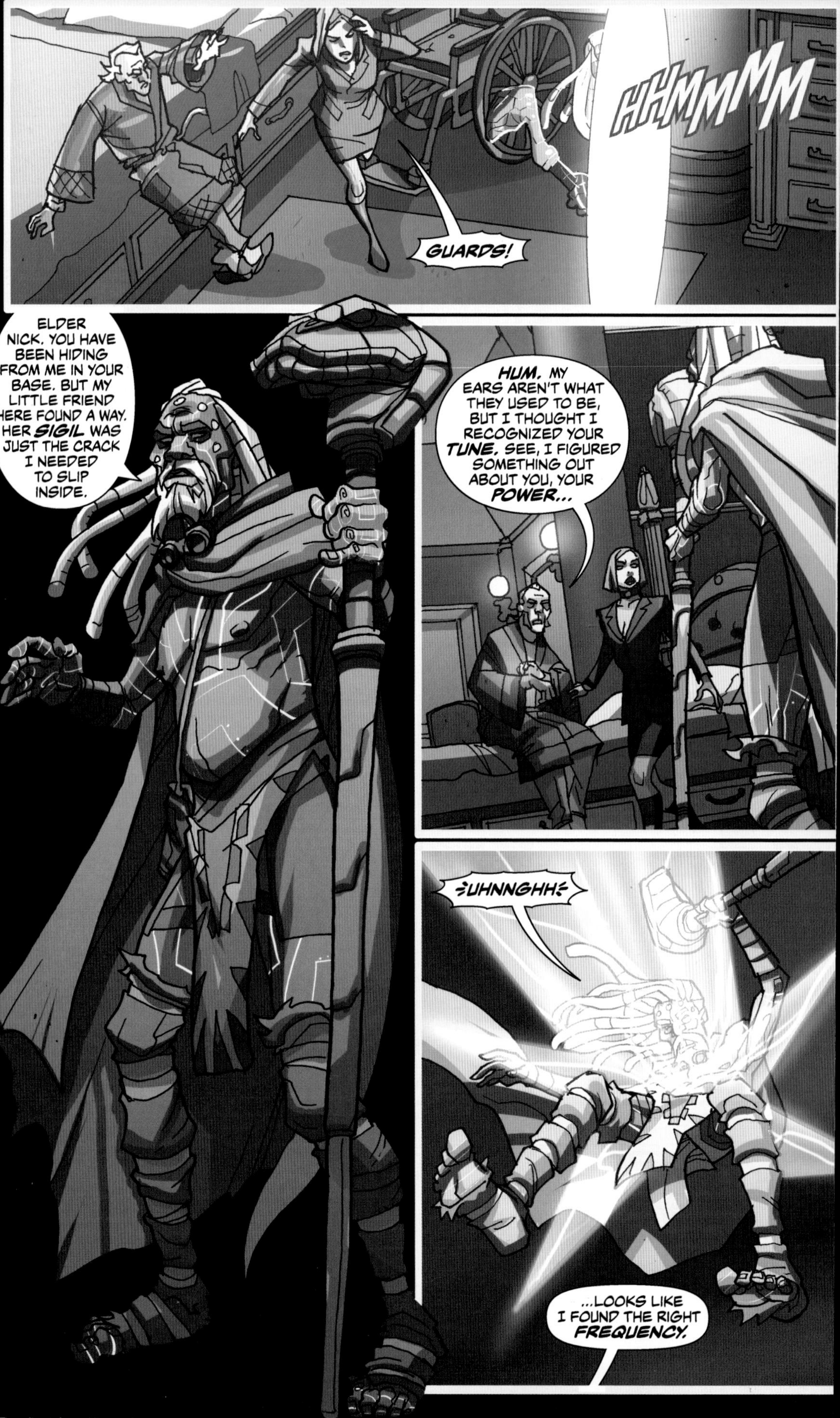
HHMMMMM
GUARDS!
ELDER NICK. YOU HAVE BEEN HIDING FROM ME IN YOUR BASE. BUT MY LITTLE FRIEND HERE FOUND A WAY. HER SIGIL WAS JUST THE CRACK I NEEDED TO SLIP INSIDE.
HUM. MY EARS AREN'T WHAT THEY USED TO BE, BUT I THOUGHT I RECOGNIZED YOUR TUNE. SEE, I FIGURED SOMETHING OUT ABOUT YOU, YOUR POWER...
UHNNGHH
...LOOKS LIKE I FOUND THE RIGHT FREQUENCY.

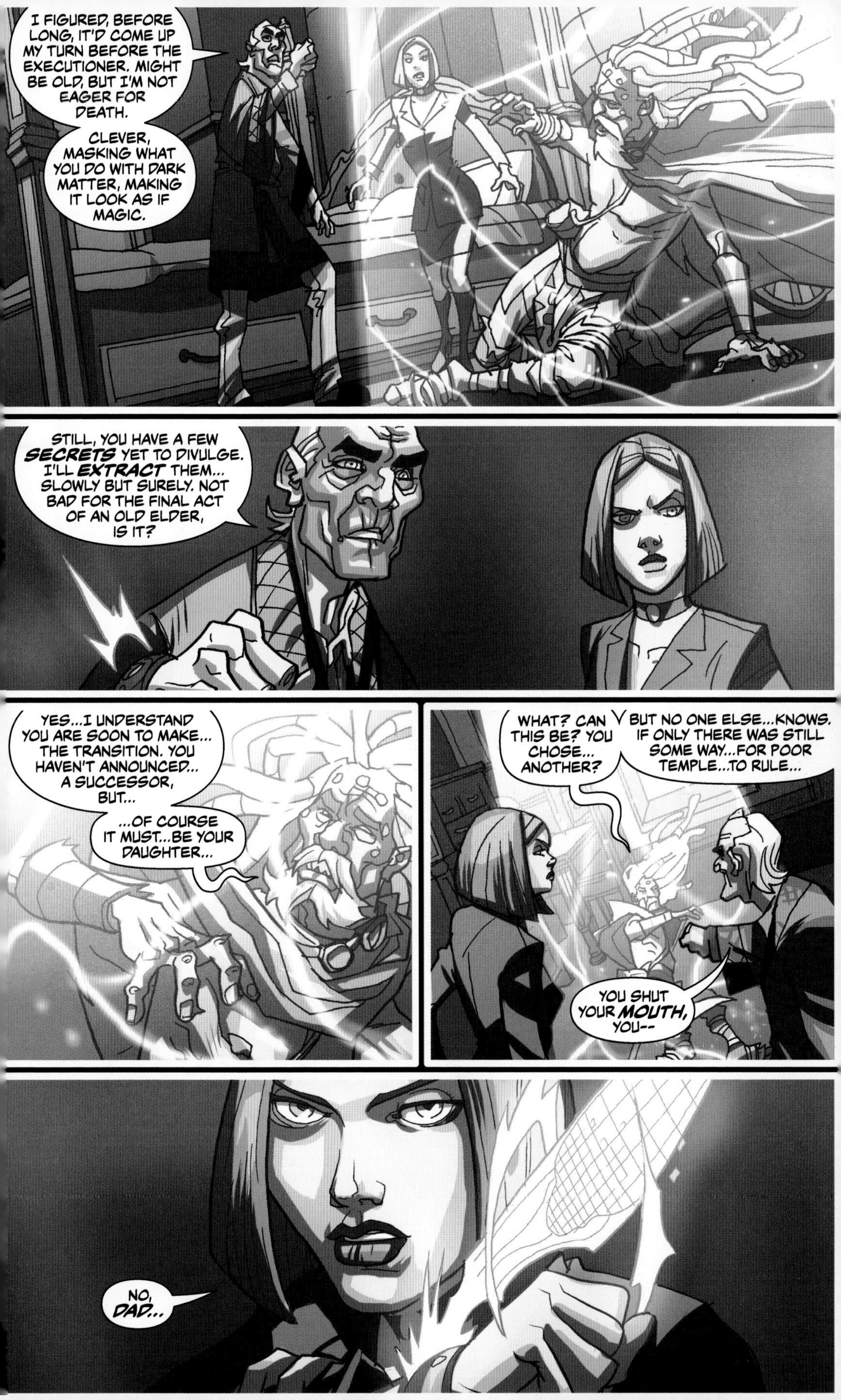
I FIGURED, BEFORE LONG, IT'D COME UP MY TURN BEFORE THE EXECUTIONER. MIGHT BE OLD, BUT I'M NOT EAGER FOR DEATH.
CLEVER, MASKING WHAT YOU DO WITH DARK MATTER, MAKING IT LOOK AS IF MAGIC.
STILL, YOU HAVE A FEW *SECRETS* YET TO DIVULGE. I'LL *EXTRACT* THEM... SLOWLY BUT SURELY. NOT BAD FOR THE FINAL ACT OF AN OLD ELDER, IS IT?
YES...I UNDERSTAND YOU ARE SOON TO MAKE... THE TRANSITION. YOU HAVEN'T ANNOUNCED... A SUCCESSOR, BUT...
...OF COURSE IT MUST...BE YOUR DAUGHTER...
WHAT? CAN THIS BE? YOU CHOSE... ANOTHER?
BUT NO ONE ELSE...KNOWS. IF ONLY THERE WAS STILL SOME WAY...FOR POOR TEMPLE...TO RULE...
YOU SHUT YOUR *MOUTH,* YOU--
NO, *DAD...*

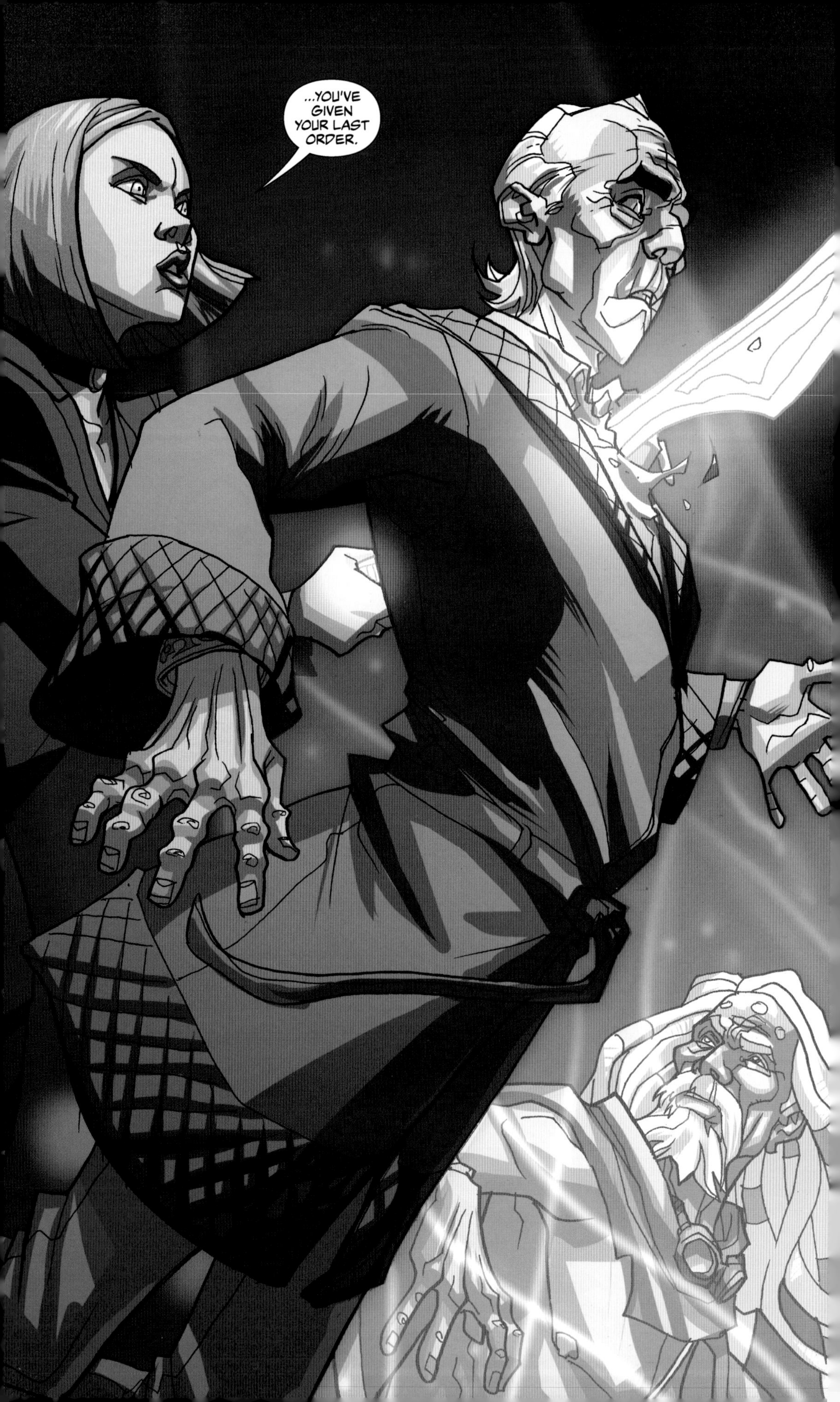
...YOU'VE GIVEN YOUR LAST ORDER.

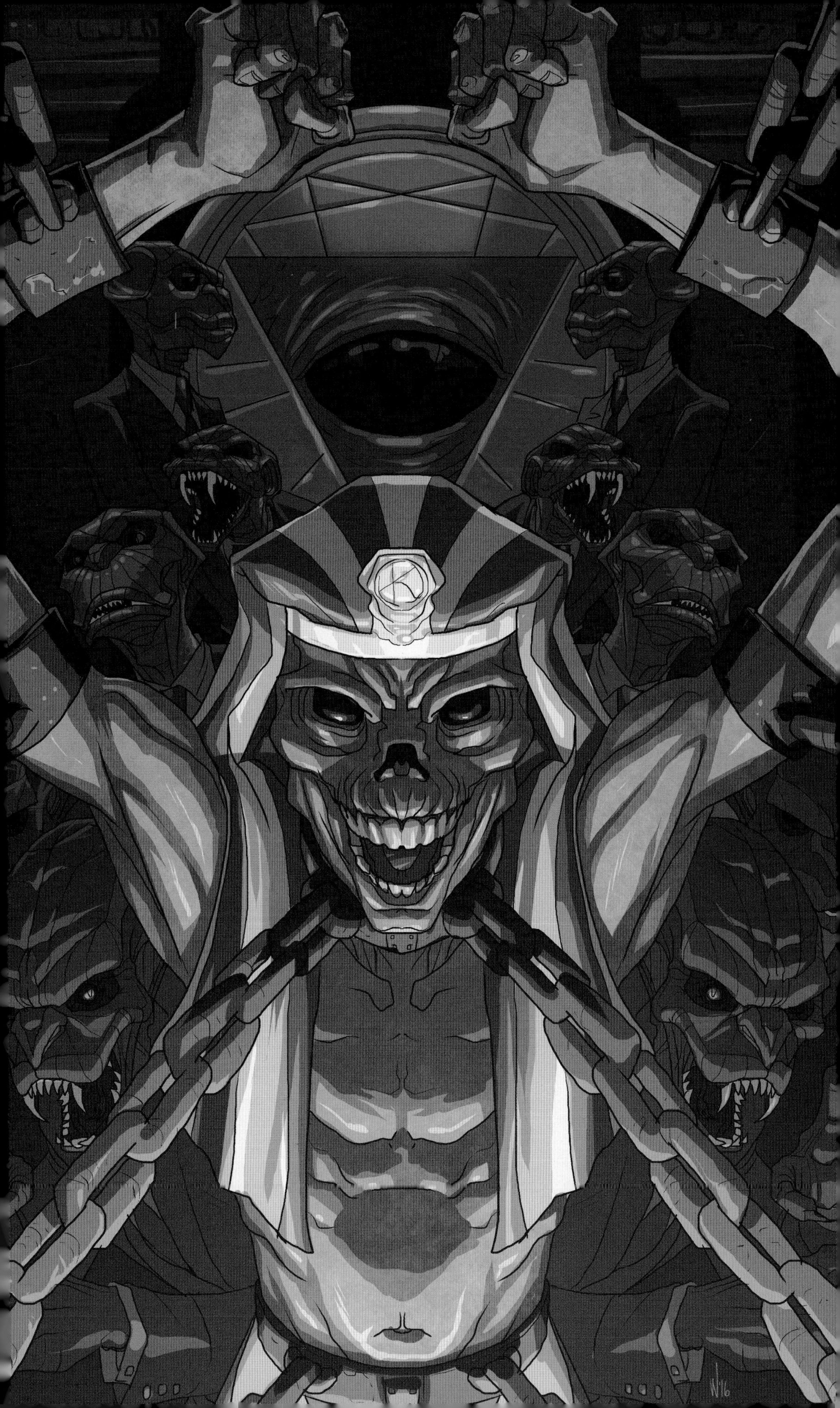

#5
CROWNS

WHEN AN ELDER DIES, THEY BECOME
PART OF THE COEMETORIUM,
A REPOSITORY OF MENTAL
ENERGY, OF MEMORIES.

They are not alive, but they can relay
all information and memories they hold
through rough speech simulation.

Elders' minds are preserved just as they
were at the moment of their death.

The Coemetorium
uses passive plasma
feeds to halt
neuron decay.

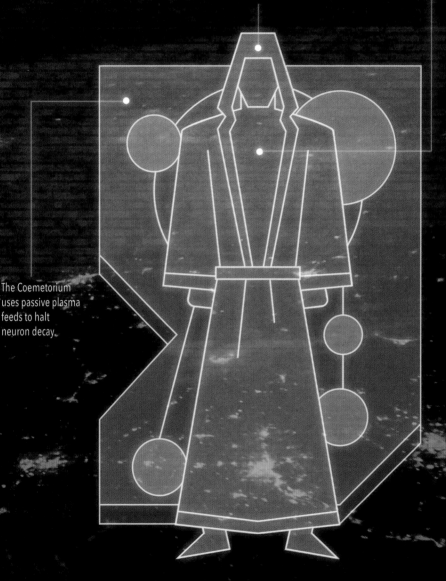

EVERY ELDER HAS BEEN PRESERVED . . . UNTIL NOW.

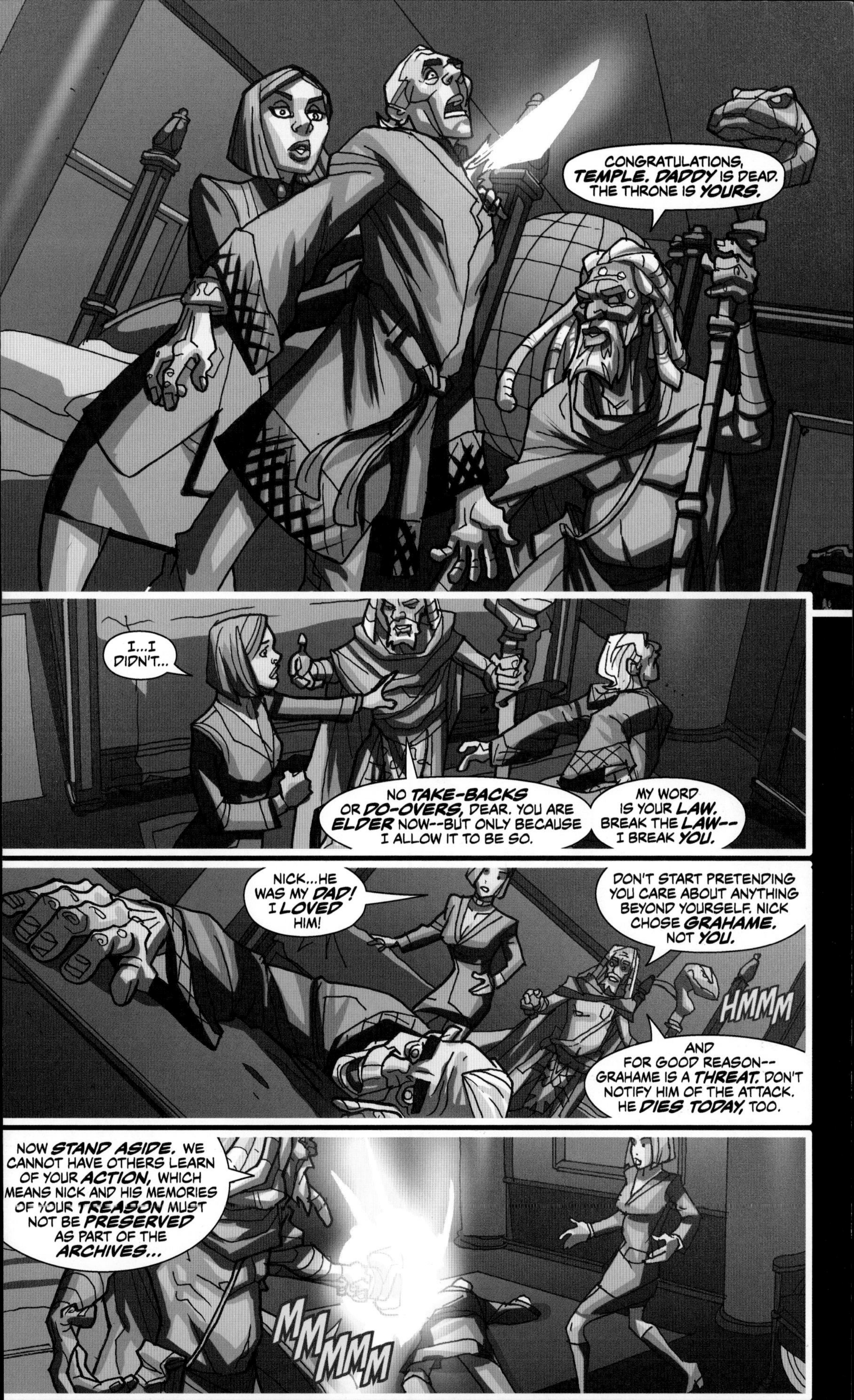
CONGRATULATIONS, TEMPLE. DADDY IS DEAD. THE THRONE IS YOURS.
I...I DIDN'T...
NO TAKE-BACKS OR DO-OVERS, DEAR. YOU ARE ELDER NOW--BUT ONLY BECAUSE I ALLOW IT TO BE SO.
MY WORD IS YOUR LAW. BREAK THE LAW-- I BREAK YOU.
NICK...HE WAS MY DAD! I LOVED HIM!
DON'T START PRETENDING YOU CARE ABOUT ANYTHING BEYOND YOURSELF. NICK CHOSE GRAHAME. NOT YOU.
HMMM
AND FOR GOOD REASON-- GRAHAME IS A THREAT. DON'T NOTIFY HIM OF THE ATTACK. HE DIES TODAY, TOO.
NOW STAND ASIDE. WE CANNOT HAVE OTHERS LEARN OF YOUR ACTION, WHICH MEANS NICK AND HIS MEMORIES OF YOUR TREASON MUST NOT BE PRESERVED AS PART OF THE ARCHIVES...
MMMMM

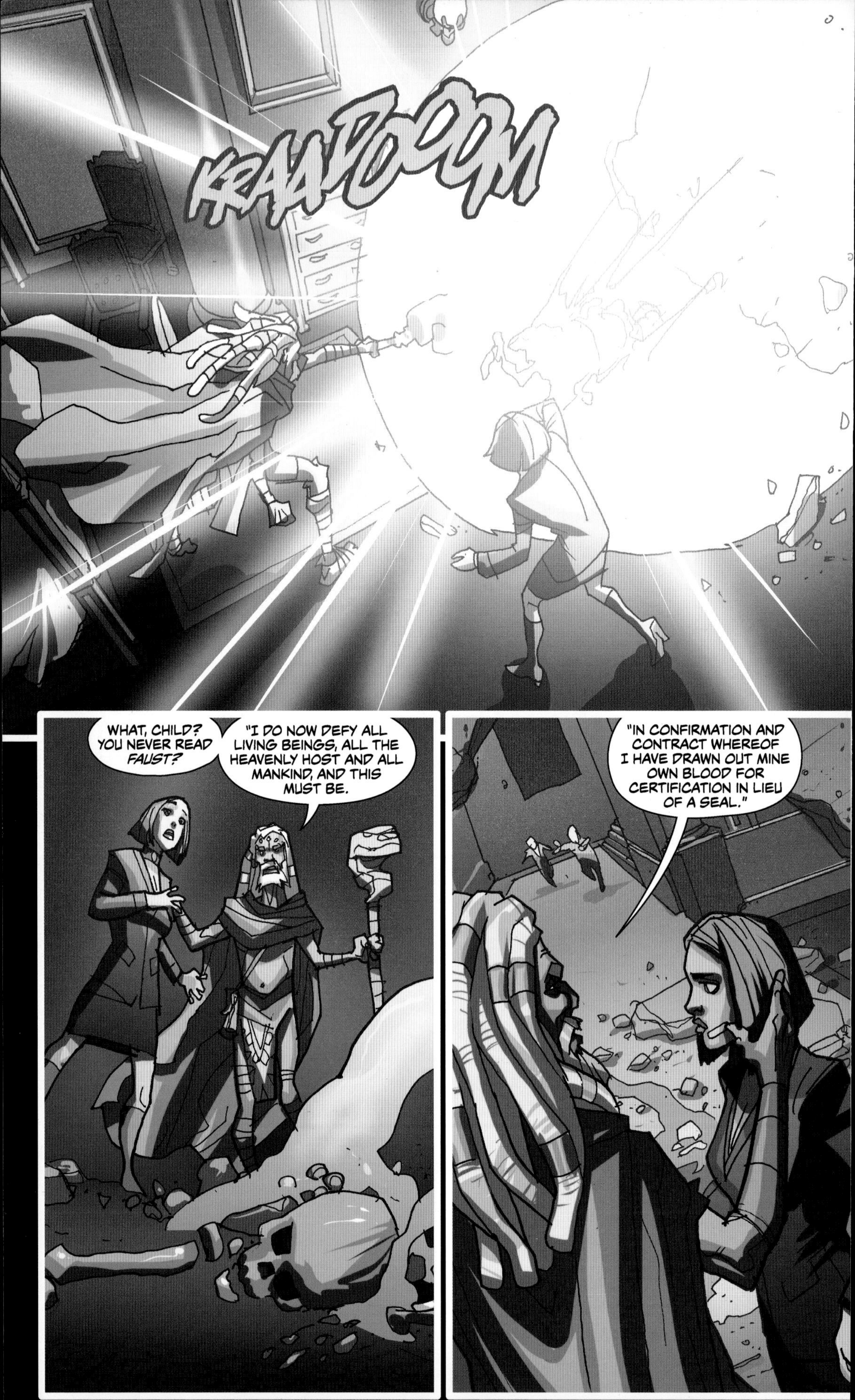
KRAADOOOM
WHAT, CHILD? YOU NEVER READ FAUST?
"I DO NOW DEFY ALL LIVING BEINGS, ALL THE HEAVENLY HOST AND ALL MANKIND, AND THIS MUST BE.
"IN CONFIRMATION AND CONTRACT WHEREOF I HAVE DRAWN OUT MINE OWN BLOOD FOR CERTIFICATION IN LIEU OF A SEAL."

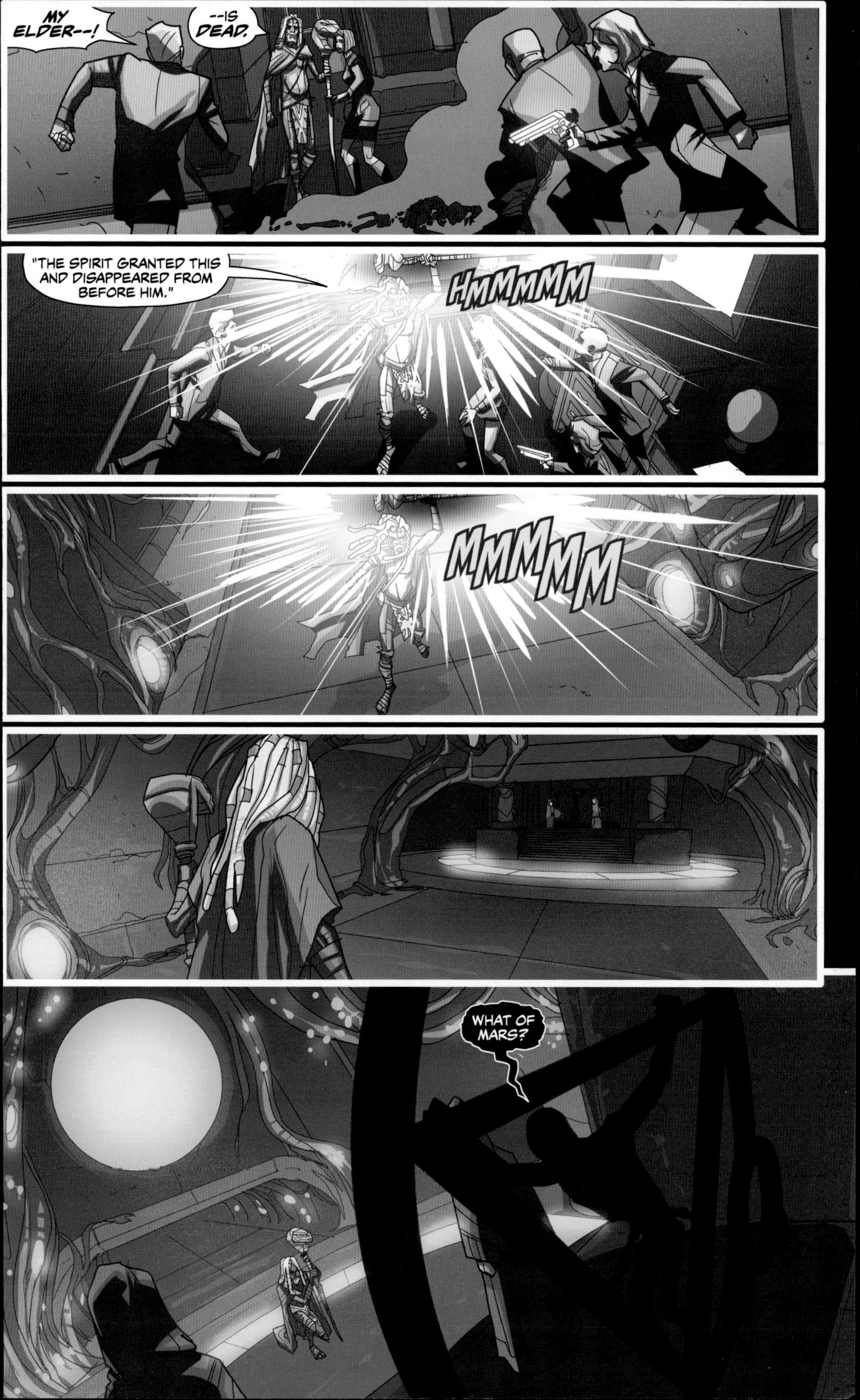
MY ELDER--!
--IS DEAD.
"THE SPIRIT GRANTED THIS AND DISAPPEARED FROM BEFORE HIM."
HMMMMM
MMMMMM
WHAT OF MARS?

IT IS DONE. NICK PUT UP A FIGHT. YOU WERE RIGHT--HE WAS MORE OF A THREAT THAN I EXPECTED. BUT TEMPLE DID AS PREDICTED. SHE BELONGS TO US--

MY APOLOGIES. SHE BELONGS TO *YOU* NOW.

BUT GRAHAME REMAINS ALIVE. HE ENDANGERS ALL OUR PLANS.

FOR NOW. MY TEAM IS IN THE FIELD. GRAHAME DOESN'T SURVIVE THE DAY. NOR DOES MARS.

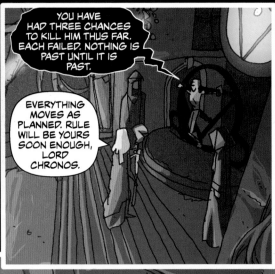

YOU HAVE HAD THREE CHANCES TO KILL HIM THUS FAR, EACH FAILED. NOTHING IS PAST UNTIL IT IS PAST.

EVERYTHING MOVES AS PLANNED. RULE WILL BE YOURS SOON ENOUGH, LORD CHRONOS.

HRGHK

DON'T JUST *STAND* THERE. WE MUST COLLECT *THE HOST BEFORE IT WEAKENS.* BRING ME ANOTHER VESSEL.

NOW!

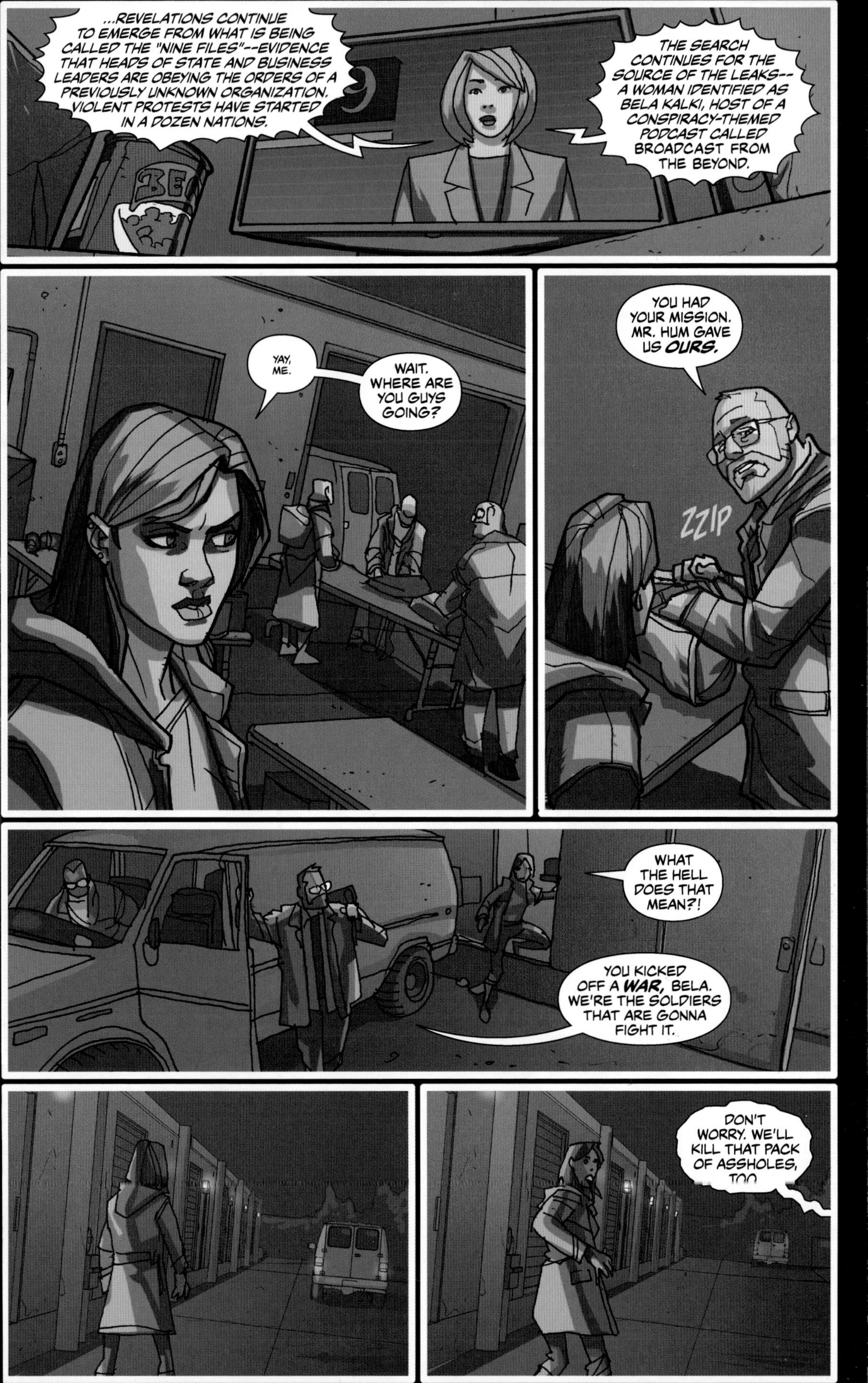
...REVELATIONS CONTINUE TO EMERGE FROM WHAT IS BEING CALLED THE "NINE FILES"--EVIDENCE THAT HEADS OF STATE AND BUSINESS LEADERS ARE OBEYING THE ORDERS OF A PREVIOUSLY UNKNOWN ORGANIZATION. VIOLENT PROTESTS HAVE STARTED IN A DOZEN NATIONS.
THE SEARCH CONTINUES FOR THE SOURCE OF THE LEAKS--A WOMAN IDENTIFIED AS BELA KALKI, HOST OF A CONSPIRACY-THEMED PODCAST CALLED BROADCAST FROM THE BEYOND.
YAY, ME.
WAIT. WHERE ARE YOU GUYS GOING?
YOU HAD YOUR MISSION. MR. HUM GAVE US **OURS.**
ZZIP
WHAT THE HELL DOES THAT MEAN?!
YOU KICKED OFF A **WAR,** BELA. WE'RE THE SOLDIERS THAT ARE GONNA FIGHT IT.
DON'T WORRY. WE'LL KILL THAT PACK OF ASSHOLES, TOO.

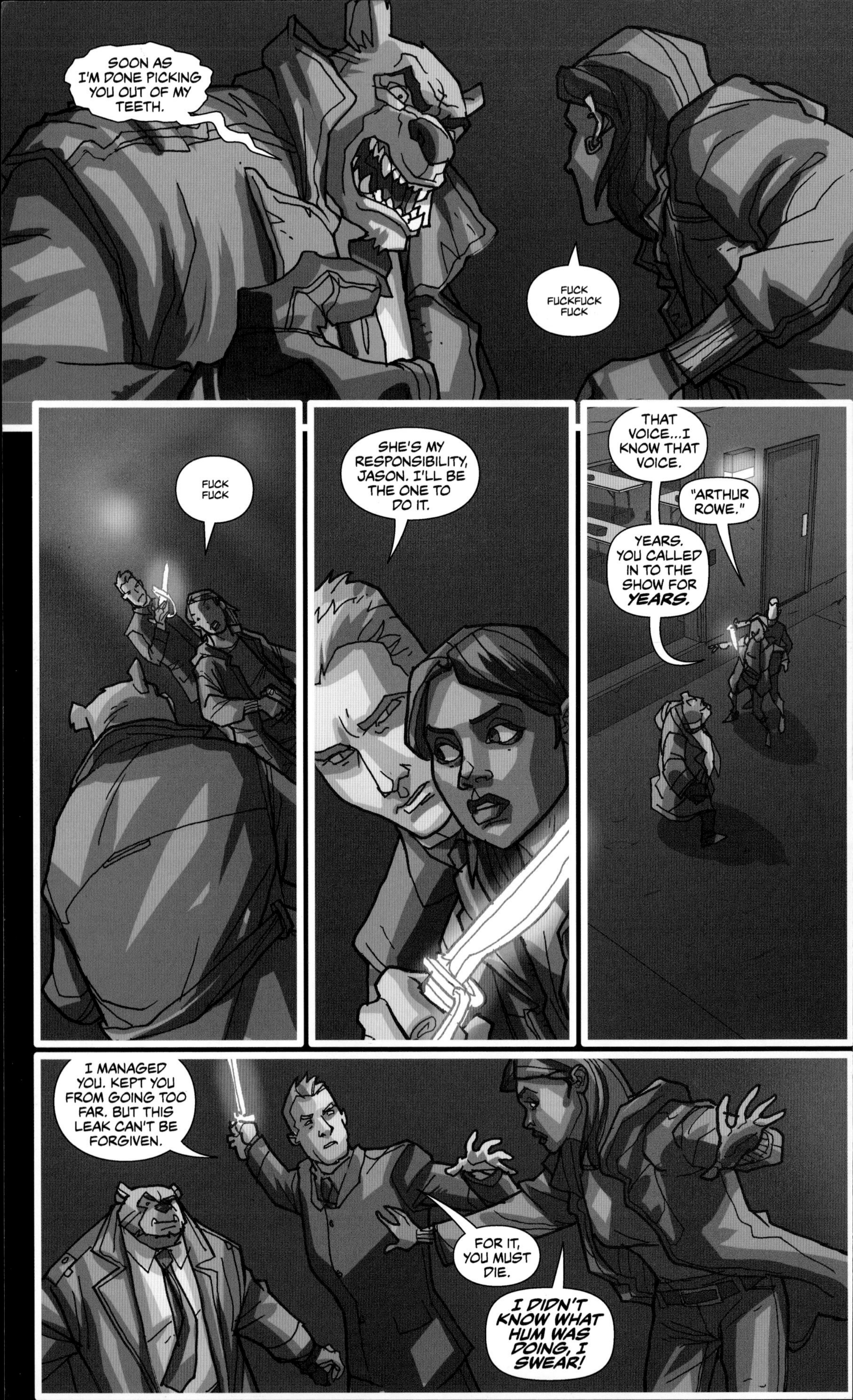
SOON AS I'M DONE PICKING YOU OUT OF MY TEETH.
FUCK FUCKFUCK FUCK
FUCK FUCK
SHE'S MY RESPONSIBILITY, JASON. I'LL BE THE ONE TO DO IT.
THAT VOICE...I KNOW THAT VOICE.
"ARTHUR ROWE."
YEARS. YOU CALLED IN TO THE SHOW FOR YEARS.
I MANAGED YOU. KEPT YOU FROM GOING TOO FAR. BUT THIS LEAK CAN'T BE FORGIVEN.
FOR IT, YOU MUST DIE.
I DIDN'T KNOW WHAT HUM WAS DOING, I SWEAR!

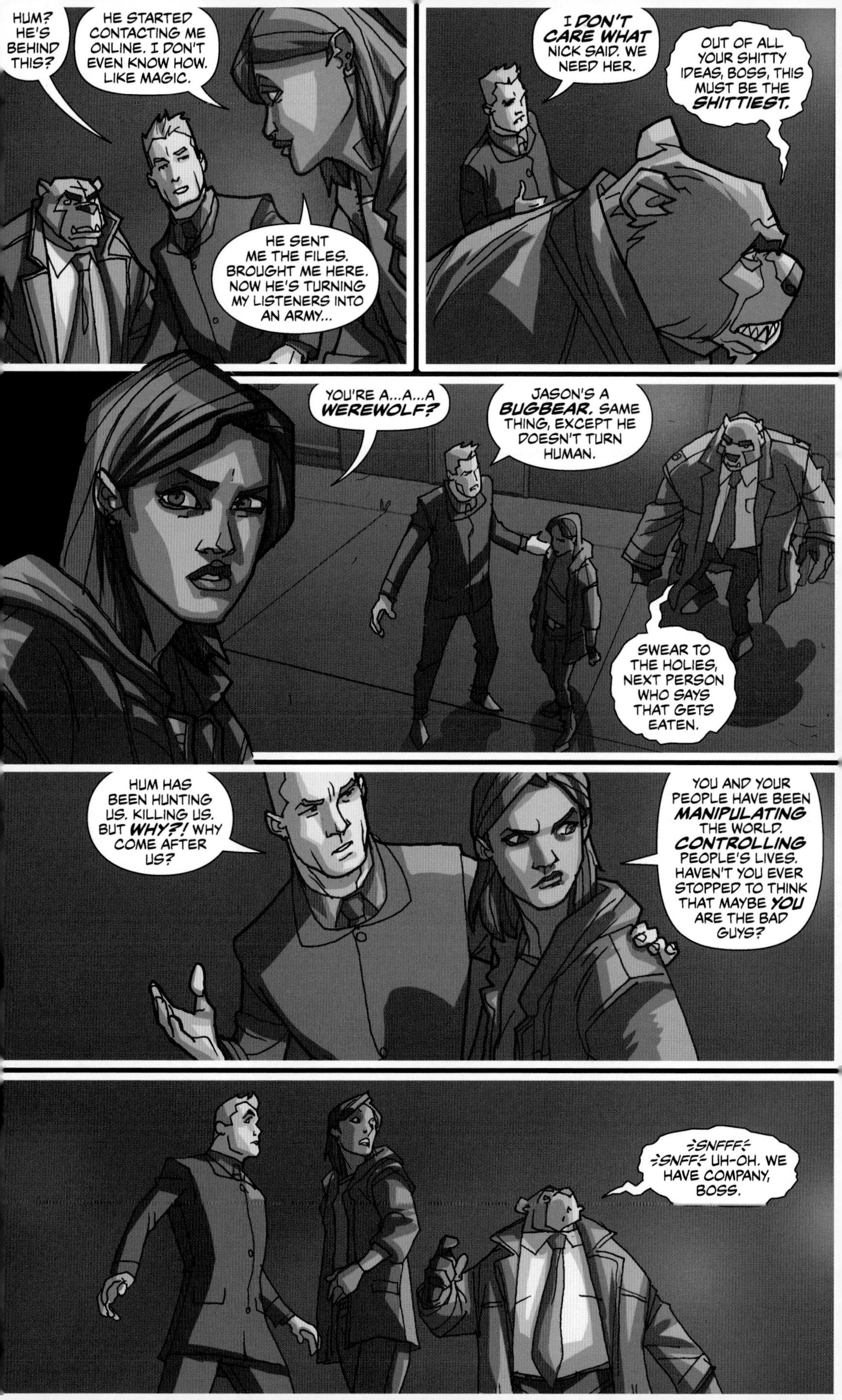
HUM? HE'S BEHIND THIS?
HE STARTED CONTACTING ME ONLINE. I DON'T EVEN KNOW HOW. LIKE MAGIC.
HE SENT ME THE FILES. BROUGHT ME HERE. NOW HE'S TURNING MY LISTENERS INTO AN ARMY...
I DON'T CARE WHAT NICK SAID. WE NEED HER.
OUT OF ALL YOUR SHITTY IDEAS, BOSS, THIS MUST BE THE SHITTIEST.
YOU'RE A...A...A WEREWOLF?
JASON'S A BUGBEAR. SAME THING, EXCEPT HE DOESN'T TURN HUMAN.
SWEAR TO THE HOLIES, NEXT PERSON WHO SAYS THAT GETS EATEN.
HUM HAS BEEN HUNTING US. KILLING US. BUT WHY?! WHY COME AFTER US?
YOU AND YOUR PEOPLE HAVE BEEN MANIPULATING THE WORLD. CONTROLLING PEOPLE'S LIVES. HAVEN'T YOU EVER STOPPED TO THINK THAT MAYBE YOU ARE THE BAD GUYS?
SNFFF SNFF UH-OH. WE HAVE COMPANY, BOSS.

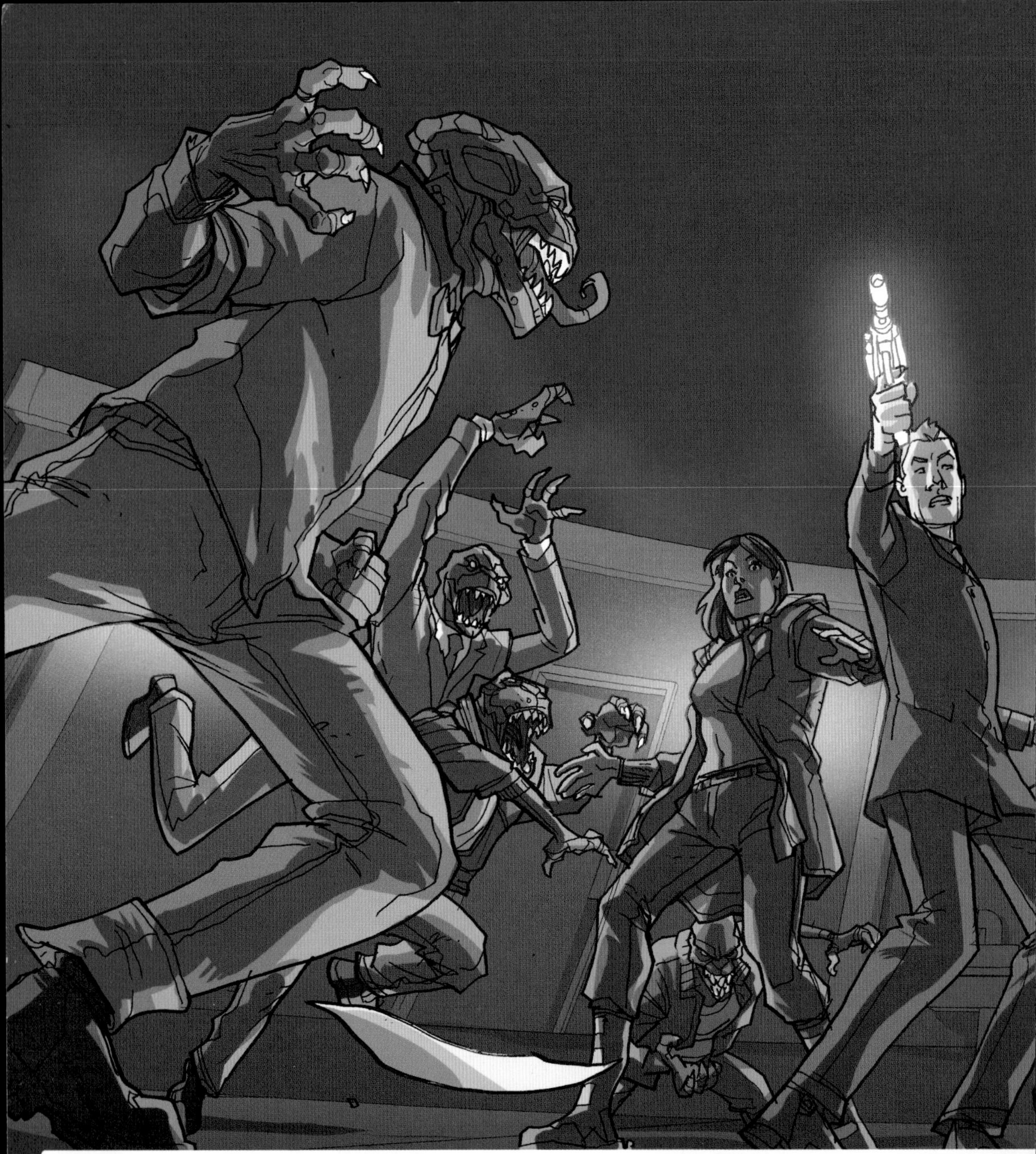

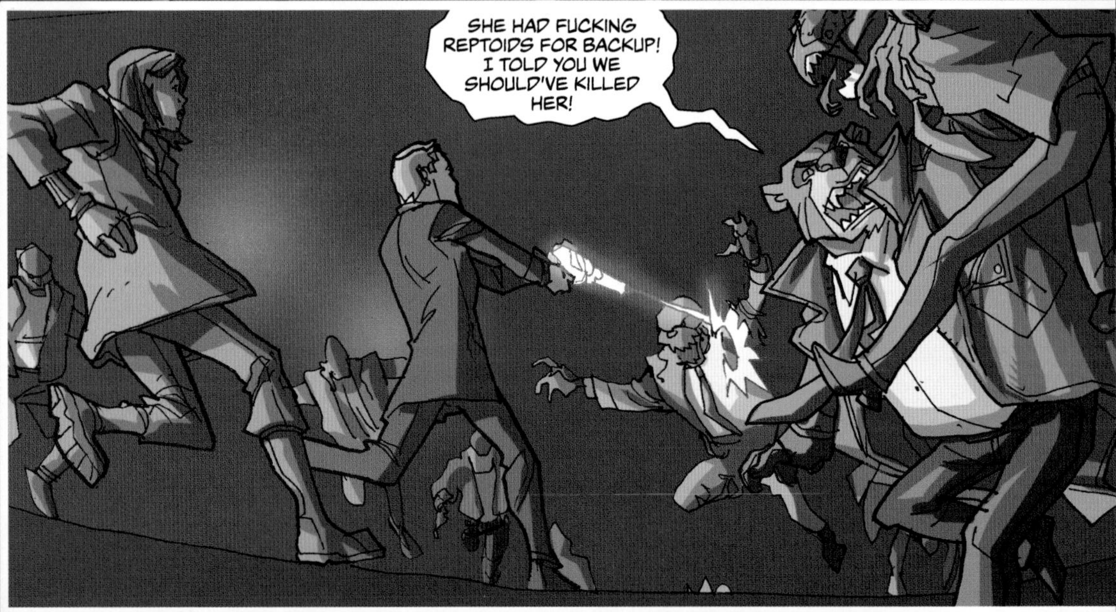
SHE HAD FUCKING REPTOIDS FOR BACKUP! I TOLD YOU WE SHOULD'VE KILLED HER!

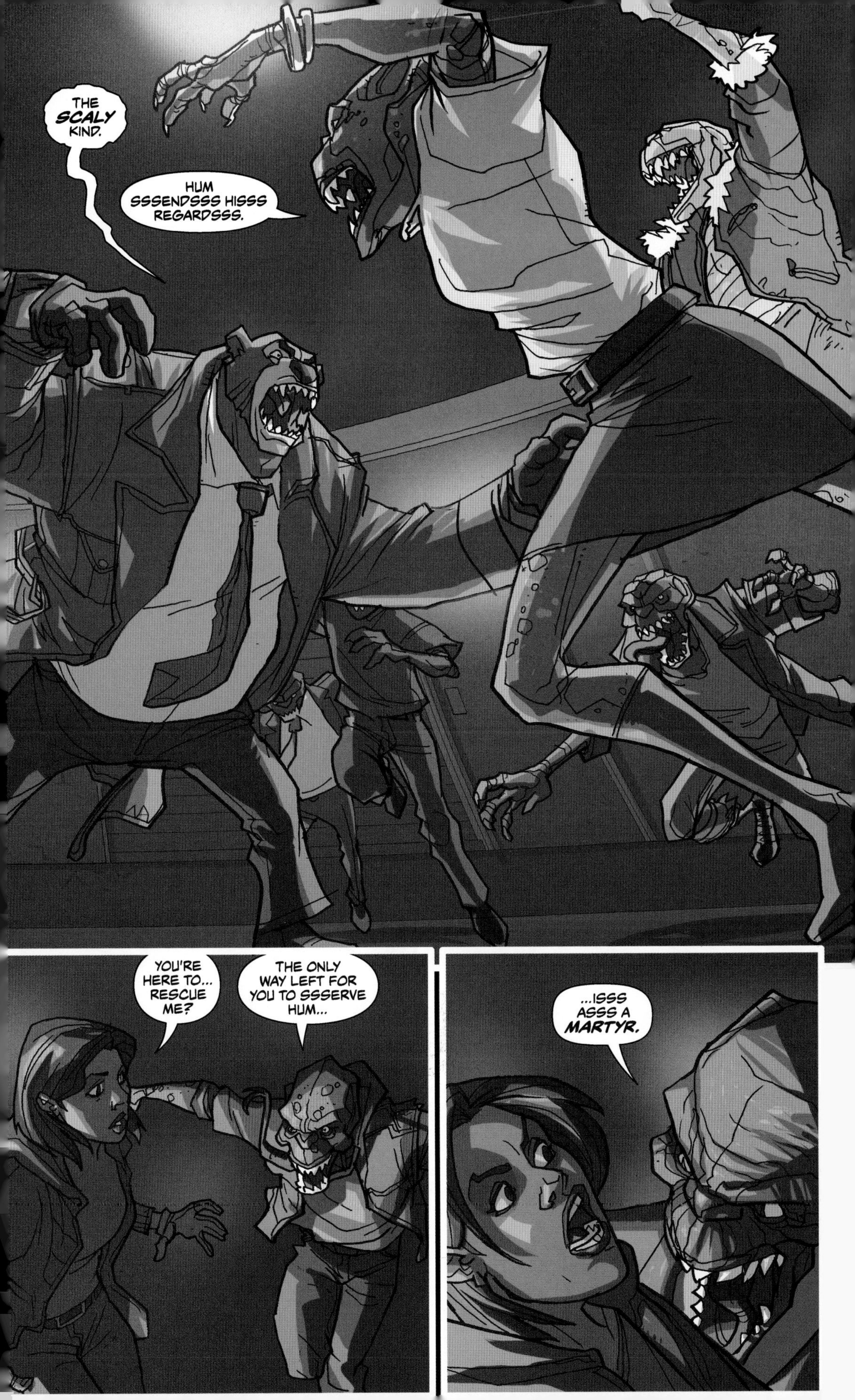
THE SCALY KIND.
HUM SSSENDSSS HISSS REGARDSSS.
YOU'RE HERE TO... RESCUE ME?
THE ONLY WAY LEFT FOR YOU TO SSSERVE HUM...
...ISSS ASSS A MARTYR.

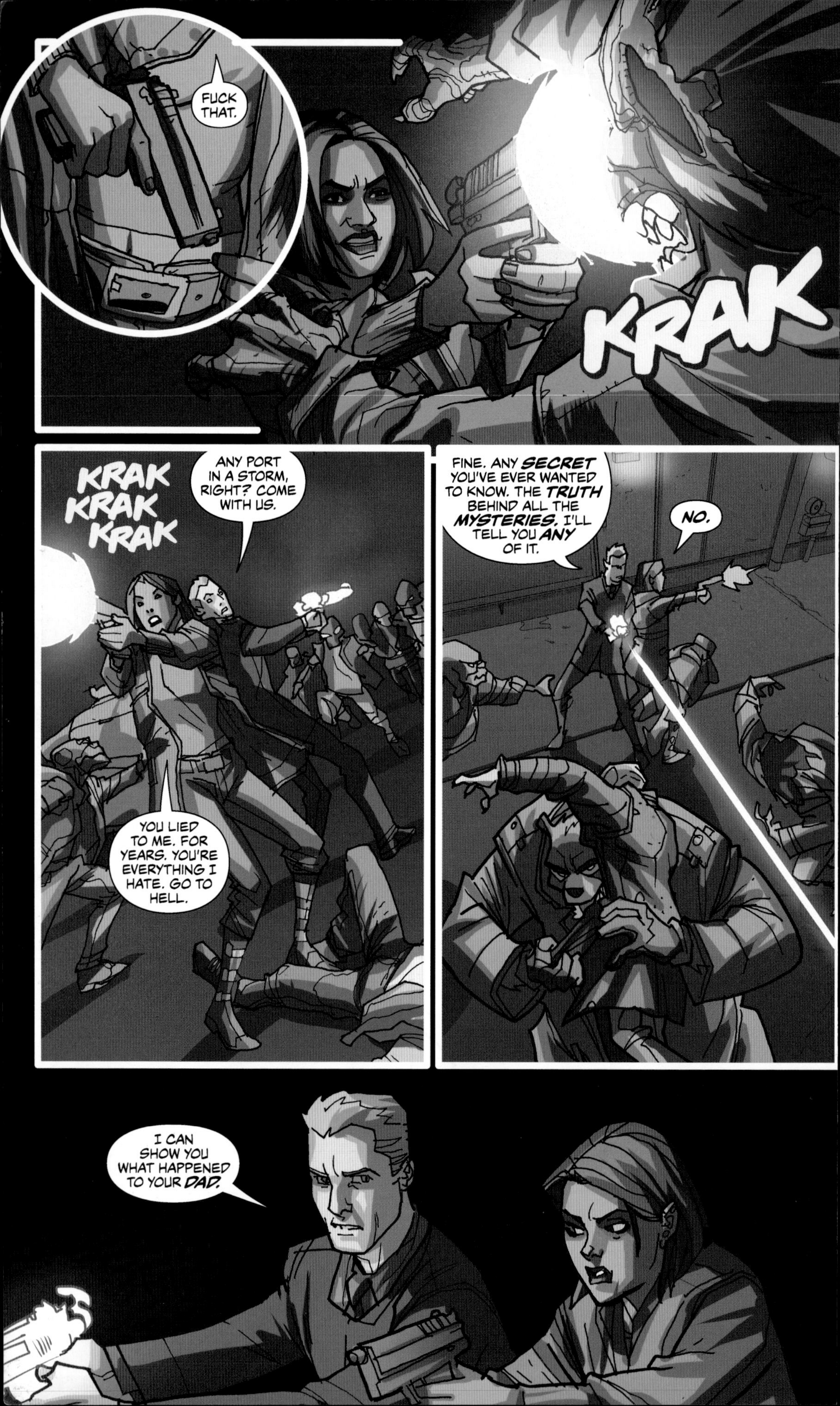
FUCK THAT.
KRAK
KRAK KRAK KRAK
ANY PORT IN A STORM, RIGHT? COME WITH US.
YOU LIED TO ME. FOR YEARS. YOU'RE EVERYTHING I HATE. GO TO HELL.
FINE. ANY SECRET YOU'VE EVER WANTED TO KNOW. THE TRUTH BEHIND ALL THE MYSTERIES. I'LL TELL YOU ANY OF IT.
NO.
I CAN SHOW YOU WHAT HAPPENED TO YOUR DAD.

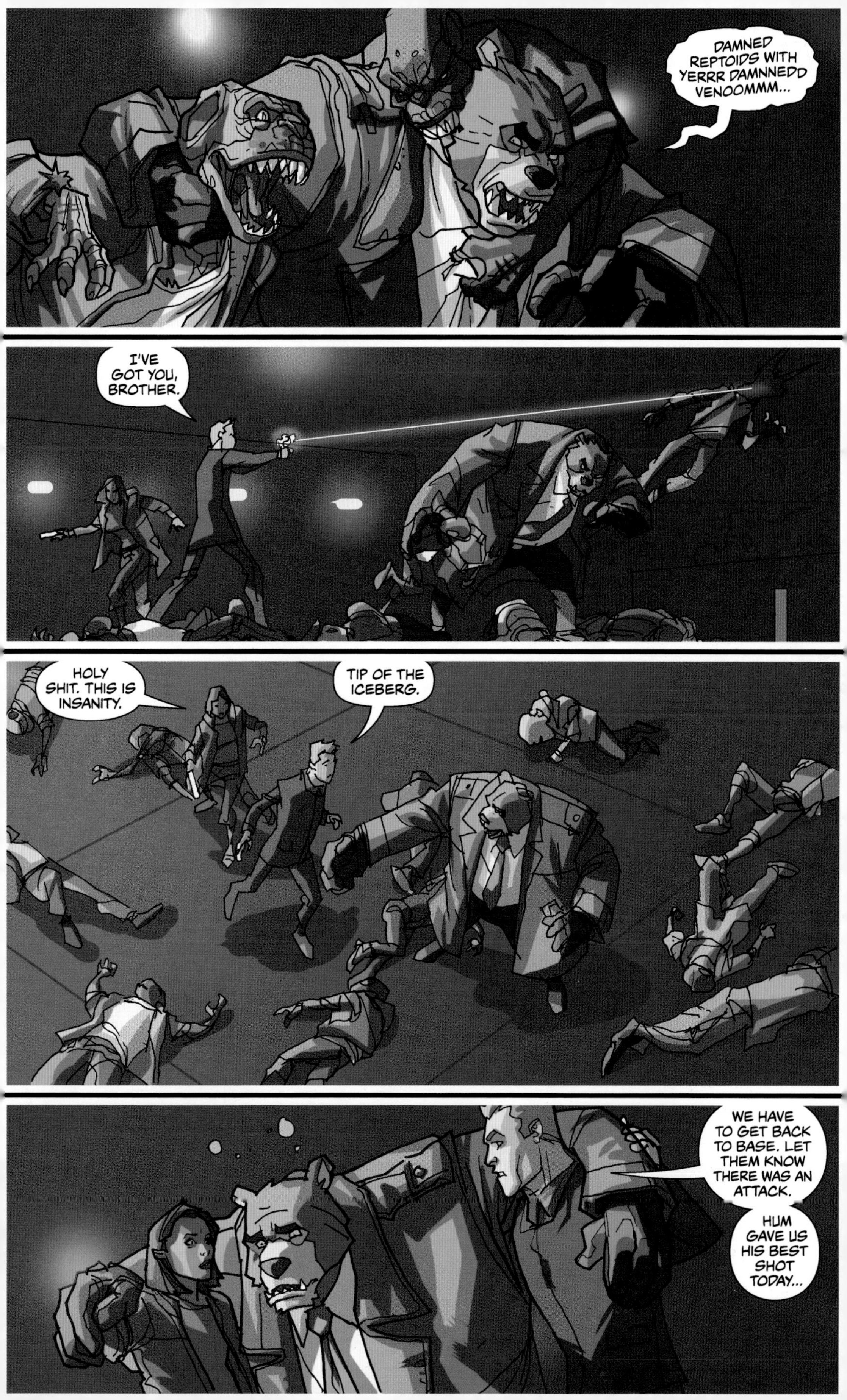
DAMNED REPTOIDS WITH YERRR DAMNNEDD VENOOMMM...
I'VE GOT YOU, BROTHER.
HOLY SHIT. THIS IS INSANITY.
TIP OF THE ICEBERG.
WE HAVE TO GET BACK TO BASE. LET THEM KNOW THERE WAS AN ATTACK.
HUM GAVE US HIS BEST SHOT TODAY...

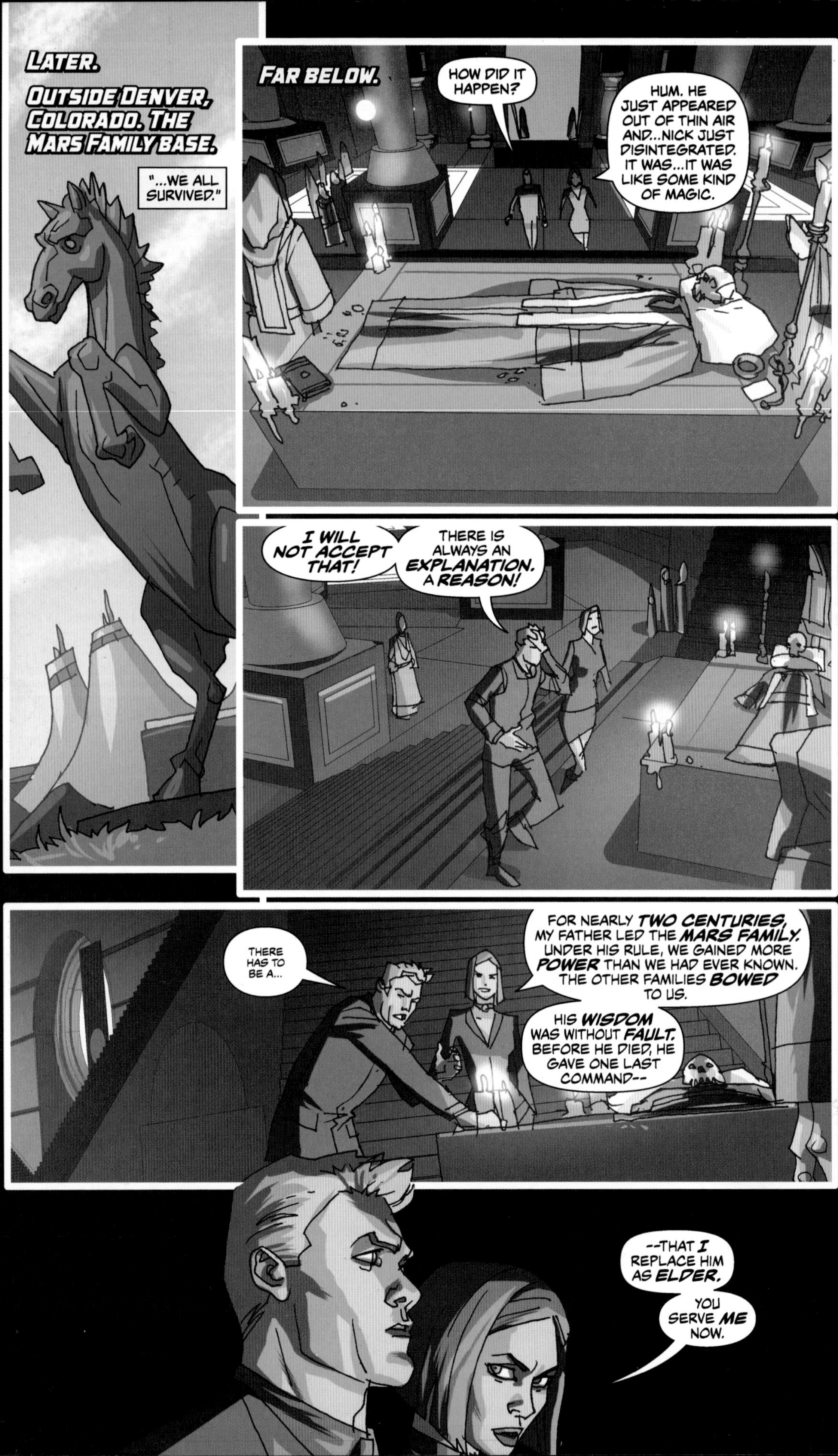
LATER.
OUTSIDE DENVER, COLORADO. THE MARS FAMILY BASE.
"...WE ALL SURVIVED."
FAR BELOW.
HOW DID IT HAPPEN?
HUM. HE JUST APPEARED OUT OF THIN AIR AND...NICK JUST DISINTEGRATED. IT WAS...IT WAS LIKE SOME KIND OF MAGIC.
I WILL NOT ACCEPT THAT!
THERE IS ALWAYS AN EXPLANATION. A REASON!
THERE HAS TO BE A...
FOR NEARLY TWO CENTURIES, MY FATHER LED THE MARS FAMILY. UNDER HIS RULE, WE GAINED MORE POWER THAN WE HAD EVER KNOWN. THE OTHER FAMILIES BOWED TO US.
HIS WISDOM WAS WITHOUT FAULT. BEFORE HE DIED, HE GAVE ONE LAST COMMAND--
--THAT I REPLACE HIM AS ELDER.
YOU SERVE ME NOW.

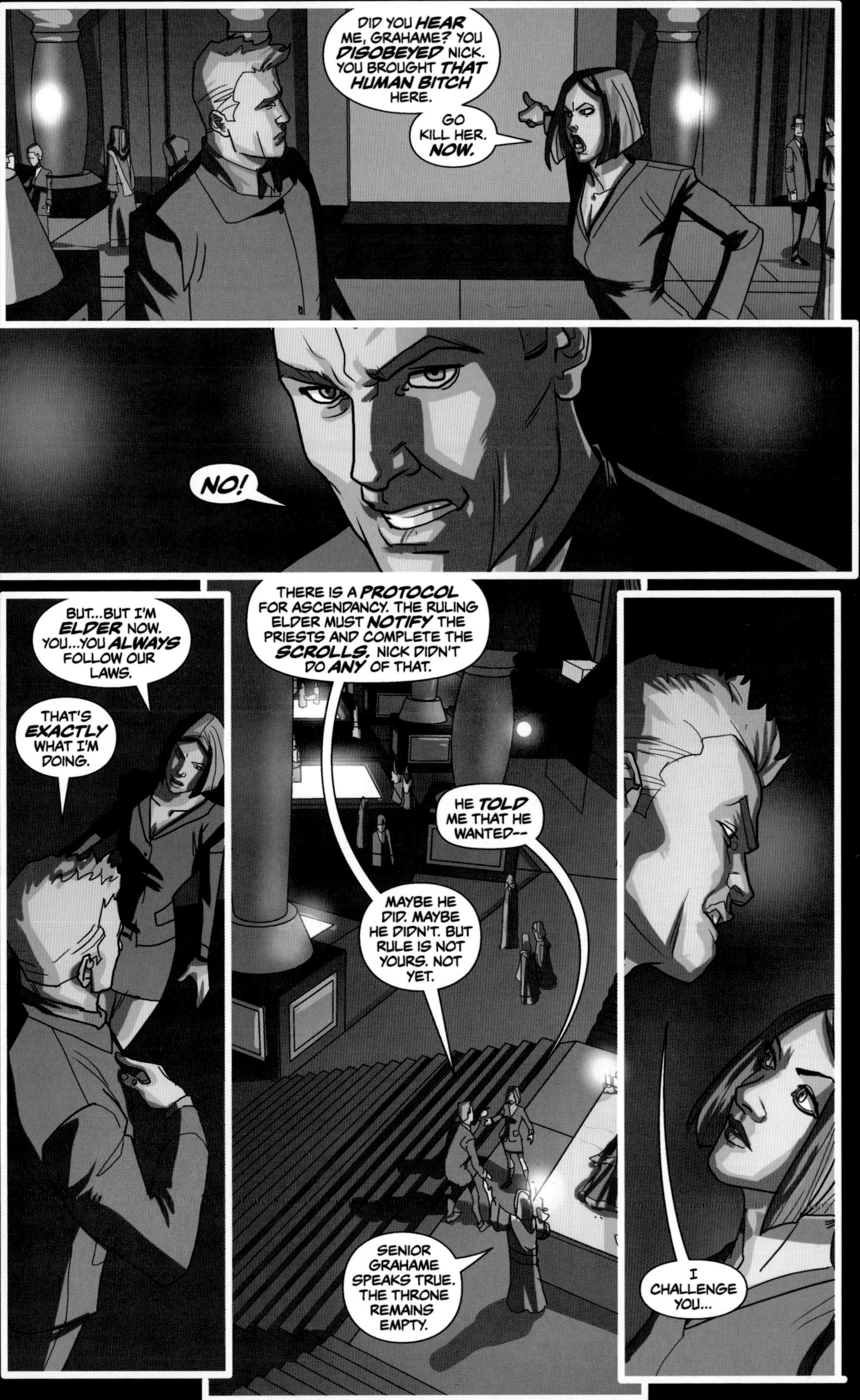
DID YOU HEAR ME, GRAHAME? YOU DISOBEYED NICK. YOU BROUGHT THAT HUMAN BITCH HERE.
GO KILL HER. NOW.
NO!
BUT...BUT I'M ELDER NOW. YOU...YOU ALWAYS FOLLOW OUR LAWS.
THAT'S EXACTLY WHAT I'M DOING.
THERE IS A PROTOCOL FOR ASCENDANCY. THE RULING ELDER MUST NOTIFY THE PRIESTS AND COMPLETE THE SCROLLS. NICK DIDN'T DO ANY OF THAT.
HE TOLD ME THAT HE WANTED--
MAYBE HE DID. MAYBE HE DIDN'T. BUT RULE IS NOT YOURS. NOT YET.
SENIOR GRAHAME SPEAKS TRUE. THE THRONE REMAINS EMPTY.
I CHALLENGE YOU...

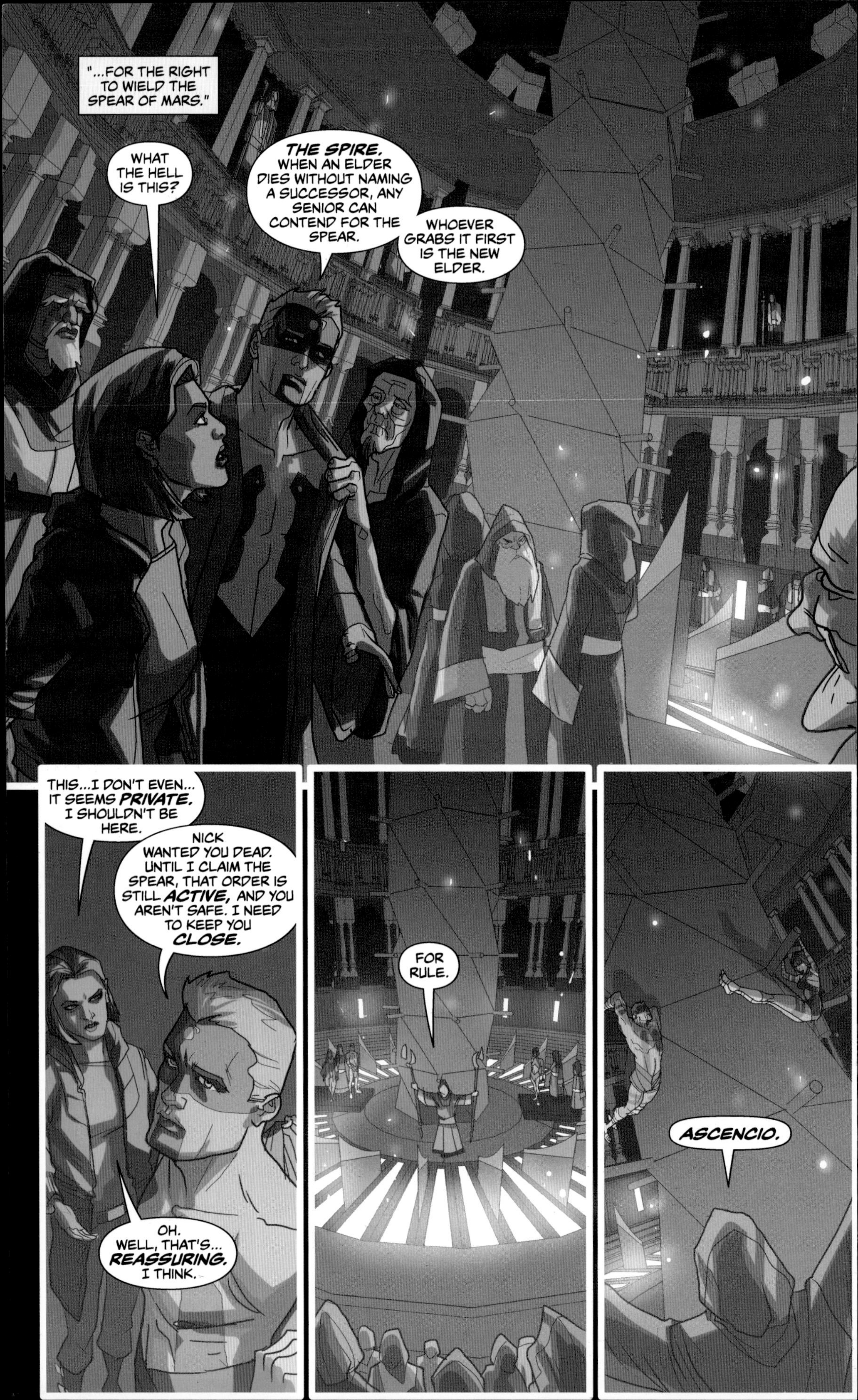
"...FOR THE RIGHT TO WIELD THE SPEAR OF MARS."
WHAT THE HELL IS THIS?
THE SPIRE. WHEN AN ELDER DIES WITHOUT NAMING A SUCCESSOR, ANY SENIOR CAN CONTEND FOR THE SPEAR.
WHOEVER GRABS IT FIRST IS THE NEW ELDER.
THIS...I DON'T EVEN... IT SEEMS ***PRIVATE.*** I SHOULDN'T BE HERE.
NICK WANTED YOU DEAD. UNTIL I CLAIM THE SPEAR, THAT ORDER IS STILL ***ACTIVE,*** AND YOU AREN'T SAFE. I NEED TO KEEP YOU ***CLOSE.***
OH. WELL, THAT'S... ***REASSURING.*** I THINK.
FOR RULE.
ASCENCIO.

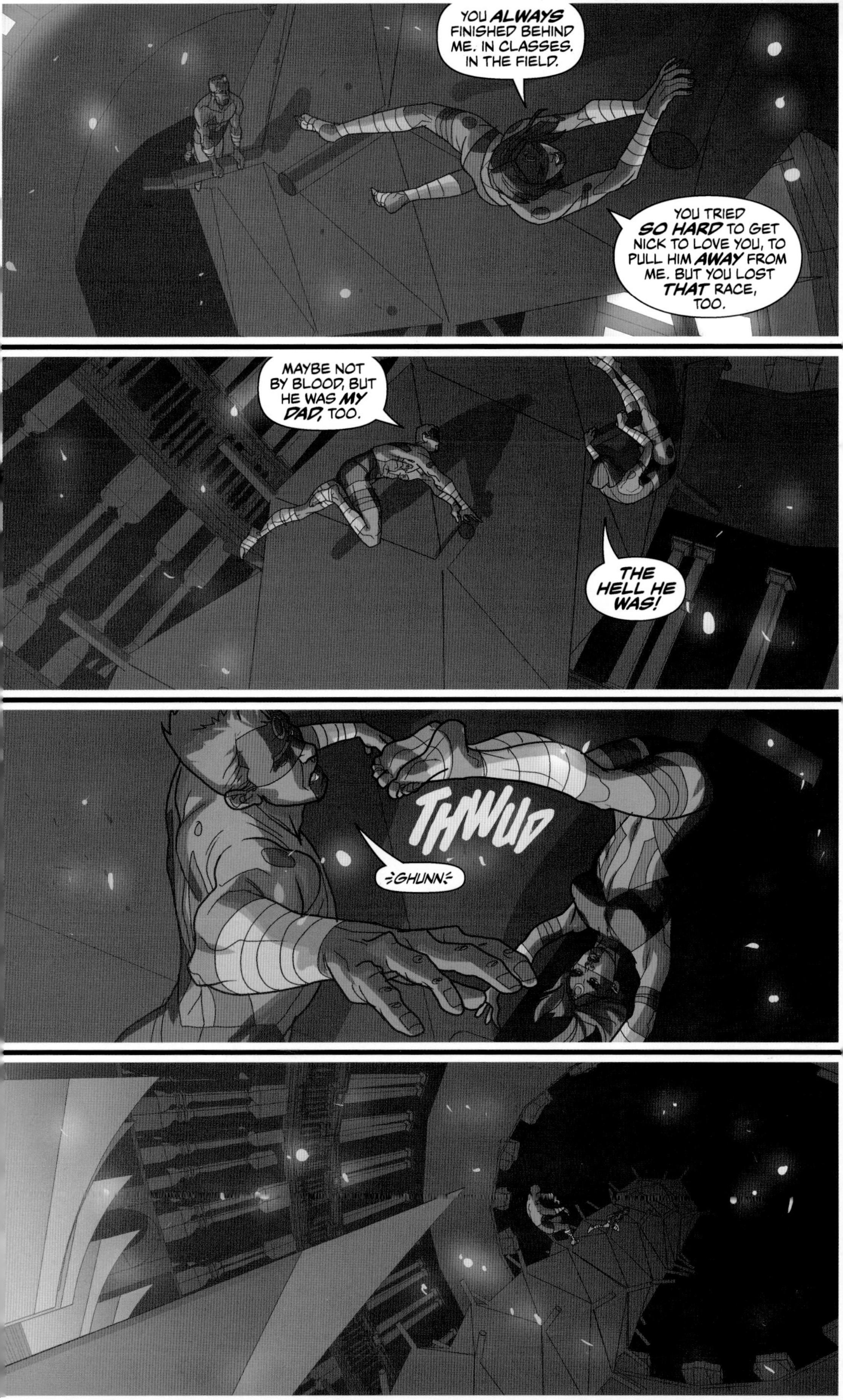
YOU ALWAYS FINISHED BEHIND ME. IN CLASSES. IN THE FIELD.
YOU TRIED SO HARD TO GET NICK TO LOVE YOU, TO PULL HIM AWAY FROM ME. BUT YOU LOST THAT RACE, TOO.
MAYBE NOT BY BLOOD, BUT HE WAS MY DAD, TOO.
THE HELL HE WAS!
THWUD
GHUNN

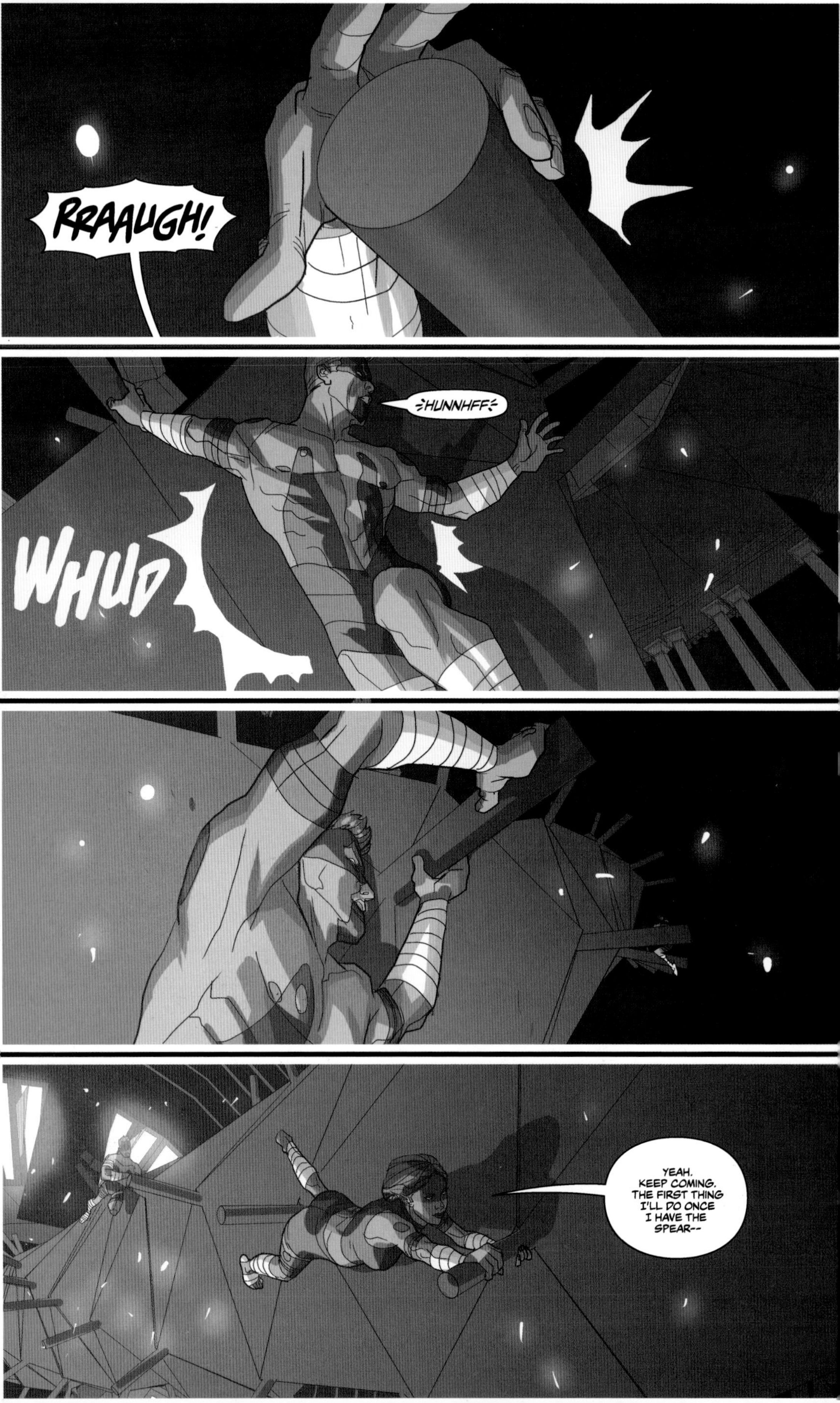
RRAAUGH!
HUNNHFF
WHUD
YEAH. KEEP COMING. THE FIRST THING I'LL DO ONCE I HAVE THE SPEAR--

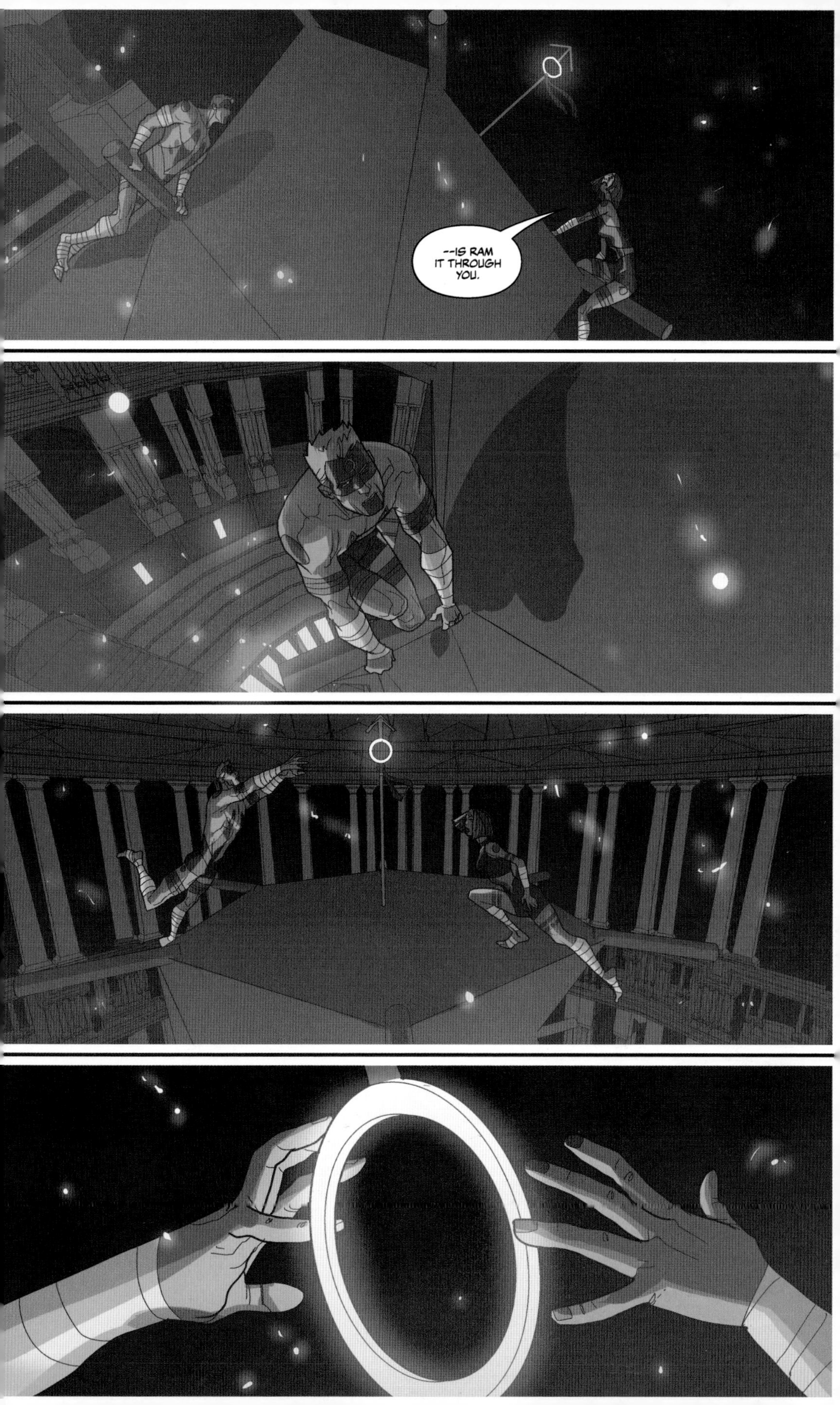
--IS RAM IT THROUGH YOU.

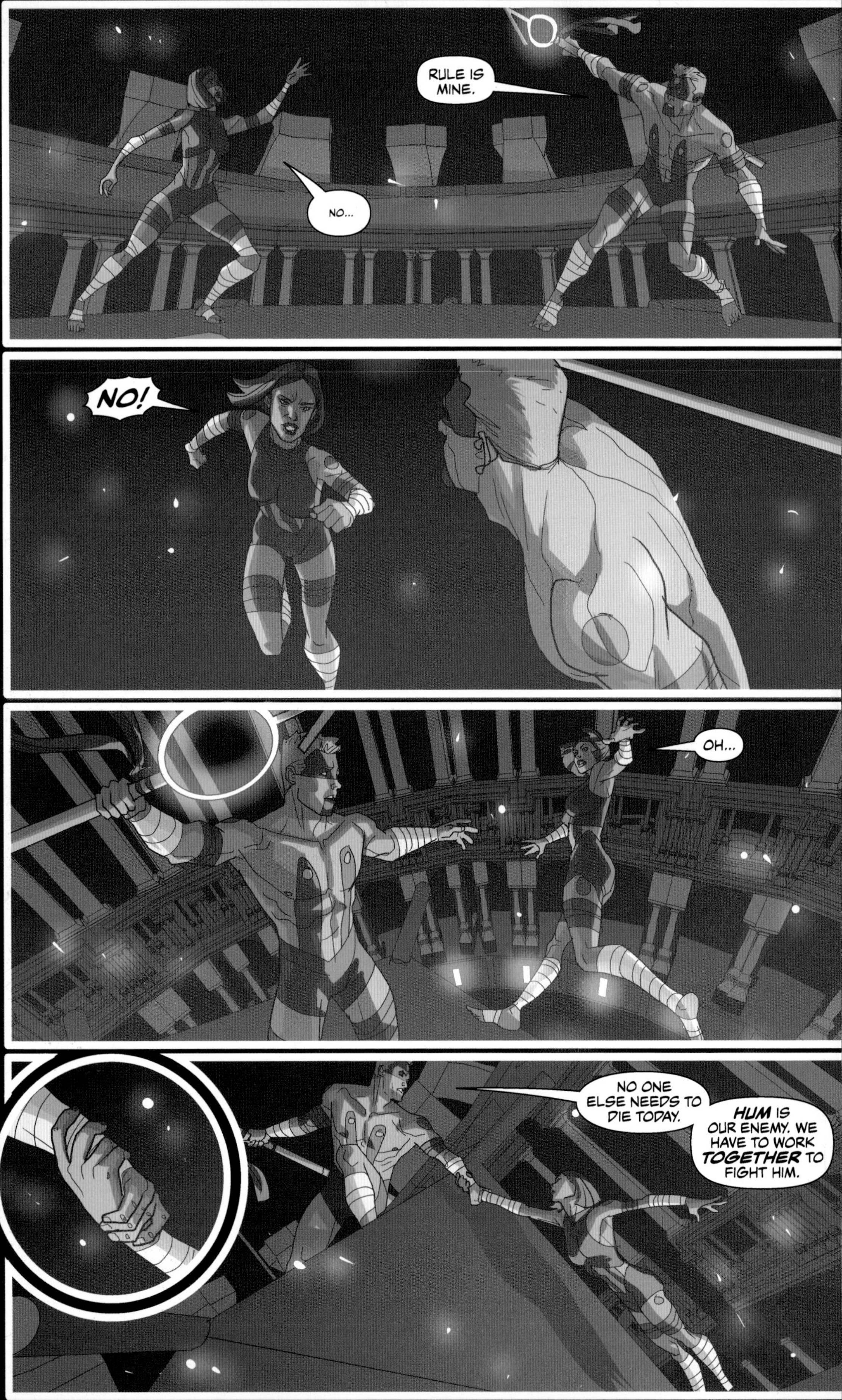
RULE IS MINE.
NO...
NO!
OH...
NO ONE ELSE NEEDS TO DIE TODAY.
HUM IS OUR ENEMY. WE HAVE TO WORK TOGETHER TO FIGHT HIM.

SO YOU'RE THE **BOSS?**

JUST OF **THIS** FAMILY. THERE ARE **EIGHT** OTHERS, EACH WITH ITS OWN ELDER.

NINE FAMILIES, CONTROLLING THE WORLD. BUGBEARS. LASER GUNS. LIZARD MEN.

IT'S **IMPOSSIBLE** THAT ALL OF THIS COULD GO ON WITHOUT PEOPLE **SEEING** IT. HOW CAN YOU HIDE **EVERYTHING?!**

WE HAVE HELP...

MEET HI LADY SPREAD RED NO SCRUB GOOD GARY HI

YUMMMS!

AAIIIIEEE!

YOU HAVE... **ALIENS?**

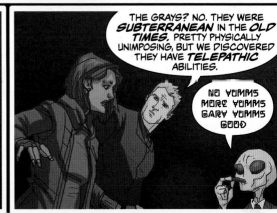

THE GRAYS? NO. THEY WERE **SUBTERRANEAN** IN THE **OLD TIMES,** PRETTY PHYSICALLY UNIMPOSING, BUT WE DISCOVERED THEY HAVE **TELEPATHIC** ABILITIES.

NO YUMMS MORE YUMMS GARY YUMMS GOOD

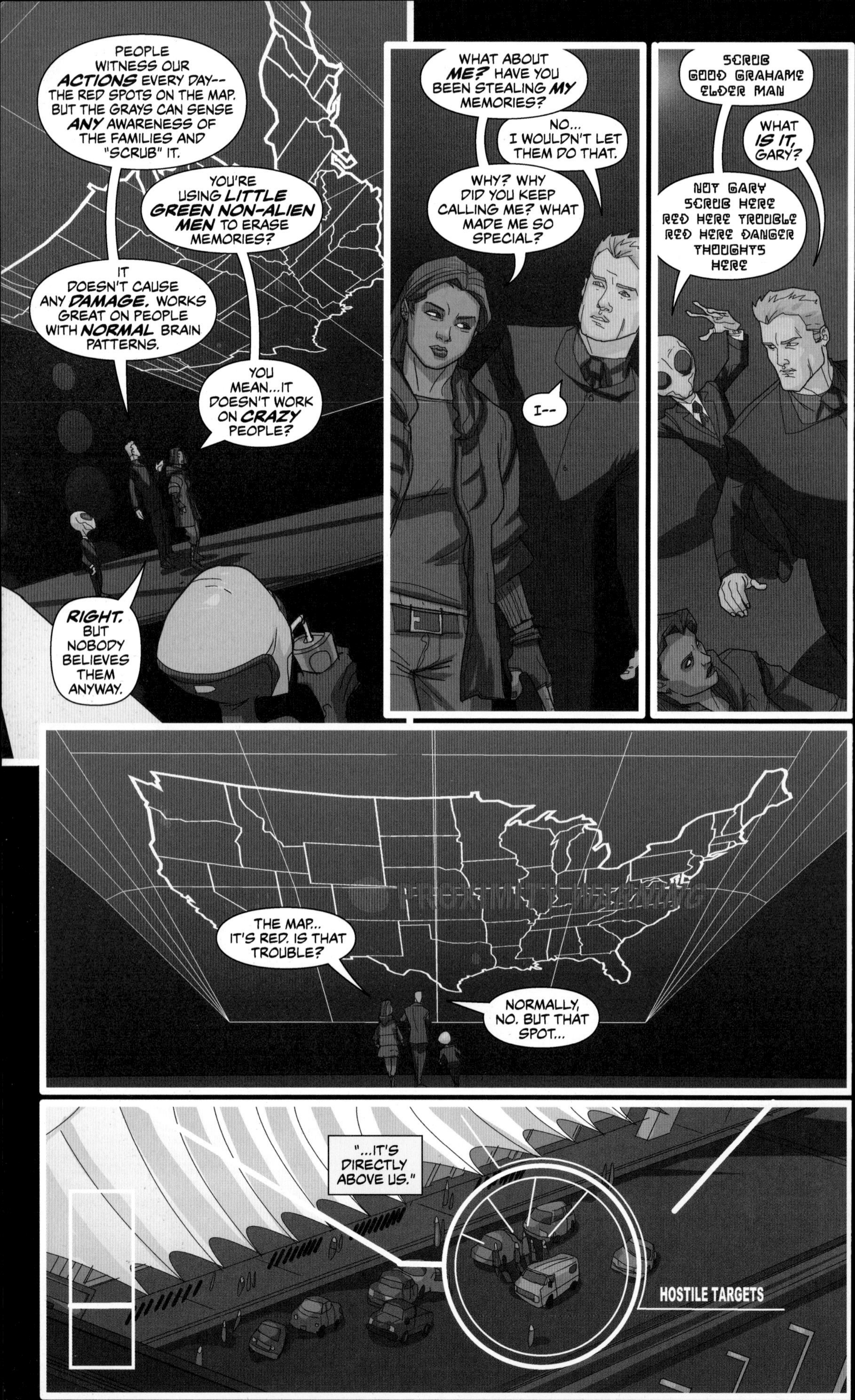
PEOPLE WITNESS OUR ACTIONS EVERY DAY-- THE RED SPOTS ON THE MAP. BUT THE GRAYS CAN SENSE ANY AWARENESS OF THE FAMILIES AND "SCRUB" IT.
YOU'RE USING LITTLE GREEN NON-ALIEN MEN TO ERASE MEMORIES?
IT DOESN'T CAUSE ANY DAMAGE. WORKS GREAT ON PEOPLE WITH NORMAL BRAIN PATTERNS.
YOU MEAN...IT DOESN'T WORK ON CRAZY PEOPLE?
RIGHT. BUT NOBODY BELIEVES THEM ANYWAY.
WHAT ABOUT ME? HAVE YOU BEEN STEALING MY MEMORIES?
NO... I WOULDN'T LET THEM DO THAT.
WHY? WHY DID YOU KEEP CALLING ME? WHAT MADE ME SO SPECIAL?
I--
SCRUB GOOD GRAHAME ELDER MAN
WHAT IS IT, GARY?
NOT GARY SCRUB HERE RED HERE TROUBLE RED HERE DANGER THOUGHTS HERE
THE MAP... IT'S RED. IS THAT TROUBLE?
NORMALLY, NO. BUT THAT SPOT...
"...IT'S DIRECTLY ABOVE US."
HOSTILE TARGETS

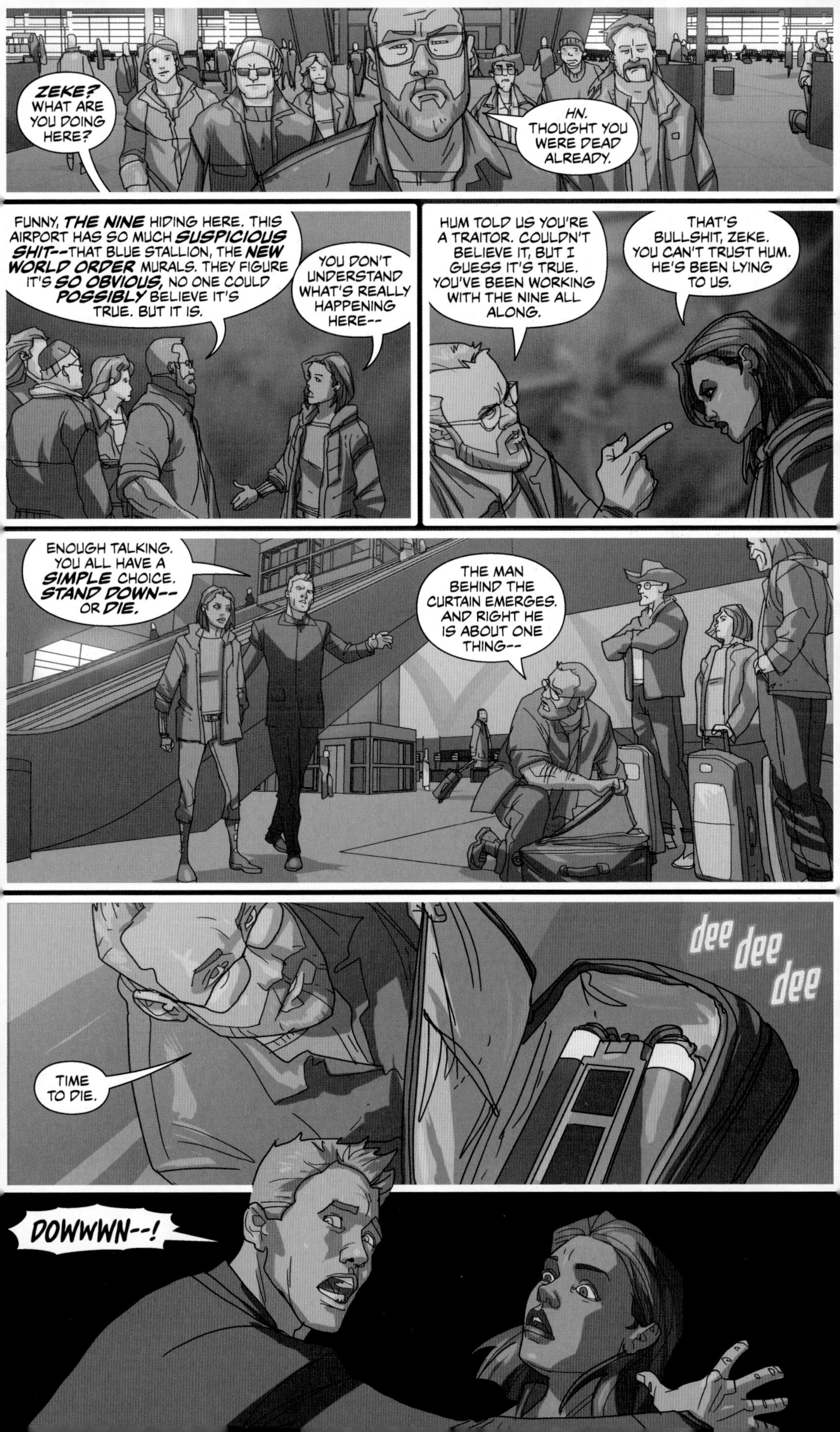
ZEKE? WHAT ARE YOU DOING HERE?
HN. THOUGHT YOU WERE DEAD ALREADY.
FUNNY, THE NINE HIDING HERE. THIS AIRPORT HAS SO MUCH SUSPICIOUS SHIT--THAT BLUE STALLION, THE NEW WORLD ORDER MURALS. THEY FIGURE IT'S SO OBVIOUS, NO ONE COULD POSSIBLY BELIEVE IT'S TRUE. BUT IT IS.
YOU DON'T UNDERSTAND WHAT'S REALLY HAPPENING HERE--
HUM TOLD US YOU'RE A TRAITOR. COULDN'T BELIEVE IT, BUT I GUESS IT'S TRUE. YOU'VE BEEN WORKING WITH THE NINE ALL ALONG.
THAT'S BULLSHIT, ZEKE. YOU CAN'T TRUST HUM. HE'S BEEN LYING TO US.
ENOUGH TALKING. YOU ALL HAVE A SIMPLE CHOICE. STAND DOWN-- OR DIE.
THE MAN BEHIND THE CURTAIN EMERGES. AND RIGHT HE IS ABOUT ONE THING--
dee dee dee
TIME TO DIE.
DOWWWN--!

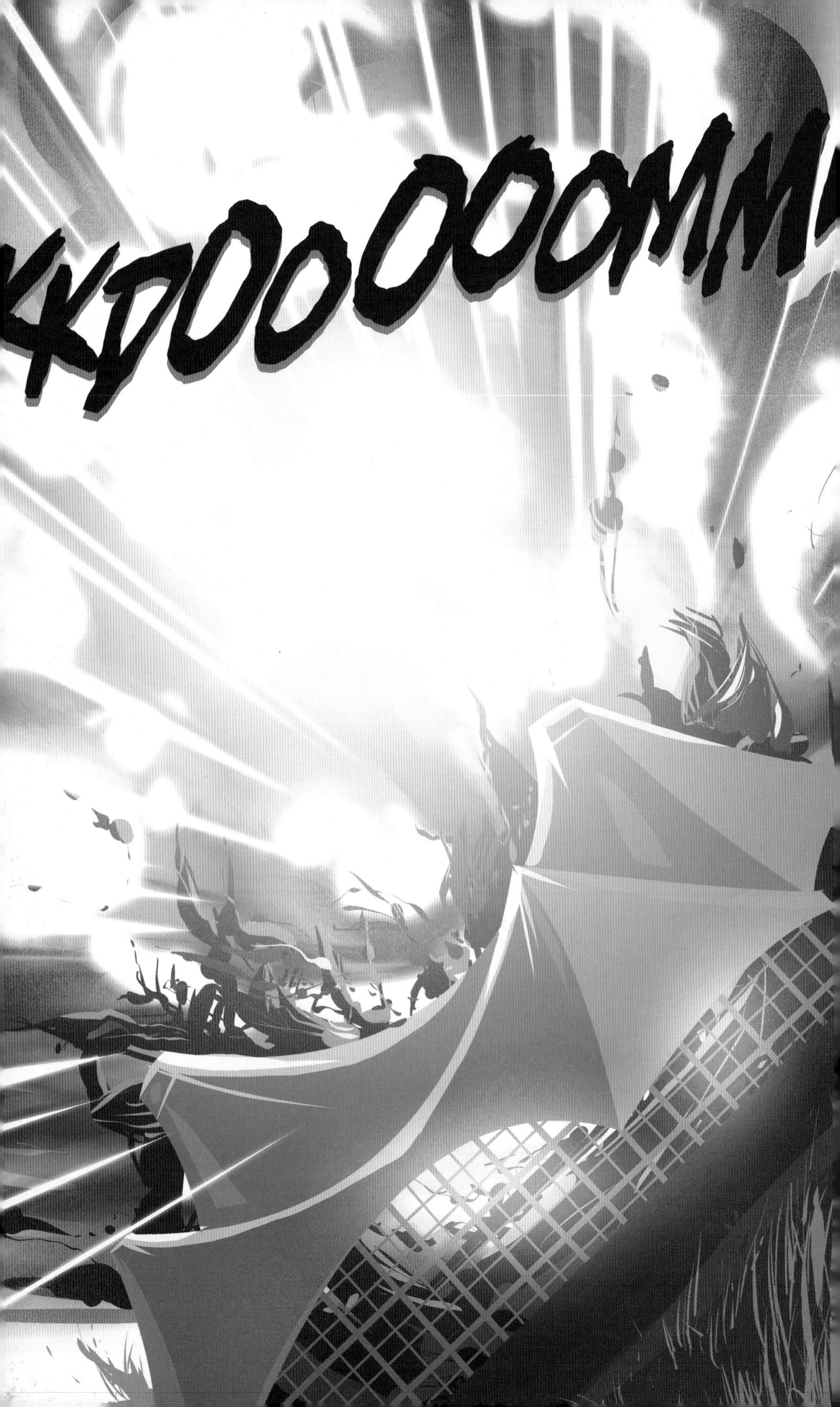
KDOOOOOMM

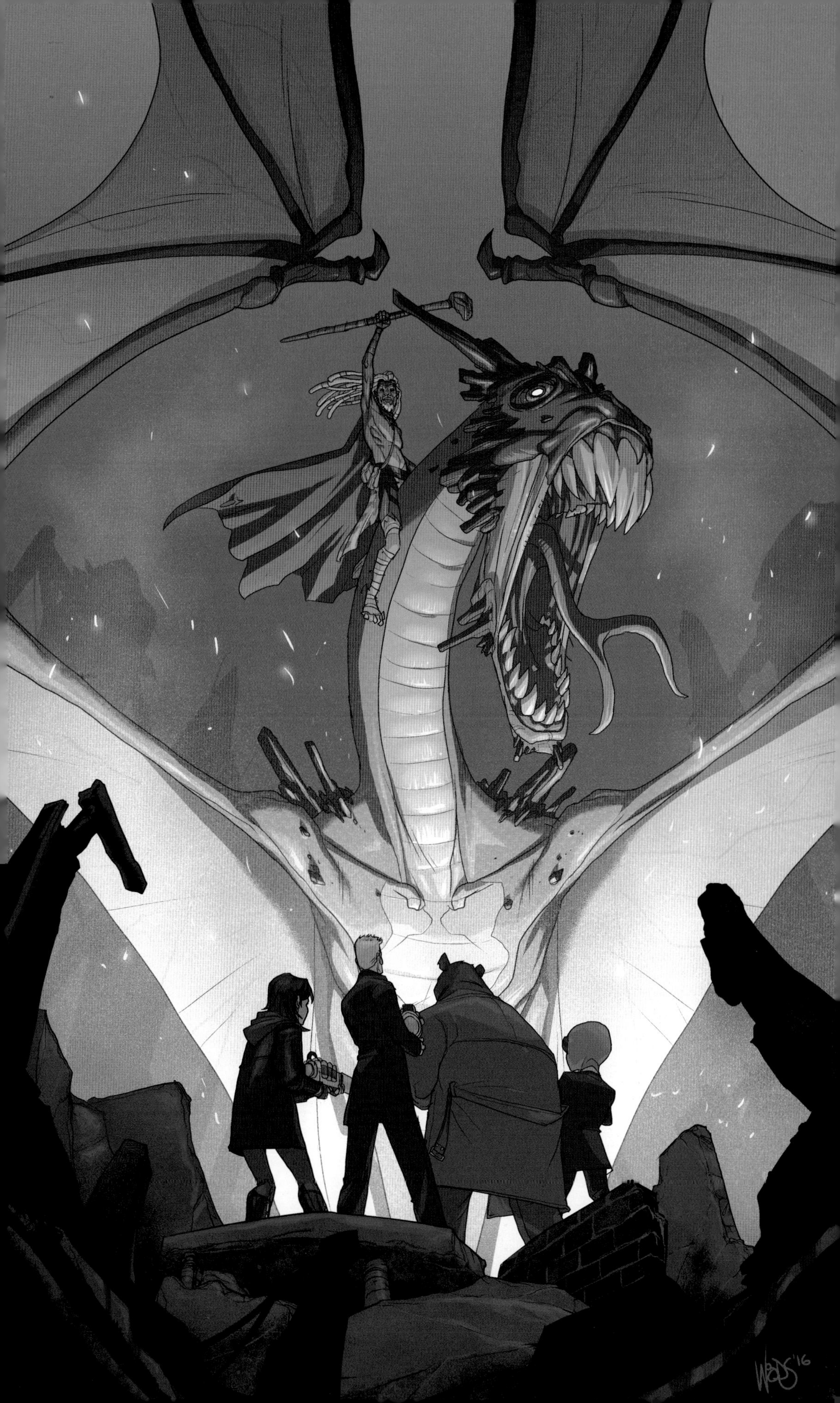

#6
CHIASMUS

LATEST REPORT FILED ON MARS FAMILY OPERATIONS.

A sudden attack on one Family leader prompted a meeting of all Families, which became an ambush at the hands of the mysterious "Hum."

Grahame, a Senior in the Mars Family, led an effort to find and kill Hum.

He and Jason, a bugbear agent, followed a lead to the Preserve, where they barely survived an attack from rogue cryptids that then broke loose.

Grahame and Jason tracked down Bela, a conspiracy theorist who had leaked a trove of information revealing Family operations.

After learning she was manipulated by Hum, Grahame and Jason returned to the Mars base . . .

. . . where they discovered that Family Elder Nick had been murdered by Hum.

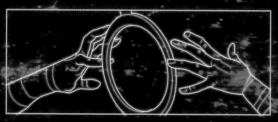

Grahame challenged fellow Senior Temple for the right to rule and defeated her, becoming Elder . . .

. . . just in time to watch as Bela's followers detonated explosives atop the Mars Family base.

"WE'RE LIVE HERE ABOVE **DENVER INTERNATIONAL AIRPORT**, WHICH SEEMS TO HAVE BEEN THE TARGET OF A **TERRORIST ATTACK**. A **DETONATION** ROCKED THE MAIN CONCOURSE MINUTES AGO, **RIPPING** IT APART.

"WE'RE STILL WAITING FOR OFFICIAL WORD ON **CASUALTIES**, BUT EVEN FROM THE SKY, WE CAN SEE **NUMEROUS DEAD** IN THE RUBBLE."

"AS OF YET, NO ORGANIZATION HAS CLAIMED **RESPONSIBILITY** FOR THE ATTACK."

HOW--?

HARD PLASMA. MY BRACELET CREATES IT.

"AFTER THE RECENT LEAK OF DOCUMENTS REVEALING THE EXISTENCE OF A SECRET GROUP THAT WAS MANIPULATING GOVERNMENTS AROUND THE WORLD, THERE HAS BEEN WIDESPREAD UNREST AND VIOLENCE. THE F.B.I. IS INVESTIGATING WHETHER THIS MIGHT BE CONNECTED."

I CAN'T BELIEVE ONE OF MY SUPPORTERS DID THIS. ALL THESE PEOPLE...THEY WERE ALL **INNOCENT**.

HUM MANIPULATED THEM TO DO THIS. JUST LIKE HE PUSHED **YOU** INTO RELEASING THE DATA. I TOLD YOU--I DON'T KNOW **WHAT** HE IS, BUT HE IS **NO HERO**.

WHY? WHY **DO THIS?** HE HAD TO KNOW THE EXPLOSION WOULDN'T **REALLY** DAMAGE YOUR FAMILY'S BASE.

THIS WASN'T THE ATTACK. IT WAS ONLY A DISTRACTION...

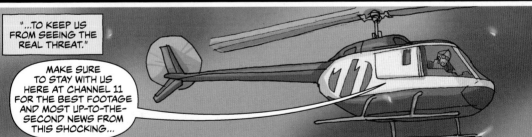

"...TO KEEP US FROM SEEING THE REAL THREAT."

MAKE SURE TO STAY WITH US HERE AT CHANNEL 11 FOR THE BEST FOOTAGE AND MOST UP-TO-THE-SECOND NEWS FROM THIS SHOCKING...

WHAT THE FLYING FUCK IS--?

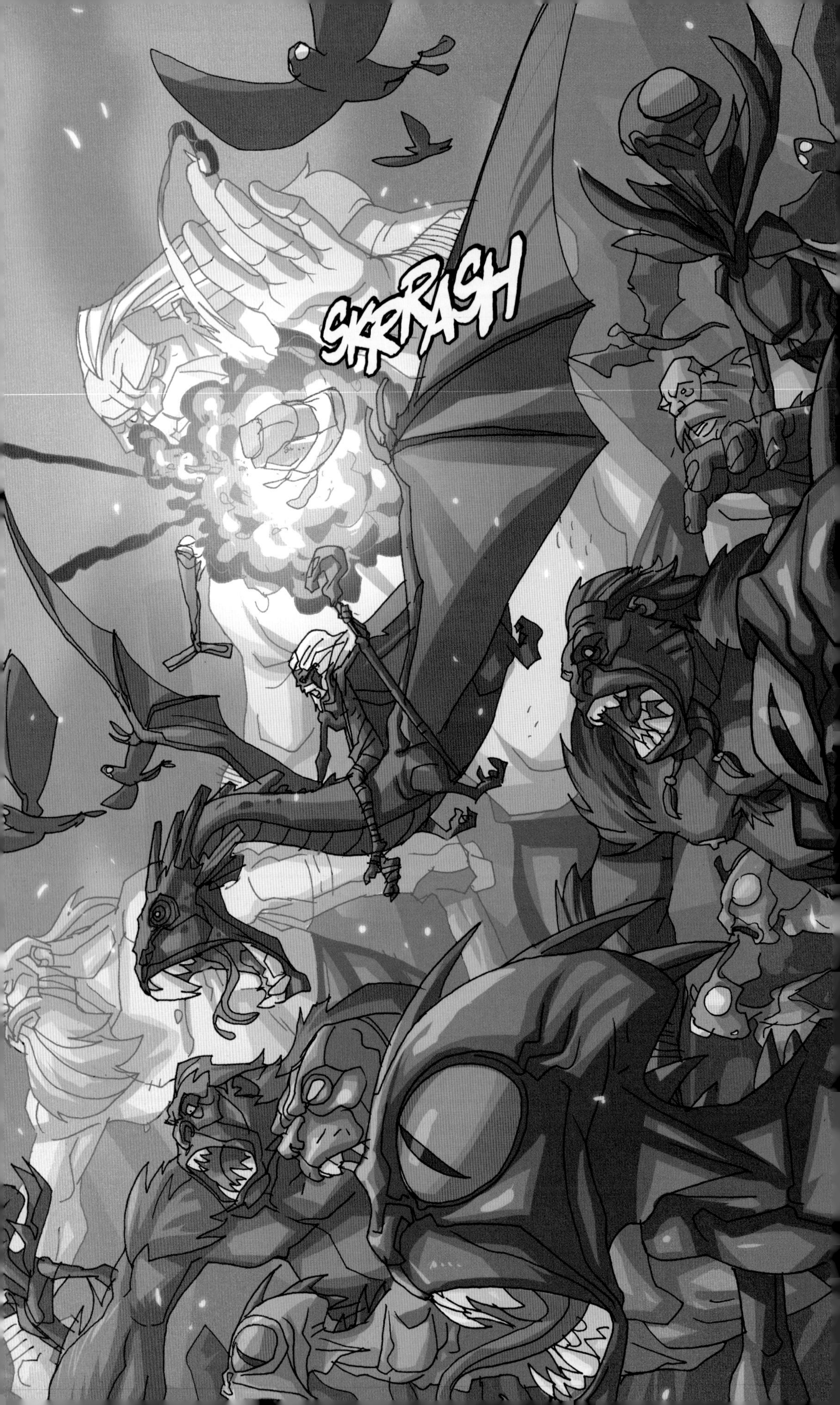
SKRRASH

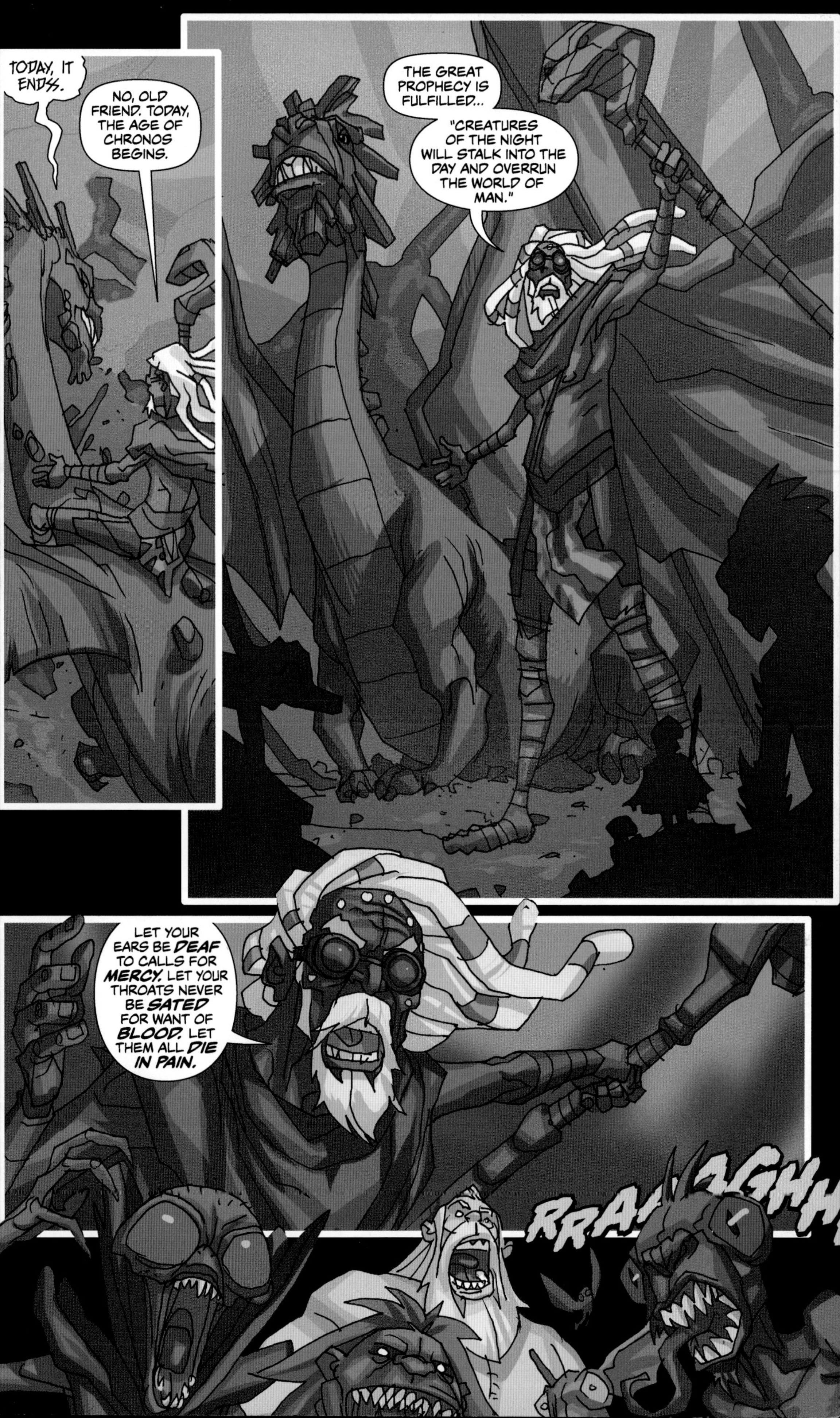
TODAY, IT ENDSS.
NO, OLD FRIEND. TODAY, THE AGE OF CHRONOS BEGINS.
THE GREAT PROPHECY IS FULFILLED...
"CREATURES OF THE NIGHT WILL STALK INTO THE DAY AND OVERRUN THE WORLD OF MAN."
LET YOUR EARS BE DEAF TO CALLS FOR MERCY. LET YOUR THROATS NEVER BE SATED FOR WANT OF BLOOD. LET THEM ALL DIE IN PAIN.
RRAAAGHH

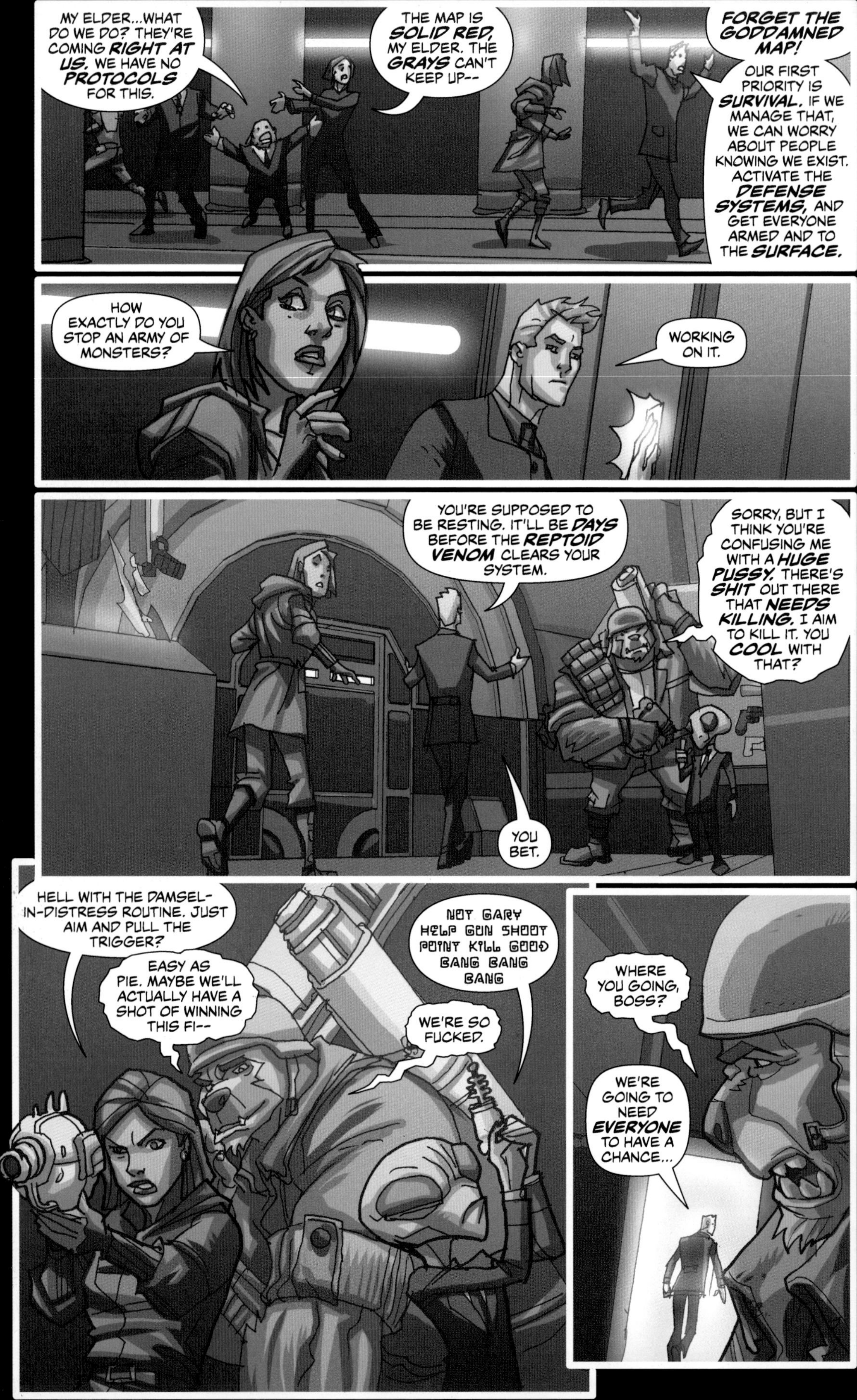
MY ELDER...WHAT DO WE DO? THEY'RE COMING RIGHT AT US. WE HAVE NO PROTOCOLS FOR THIS.
THE MAP IS SOLID RED, MY ELDER. THE GRAYS CAN'T KEEP UP--
FORGET THE GODDAMNED MAP!
OUR FIRST PRIORITY IS SURVIVAL. IF WE MANAGE THAT, WE CAN WORRY ABOUT PEOPLE KNOWING WE EXIST. ACTIVATE THE DEFENSE SYSTEMS, AND GET EVERYONE ARMED AND TO THE SURFACE.
HOW EXACTLY DO YOU STOP AN ARMY OF MONSTERS?
WORKING ON IT.
YOU'RE SUPPOSED TO BE RESTING. IT'LL BE DAYS BEFORE THE REPTOID VENOM CLEARS YOUR SYSTEM.
SORRY, BUT I THINK YOU'RE CONFUSING ME WITH A HUGE PUSSY. THERE'S SHIT OUT THERE THAT NEEDS KILLING. I AIM TO KILL IT. YOU COOL WITH THAT?
YOU BET.
HELL WITH THE DAMSEL-IN-DISTRESS ROUTINE. JUST AIM AND PULL THE TRIGGER?
EASY AS PIE. MAYBE WE'LL ACTUALLY HAVE A SHOT OF WINNING THIS FI--
NOT GARY HELP GUN SHOOT POINT KILL GOOD BANG BANG BANG
WE'RE SO FUCKED.
WHERE YOU GOING, BOSS?
WE'RE GOING TO NEED EVERYONE TO HAVE A CHANCE...

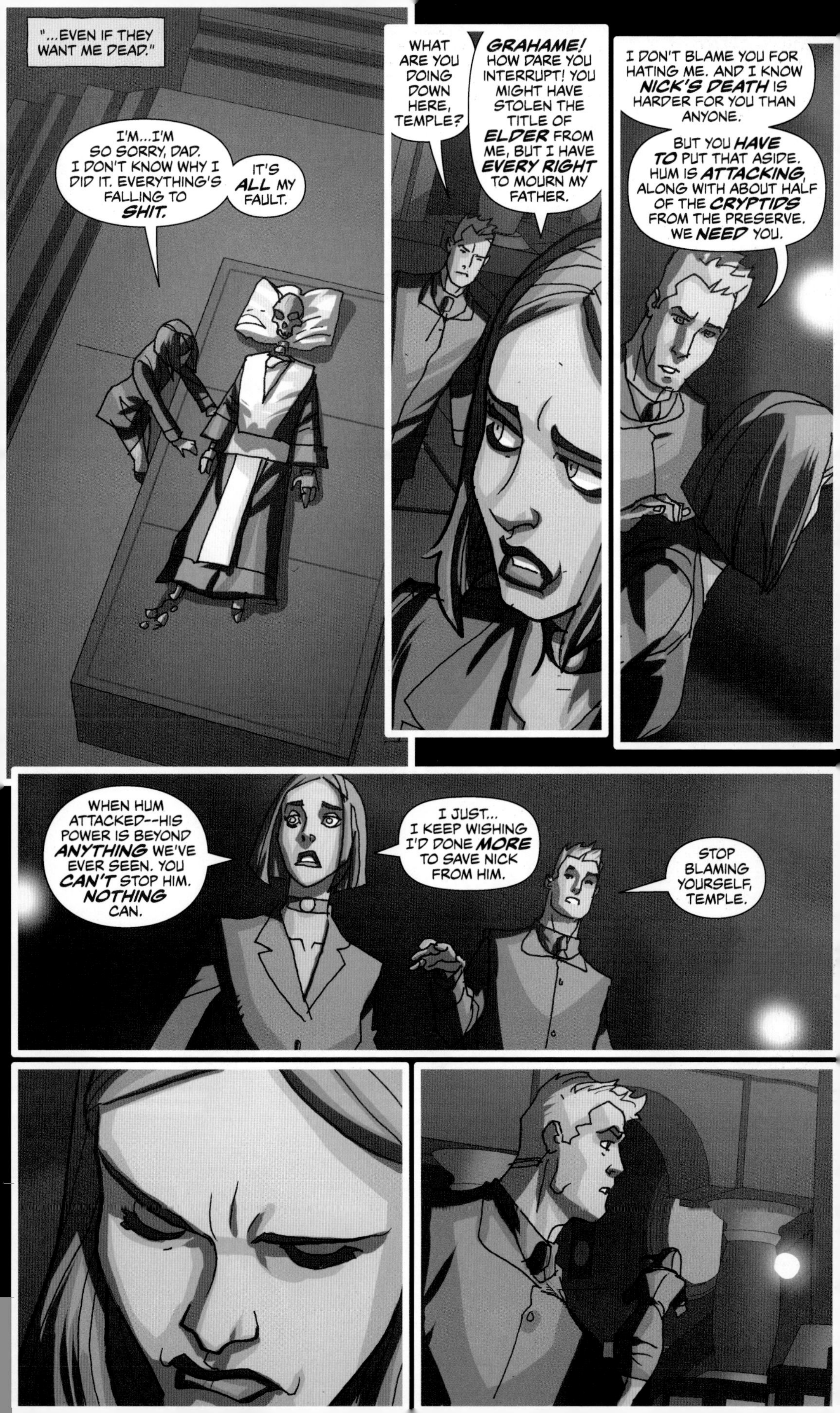
"...EVEN IF THEY WANT ME DEAD."
I'M...I'M SO SORRY, DAD. I DON'T KNOW WHY I DID IT. EVERYTHING'S FALLING TO SHIT.
IT'S ALL MY FAULT.
WHAT ARE YOU DOING DOWN HERE, TEMPLE?
GRAHAME! HOW DARE YOU INTERRUPT! YOU MIGHT HAVE STOLEN THE TITLE OF ELDER FROM ME, BUT I HAVE EVERY RIGHT TO MOURN MY FATHER.
I DON'T BLAME YOU FOR HATING ME. AND I KNOW NICK'S DEATH IS HARDER FOR YOU THAN ANYONE.
BUT YOU HAVE TO PUT THAT ASIDE. HUM IS ATTACKING, ALONG WITH ABOUT HALF OF THE CRYPTIDS FROM THE PRESERVE. WE NEED YOU.
WHEN HUM ATTACKED--HIS POWER IS BEYOND ANYTHING WE'VE EVER SEEN. YOU CAN'T STOP HIM. NOTHING CAN.
I JUST... I KEEP WISHING I'D DONE MORE TO SAVE NICK FROM HIM.
STOP BLAMING YOURSELF, TEMPLE.

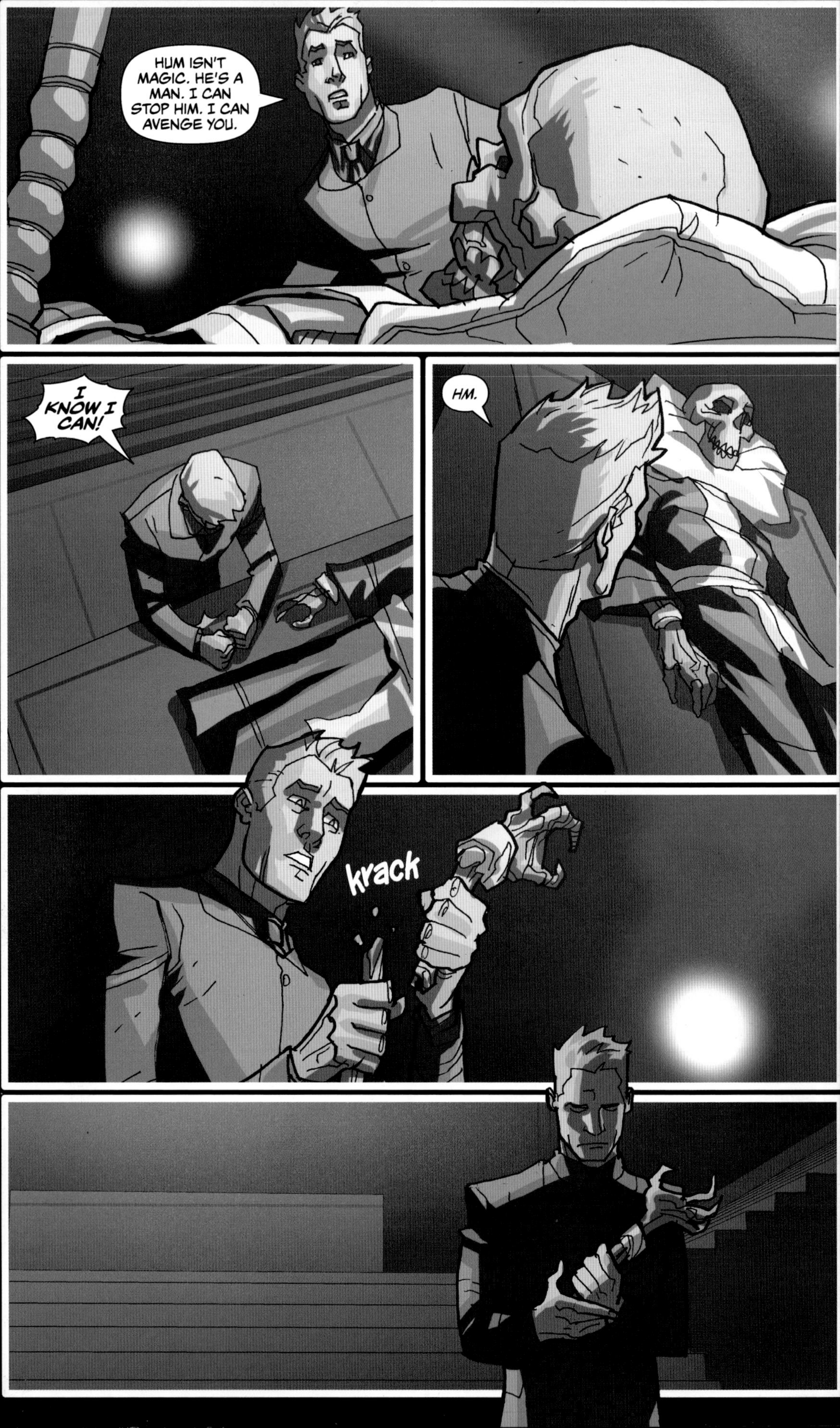
HUM ISN'T MAGIC. HE'S A MAN. I CAN STOP HIM. I CAN AVENGE YOU.
I KNOW I CAN!
HM.
krack

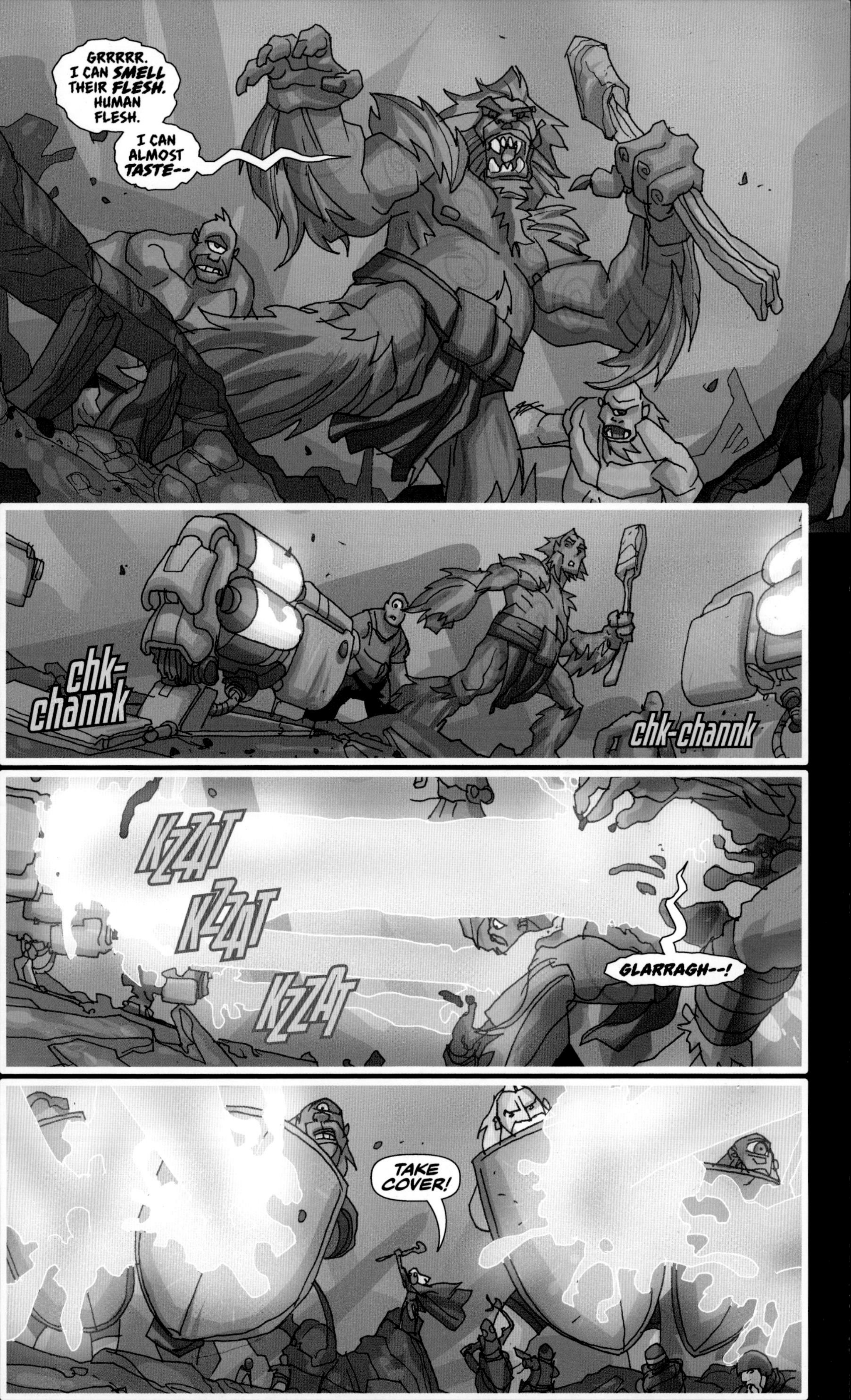
GRRRRR. I CAN SMELL THEIR FLESH. HUMAN FLESH.
I CAN ALMOST TASTE--
chk-channk
chk-channk
KZZAT
KZZAT
KZZAT
GLARRAGH--!
TAKE COVER!

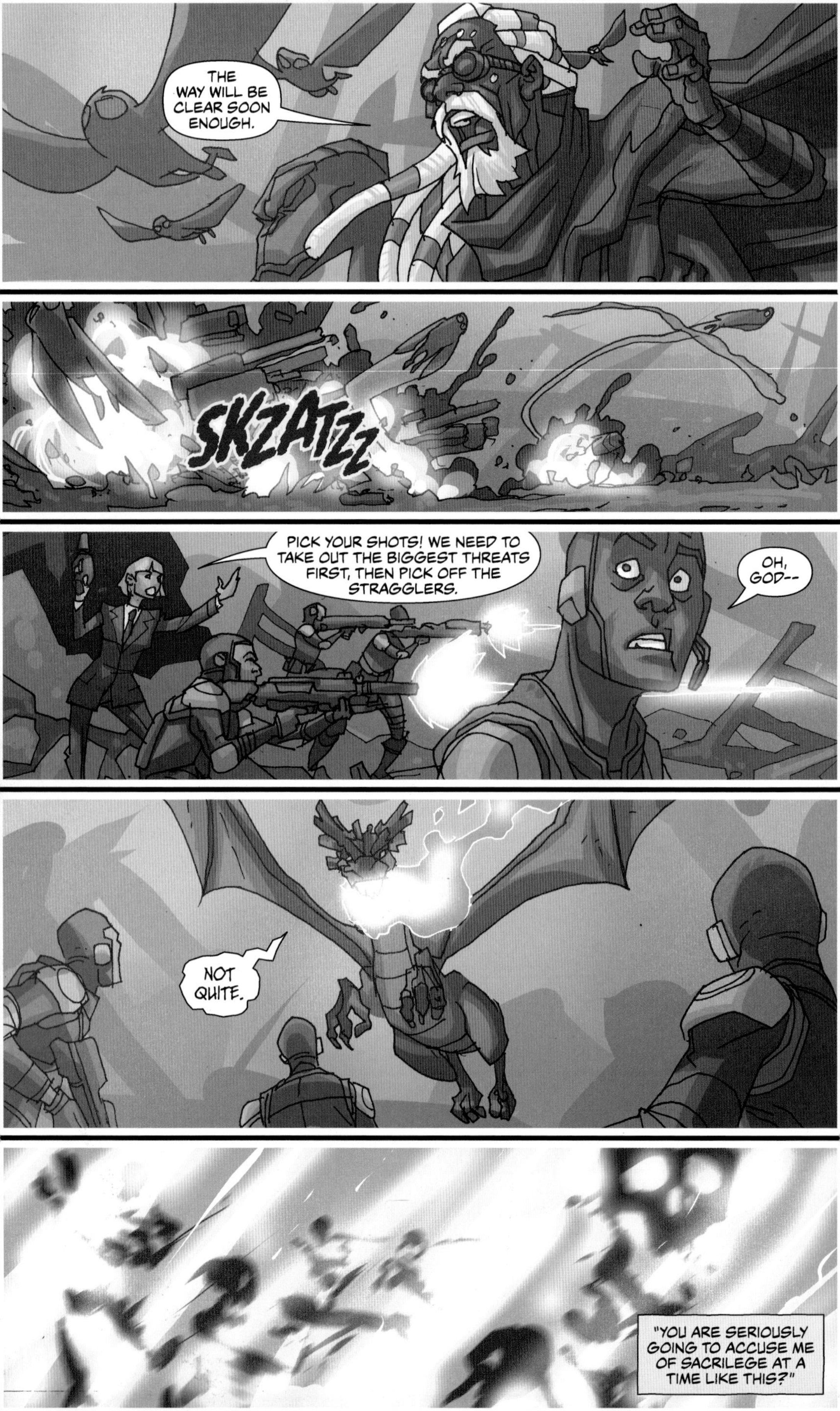
THE WAY WILL BE CLEAR SOON ENOUGH.
SKZATZZ
PICK YOUR SHOTS! WE NEED TO TAKE OUT THE BIGGEST THREATS FIRST, THEN PICK OFF THE STRAGGLERS.
OH, GOD--
NOT QUITE.
"YOU ARE SERIOUSLY GOING TO ACCUSE ME OF SACRILEGE AT A TIME LIKE THIS?"

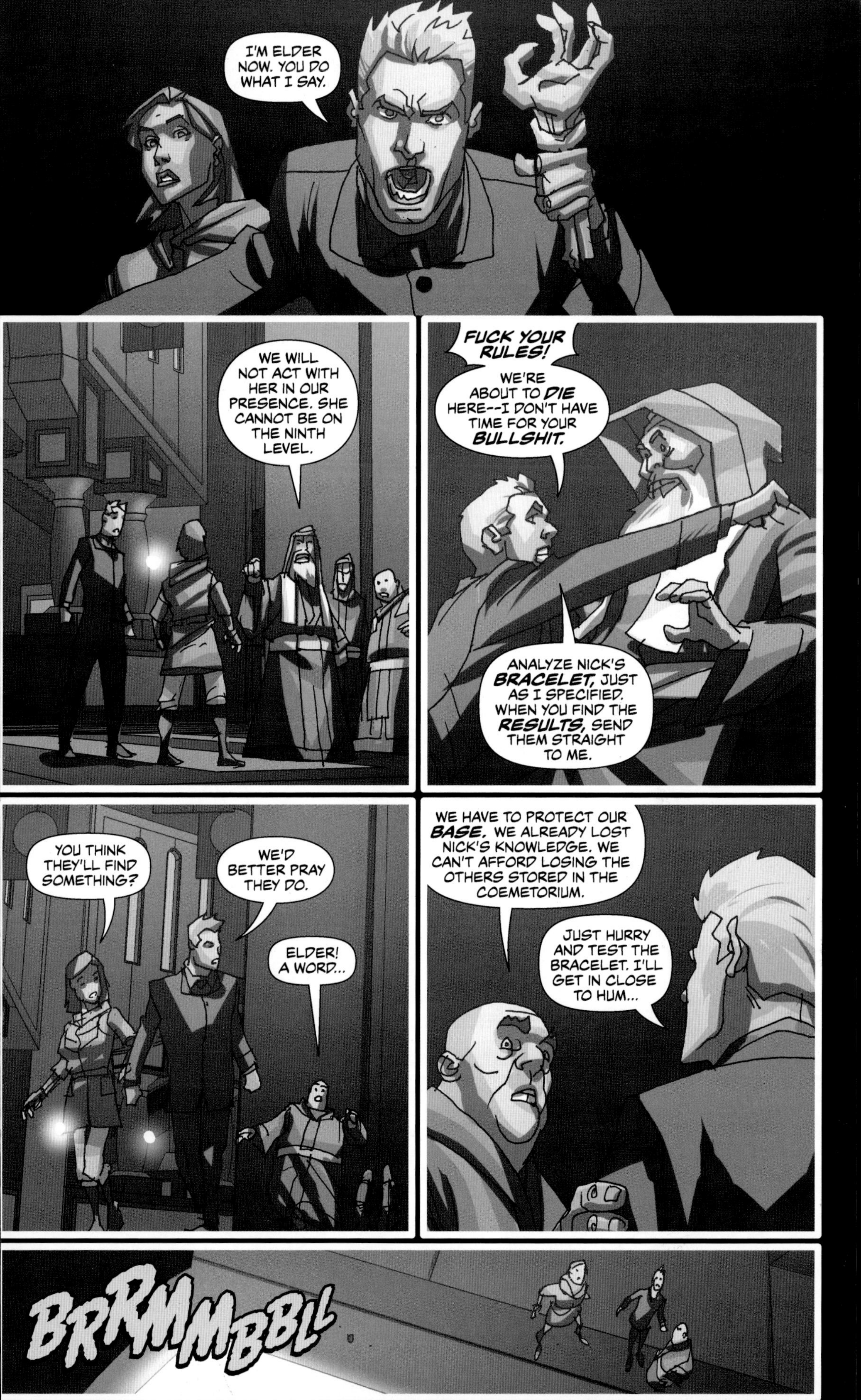
I'M ELDER NOW. YOU DO WHAT I SAY.
WE WILL NOT ACT WITH HER IN OUR PRESENCE. SHE CANNOT BE ON THE NINTH LEVEL.
FUCK YOUR RULES!
WE'RE ABOUT TO DIE HERE--I DON'T HAVE TIME FOR YOUR BULLSHIT.
ANALYZE NICK'S BRACELET, JUST AS I SPECIFIED. WHEN YOU FIND THE RESULTS, SEND THEM STRAIGHT TO ME.
YOU THINK THEY'LL FIND SOMETHING?
WE'D BETTER PRAY THEY DO.
ELDER! A WORD...
WE HAVE TO PROTECT OUR BASE. WE ALREADY LOST NICK'S KNOWLEDGE. WE CAN'T AFFORD LOSING THE OTHERS STORED IN THE COEMETORIUM.
JUST HURRY AND TEST THE BRACELET. I'LL GET IN CLOSE TO HUM...
BRRMMBBLL

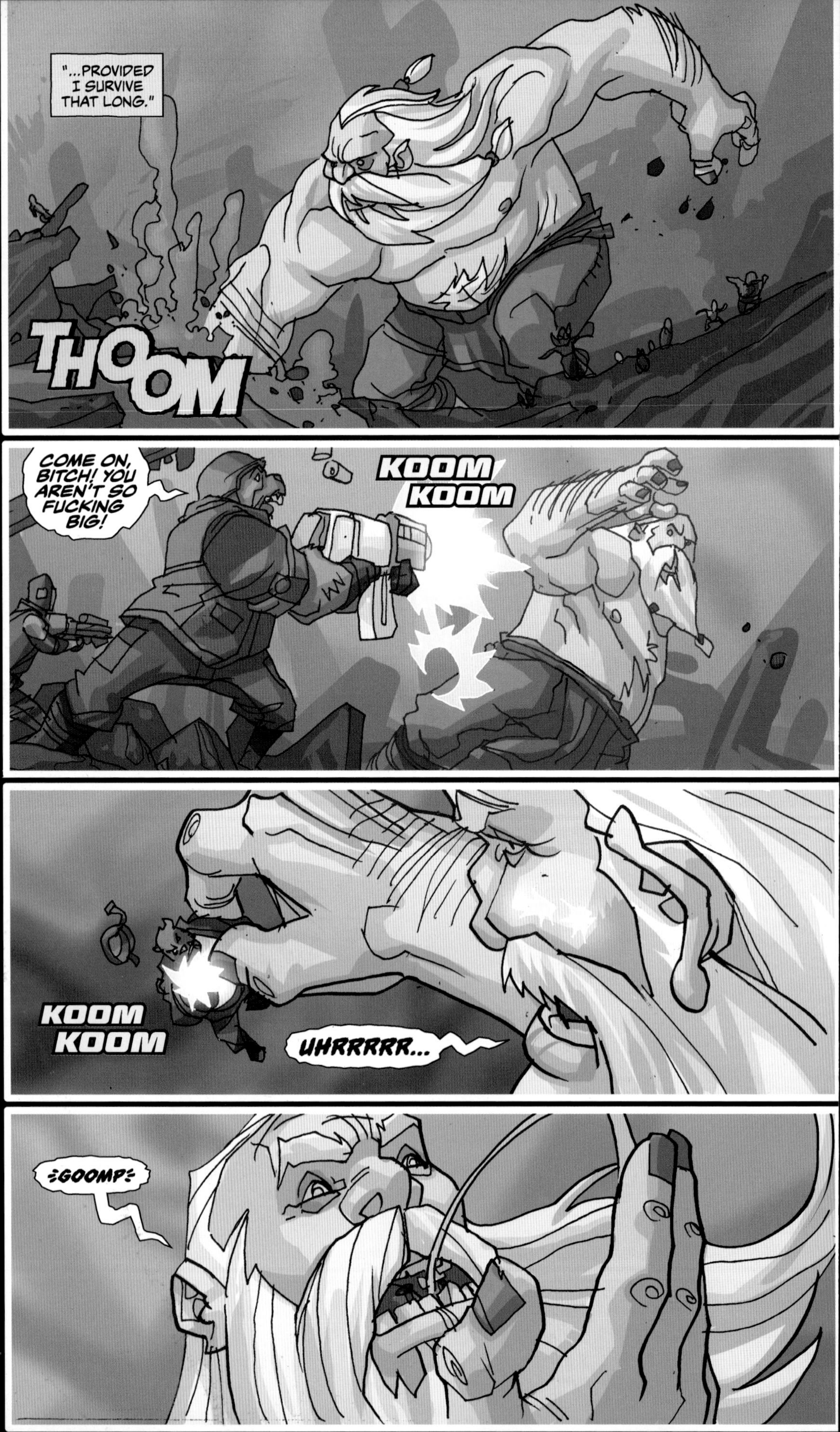
"...PROVIDED I SURVIVE THAT LONG."
THOOOM
COME ON, BITCH! YOU AREN'T SO FUCKING BIG!
KOOM KOOM
KOOM KOOM
UHRRRRR...
GOOMP

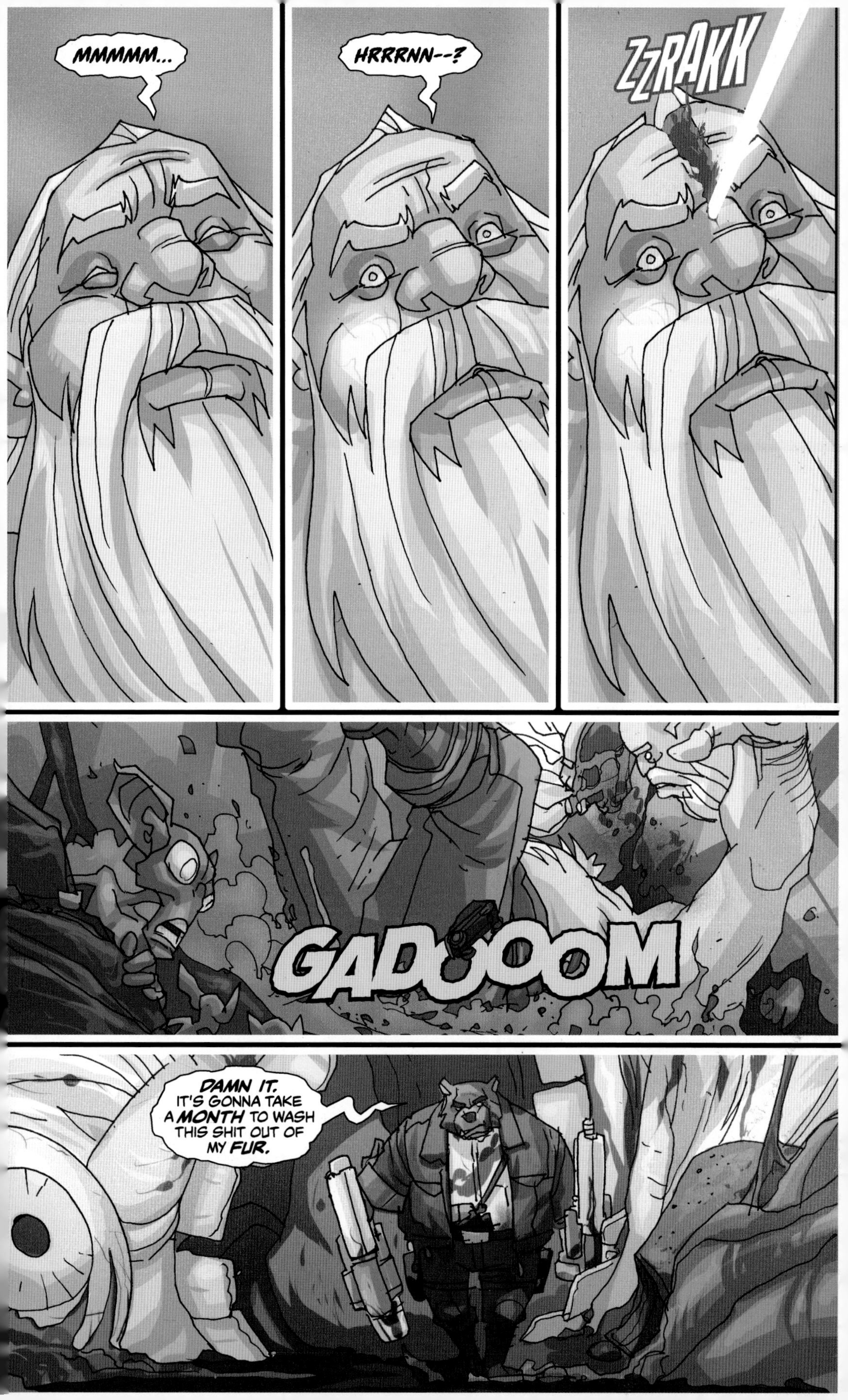
MMMMM...
HRRRNN--?
ZZRAKK
GADOOOM
DAMN IT. IT'S GONNA TAKE A MONTH TO WASH THIS SHIT OUT OF MY FUR.

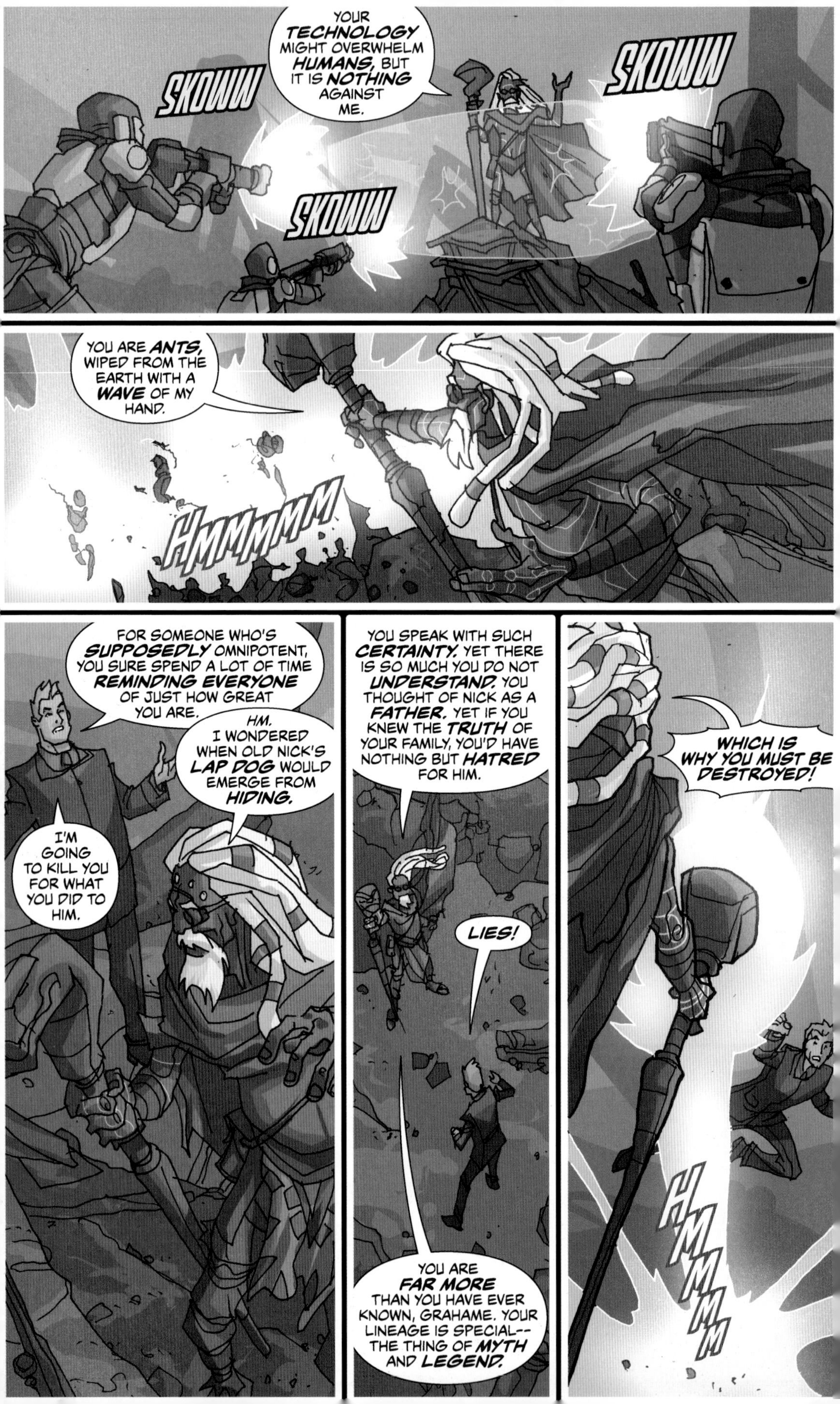
YOUR TECHNOLOGY MIGHT OVERWHELM HUMANS, BUT IT IS NOTHING AGAINST ME.
SKOWW
SKOWW
SKOWW
YOU ARE ANTS, WIPED FROM THE EARTH WITH A WAVE OF MY HAND.
HMMMMM
FOR SOMEONE WHO'S SUPPOSEDLY OMNIPOTENT, YOU SURE SPEND A LOT OF TIME REMINDING EVERYONE OF JUST HOW GREAT YOU ARE.
HM. I WONDERED WHEN OLD NICK'S LAP DOG WOULD EMERGE FROM HIDING.
I'M GOING TO KILL YOU FOR WHAT YOU DID TO HIM.
YOU SPEAK WITH SUCH CERTAINTY. YET THERE IS SO MUCH YOU DO NOT UNDERSTAND. YOU THOUGHT OF NICK AS A FATHER. YET IF YOU KNEW THE TRUTH OF YOUR FAMILY, YOU'D HAVE NOTHING BUT HATRED FOR HIM.
LIES!
YOU ARE FAR MORE THAN YOU HAVE EVER KNOWN, GRAHAME. YOUR LINEAGE IS SPECIAL-- THE THING OF MYTH AND LEGEND.
WHICH IS WHY YOU MUST BE DESTROYED!
HMMMM

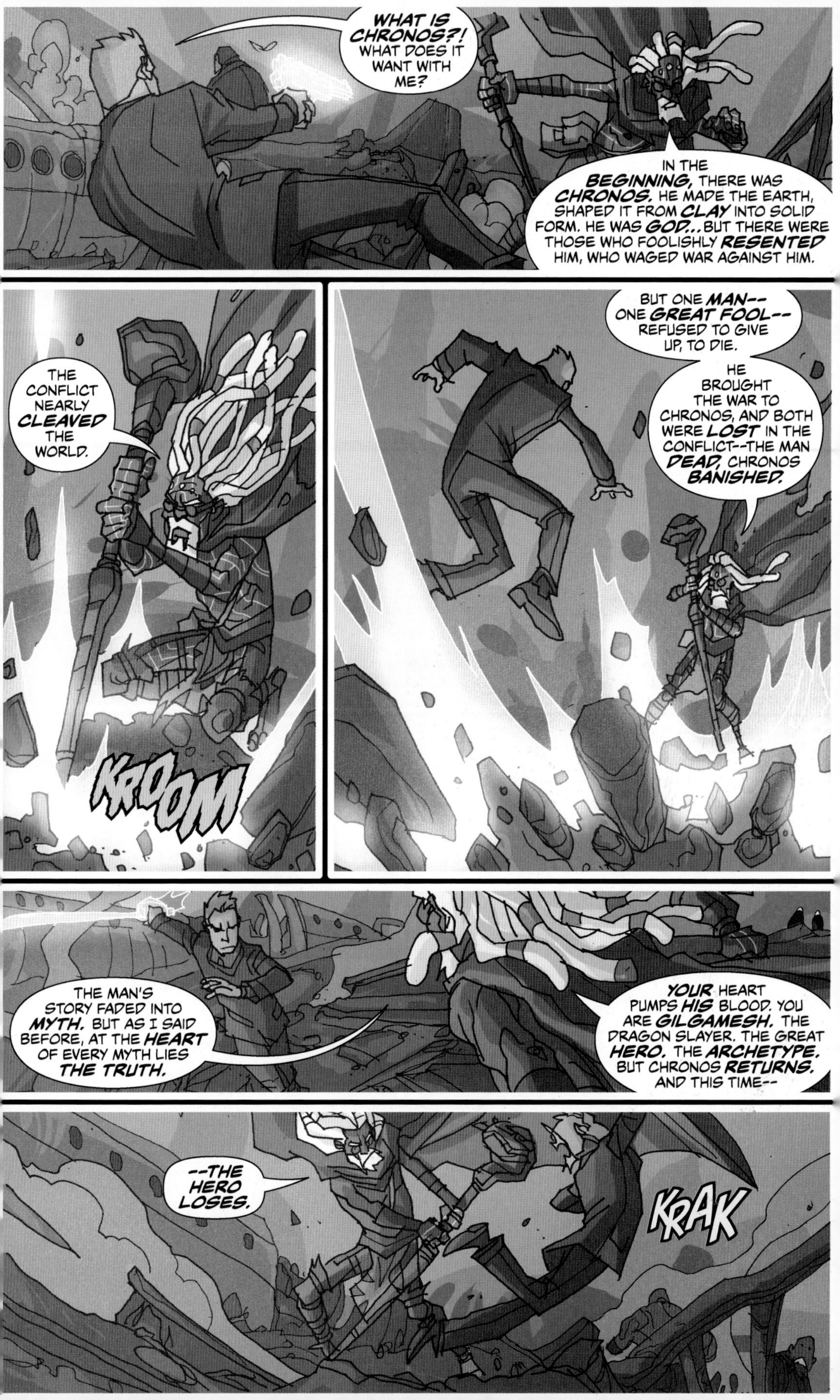
WHAT IS CHRONOS?! WHAT DOES IT WANT WITH ME?
IN THE BEGINNING, THERE WAS CHRONOS. HE MADE THE EARTH, SHAPED IT FROM CLAY INTO SOLID FORM. HE WAS GOD... BUT THERE WERE THOSE WHO FOOLISHLY RESENTED HIM, WHO WAGED WAR AGAINST HIM.
THE CONFLICT NEARLY CLEAVED THE WORLD.
KROOM
BUT ONE MAN-- ONE GREAT FOOL-- REFUSED TO GIVE UP, TO DIE.
HE BROUGHT THE WAR TO CHRONOS, AND BOTH WERE LOST IN THE CONFLICT--THE MAN DEAD, CHRONOS BANISHED.
THE MAN'S STORY FADED INTO MYTH. BUT AS I SAID BEFORE, AT THE HEART OF EVERY MYTH LIES THE TRUTH.
YOUR HEART PUMPS HIS BLOOD. YOU ARE GILGAMESH. THE DRAGON SLAYER. THE GREAT HERO. THE ARCHETYPE. BUT CHRONOS RETURNS. AND THIS TIME--
--THE HERO LOSES.
KRAK

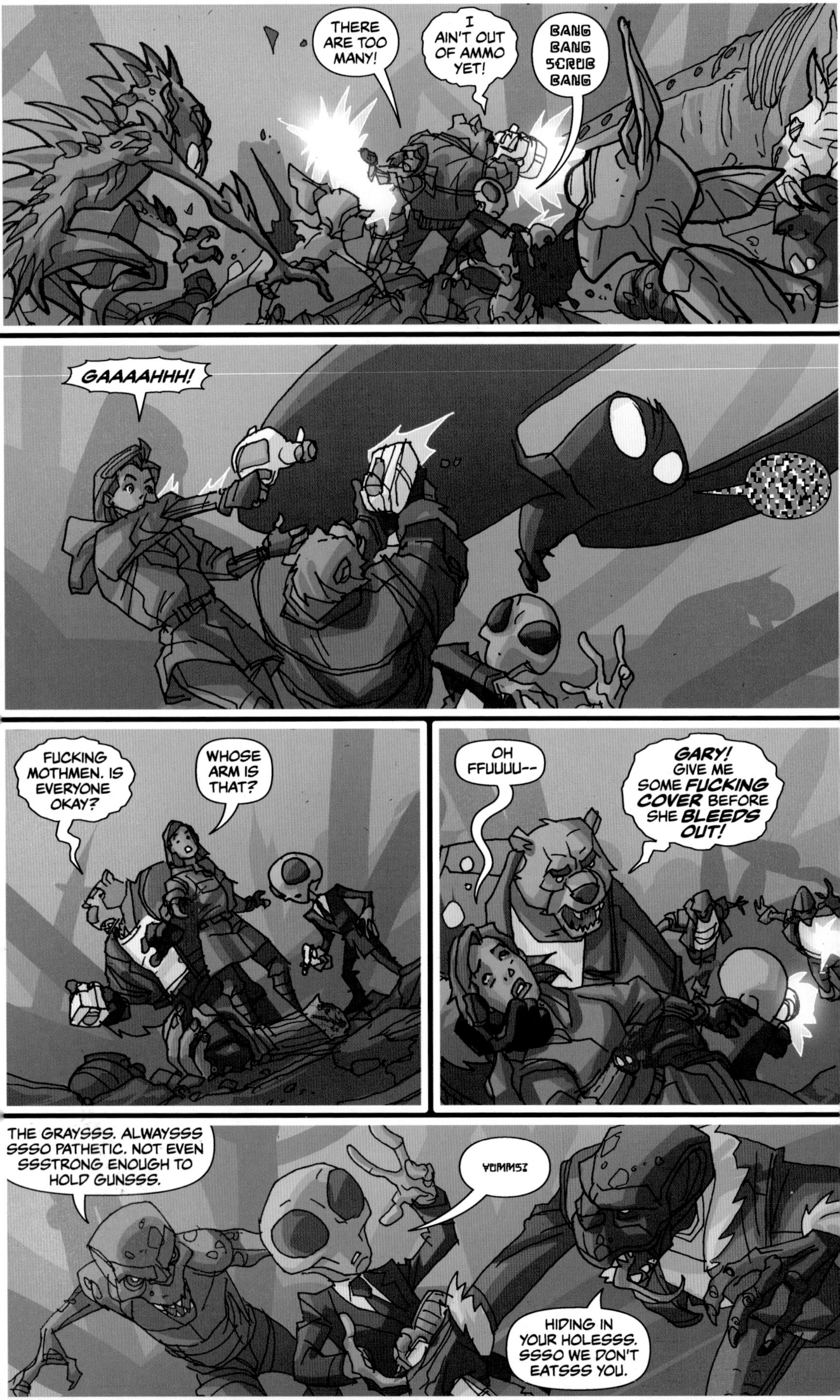
THERE ARE TOO MANY!
I AIN'T OUT OF AMMO YET!
BANG BANG SCRUB BANG
GAAAAHHH!
FUCKING MOTHMEN. IS EVERYONE OKAY?
WHOSE ARM IS THAT?
OH FFUUUU--
GARY! GIVE ME SOME FUCKING COVER BEFORE SHE BLEEDS OUT!
THE GRAYSSS. ALWAYSSS SSSO PATHETIC. NOT EVEN SSSTRONG ENOUGH TO HOLD GUNSSS.
HIDING IN YOUR HOLESSS. SSSO WE DON'T EATSSS YOU.

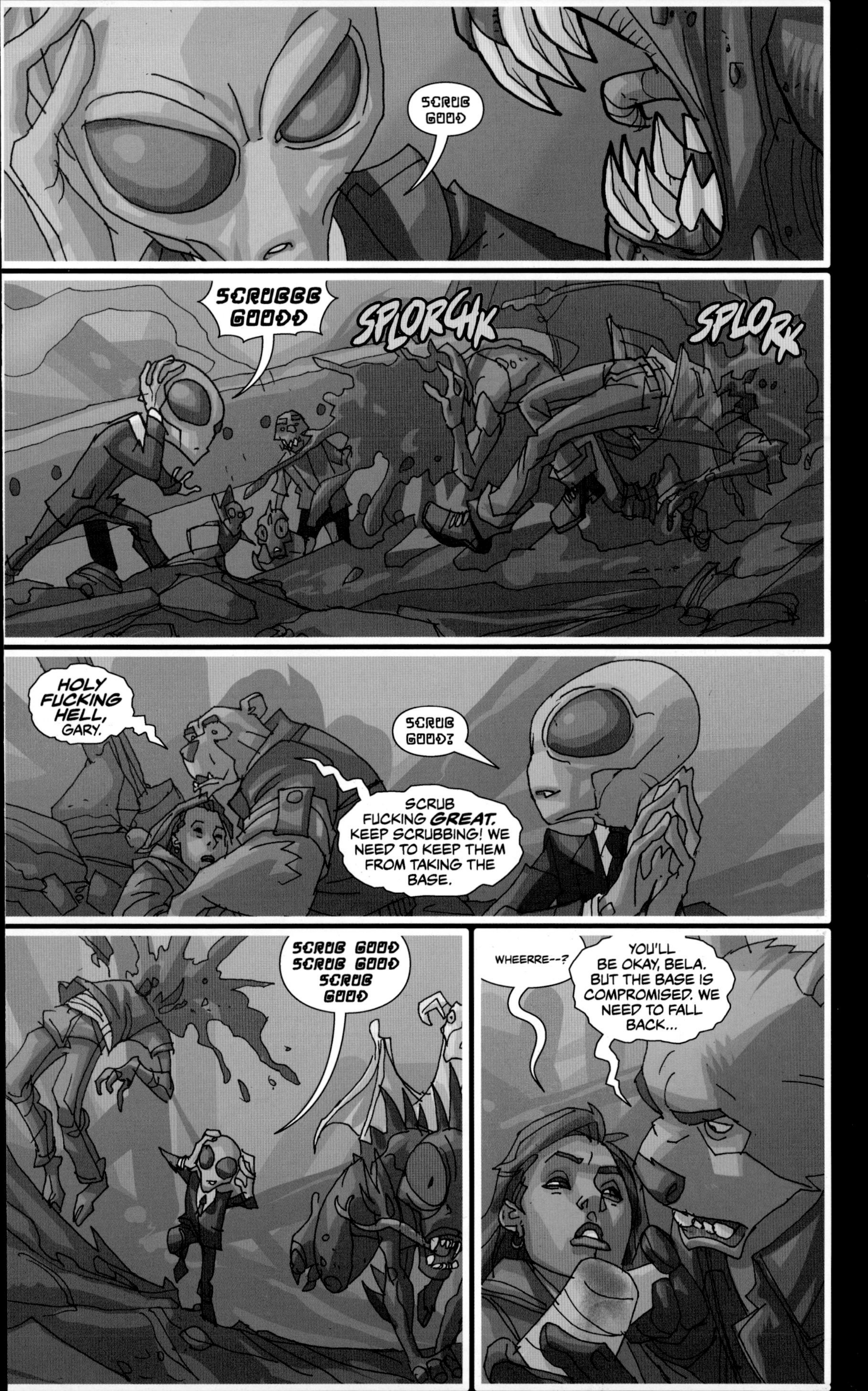
SCRUB GOOD
SCRUBBBB GOOOD
SPLORCHK
SPLORK
HOLY FUCKING HELL, GARY.
SCRUB GOOD?
SCRUB FUCKING GREAT. KEEP SCRUBBING! WE NEED TO KEEP THEM FROM TAKING THE BASE.
SCRUB GOOD SCRUB GOOD SCRUB GOOD
WHEERRE--?
YOU'LL BE OKAY, BELA. BUT THE BASE IS COMPROMISED. WE NEED TO FALL BACK...

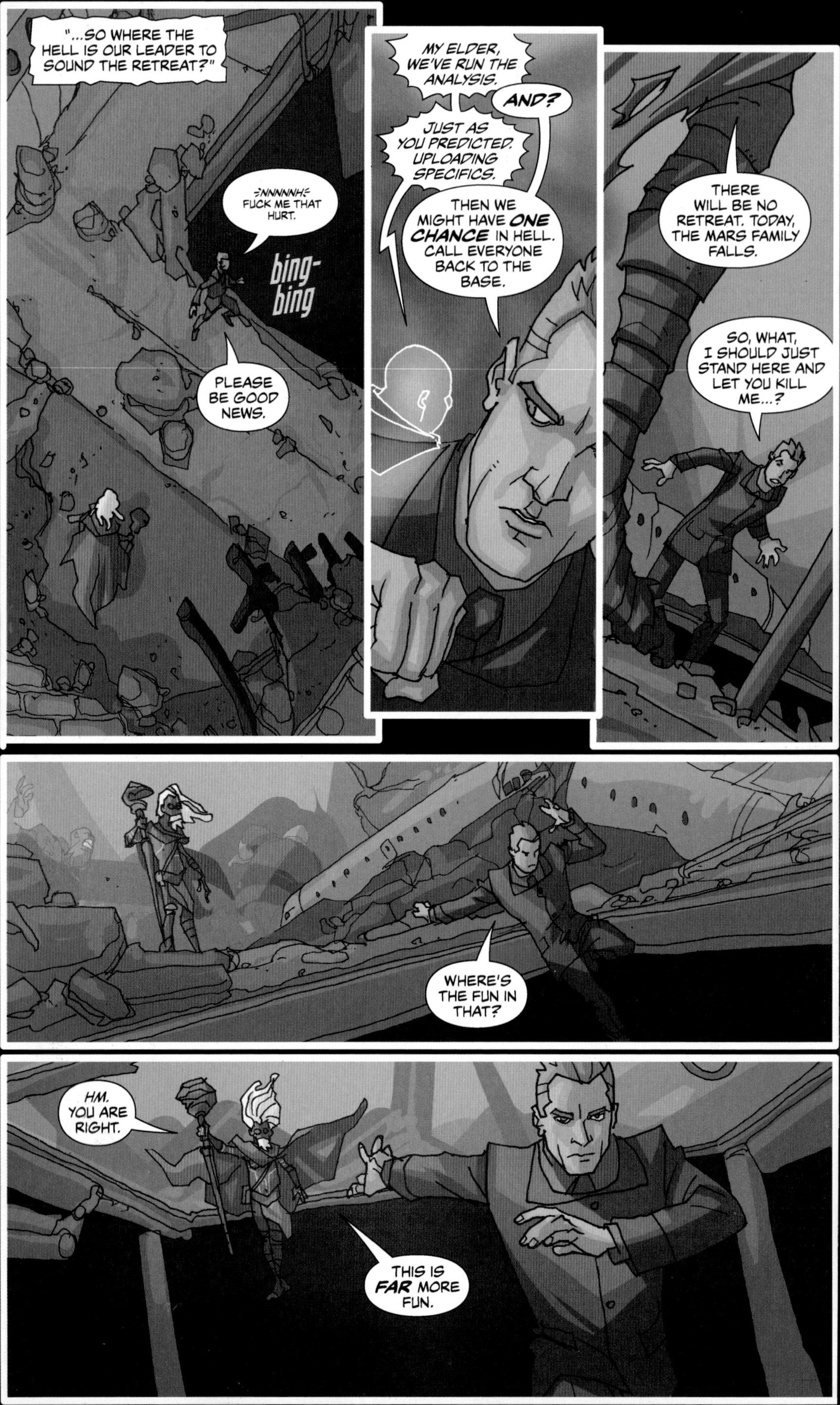
"...SO WHERE THE HELL IS OUR LEADER TO SOUND THE RETREAT?"
=NNNNNH= FUCK ME THAT HURT.
bing-bing
PLEASE BE GOOD NEWS.
MY ELDER, WE'VE RUN THE ANALYSIS.
AND?
JUST AS YOU PREDICTED. UPLOADING SPECIFICS.
THEN WE MIGHT HAVE ONE CHANCE IN HELL. CALL EVERYONE BACK TO THE BASE.
THERE WILL BE NO RETREAT. TODAY, THE MARS FAMILY FALLS.
SO, WHAT, I SHOULD JUST STAND HERE AND LET YOU KILL ME...?
WHERE'S THE FUN IN THAT?
HM. YOU ARE RIGHT.
THIS IS FAR MORE FUN.

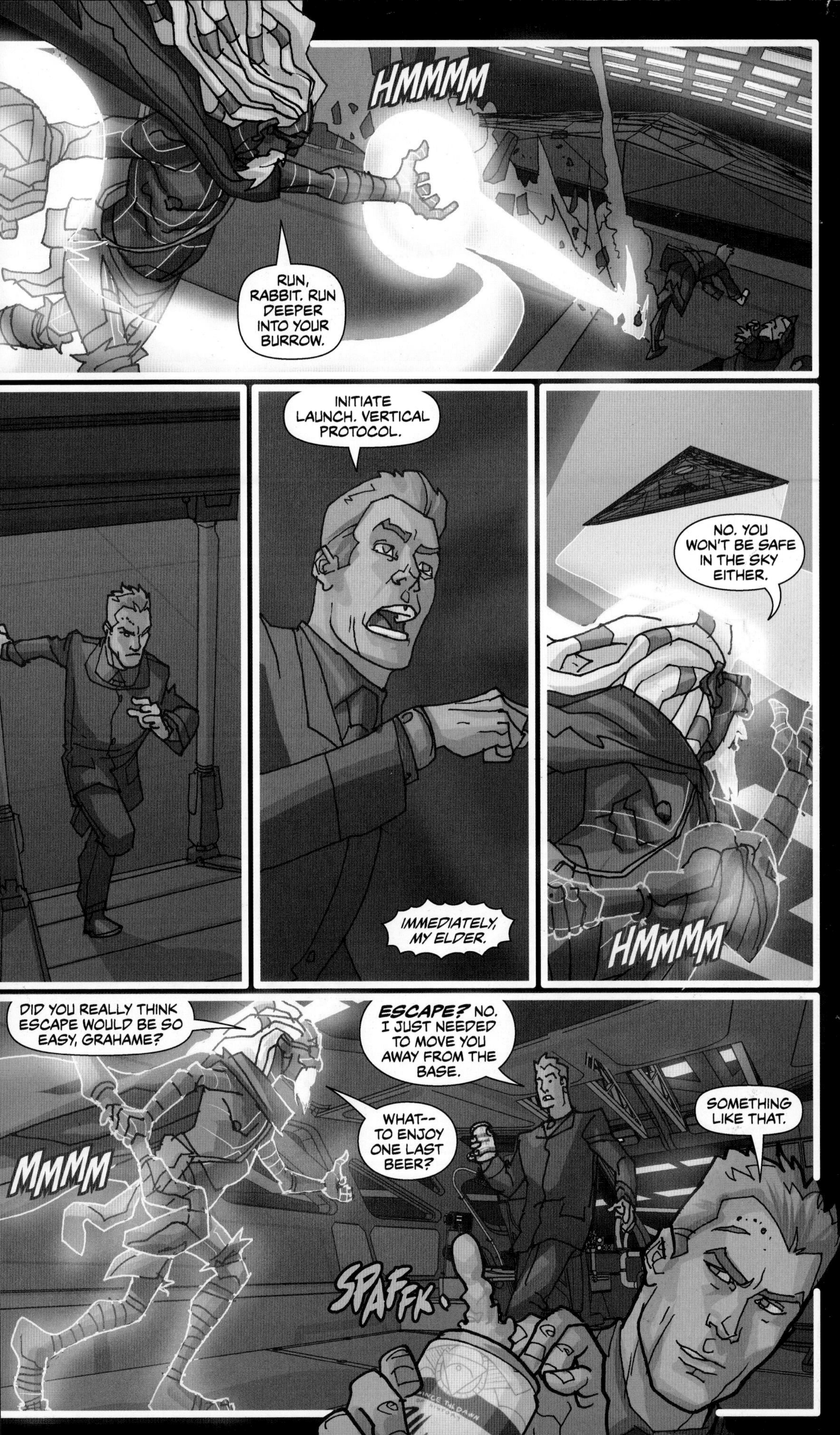
HMMMM
RUN, RABBIT. RUN DEEPER INTO YOUR BURROW.
INITIATE LAUNCH. VERTICAL PROTOCOL.
IMMEDIATELY, MY ELDER.
NO. YOU WON'T BE SAFE IN THE SKY EITHER.
HMMMM
DID YOU REALLY THINK ESCAPE WOULD BE SO EASY, GRAHAME?
ESCAPE? NO. I JUST NEEDED TO MOVE YOU AWAY FROM THE BASE.
WHAT-- TO ENJOY ONE LAST BEER?
SOMETHING LIKE THAT.
MMMM
SPAFFK

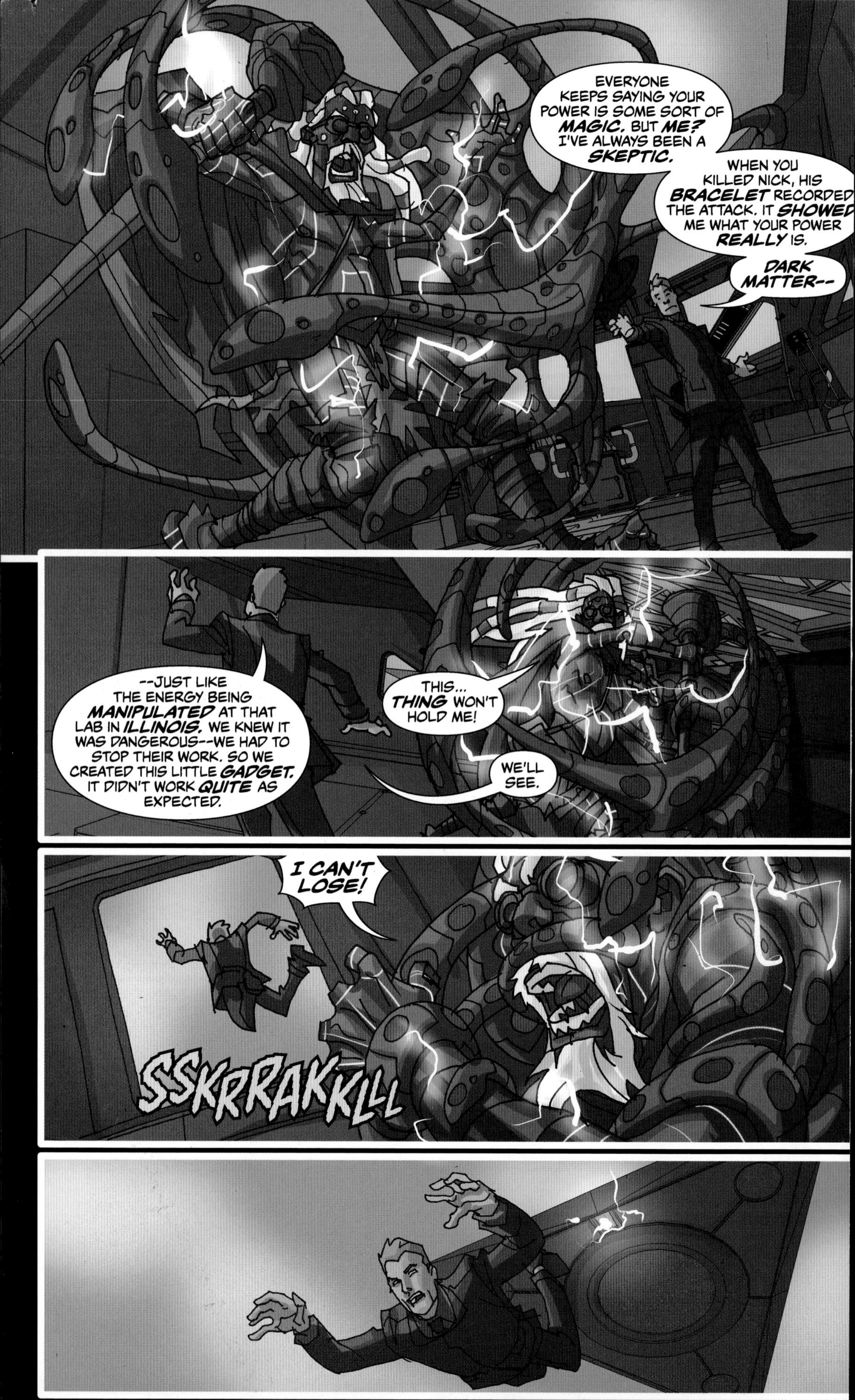
EVERYONE KEEPS SAYING YOUR POWER IS SOME SORT OF MAGIC. BUT ME? I'VE ALWAYS BEEN A SKEPTIC.
WHEN YOU KILLED NICK, HIS BRACELET RECORDED THE ATTACK. IT SHOWED ME WHAT YOUR POWER REALLY IS.
DARK MATTER--
--JUST LIKE THE ENERGY BEING MANIPULATED AT THAT LAB IN ILLINOIS. WE KNEW IT WAS DANGEROUS--WE HAD TO STOP THEIR WORK. SO WE CREATED THIS LITTLE GADGET. IT DIDN'T WORK QUITE AS EXPECTED.
THIS... THING WON'T HOLD ME!
WE'LL SEE.
I CAN'T LOSE!
SSKRRAKKLLL

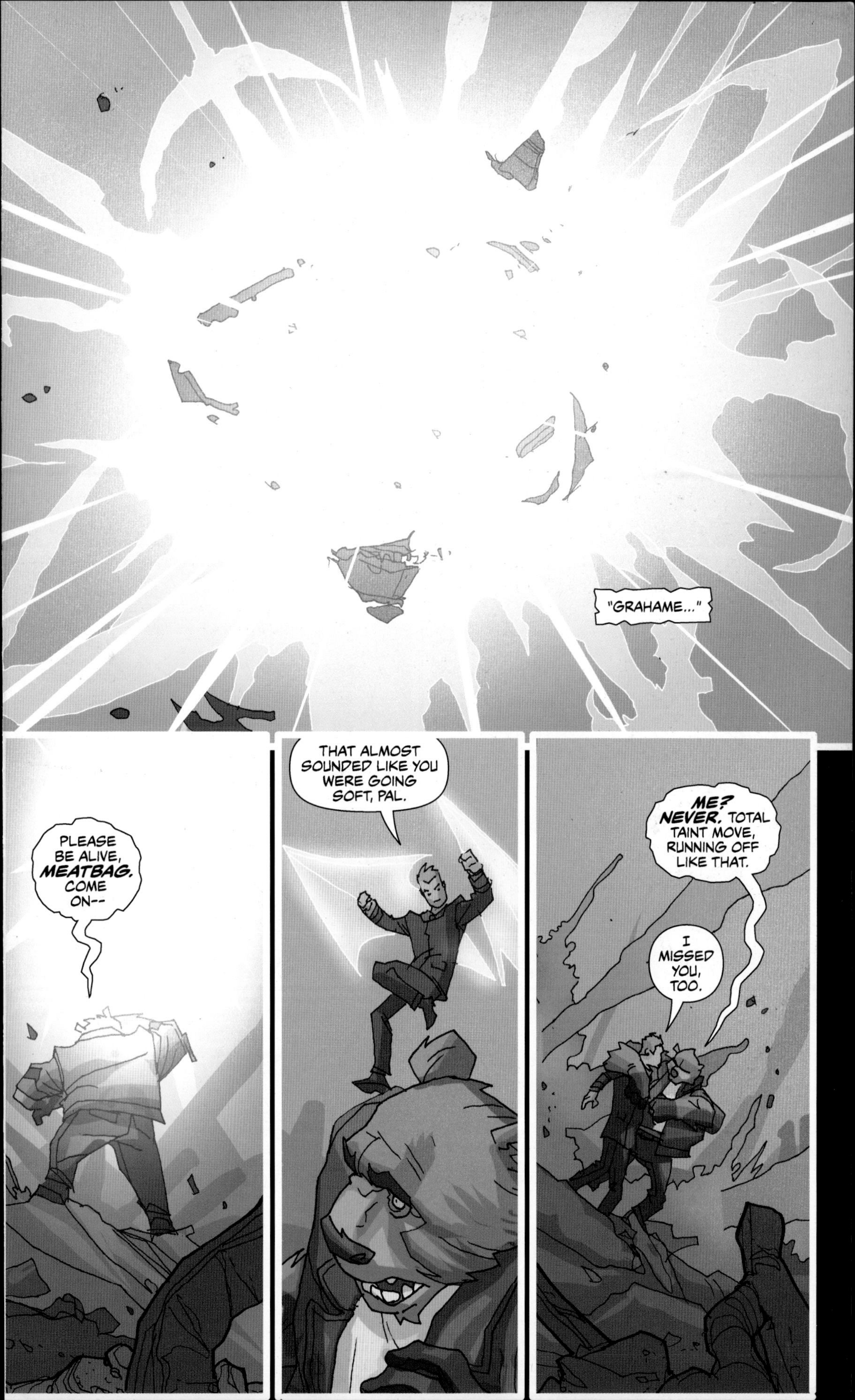
"GRAHAME..."
PLEASE BE ALIVE, MEATBAG. COME ON--
THAT ALMOST SOUNDED LIKE YOU WERE GOING SOFT, PAL.
ME? NEVER. TOTAL TAINT MOVE, RUNNING OFF LIKE THAT.
I MISSED YOU, TOO.

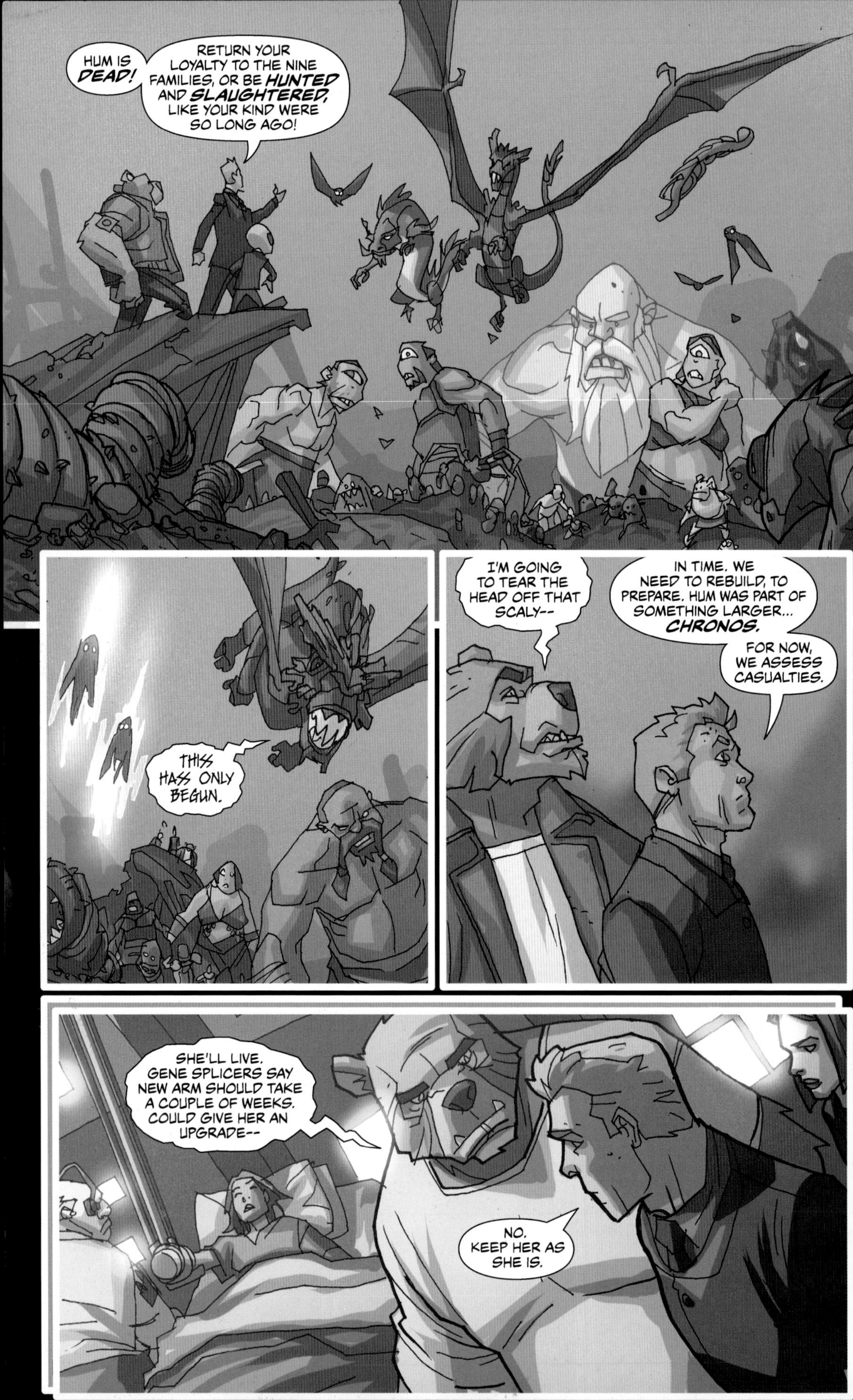
HUM IS DEAD!
RETURN YOUR LOYALTY TO THE NINE FAMILIES, OR BE HUNTED AND SLAUGHTERED, LIKE YOUR KIND WERE SO LONG AGO!
THISS HASS ONLY BEGUN.
I'M GOING TO TEAR THE HEAD OFF THAT SCALY--
IN TIME. WE NEED TO REBUILD, TO PREPARE. HUM WAS PART OF SOMETHING LARGER... CHRONOS.
FOR NOW, WE ASSESS CASUALTIES.
SHE'LL LIVE. GENE SPLICERS SAY NEW ARM SHOULD TAKE A COUPLE OF WEEKS. COULD GIVE HER AN UPGRADE--
NO. KEEP HER AS SHE IS.

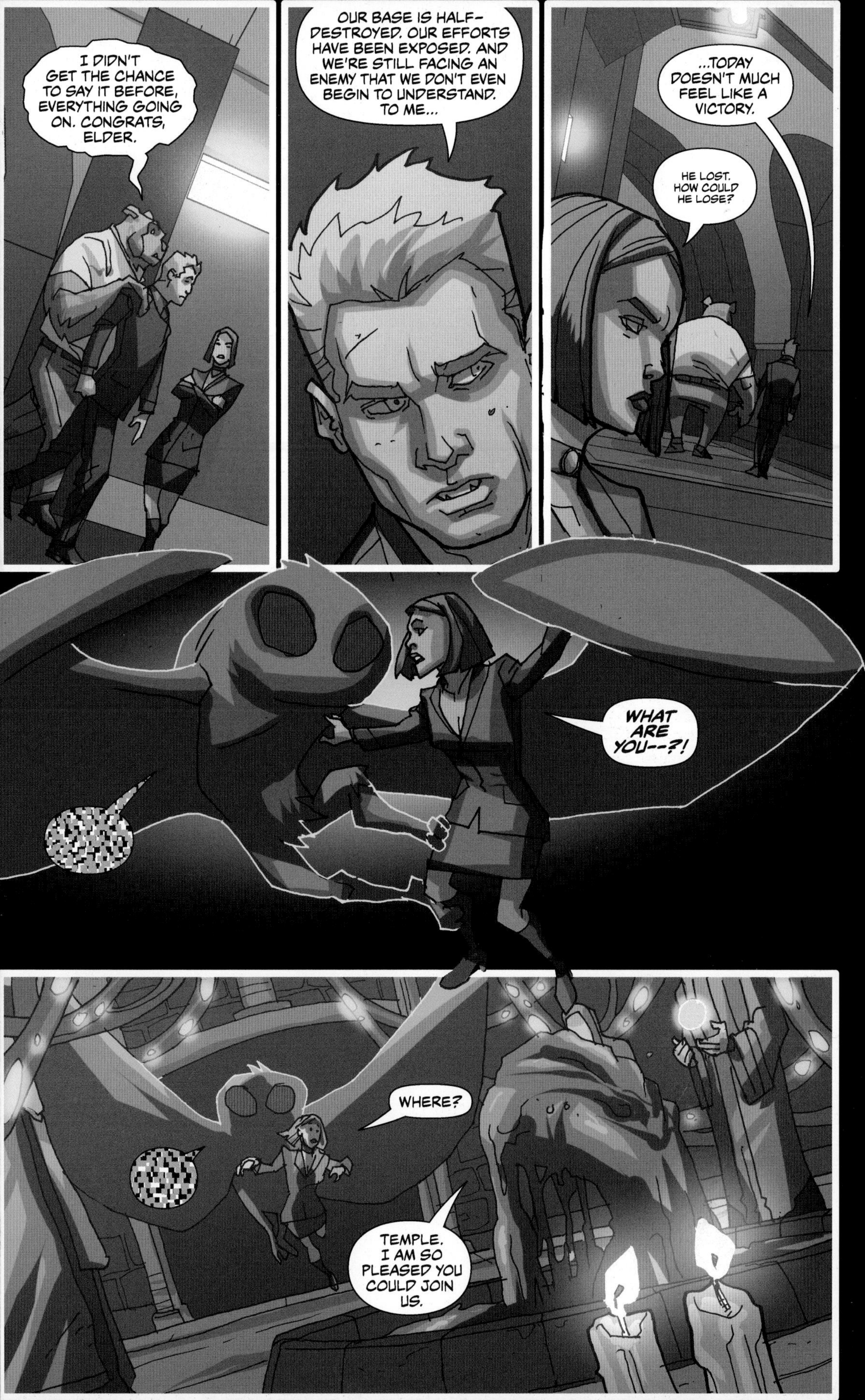
I DIDN'T GET THE CHANCE TO SAY IT BEFORE, EVERYTHING GOING ON. CONGRATS, ELDER.
OUR BASE IS HALF-DESTROYED. OUR EFFORTS HAVE BEEN EXPOSED. AND WE'RE STILL FACING AN ENEMY THAT WE DON'T EVEN BEGIN TO UNDERSTAND. TO ME...
...TODAY DOESN'T MUCH FEEL LIKE A VICTORY.
HE LOST. HOW COULD HE LOSE?
WHAT ARE YOU--?!
WHERE?
TEMPLE. I AM SO PLEASED YOU COULD JOIN US.

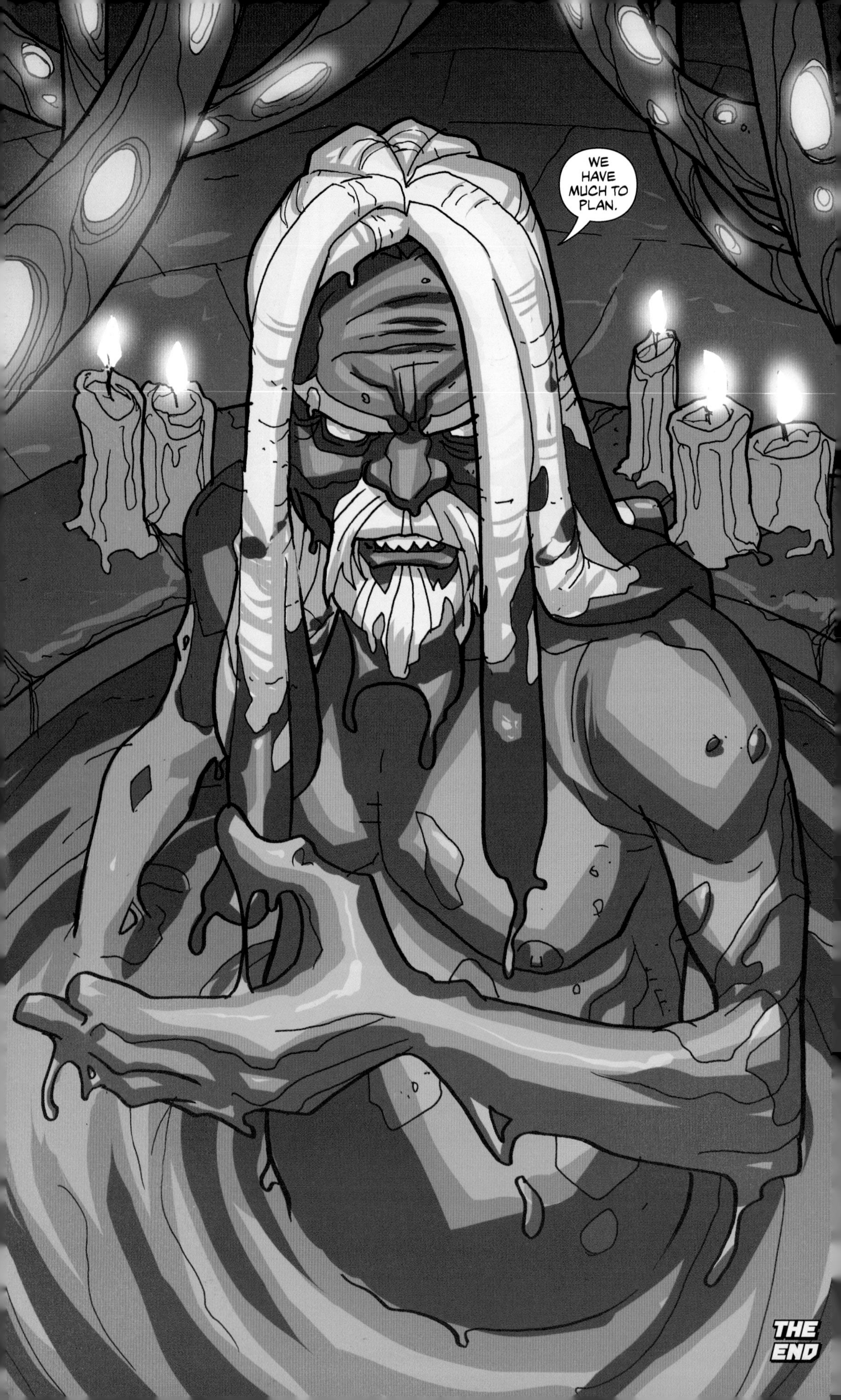
WE HAVE MUCH TO PLAN.
THE END

A PRIMER ON THE WORLD OF CRYPTOCRACY

•————————————————————•

WHEN WE SET OUT TO DEBUT THIS SERIES, PETE HAD THE IDEA OF TELLING A STORY
ABOUT THE SECRET HISTORY OF GARY THE GRAY, SOMETHING TO SHARE FOR FREE TO
HOOK READERS ON THIS WORLD. PETE CAME UP WITH THE STORY, AND WE KNOCKED
OUT A FUN LITTLE ADVANCE LOOK AT THE VARIOUS ENTITIES THAT EXIST WITHIN
CRYPTOCRACY, ALL SET IN THAT BASTION OF CONSPIRACY, ROSWELL, NEW MEXICO.

THE STORY DEBUTED ON BLEEDINGCOOL.COM AND WAS RELEASED FOR FREE TO FANS.
AND NOW WE'RE INCLUDING IT HERE AS WELL, SO THAT YOU ALL CAN KNOW JUST WHY
THE GRAYS SO LOVE THEIR SNACKS (WHICH, BY THE WAY, WAS ALL PETE'S GENIUS).

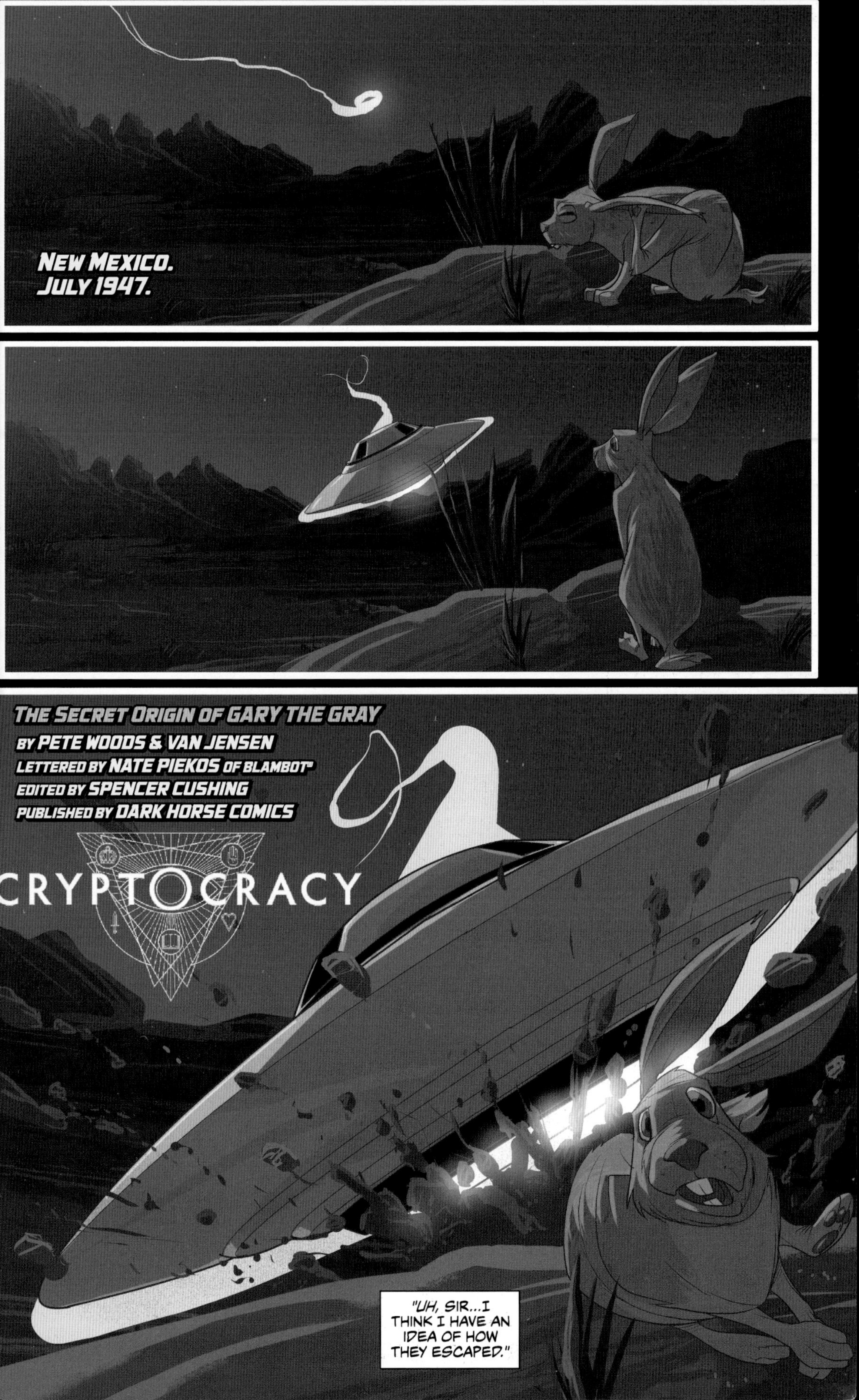

NEW MEXICO.
JULY 1947.
THE SECRET ORIGIN OF GARY THE GRAY
BY PETE WOODS & VAN JENSEN
LETTERED BY NATE PIEKOS OF BLAMBOT
EDITED BY SPENCER CUSHING
PUBLISHED BY DARK HORSE COMICS
CRYPTOCRACY
"UH, SIR...I THINK I HAVE AN IDEA OF HOW THEY ESCAPED."

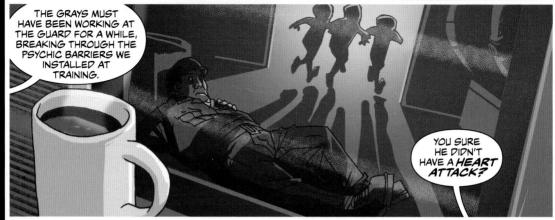

THE GRAYS MUST HAVE BEEN WORKING AT THE GUARD FOR A WHILE, BREAKING THROUGH THE PSYCHIC BARRIERS WE INSTALLED AT TRAINING.

YOU SURE HE DIDN'T HAVE A *HEART ATTACK?*

HE PASSED A PHYSICAL JUST A FEW MONTHS AGO.

I DON'T KNOW HOW HE PUT ON SO MUCH WEIGHT SO QUICKLY. BUT WE'RE PRETTY CERTAIN THEY *SCRUBBED* HIM, THEN TOOK OFF IN A *DISK.*

HOW'D THEY LEARN TO FLY? THE GRAYS CAN'T EVEN *TALK.*

MUST'VE PICKED A BIT UP TELEPATHICALLY. BUT THE FLIGHT PATH WAS *ERRATIC* AS HELL. IT'D BE A MIRACLE IF THEY MADE IT VERY FAR.

"FIND THEM. FAST. WE NEED TO *SANITIZE* THIS--*QUICKLY.*"

ΥΡΙΡΙΡΙΡΙ

ΥΡΙΡΙΡΙΡΙΡΙ

AAAGGHH!

ΥΡΙΡΙΡΙΡΙ

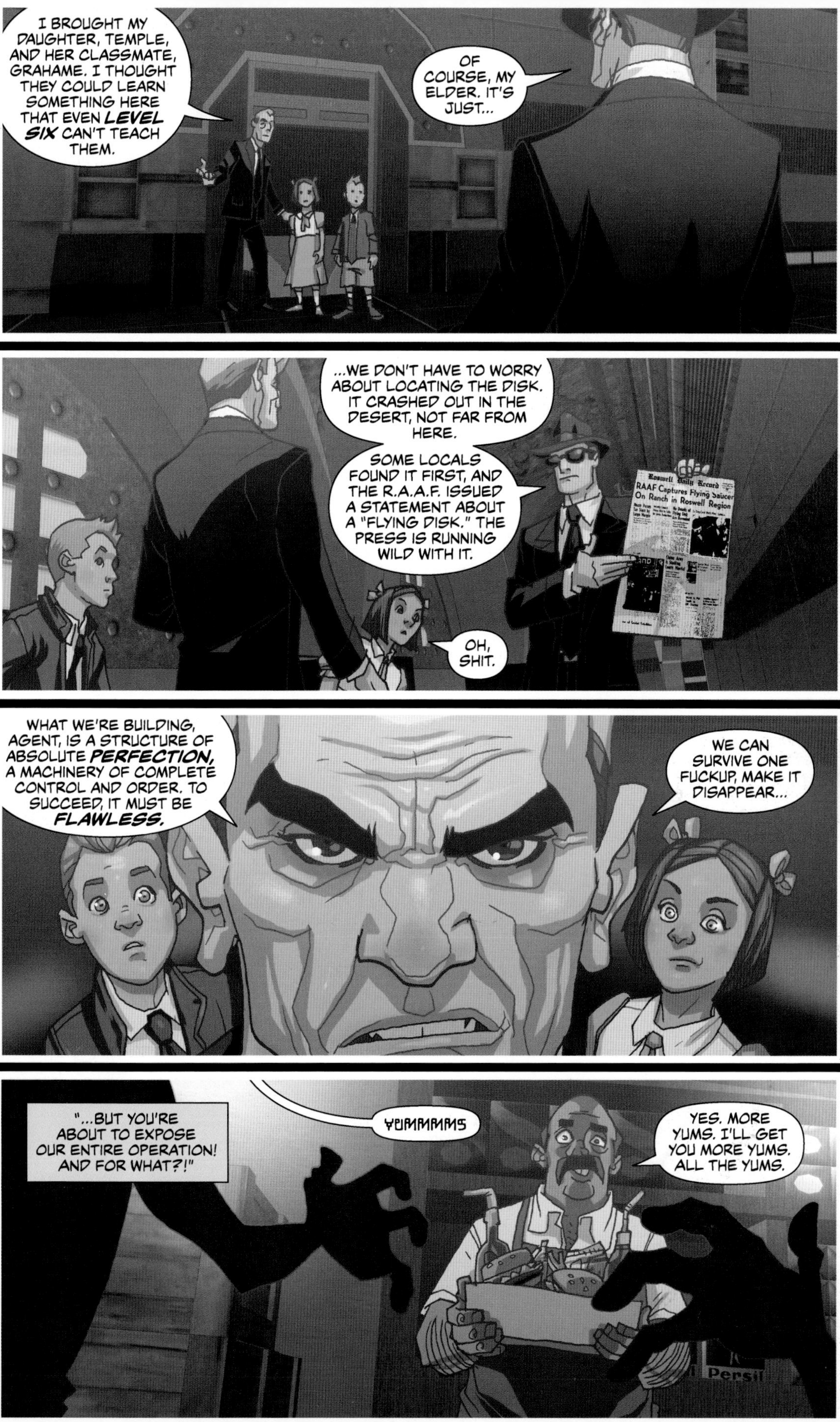
I BROUGHT MY DAUGHTER, TEMPLE, AND HER CLASSMATE, GRAHAME. I THOUGHT THEY COULD LEARN SOMETHING HERE THAT EVEN **LEVEL SIX** CAN'T TEACH THEM.
OF COURSE, MY ELDER. IT'S JUST...
...WE DON'T HAVE TO WORRY ABOUT LOCATING THE DISK. IT CRASHED OUT IN THE DESERT, NOT FAR FROM HERE.
SOME LOCALS FOUND IT FIRST, AND THE R.A.A.F. ISSUED A STATEMENT ABOUT A "FLYING DISK." THE PRESS IS RUNNING WILD WITH IT.
Roswell Daily Record
RAAF Captures Flying Saucer On Ranch in Roswell Region
OH, SHIT.
WHAT WE'RE BUILDING, AGENT, IS A STRUCTURE OF ABSOLUTE **PERFECTION,** A MACHINERY OF COMPLETE CONTROL AND ORDER. TO SUCCEED, IT MUST BE **FLAWLESS.**
WE CAN SURVIVE ONE FUCKUP, MAKE IT DISAPPEAR...
"...BUT YOU'RE ABOUT TO EXPOSE OUR ENTIRE OPERATION! AND FOR WHAT?!"
YUMMMMS
YES. MORE YUMS. I'LL GET YOU MORE YUMS. ALL THE YUMS.
Persil

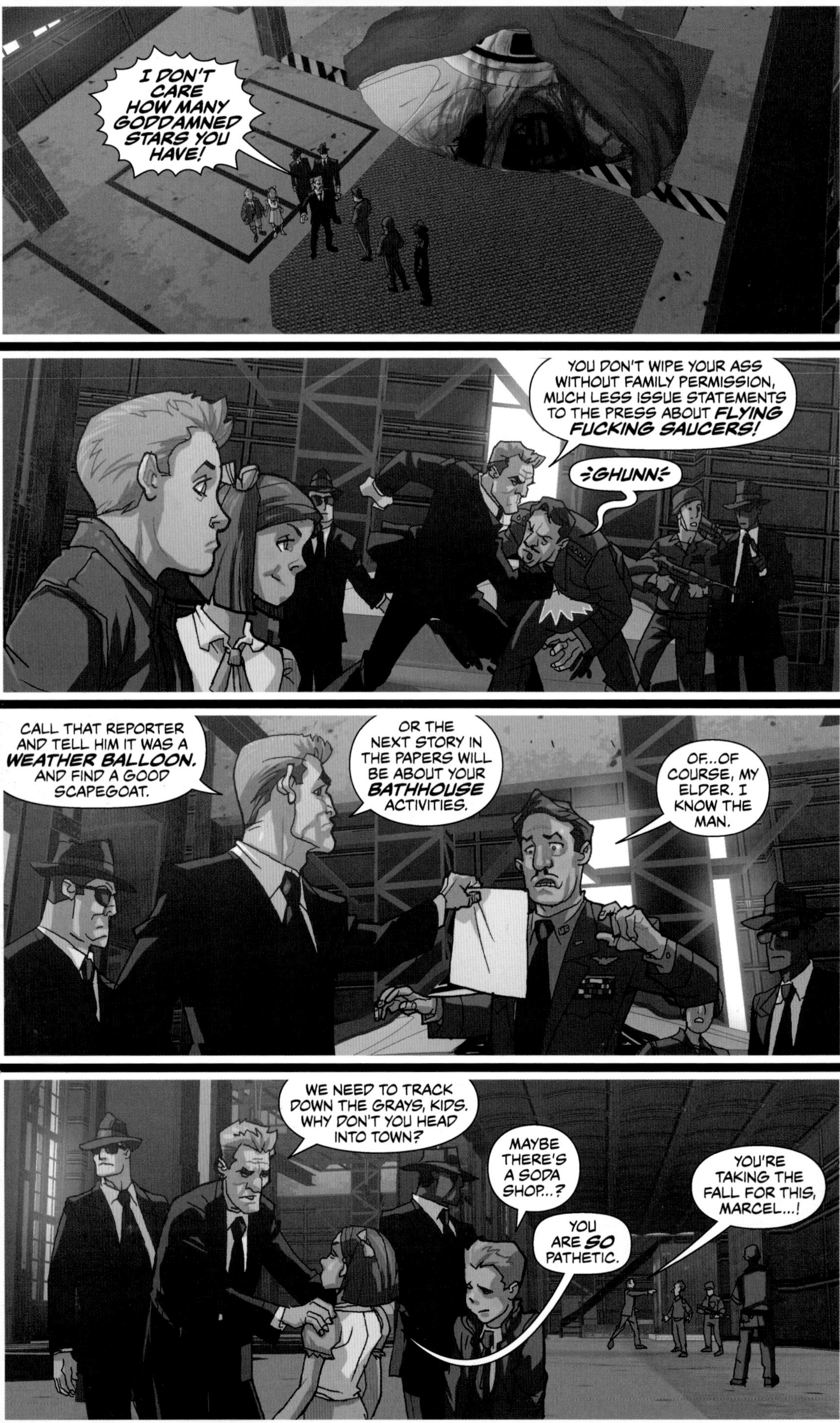
I DON'T CARE HOW MANY GODDAMNED STARS YOU HAVE!
YOU DON'T WIPE YOUR ASS WITHOUT FAMILY PERMISSION, MUCH LESS ISSUE STATEMENTS TO THE PRESS ABOUT FLYING FUCKING SAUCERS!
GHUNN
CALL THAT REPORTER AND TELL HIM IT WAS A WEATHER BALLOON. AND FIND A GOOD SCAPEGOAT.
OR THE NEXT STORY IN THE PAPERS WILL BE ABOUT YOUR BATHHOUSE ACTIVITIES.
OF...OF COURSE, MY ELDER. I KNOW THE MAN.
WE NEED TO TRACK DOWN THE GRAYS, KIDS. WHY DON'T YOU HEAD INTO TOWN?
MAYBE THERE'S A SODA SHOP...?
YOU ARE SO PATHETIC.
YOU'RE TAKING THE FALL FOR THIS, MARCEL...!

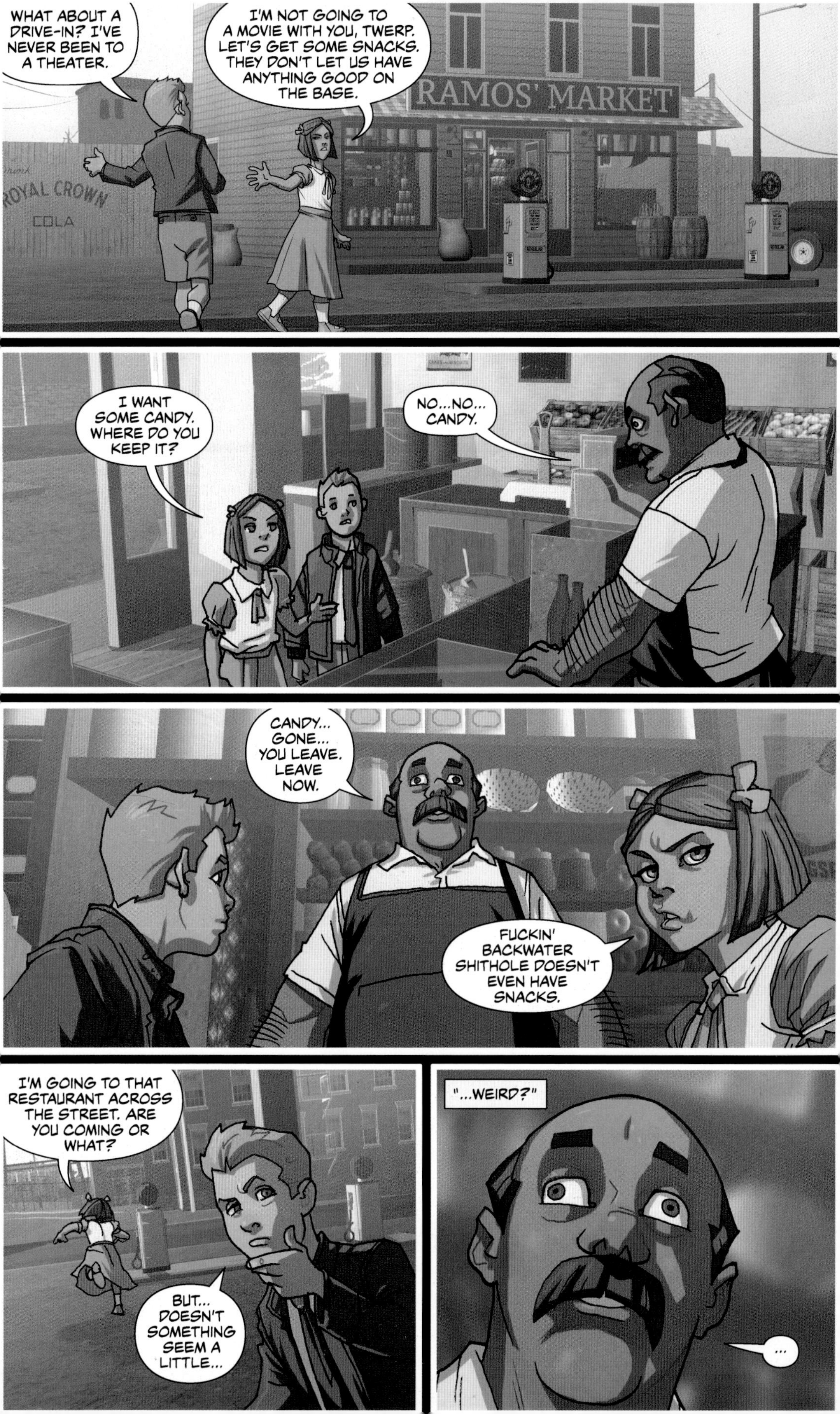
WHAT ABOUT A DRIVE-IN? I'VE NEVER BEEN TO A THEATER.
I'M NOT GOING TO A MOVIE WITH YOU, TWERP. LET'S GET SOME SNACKS. THEY DON'T LET US HAVE ANYTHING GOOD ON THE BASE.
RAMOS' MARKET
ROYAL CROWN
COLA
I WANT SOME CANDY. WHERE DO YOU KEEP IT?
NO...NO... CANDY.
CANDY... GONE... YOU LEAVE. LEAVE NOW.
FUCKIN' BACKWATER SHITHOLE DOESN'T EVEN HAVE SNACKS.
I'M GOING TO THAT RESTAURANT ACROSS THE STREET. ARE YOU COMING OR WHAT?
BUT... DOESN'T SOMETHING SEEM A LITTLE...
"...WEIRD?"
...

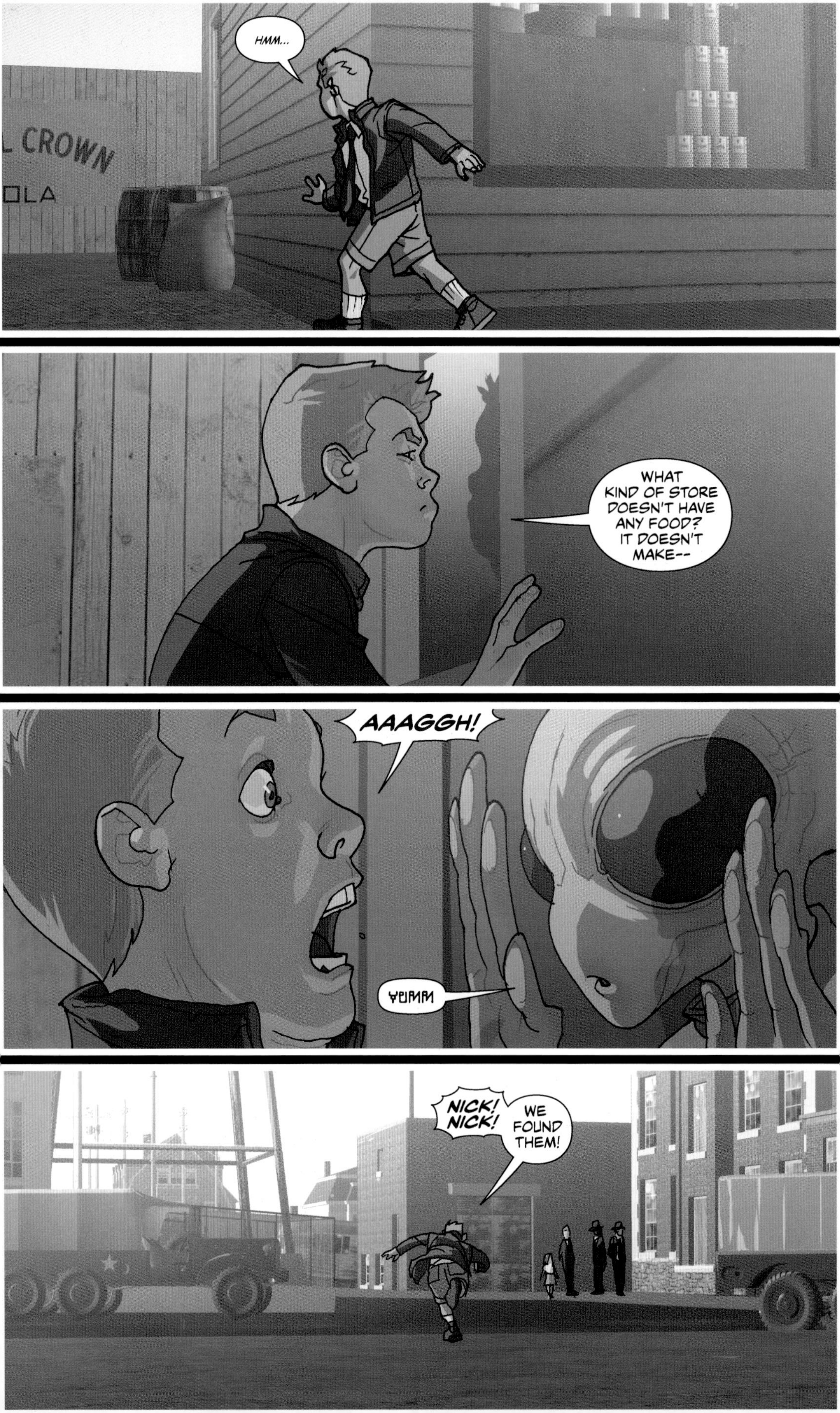
HMM...
L CROWN
OLA
WHAT KIND OF STORE DOESN'T HAVE ANY FOOD? IT DOESN'T MAKE--
AAAGGH!
NICK! NICK!
WE FOUND THEM!

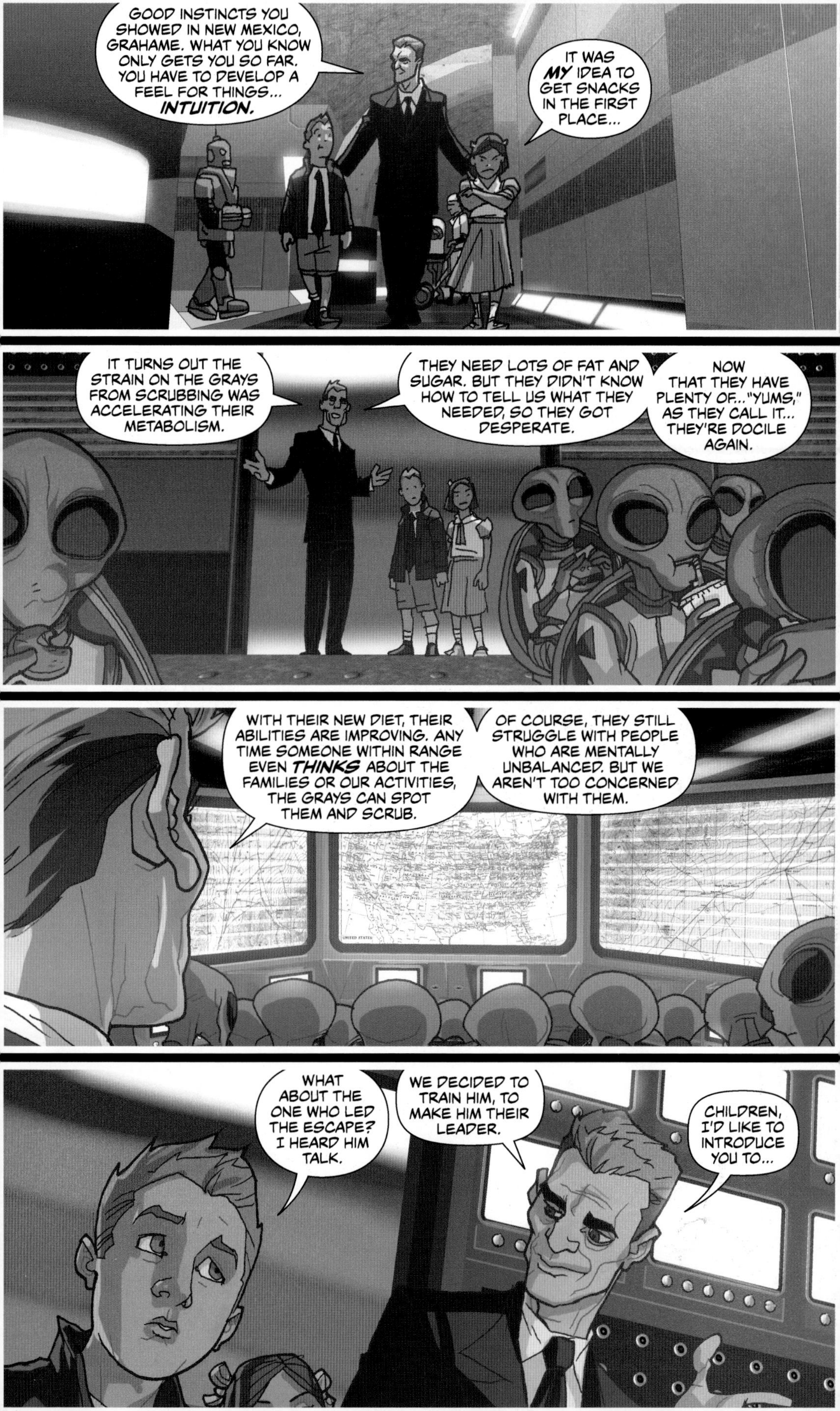
GOOD INSTINCTS YOU SHOWED IN NEW MEXICO, GRAHAME. WHAT YOU KNOW ONLY GETS YOU SO FAR. YOU HAVE TO DEVELOP A FEEL FOR THINGS... INTUITION.
IT WAS MY IDEA TO GET SNACKS IN THE FIRST PLACE...
IT TURNS OUT THE STRAIN ON THE GRAYS FROM SCRUBBING WAS ACCELERATING THEIR METABOLISM.
THEY NEED LOTS OF FAT AND SUGAR. BUT THEY DIDN'T KNOW HOW TO TELL US WHAT THEY NEEDED, SO THEY GOT DESPERATE.
NOW THAT THEY HAVE PLENTY OF..."YUMS," AS THEY CALL IT... THEY'RE DOCILE AGAIN.
WITH THEIR NEW DIET, THEIR ABILITIES ARE IMPROVING. ANY TIME SOMEONE WITHIN RANGE EVEN THINKS ABOUT THE FAMILIES OR OUR ACTIVITIES, THE GRAYS CAN SPOT THEM AND SCRUB.
OF COURSE, THEY STILL STRUGGLE WITH PEOPLE WHO ARE MENTALLY UNBALANCED. BUT WE AREN'T TOO CONCERNED WITH THEM.
WHAT ABOUT THE ONE WHO LED THE ESCAPE? I HEARD HIM TALK.
WE DECIDED TO TRAIN HIM, TO MAKE HIM THEIR LEADER.
CHILDREN, I'D LIKE TO INTRODUCE YOU TO...

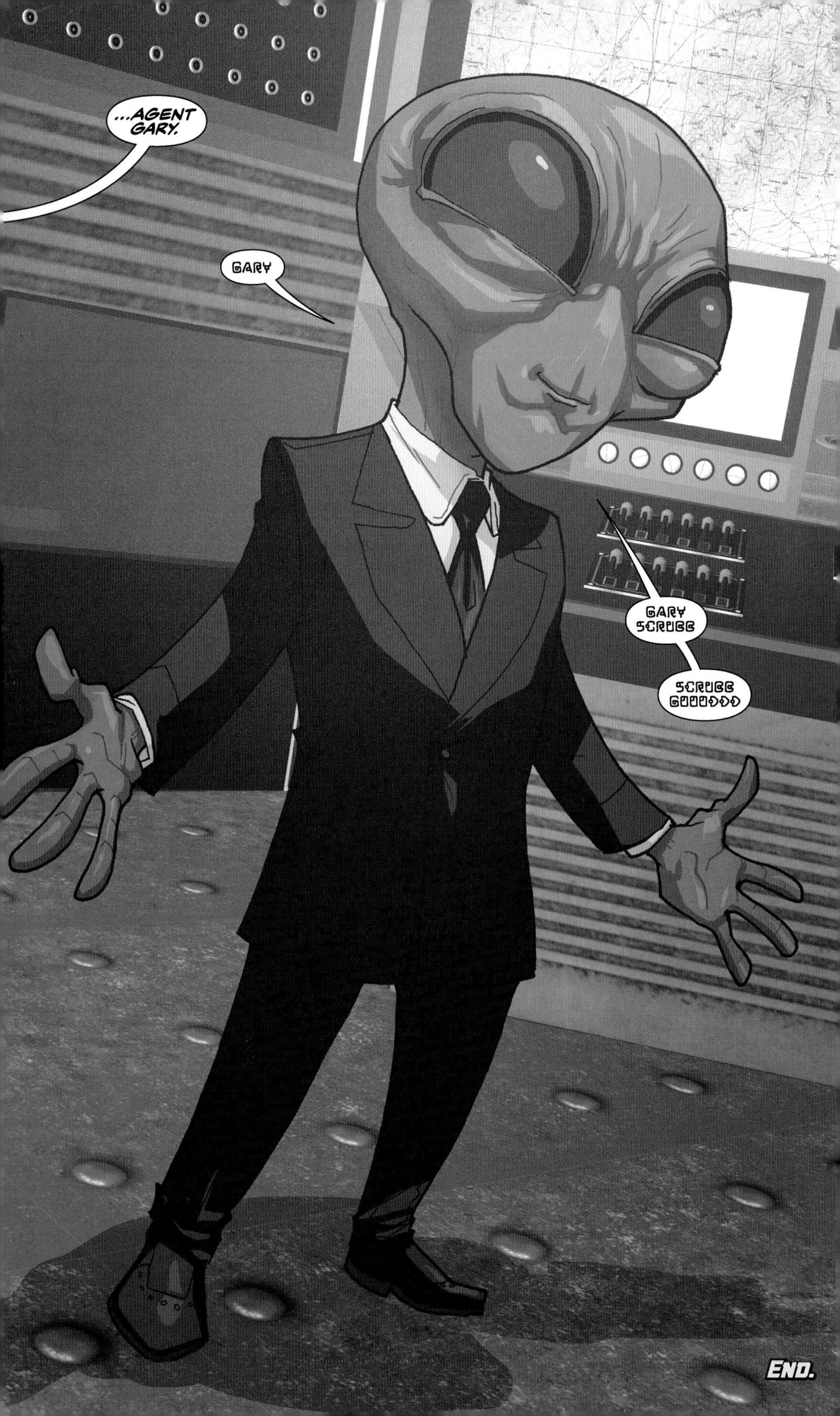
...AGENT GARY.
GARY
GARY SCRUBB
SCRUBB GUUUDDD
END.

UNLOCKING THE CRYPTOCRACY™

A SKETCHBOOK

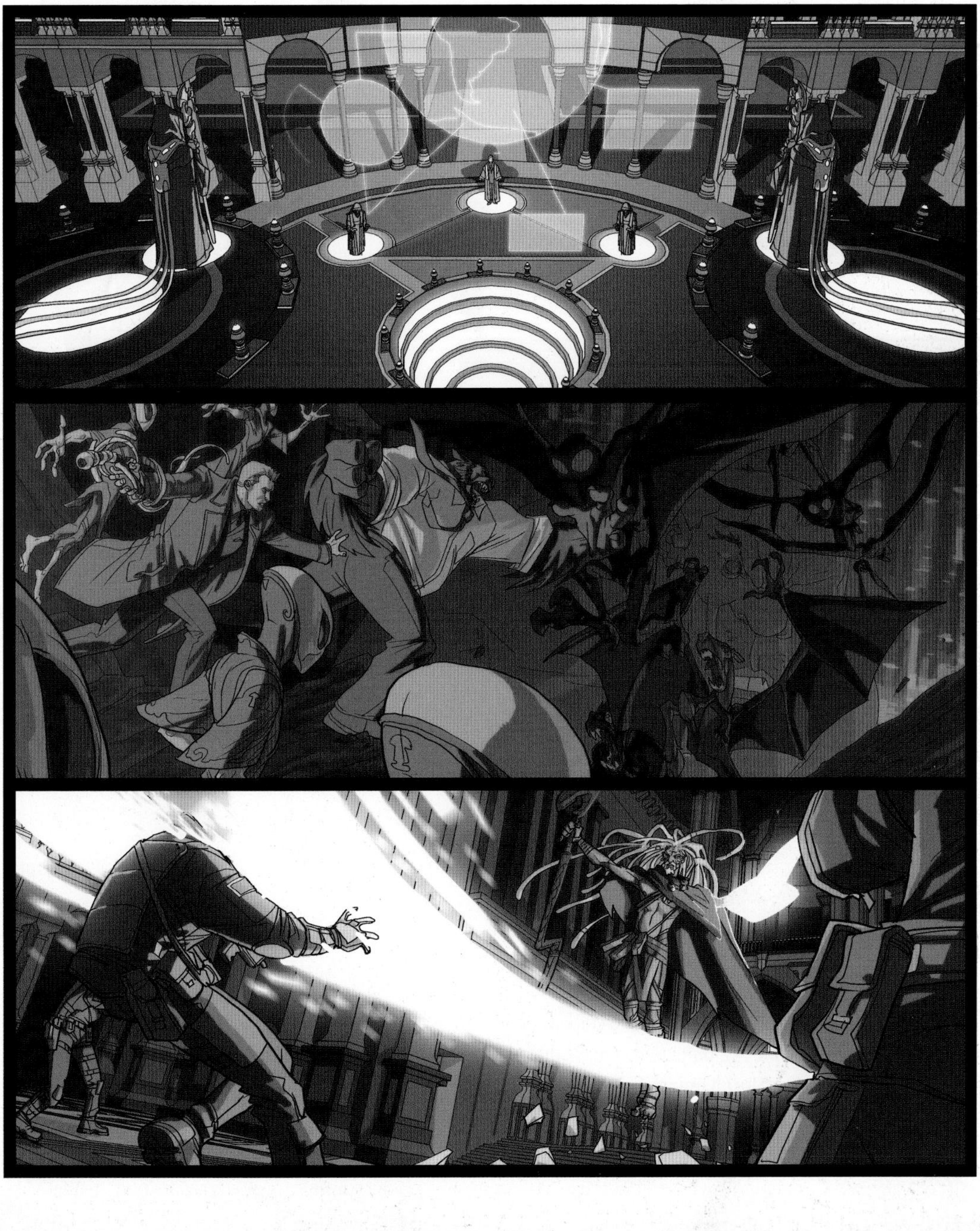

GRAHAME

Van: Grahame was a bit of a tough nut to crack. He's heroic but also a rule follower. A warrior but not ferocious. Initially, he had the look of a pulp hero, and we dialed that back a bit, making him more of an upper-middle-management type who just happens to be the ultimate Man in Black.

HUM

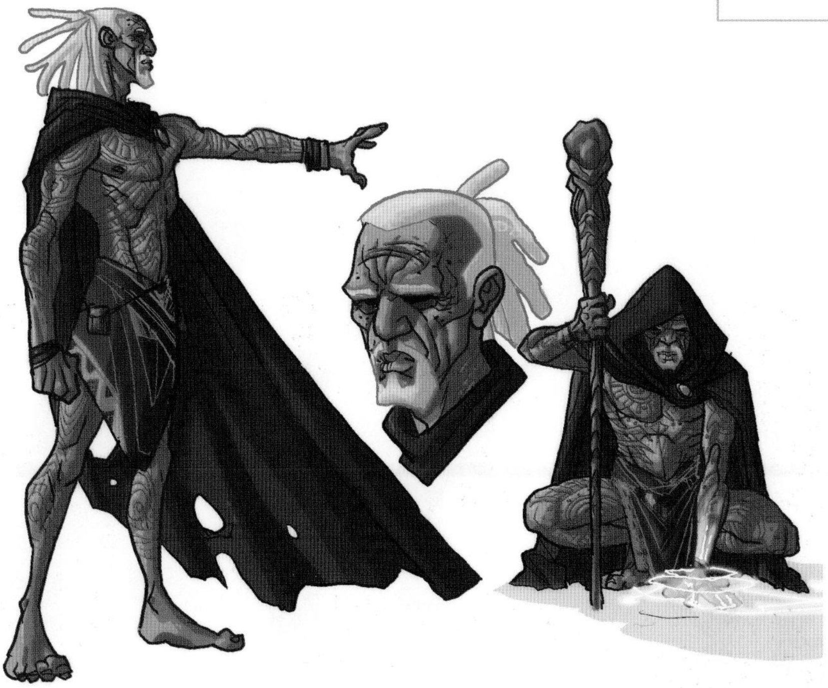

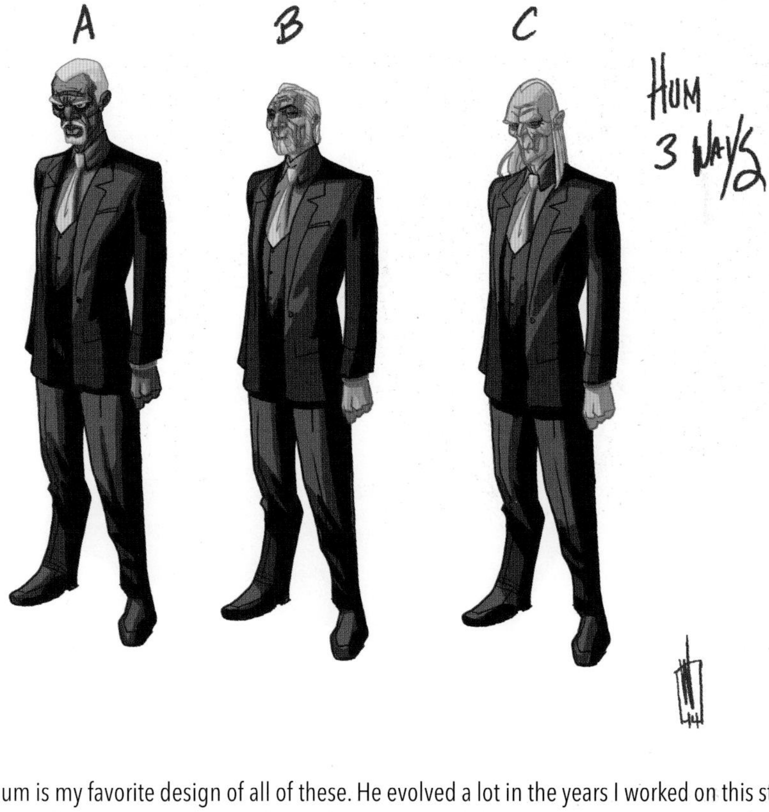
A
B
C
HUM
3 WAYS

Van: Hum is my favorite design of all of these. He evolved a lot in the years I worked on this story, but it was really Pete's idea of giving him a shamanistic look that brought the character to life.

BELA & NICK

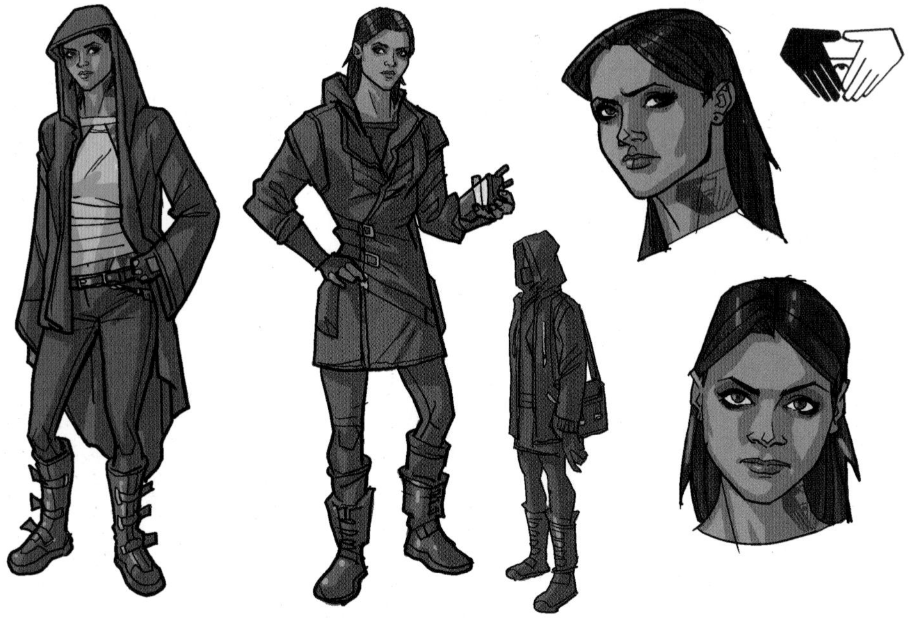

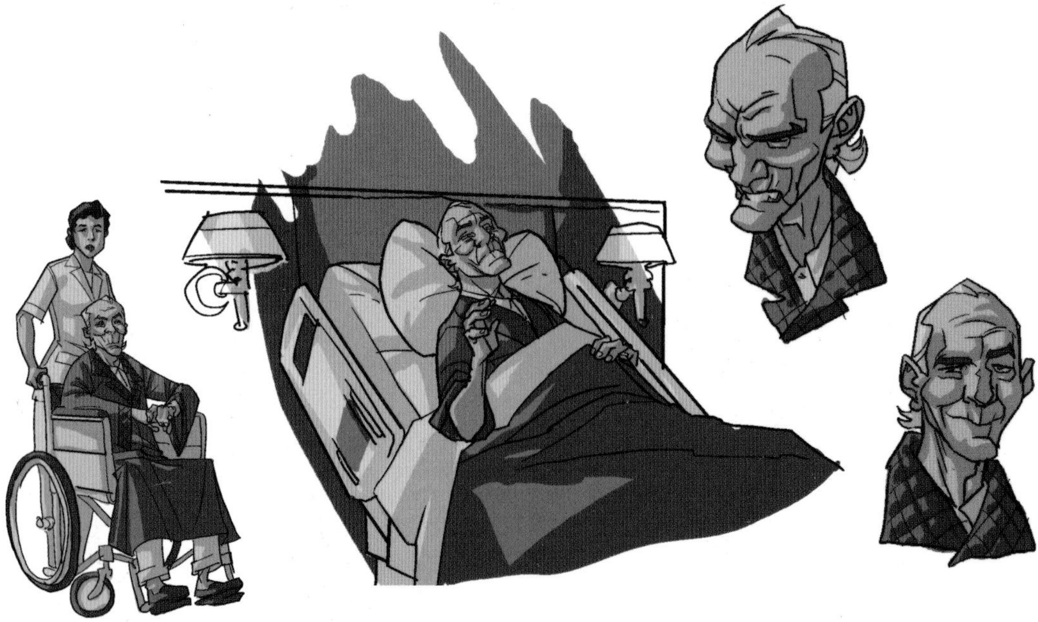

Van: Bela and Nick didn't change a great deal. Just really sharp designs from Pete. Jason is super fun and weird, an *amazing* design from Pete. You'll see here that Temple originally was called "Chase." At first, the character was going to be male. Because this was a villain, I'd intended to give him the same name as our dog, who is a bit of a handful. But he became she, and Chase became Temple. (If you read this, Chase the dog, please accept my apologies.)

JASON & TEMPLE

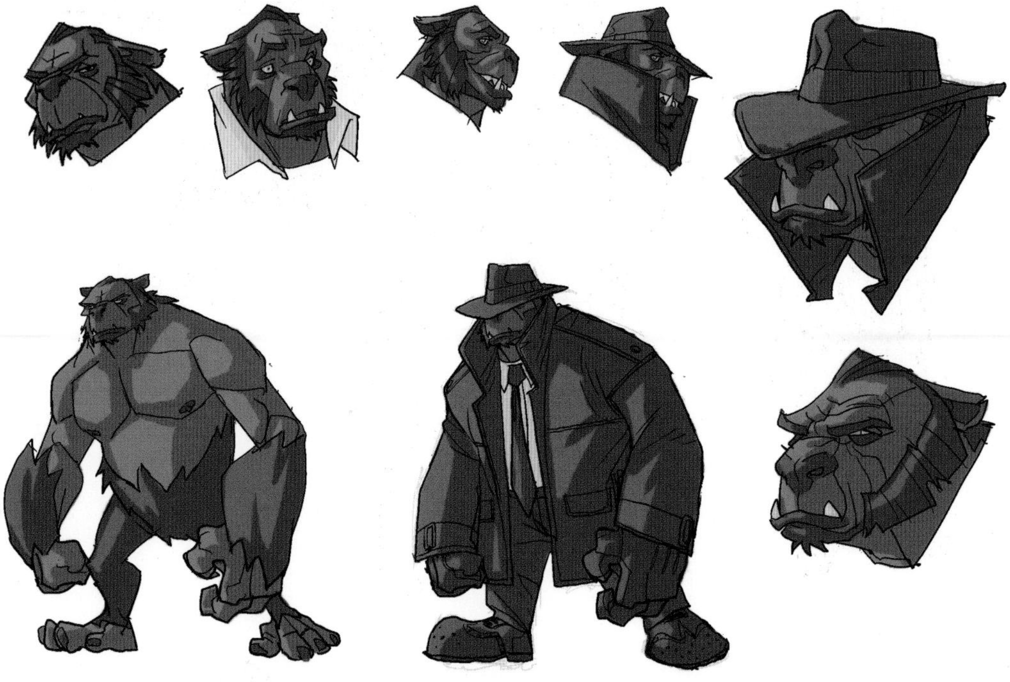

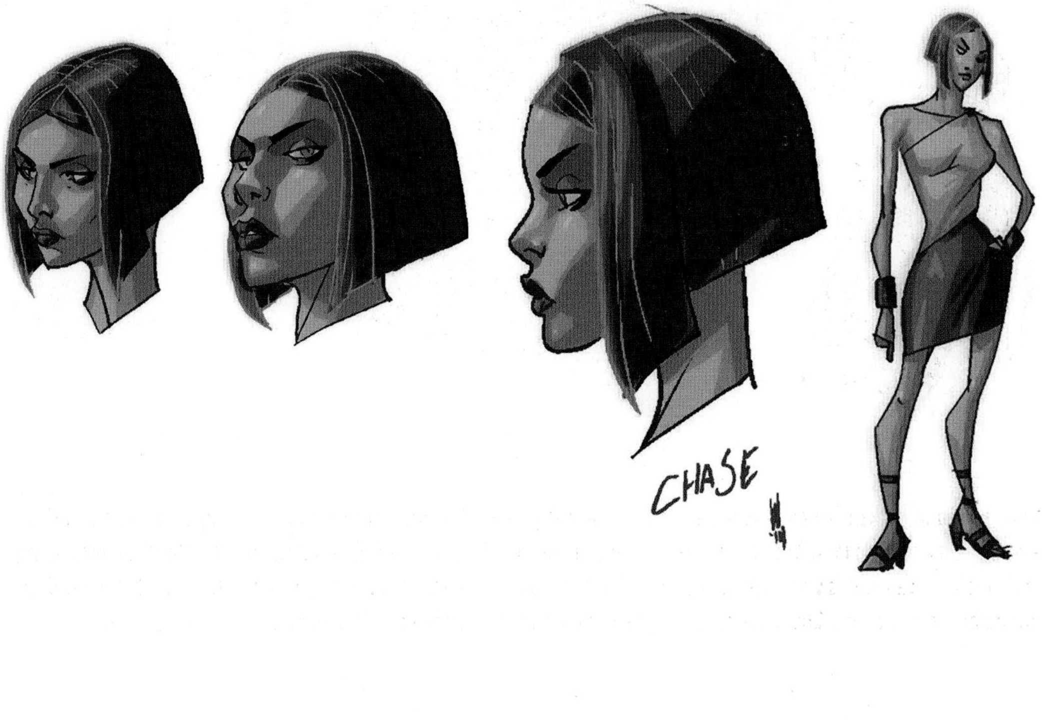
CHASE

THE CRYPTOCRACY SYMBOL

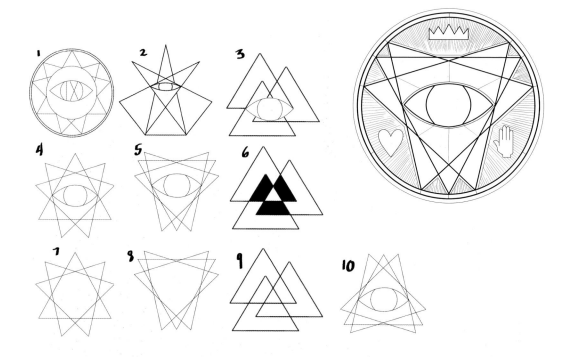

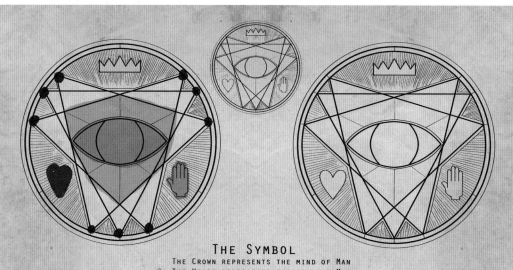

THE SYMBOL

THE CROWN REPRESENTS THE MIND OF MAN
2. THE HEART REPRESENTS THE SOUL OF MAN
. THE HAND REPRESENTS THE WORKS OF MAN
. THE EYE REPRESENTS THE WATCHFUL EYE OF THE NINE FAMILIES
5. THE POINTS OF THE TRIANGLES REPRESENT THE NINE FAMILES
6. THE TRIANGLES REPRESENT THE UNIFIED PURPOSE OF THE NINE FAMILIES
7. THE RADIATING LINES FROM THE CENTER REPRESENT THE LIGHT OF WISDOM
. BEHIND THE EYE AND HIDDEN IN THE CENTER IS A HINT OF A TESSERACT SYMBOL OF THE FAMILIES'
JOURNEY FROM THE FUTURE.

WHEN HEADS
OF THE FAMILIES COMMUNICATE THE DOCUMENTS ARE STAMPED WITH THE
CIRCLE, THE TRIANGLES, AND THE TESSERACT ONLY. IT IS VERY RARELY
SEEN.

ANCIENT MAN HAS BASTARDIZED THE SYMBOL. THE UNITED TRIANGLES WERE TAKEN TO REPRESENT
A GOAT'S HEAD, A DEMON'S HEAD, AND LATER A PENTAGRAM.

ROUGH COVER CONCEPTS

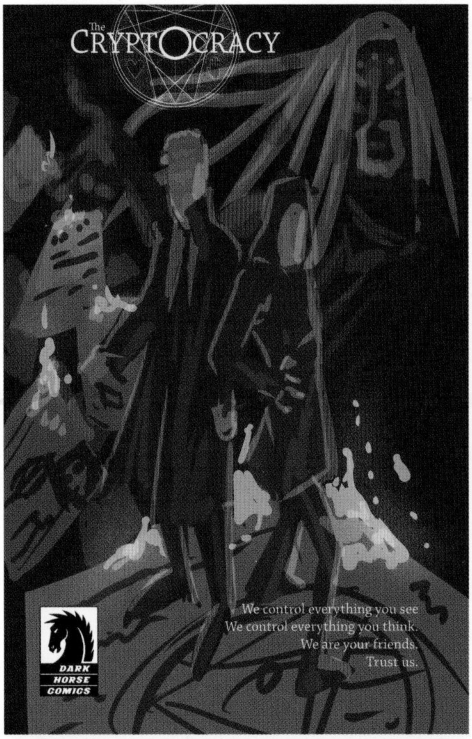
The CRYPTOCRACY
We control everything you see
We control everything you think.
We are your friends.
Trust us.
DARK HORSE COMICS

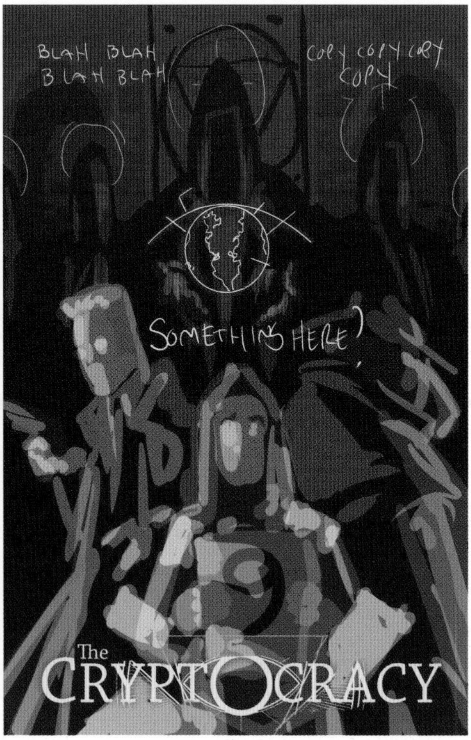
BLAH BLAH
BLAH BLAH
COPY COPY COPY
COPY
SOMETHING HERE?
The CRYPTOCRACY

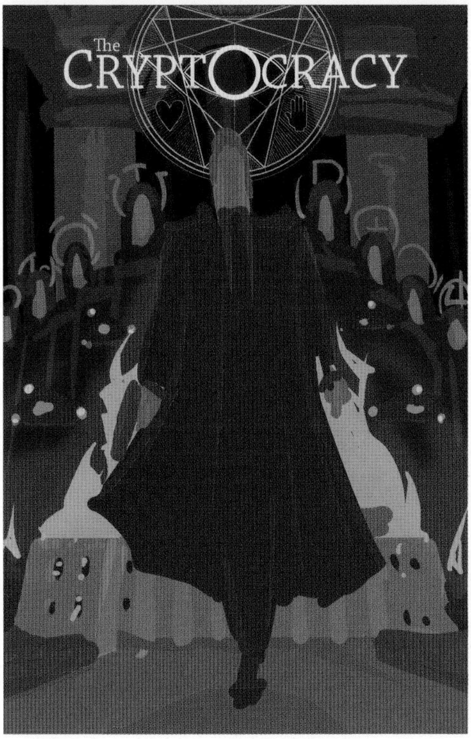
The CRYPTOCRACY

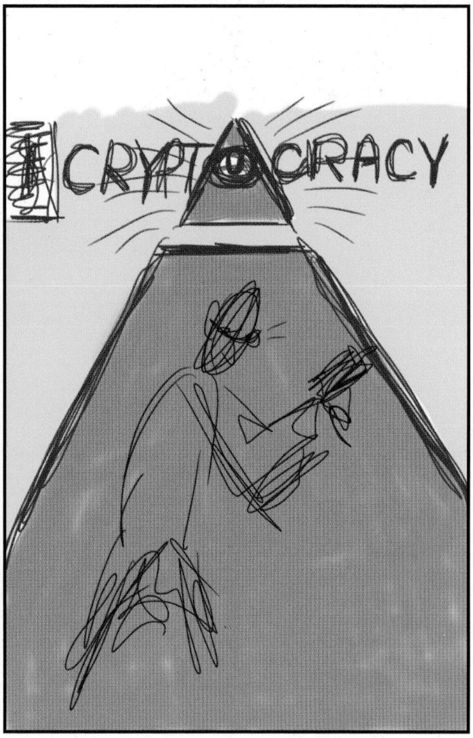
CRYPTOCRACY

Van: The title changed so many times over the years. *Cryptocracy* came about really late. I realized it had eleven letters, and the o was the central letter, which meant it could be used as the all-seeing eye in a symmetrical logo design. Pete and the Dark Horse design team ran wild with that idea.

AND YOUR HOST . . .

Haland,
Aaron
Lewis,
Clyde
Noory,
George
Martin,
Abby
Icke,
David
Richard,
Syrett
Ventura,
Jesse
Corbett,
James
Bela

Pete had the great idea of taking some of the big names from conspiracy media and inserting them into the comic itself. So we set it up that the Cryptocracy had a watch list, including our fictional character Bela, but also a lot of real-life hosts. It was this panel that actually got us on the air as guests on some amazing podcasts and radio shows, including the legendary *Coast to Coast AM*. Cue up the synthesizer and strap on your tinfoil hat.

ABOVE YOUR PAY GRADE . . .

OUTER RING
INNER RING
LOWEST SECURITY
HIGHEST SECURITY

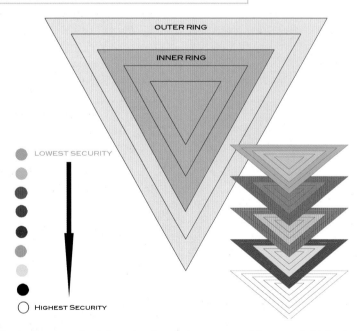

The world of the Cryptocracy is divided into levels. Which one are you? Since you hold this book in your hands, you're at least in level three. Want to dig deeper? Make sure to spread the word far and wide. How else are we going to defeat THEM?

Protect Yourself From Thought Invasion!!

Follow our 7-step guide to keeping THEM out of your brain

1. Purchase (or steal) aluminum foil

2. Tear out a head's worth of foil

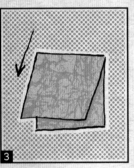

3. Fold sheet in half

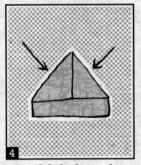

4. Fold left and right sides in

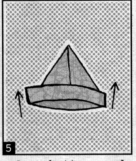

5. Open bottom, and fold each flap up

6. Place hat on head and adjust fit

7. Enjoy, and watch out for the black helicopters!

From your friends, the Beyonders! Take a photo of yourself wearing your hat and share it online.

Make sure to tag it **#Cryptocracy** to let them know they can't steal your thoughts!

And don't miss an episode of "Broadcast from the Beyond"!

BROADCAST
(((FROM THE)))
BEYOND

To learn more secrets of the shadow state, don't miss an issue of **CRYPTOCRACY**, brought to you by truth seekers Van Jensen and Pete Woods and Dark Horse Comics.

DARK HORSE COMICS

CREATIVE GIANTS!

GET YOUR FIX OF DARK HORSE BOOKS FROM THESE INSPIRED CREATORS!

MESMO DELIVERY SECOND EDITION

Rafael Grampá

Eisner Award–winning artist Rafael Grampá (5, Hellblazer) makes his full-length comics debut with the critically acclaimed graphic novel *Mesmo Delivery*—a kinetic, bloody romp starring Rufo, an ex-boxer; Sangrecco, an Elvis impersonator; and a ragtag crew of overly confident drunks who pick the wrong delivery men to mess with.

ISBN 978-1-61655-457-6 | $14.99

SIN TITULO

Cameron Stewart

Following the death of his grandfather, Alex Mackay discovers a mysterious photograph in the old man's belongings that sets him on an adventure like no other—where dreams and reality merge, family secrets are laid bare, and lives are irrevocably altered.

ISBN 978-1-61655-248-0 | $19.99

DE:TALES

Fábio Moon and Gabriel Bá

Brazilian twins Fábio Moon and Gabriel Bá's (*Daytripper*, *Pixu*) most personal work to date. Brimming with all the details of human life, their charming tales move from the urban reality of their home in São Paulo to the magical realism of their Latin American background.

ISBN 978-1-59582-557-5 | $19.99

THE TRUE LIVES OF THE FABULOUS KILLJOYS

Gerard Way, Shaun Simon, and Becky Cloonan

Years ago, the Killjoys fought against the tyrannical megacorporation Better Living Industries. Today, the followers of the original Killjoys languish in the desert and the fight for freedom fades. It's left to the Girl to take down BLI!

ISBN 978-1-59582-462-2 | $19.99

DEMO

Brian Wood and Becky Cloonan

It's hard enough being a teenager. Now try being a teenager with *powers*. A chronicle of the lives of young people on separate journeys to self-discovery in a world—just like our own—where being different is feared.

ISBN 978-1-61655-682-2 | $24.99

SABERTOOTH SWORDSMAN

Damon Gentry and Aaron Conley

When his village is enslaved and his wife kidnapped by the malevolent Mastodon Mathematician, a simple farmer must find his inner warrior—the Sabertooth Swordsman!

ISBN 978-1-61655-176-6 | $17.99

JAYBIRD

Jaakko and Lauri Ahonen

Disney meets Kafka in this beautiful, intense, original tale! A very small, very scared little bird lives an isolated life in a great big house with his infirm mother. He's never been outside the house, and he never will if his mother has anything to say about it.

ISBN 978-1-61655-469-9 | $19.99

MONSTERS! & OTHER STORIES

Gustavo Duarte

Newcomer Gustavo Duarte spins wordless tales inspired by Godzilla, King Kong, and Pixar, brimming with humor, charm, and delightfully twisted horror!

ISBN 978-1-61655-309-8 | $12.99

SACRIFICE

Sam Humphries and Dalton Rose

What happens when a troubled youth is plucked from modern society and thrust though time and space into the heart of the Aztec civilization—one of the most bloodthirsty times in human history?

ISBN 978-1-59582-985-6 | $19.99